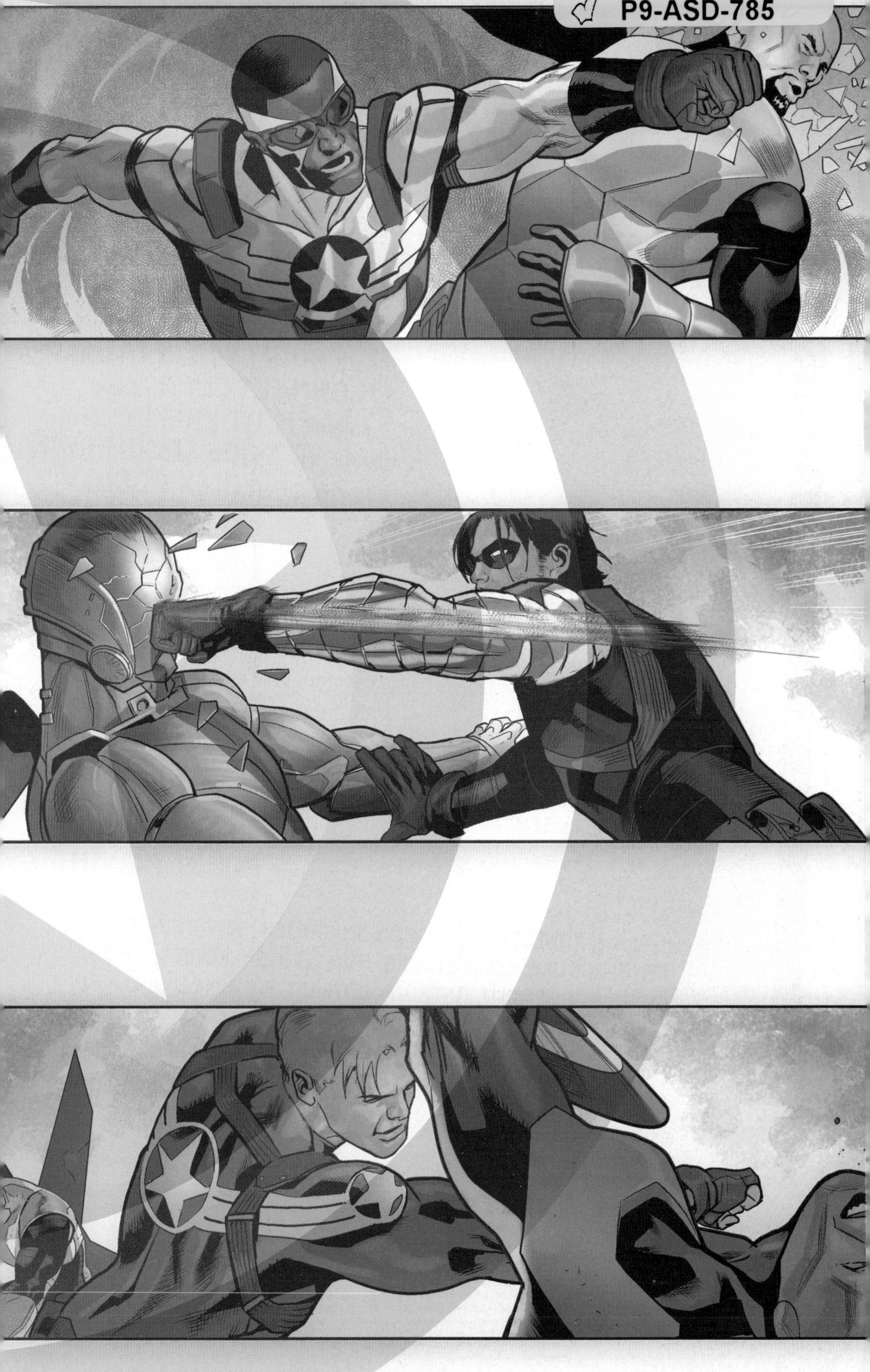

●●●○ Speed Walk 19:40 75%

STANDOFF

writer **NICK SPENCER**

Assault on Pleasant Hill Alpha
artist **JESÚS SAIZ**
letterer **VC'S CLAYTON COWLES**
cover art **JESÚS SAIZ**

Captain America: Sam Wilson #7
artists **ANGEL UNZUETA** (Sam) & **DANIEL ACUÑA** (Steve)
colorist **MATT YACKEY** (Sam)
letterer **VC'S JOE CARAMAGNA**
cover art **ALEX ROSS**

Captain America: Sam Wilson #8
artist **PAUL RENAUD**
colorist **DONO SÁNCHEZ-ALMARA** (pgs. 11-13)
letterer **VC'S JOE CARAMAGNA**
cover art **PAUL RENAUD**

Assault on Pleasant Hill Omega
artists **DANIEL ACUÑA**
with **Angel Unzueta**
colorists **DANIEL ACUÑA**
with **Matt Wilson**
letterer **VC'S CLAYTON COWLES**
cover art **DANIEL ACUÑA**

assistant editor **ALANNA SMITH**
editors **TOM BREVOORT**
with **KATIE KUBERT**

researchers **RONALD BYRD, MADISON CARTER, JEFF CHRISTIANSEN, PATRICK DUKE, KEVIN GARCIA, ROB LONDON, KEVIN WASSER, JACOB ROUGEMONT, ANTHONY COTILLETTA & MIKE O'SULLIVAN**

Captain America created by **Joe Simon & Jack Kirby**

collection editor **SARAH BRUNSTAD**
associate manager, digital assets **JOE HOCHSTEIN**
associate managing editor **KATERI WOODY**
senior editor, special projects **JENNIFER GRÜNWALD**
editor, special projects **MARK D. BEAZLEY**

vp, production & special projects **JEFF YOUNGQUIST**
svp print, sales & marketing **DAVID GABRIEL**
editor in chief **AXEL ALONSO**
chief creative officer **JOE QUESADA**
publisher **DAN BUCKLEY**
executive producer **ALAN FINE**

CAPTAIN AMERICA: SAM WILSON VOL. 2 — STANDOFF. Contains material originally published in magazine form as CAPTAIN AMERICA: SAM WILSON #7-8, ASSAULT ON PLEASANT HILL ALPHA #1 and ASSAULT ON PLEASANT HILL OMEGA #1. First printing 2016. ISBN# 978-0-7851-9641-9. Published by MARVEL WORLDWIDE, INC., a subsidiary of MARVEL ENTERTAINMENT, LLC. OFFICE OF PUBLICATION: 135 West 50th Street, New York, NY 10020. **Printed in the U.S.A.** ALAN FINE, President, Marvel Entertainment; DAN BUCKLEY, President, TV, Publishing & Brand Management; JOE QUESADA, Chief Creative Officer; TOM BREVOORT, SVP of Publishing; DAVID BOGART, SVP of Business Affairs & Operations, Publishing & Partnership; C.B. CEBULSKI, VP of Brand Management & Development, Asia; DAVID GABRIEL, SVP of Sales & Marketing, Publishing; JEFF YOUNGQUIST, VP of Production & Special Projects; DAN CARR, Executive Director of Publishing Technology; ALEX MORALES, Director of Publishing Operations; SUSAN CRESPI, Production Manager; STAN LEE, Chairman Emeritus. For information regarding advertising in Marvel Comics or on Marvel.com, please contact Vit DeBellis, Integrated Sales Manager, at vdebellis@marvel.com. For Marvel subscription inquiries, please call 888-511-5480. **Manufactured between 8/5/2016 and 9/12/2016 by LSC COMMUNICATIONS INC., ROANOKE, VA, USA.**

10 9 8 7 6 5 4 3 2 1

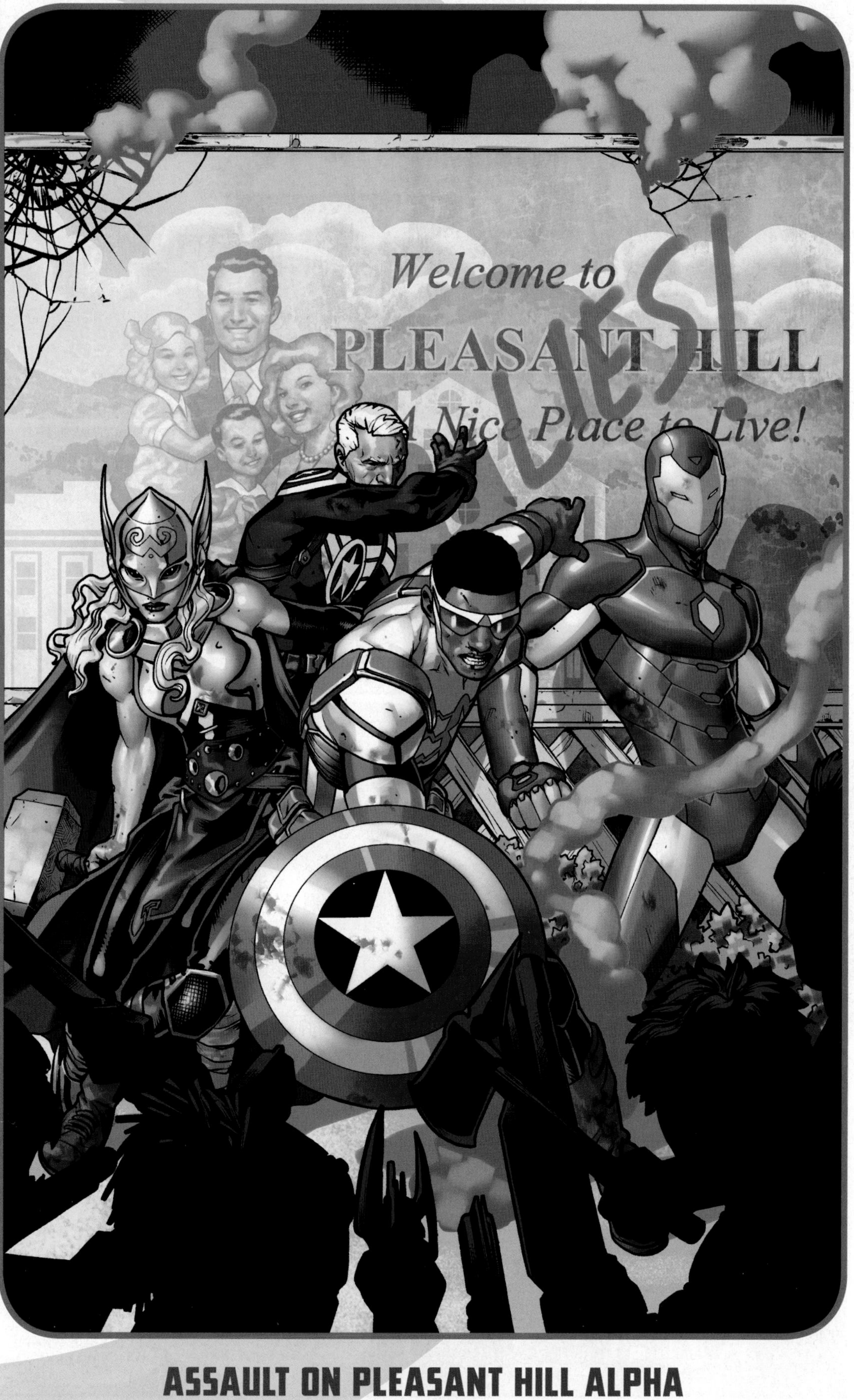

Welcome to
PLEASANT HILL
A Nice Place to Live!
LIES!

ASSAULT ON PLEASANT HILL ALPHA

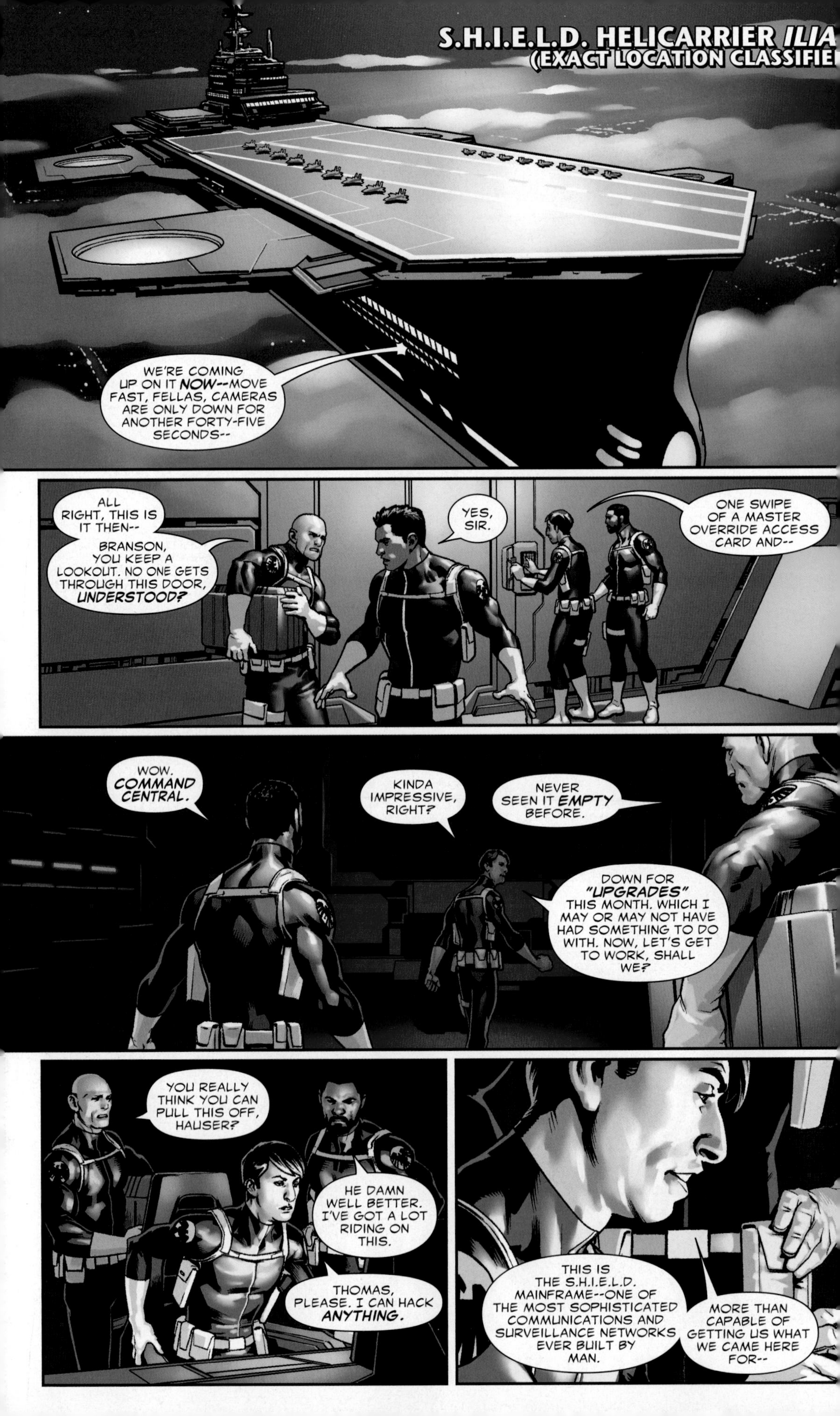
S.H.I.E.L.D. HELICARRIER ILIA
(EXACT LOCATION CLASSIFIE
WE'RE COMING UP ON IT NOW--MOVE FAST, FELLAS, CAMERAS ARE ONLY DOWN FOR ANOTHER FORTY-FIVE SECONDS--
ALL RIGHT, THIS IS IT THEN--
BRANSON, YOU KEEP A LOOKOUT. NO ONE GETS THROUGH THIS DOOR, UNDERSTOOD?
YES, SIR.
ONE SWIPE OF A MASTER OVERRIDE ACCESS CARD AND--
WOW. COMMAND CENTRAL.
KINDA IMPRESSIVE, RIGHT?
NEVER SEEN IT EMPTY BEFORE.
DOWN FOR "UPGRADES" THIS MONTH. WHICH I MAY OR MAY NOT HAVE HAD SOMETHING TO DO WITH. NOW, LET'S GET TO WORK, SHALL WE?
YOU REALLY THINK YOU CAN PULL THIS OFF, HAUSER?
HE DAMN WELL BETTER. I'VE GOT A LOT RIDING ON THIS.
THOMAS, PLEASE. I CAN HACK ANYTHING.
THIS IS THE S.H.I.E.L.D. MAINFRAME--ONE OF THE MOST SOPHISTICATED COMMUNICATIONS AND SURVEILLANCE NETWORKS EVER BUILT BY MAN.
MORE THAN CAPABLE OF GETTING US WHAT WE CAME HERE FOR--

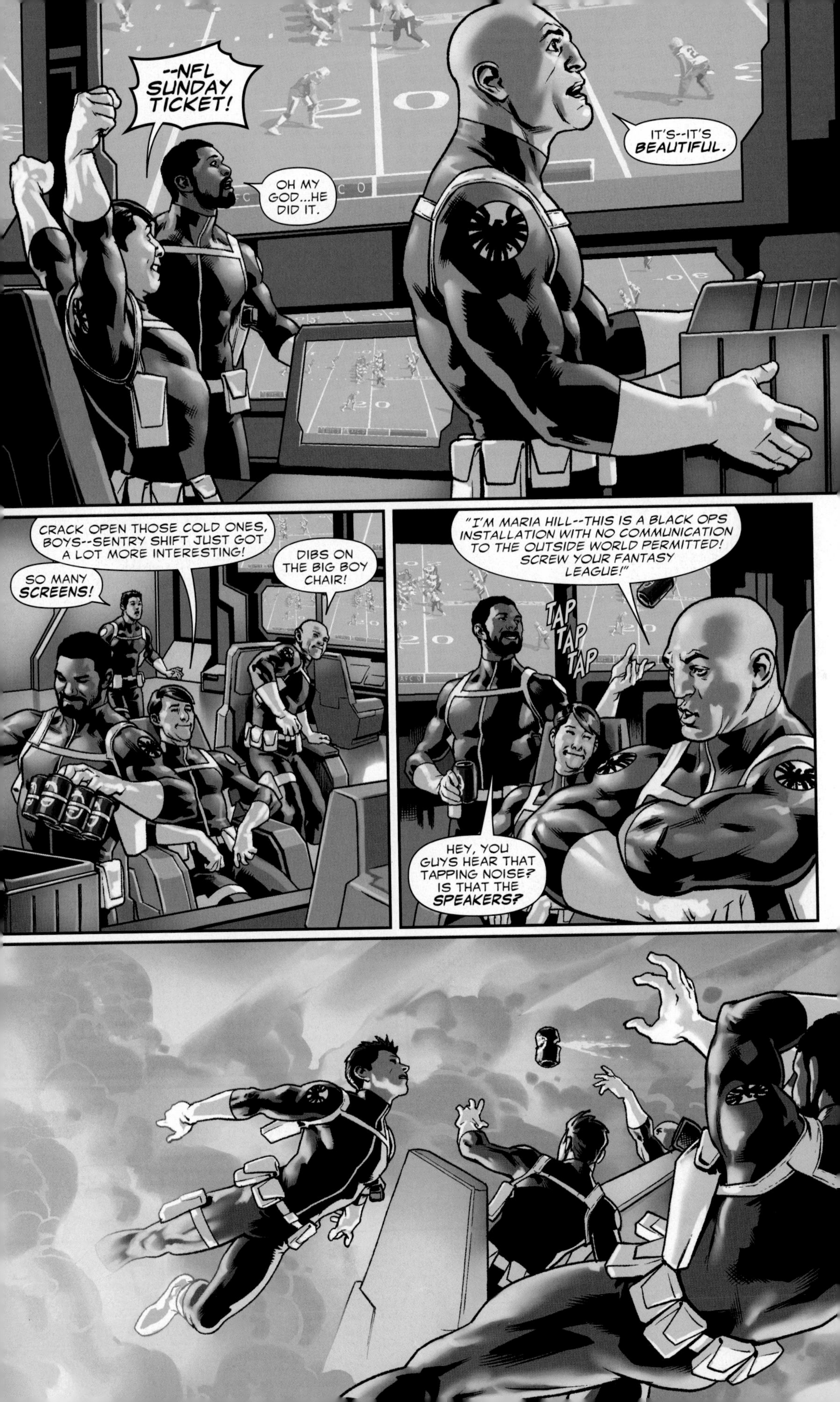
--NFL SUNDAY TICKET!
OH MY GOD...HE DID IT.
IT'S--IT'S BEAUTIFUL.
CRACK OPEN THOSE COLD ONES, BOYS--SENTRY SHIFT JUST GOT A LOT MORE INTERESTING!
SO MANY SCREENS!
DIBS ON THE BIG BOY CHAIR!
"I'M MARIA HILL--THIS IS A BLACK OPS INSTALLATION WITH NO COMMUNICATION TO THE OUTSIDE WORLD PERMITTED! SCREW YOUR FANTASY LEAGUE!"
TAP TAP TAP
HEY, YOU GUYS HEAR THAT TAPPING NOISE? IS THAT THE SPEAKERS?

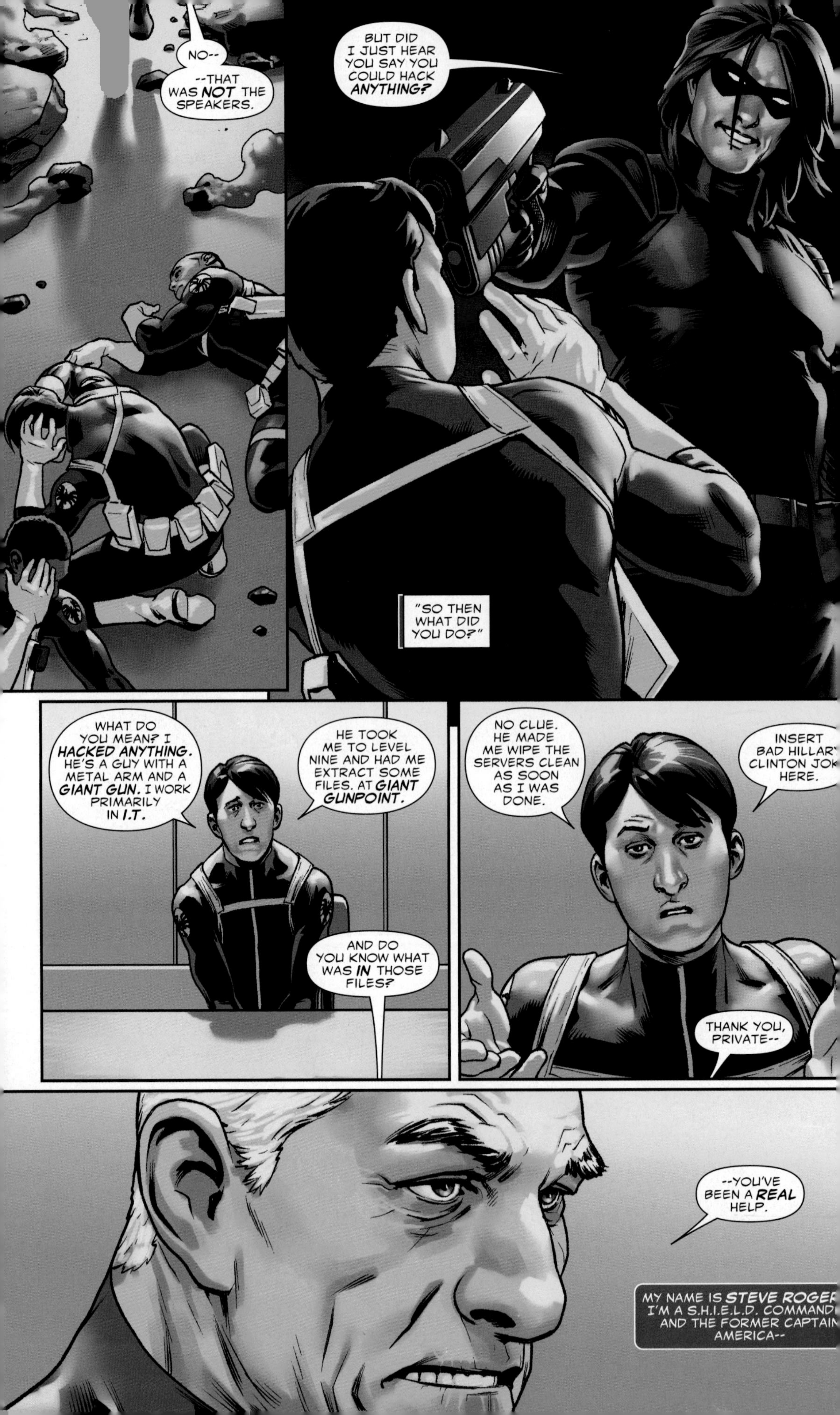

NO--
--THAT WAS NOT THE SPEAKERS.
BUT DID I JUST HEAR YOU SAY YOU COULD HACK ANYTHING?
"SO THEN WHAT DID YOU DO?"
WHAT DO YOU MEAN? I HACKED ANYTHING. HE'S A GUY WITH A METAL ARM AND A GIANT GUN. I WORK PRIMARILY IN I.T.
HE TOOK ME TO LEVEL NINE AND HAD ME EXTRACT SOME FILES. AT GIANT GUNPOINT.
AND DO YOU KNOW WHAT WAS IN THOSE FILES?
NO CLUE. HE MADE ME WIPE THE SERVERS CLEAN AS SOON AS I WAS DONE.
INSERT BAD HILLAR CLINTON JOK HERE.
THANK YOU, PRIVATE--
--YOU'VE BEEN A REAL HELP.
MY NAME IS STEVE ROGER I'M A S.H.I.E.L.D. COMMAND AND THE FORMER CAPTAIN AMERICA--

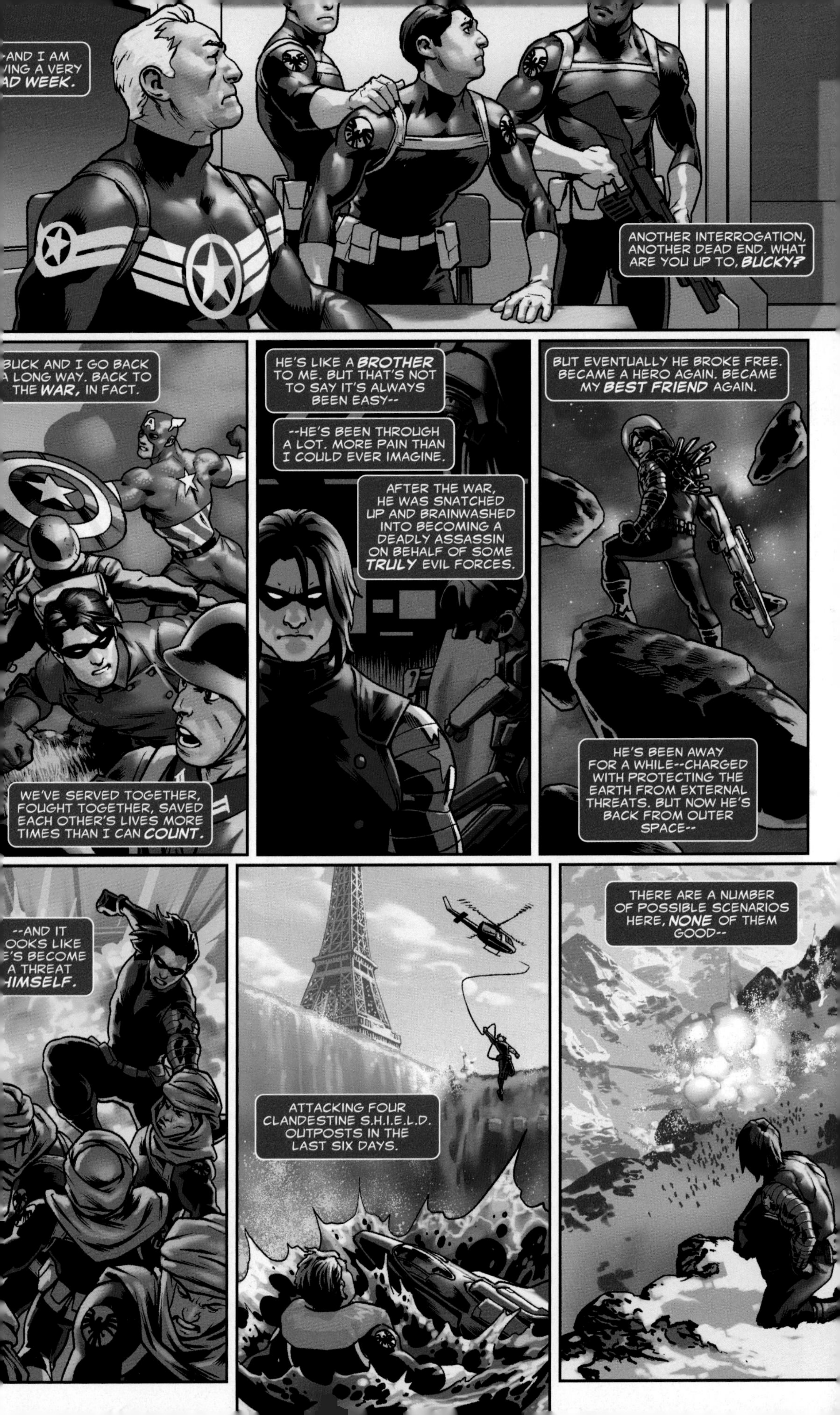

-AND I AM
VING A VERY
AD WEEK.
ANOTHER INTERROGATION, ANOTHER DEAD END. WHAT ARE YOU UP TO, BUCKY?
BUCK AND I GO BACK A LONG WAY. BACK TO THE WAR, IN FACT.
WE'VE SERVED TOGETHER, FOUGHT TOGETHER, SAVED EACH OTHER'S LIVES MORE TIMES THAN I CAN COUNT.
HE'S LIKE A BROTHER TO ME. BUT THAT'S NOT TO SAY IT'S ALWAYS BEEN EASY--
--HE'S BEEN THROUGH A LOT. MORE PAIN THAN I COULD EVER IMAGINE.
AFTER THE WAR, HE WAS SNATCHED UP AND BRAINWASHED INTO BECOMING A DEADLY ASSASSIN ON BEHALF OF SOME TRULY EVIL FORCES.
BUT EVENTUALLY HE BROKE FREE. BECAME A HERO AGAIN. BECAME MY BEST FRIEND AGAIN.
HE'S BEEN AWAY FOR A WHILE--CHARGED WITH PROTECTING THE EARTH FROM EXTERNAL THREATS. BUT NOW HE'S BACK FROM OUTER SPACE--
--AND IT
OOKS LIKE
E'S BECOME
A THREAT
HIMSELF.
ATTACKING FOUR CLANDESTINE S.H.I.E.L.D. OUTPOSTS IN THE LAST SIX DAYS.
THERE ARE A NUMBER OF POSSIBLE SCENARIOS HERE, NONE OF THEM GOOD--

THE WORST POSSIBILITY BEING THAT HIS OLD WINTER SOLDIER PROGRAMMING IS SOMEHOW REASSERTING ITSELF.

I DON'T *WANT* TO BELIEVE THAT'S THE CASE HERE--BUT HOW ELSE CAN I EXPLAIN THIS?

IT'S NOT JUST THAT HE'S TARGETING HIS ALLIES-- IT'S THAT I KNOW, IF BUCK WERE HIMSELF AND HE WERE DOING SOMETHING THIS RISKY--SOMETHING THAT LOOKED THIS *BAD*--

--HE'D TALK TO HIS *BEST FRIEND* ABOUT IT FIRST.

THAT'S WHAT'S BEEN DOGGING ME AS I'VE CHASED HIM ACROSS THESE BLACK OPS SITES--

--BUT HERE, I FINALLY GET THE HOPE I'VE BEEN DESPERATE FOR--EVEN IF IT IS JUST A *GLIMMER*--

--AT LEAST IT'S SOMETHING.

UM, COMMANDER ROGERS?

BUT IF THERE'S ONE THING I'VE LEARNED--

UH, BEFORE I GO, SIR--I WAS JUST WONDERING--IS THERE ANY CHANCE YOU COULD NOT TELL DIRECTO HILL ABOUT THE FOOTBA THING? SHE...DOESN'T REALL HAVE THE BEST SENSE OF HUMOR ABOUT THIS STUFF.

AND I CANNOT GO BACK TO SUBSTITUTE TEACHING.

--IT'S TH THINGS C ALWAYS C WORSE

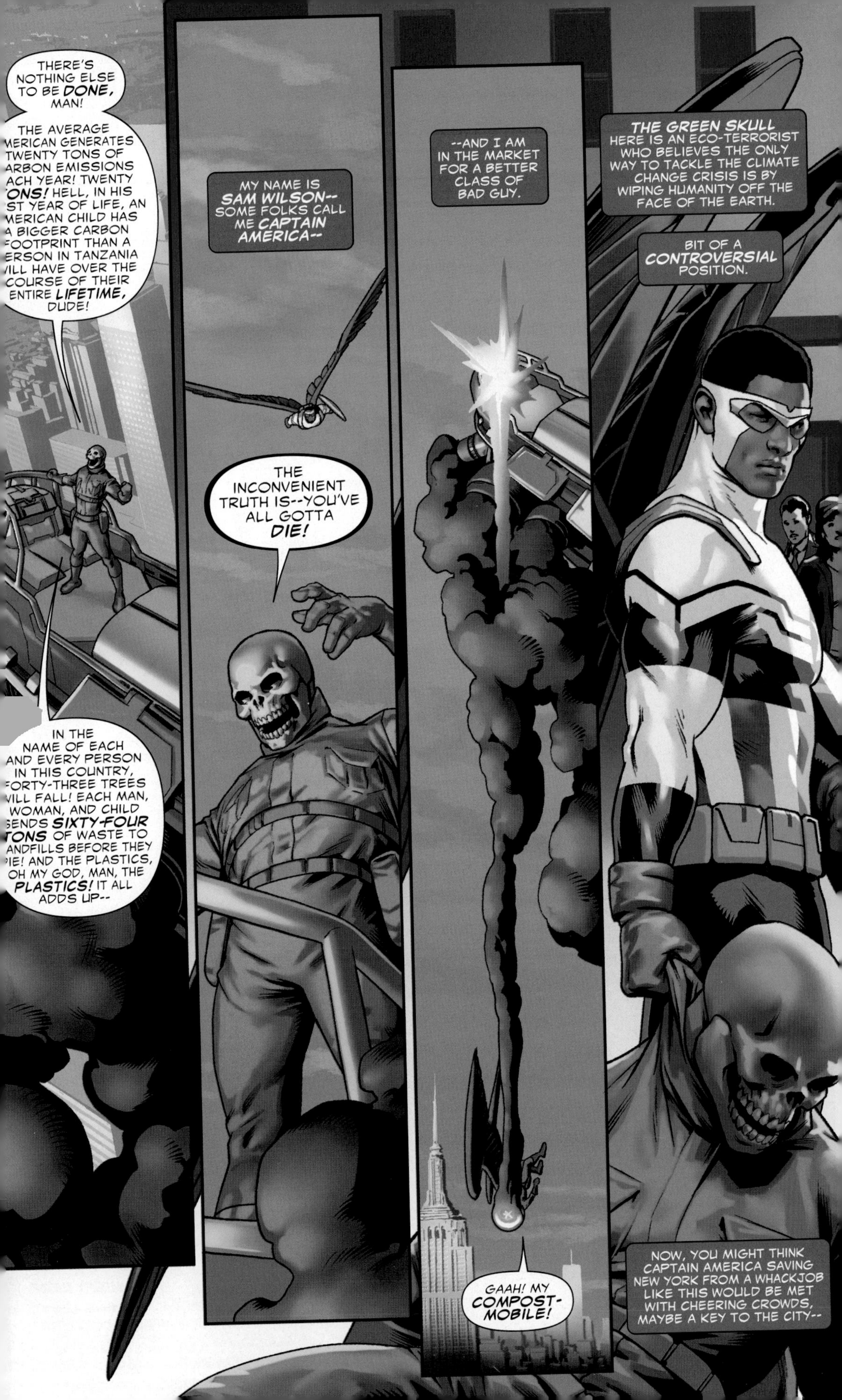

THERE'S NOTHING ELSE TO BE DONE, MAN!
THE AVERAGE MERICAN GENERATES TWENTY TONS OF ARBON EMISSIONS ACH YEAR! TWENTY ONS! HELL, IN HIS ST YEAR OF LIFE, AN MERICAN CHILD HAS A BIGGER CARBON FOOTPRINT THAN A ERSON IN TANZANIA VILL HAVE OVER THE COURSE OF THEIR ENTIRE LIFETIME, DUDE!
IN THE NAME OF EACH AND EVERY PERSON IN THIS COUNTRY, ORTY-THREE TREES VILL FALL! EACH MAN, WOMAN, AND CHILD SENDS SIXTY-FOUR ONS OF WASTE TO ANDFILLS BEFORE THEY IE! AND THE PLASTICS, OH MY GOD, MAN, THE PLASTICS! IT ALL ADDS UP--
MY NAME IS SAM WILSON-- SOME FOLKS CALL ME CAPTAIN AMERICA--
THE INCONVENIENT TRUTH IS--YOU'VE ALL GOTTA DIE!
--AND I AM IN THE MARKET FOR A BETTER CLASS OF BAD GUY.
GAAH! MY COMPOST-MOBILE!
THE GREEN SKULL HERE IS AN ECO-TERRORIST WHO BELIEVES THE ONLY WAY TO TACKLE THE CLIMATE CHANGE CRISIS IS BY WIPING HUMANITY OFF THE FACE OF THE EARTH.
BIT OF A CONTROVERSIAL POSITION.
NOW, YOU MIGHT THINK CAPTAIN AMERICA SAVING NEW YORK FROM A WHACKJOB LIKE THIS WOULD BE MET WITH CHEERING CROWDS, MAYBE A KEY TO THE CITY--

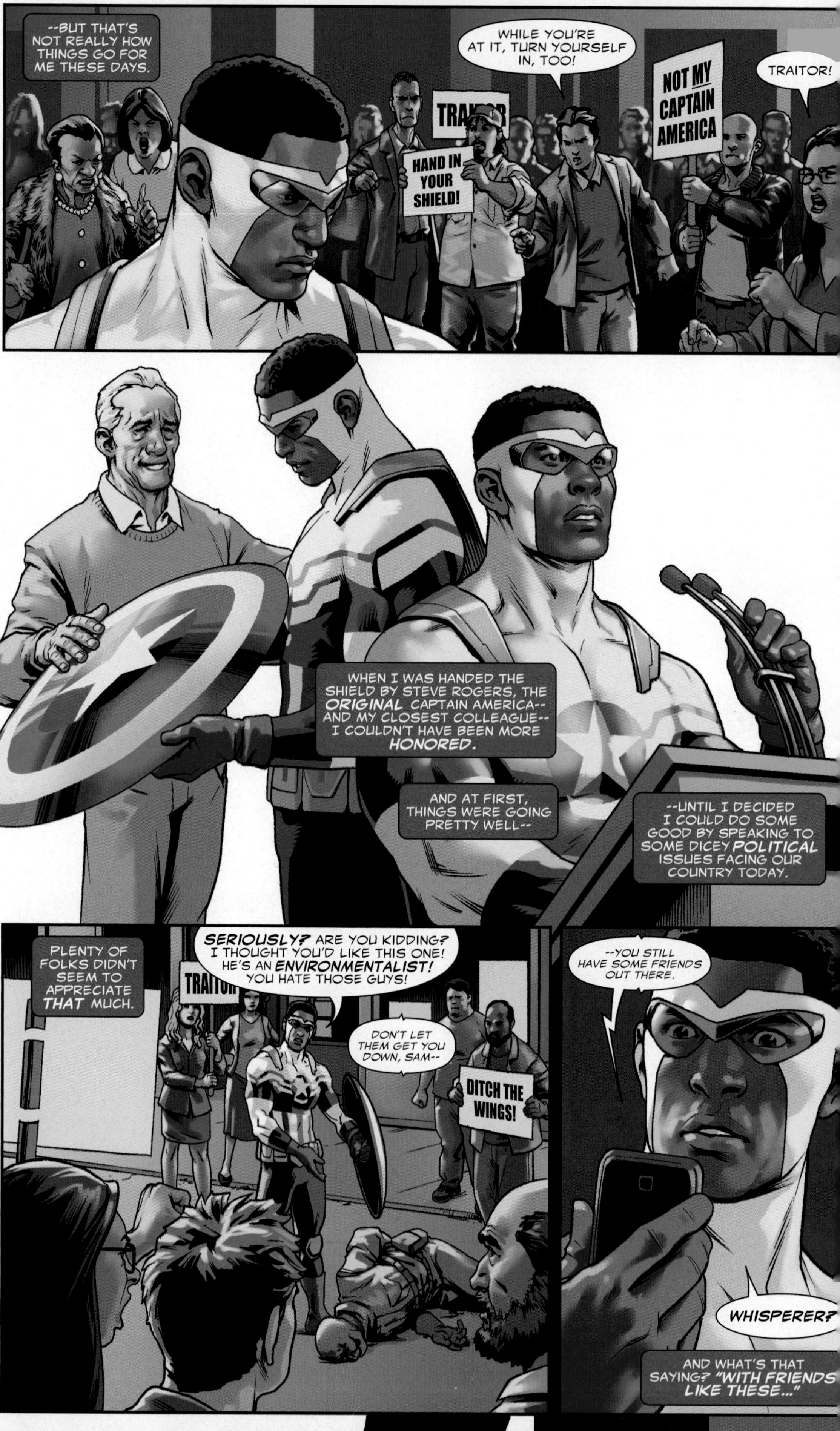

--BUT THAT'S NOT REALLY HOW THINGS GO FOR ME THESE DAYS.
HAND IN YOUR SHIELD!
WHILE YOU'RE AT IT, TURN YOURSELF IN, TOO!
NOT MY CAPTAIN AMERICA
TRAITOR!
WHEN I WAS HANDED THE SHIELD BY STEVE ROGERS, THE ORIGINAL CAPTAIN AMERICA-- AND MY CLOSEST COLLEAGUE-- I COULDN'T HAVE BEEN MORE HONORED.
AND AT FIRST, THINGS WERE GOING PRETTY WELL--
--UNTIL I DECIDED I COULD DO SOME GOOD BY SPEAKING TO SOME DICEY POLITICAL ISSUES FACING OUR COUNTRY TODAY.
PLENTY OF FOLKS DIDN'T SEEM TO APPRECIATE THAT MUCH.
SERIOUSLY? ARE YOU KIDDING? I THOUGHT YOU'D LIKE THIS ONE! HE'S AN ENVIRONMENTALIST! YOU HATE THOSE GUYS!
DON'T LET THEM GET YOU DOWN, SAM--
DITCH THE WINGS!
--YOU STILL HAVE SOME FRIENDS OUT THERE.
WHISPERER?
AND WHAT'S THAT SAYING? "WITH FRIENDS LIKE THESE..."

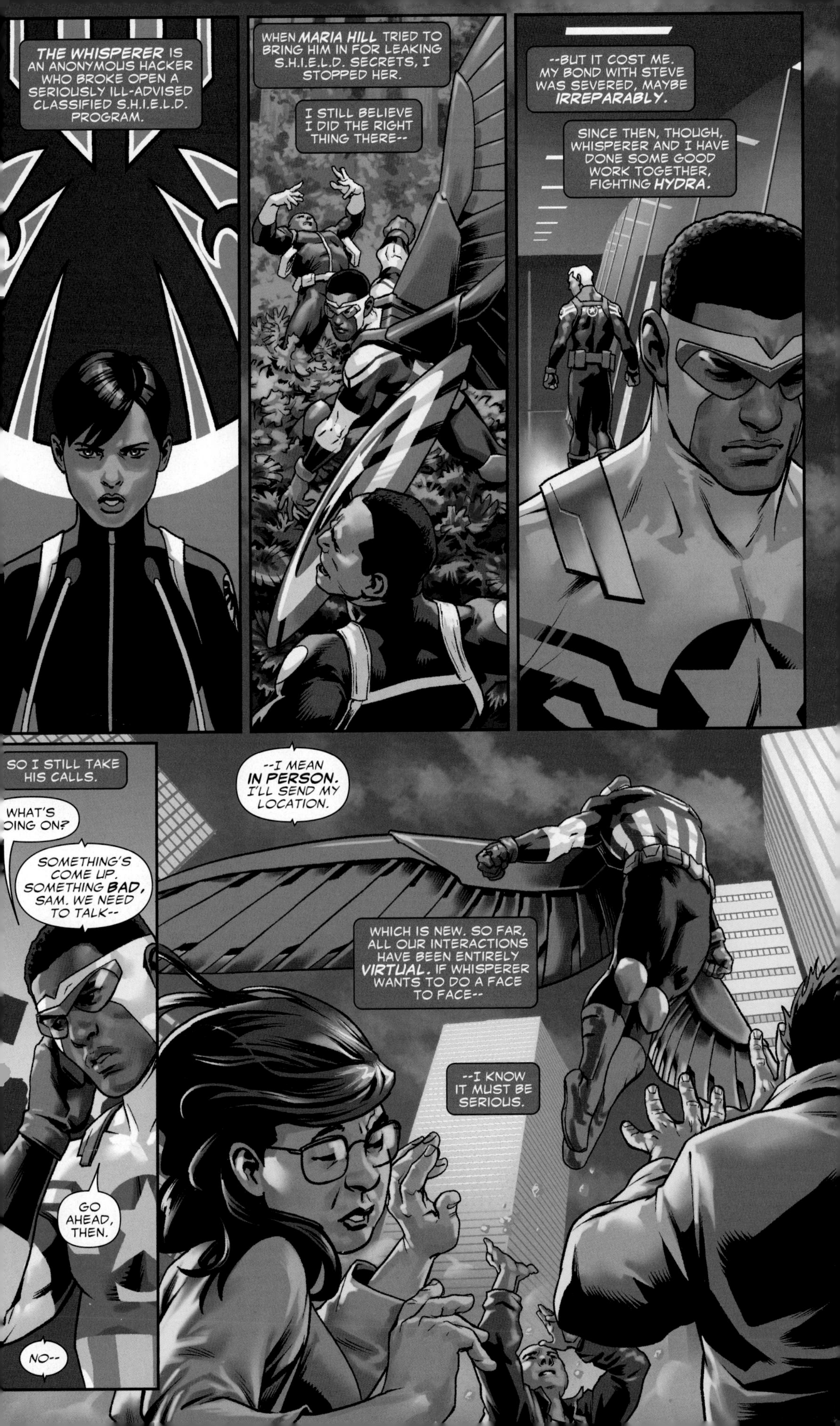
THE WHISPERER IS AN ANONYMOUS HACKER WHO BROKE OPEN A SERIOUSLY ILL-ADVISED CLASSIFIED S.H.I.E.L.D. PROGRAM.
WHEN MARIA HILL TRIED TO BRING HIM IN FOR LEAKING S.H.I.E.L.D. SECRETS, I STOPPED HER.
I STILL BELIEVE I DID THE RIGHT THING THERE--
--BUT IT COST ME. MY BOND WITH STEVE WAS SEVERED, MAYBE IRREPARABLY.
SINCE THEN, THOUGH, WHISPERER AND I HAVE DONE SOME GOOD WORK TOGETHER, FIGHTING HYDRA.
SO I STILL TAKE HIS CALLS.
WHAT'S OING ON?
SOMETHING'S COME UP. SOMETHING BAD, SAM. WE NEED TO TALK--
--I MEAN IN PERSON. I'LL SEND MY LOCATION.
WHICH IS NEW. SO FAR, ALL OUR INTERACTIONS HAVE BEEN ENTIRELY VIRTUAL. IF WHISPERER WANTS TO DO A FACE TO FACE--
--I KNOW IT MUST BE SERIOUS.
GO AHEAD, THEN.
NO--

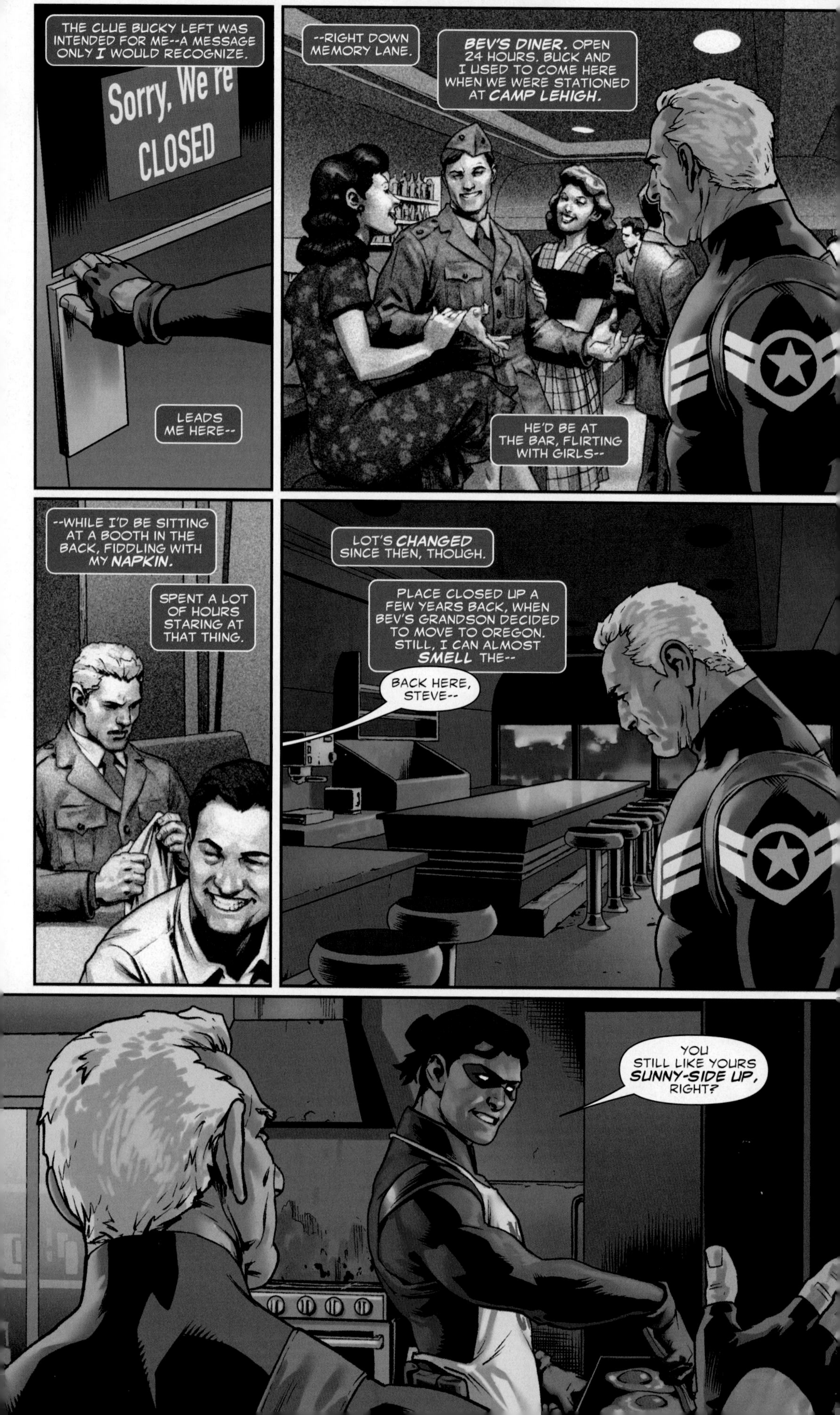
THE CLUE BUCKY LEFT WAS INTENDED FOR ME--A MESSAGE ONLY I WOULD RECOGNIZE.
Sorry, We're CLOSED
LEADS ME HERE--
--RIGHT DOWN MEMORY LANE.
BEV'S DINER. OPEN 24 HOURS. BUCK AND I USED TO COME HERE WHEN WE WERE STATIONED AT CAMP LEHIGH.
HE'D BE AT THE BAR, FLIRTING WITH GIRLS--
--WHILE I'D BE SITTING AT A BOOTH IN THE BACK, FIDDLING WITH MY NAPKIN.
SPENT A LOT OF HOURS STARING AT THAT THING.
LOT'S CHANGED SINCE THEN, THOUGH.
PLACE CLOSED UP A FEW YEARS BACK, WHEN BEV'S GRANDSON DECIDED TO MOVE TO OREGON. STILL, I CAN ALMOST SMELL THE--
BACK HERE, STEVE--
YOU STILL LIKE YOURS SUNNY-SIDE UP, RIGHT?

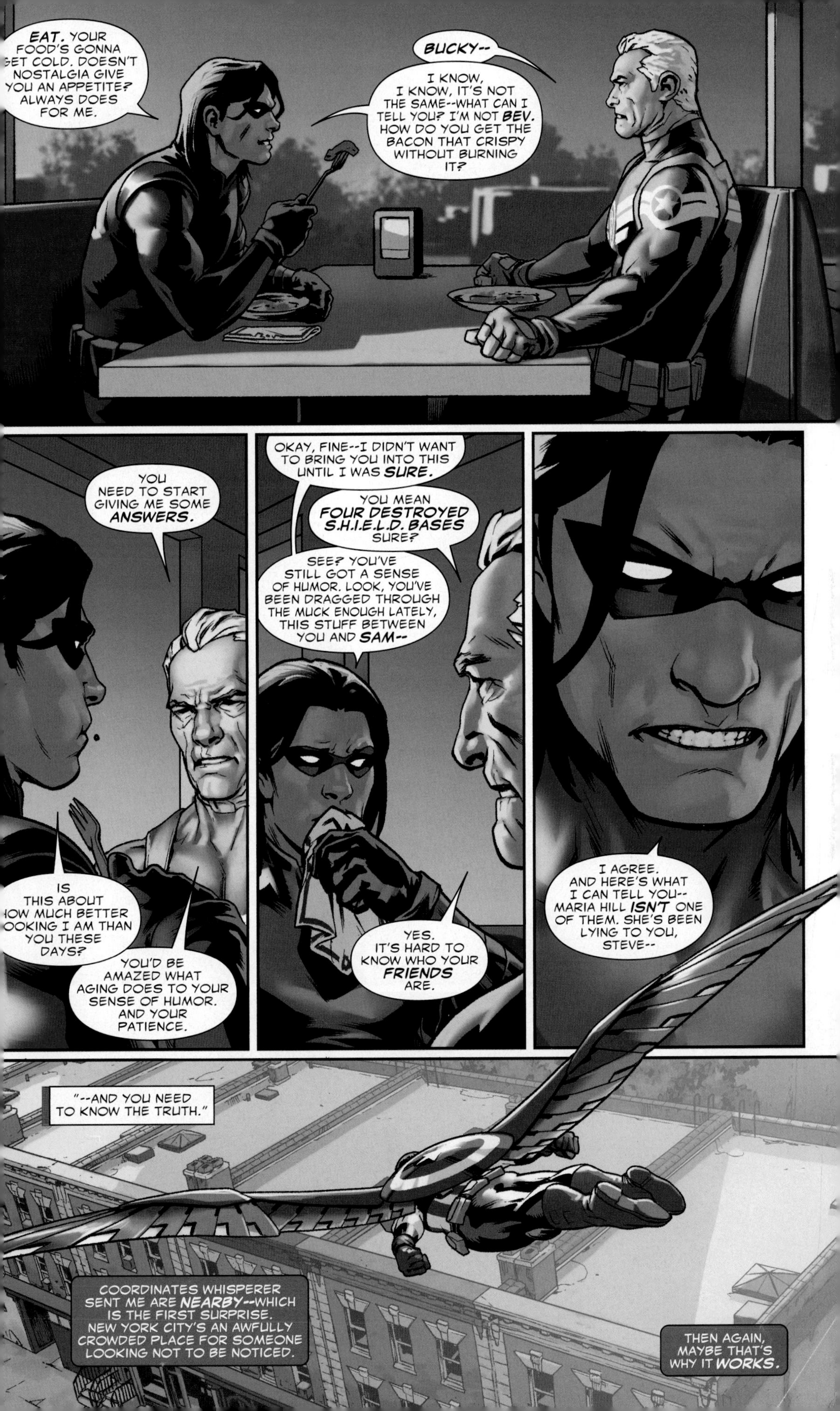
EAT. YOUR FOOD'S GONNA GET COLD. DOESN'T NOSTALGIA GIVE YOU AN APPETITE? ALWAYS DOES FOR ME.
BUCKY--
I KNOW, I KNOW, IT'S NOT THE SAME--WHAT CAN I TELL YOU? I'M NOT BEV. HOW DO YOU GET THE BACON THAT CRISPY WITHOUT BURNING IT?
YOU NEED TO START GIVING ME SOME ANSWERS.
IS THIS ABOUT HOW MUCH BETTER LOOKING I AM THAN YOU THESE DAYS?
YOU'D BE AMAZED WHAT AGING DOES TO YOUR SENSE OF HUMOR. AND YOUR PATIENCE.
OKAY, FINE--I DIDN'T WANT TO BRING YOU INTO THIS UNTIL I WAS SURE.
YOU MEAN FOUR DESTROYED S.H.I.E.L.D. BASES SURE?
SEE? YOU'VE STILL GOT A SENSE OF HUMOR. LOOK, YOU'VE BEEN DRAGGED THROUGH THE MUCK ENOUGH LATELY, THIS STUFF BETWEEN YOU AND SAM--
YES. IT'S HARD TO KNOW WHO YOUR FRIENDS ARE.
I AGREE. AND HERE'S WHAT I CAN TELL YOU-- MARIA HILL ISN'T ONE OF THEM. SHE'S BEEN LYING TO YOU, STEVE--
"--AND YOU NEED TO KNOW THE TRUTH."
COORDINATES WHISPERER SENT ME ARE NEARBY--WHICH IS THE FIRST SURPRISE. NEW YORK CITY'S AN AWFULLY CROWDED PLACE FOR SOMEONE LOOKING NOT TO BE NOTICED.
THEN AGAIN, MAYBE THAT'S WHY IT WORKS.

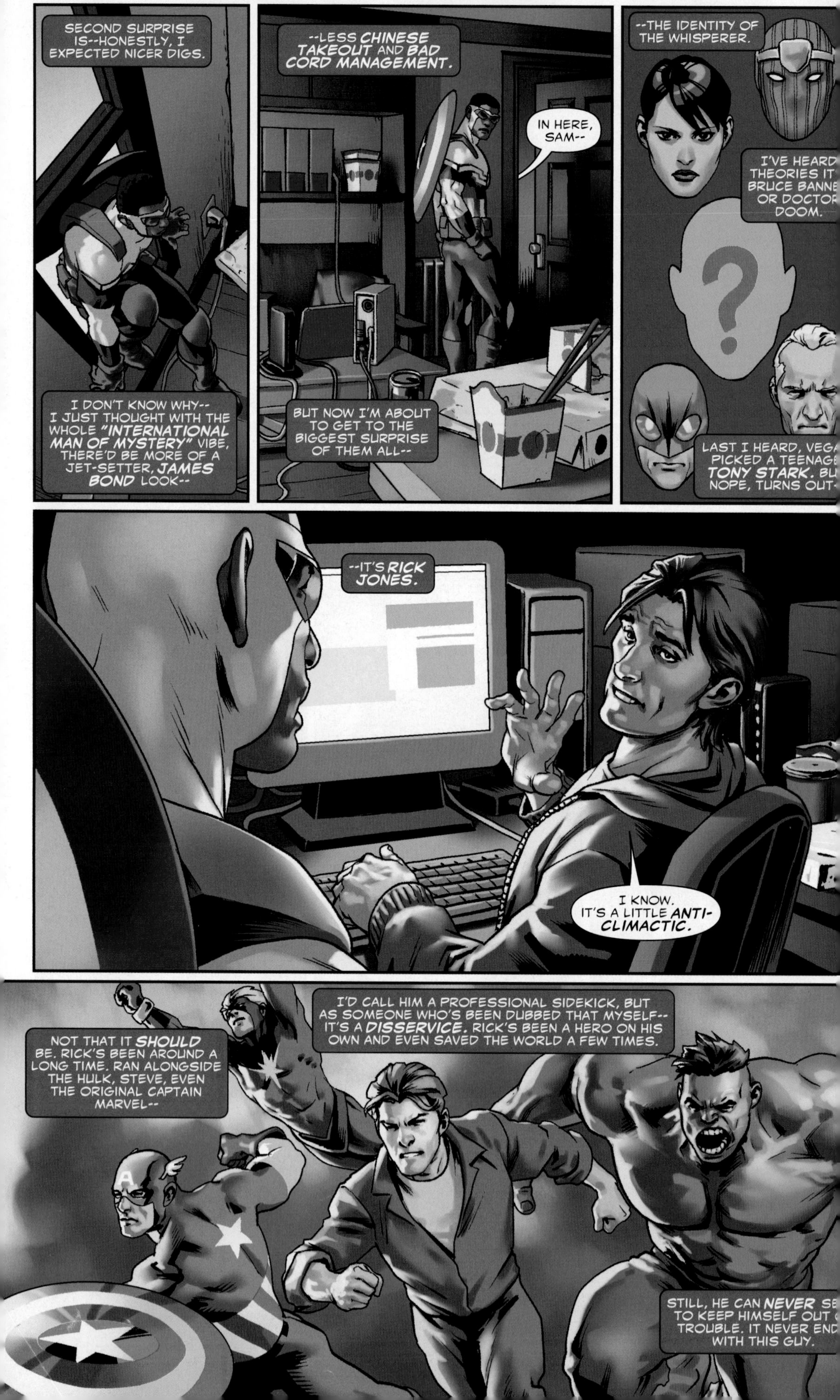
SECOND SURPRISE IS--HONESTLY, I EXPECTED NICER DIGS.
I DON'T KNOW WHY-- I JUST THOUGHT WITH THE WHOLE "INTERNATIONAL MAN OF MYSTERY" VIBE, THERE'D BE MORE OF A JET-SETTER, JAMES BOND LOOK--
--LESS CHINESE TAKEOUT AND BAD CORD MANAGEMENT.
IN HERE, SAM--
BUT NOW I'M ABOUT TO GET TO THE BIGGEST SURPRISE OF THEM ALL--
--THE IDENTITY OF THE WHISPERER.
I'VE HEARD THEORIES IT BRUCE BANNE OR DOCTOR DOOM.
LAST I HEARD, VEGA PICKED A TEENAGE TONY STARK. BU NOPE, TURNS OUT-
--IT'S RICK JONES.
I KNOW. IT'S A LITTLE ANTI-CLIMACTIC.
NOT THAT IT SHOULD BE. RICK'S BEEN AROUND A LONG TIME. RAN ALONGSIDE THE HULK, STEVE, EVEN THE ORIGINAL CAPTAIN MARVEL--
I'D CALL HIM A PROFESSIONAL SIDEKICK, BUT AS SOMEONE WHO'S BEEN DUBBED THAT MYSELF-- IT'S A DISSERVICE. RICK'S BEEN A HERO ON HIS OWN AND EVEN SAVED THE WORLD A FEW TIMES.
STILL, HE CAN NEVER SE TO KEEP HIMSELF OUT TROUBLE. IT NEVER END WITH THIS GUY.

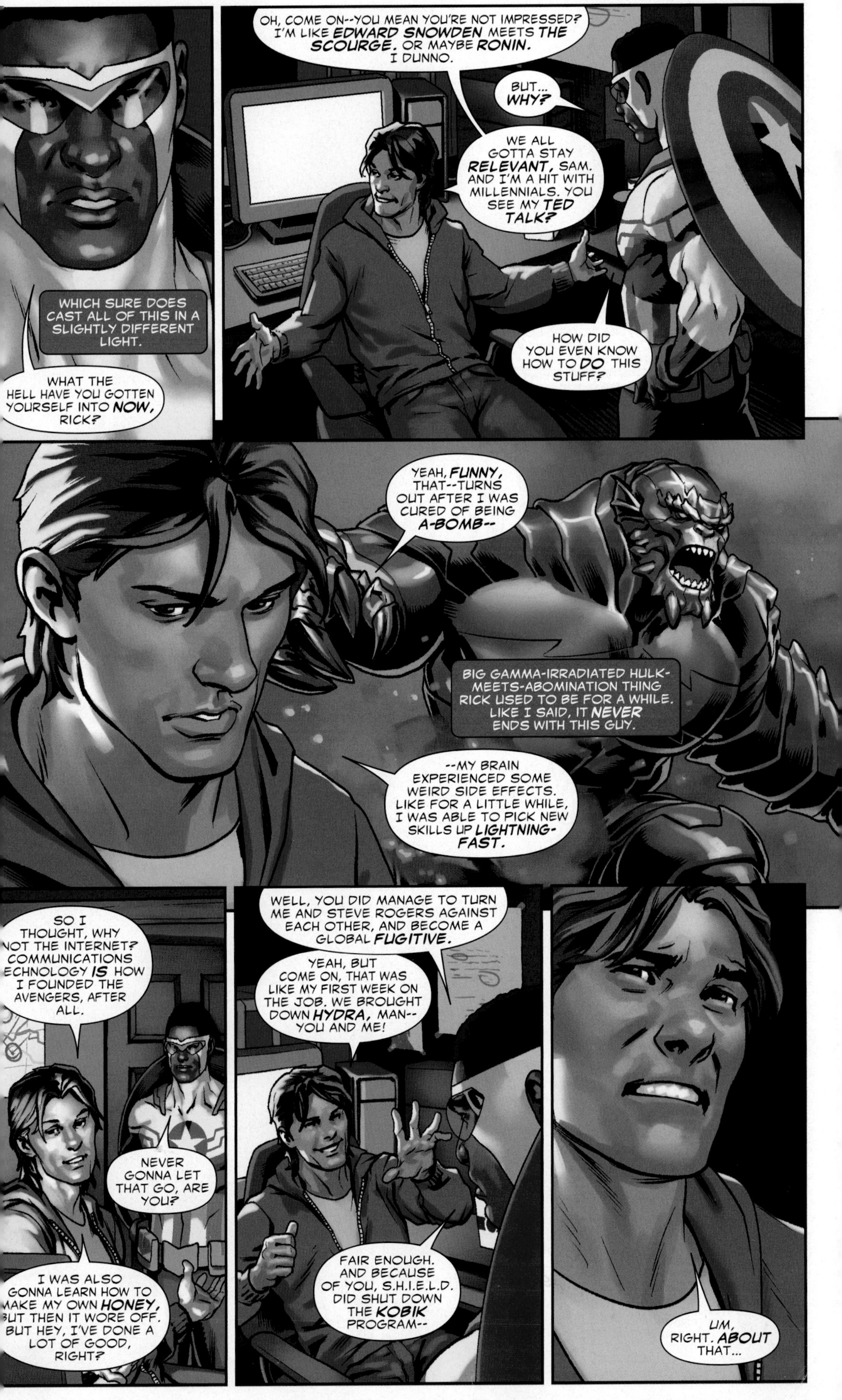
WHICH SURE DOES CAST ALL OF THIS IN A SLIGHTLY DIFFERENT LIGHT.
WHAT THE HELL HAVE YOU GOTTEN YOURSELF INTO NOW, RICK?
OH, COME ON--YOU MEAN YOU'RE NOT IMPRESSED? I'M LIKE EDWARD SNOWDEN MEETS THE SCOURGE. OR MAYBE RONIN. I DUNNO.
BUT... WHY?
WE ALL GOTTA STAY RELEVANT, SAM. AND I'M A HIT WITH MILLENNIALS. YOU SEE MY TED TALK?
HOW DID YOU EVEN KNOW HOW TO DO THIS STUFF?
YEAH, FUNNY, THAT--TURNS OUT AFTER I WAS CURED OF BEING A-BOMB--
BIG GAMMA-IRRADIATED HULK-MEETS-ABOMINATION THING RICK USED TO BE FOR A WHILE. LIKE I SAID, IT NEVER ENDS WITH THIS GUY.
--MY BRAIN EXPERIENCED SOME WEIRD SIDE EFFECTS. LIKE FOR A LITTLE WHILE, I WAS ABLE TO PICK NEW SKILLS UP LIGHTNING-FAST.
SO I THOUGHT, WHY NOT THE INTERNET? COMMUNICATIONS ECHNOLOGY IS HOW I FOUNDED THE AVENGERS, AFTER ALL.
NEVER GONNA LET THAT GO, ARE YOU?
I WAS ALSO GONNA LEARN HOW TO MAKE MY OWN HONEY, BUT THEN IT WORE OFF. BUT HEY, I'VE DONE A LOT OF GOOD, RIGHT?
WELL, YOU DID MANAGE TO TURN ME AND STEVE ROGERS AGAINST EACH OTHER, AND BECOME A GLOBAL FUGITIVE.
YEAH, BUT COME ON, THAT WAS LIKE MY FIRST WEEK ON THE JOB. WE BROUGHT DOWN HYDRA, MAN--YOU AND ME!
FAIR ENOUGH. AND BECAUSE OF YOU, S.H.I.E.L.D. DID SHUT DOWN THE KOBIK PROGRAM--
UM, RIGHT. ABOUT THAT...

"KOBIK. S.H.I.E.L.D.'S SECRET INITIATIVE TO USE COSMIC CUBE FRAGMENTS TO ALTER REALITY IN THE INTEREST OF GLOBAL SECURITY, OR ACCORDING TO MARIA HILL'S WHIMS, PLENTY SAID--

"EITHER WAY, ONCE THE WHISPERER LEAKS THE DETAILS OF ITS EXISTENCE TO THE PUBLIC, AND CAPTAIN AMERICAS BOTH PRESENT AND FORMER STRONGLY CONDEMN IT, IT GOES UP IN FLAMES--"

--EXCEPT IT DIDN'T.

WHAT ARE YOU SAYING RICK?

TURNS OUT SCIENTISTS HAVE GAMBLING DEBTS AND NAKED SELFIES JUST LIKE THE REST OF US. ONE WAY OR ANOTHER, SHE GOT TO ALL OF THEM.

WOMAN IS TENACIOUS, YOU HAVE TO GIVE HER THAT.

BUT IF THE CUBE FRAGMENTS ARE STILL OUT THERE, THAT MEANS--

SHE'S USING THEM. YEAH--THAT MUCH I KNOW. BUT--

I CAN'T SAY HOW SHE'S USING THEM. THAT'S THE PART I DON'T KNOW YET.

BUT I INTEND TO FIND OUT.

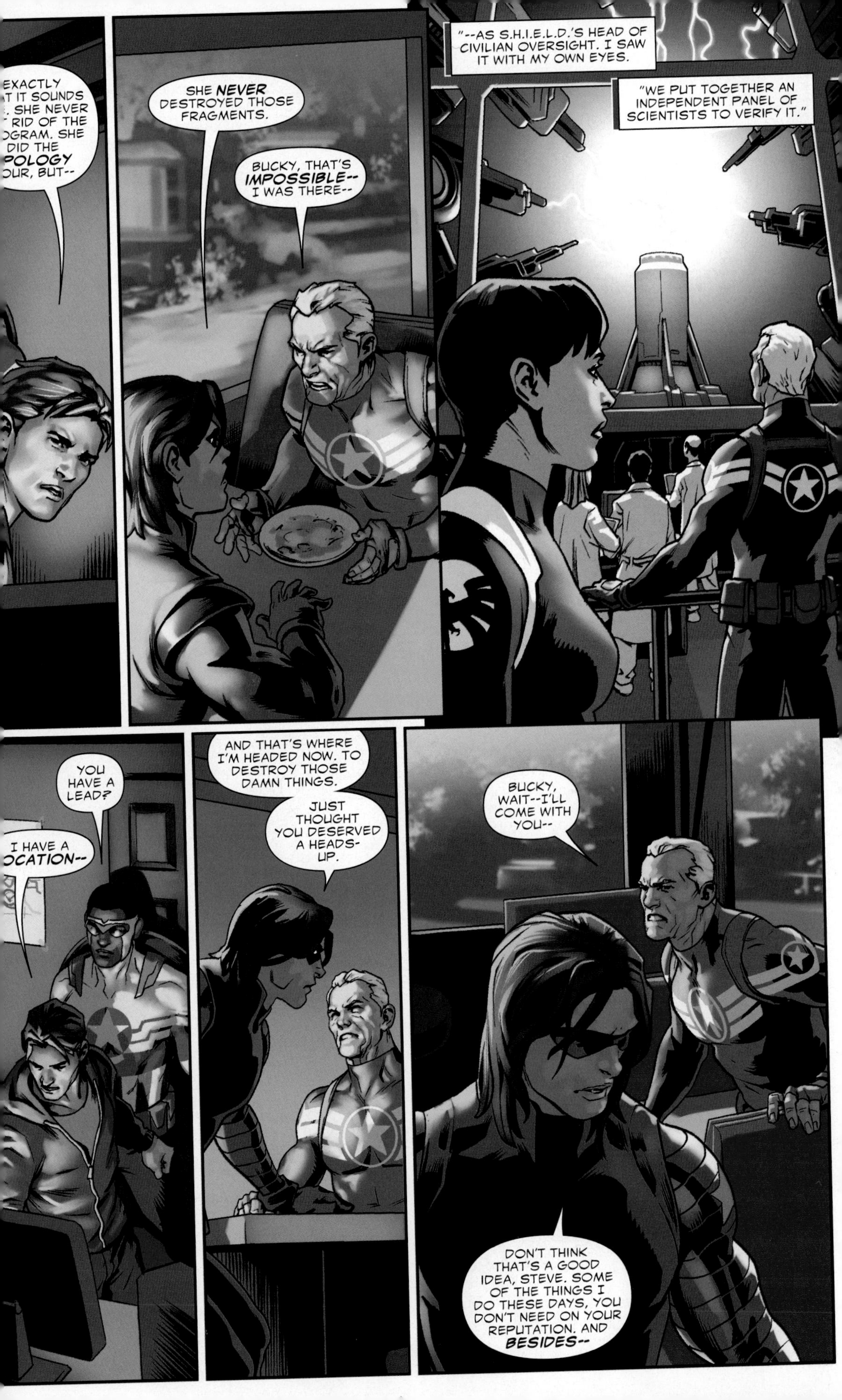

EXACTLY
AT IT SOUNDS
. SHE NEVER
RID OF THE
OGRAM. SHE
DID THE
POLOGY
OUR, BUT--
SHE NEVER DESTROYED THOSE FRAGMENTS.
BUCKY, THAT'S IMPOSSIBLE-- I WAS THERE--
"--AS S.H.I.E.L.D.'S HEAD OF CIVILIAN OVERSIGHT. I SAW IT WITH MY OWN EYES.
"WE PUT TOGETHER AN INDEPENDENT PANEL OF SCIENTISTS TO VERIFY IT."
YOU HAVE A LEAD?
I HAVE A
OCATION--
AND THAT'S WHERE I'M HEADED NOW. TO DESTROY THOSE DAMN THINGS.
JUST THOUGHT YOU DESERVED A HEADS-UP.
BUCKY, WAIT--I'LL COME WITH YOU--
DON'T THINK THAT'S A GOOD IDEA, STEVE. SOME OF THE THINGS I DO THESE DAYS, YOU DON'T NEED ON YOUR REPUTATION. AND BESIDES--

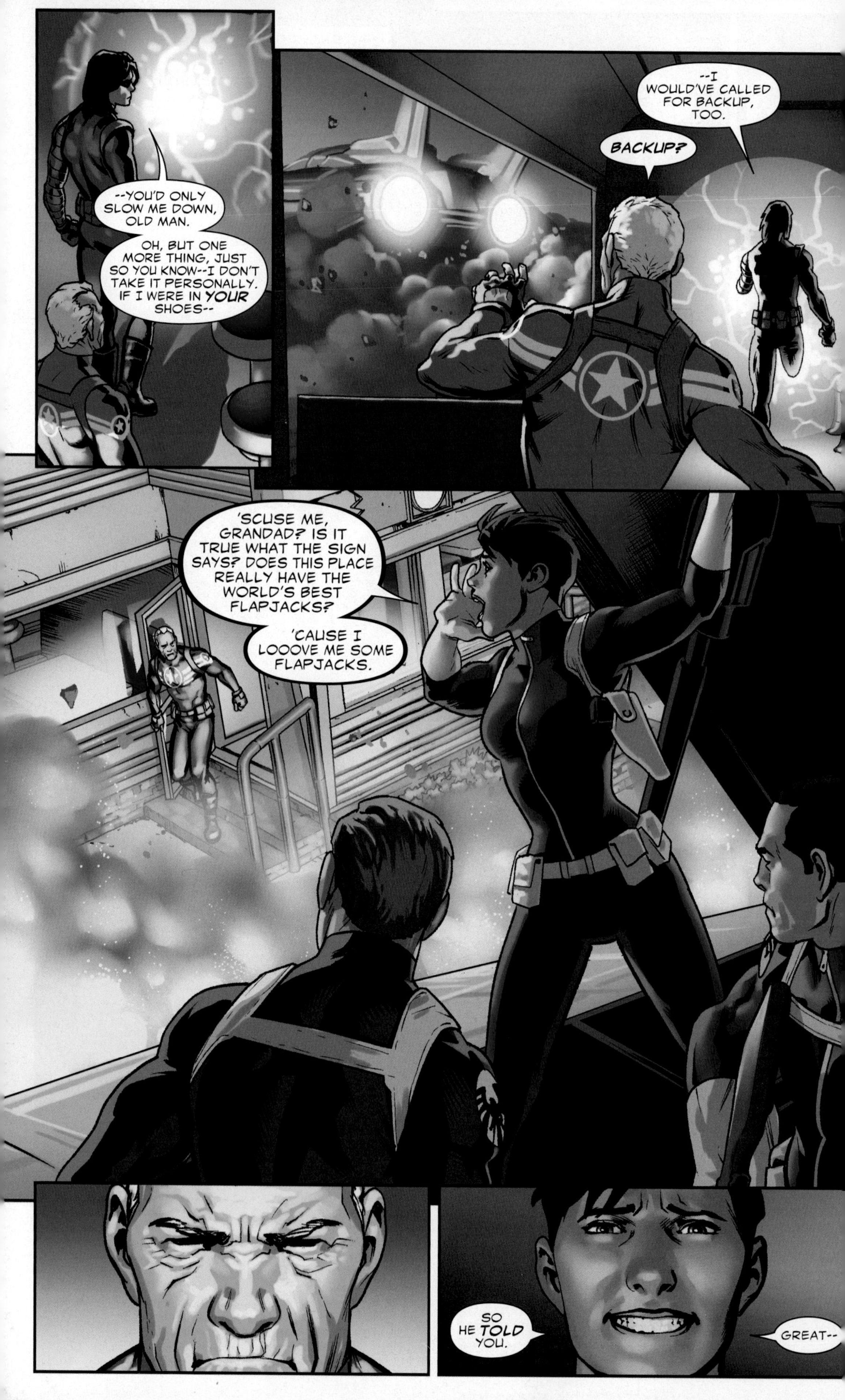
--YOU'D ONLY SLOW ME DOWN, OLD MAN.
OH, BUT ONE MORE THING, JUST SO YOU KNOW--I DON'T TAKE IT PERSONALLY. IF I WERE IN YOUR SHOES--
--I WOULD'VE CALLED FOR BACKUP, TOO.
BACKUP?
'SCUSE ME, GRANDAD? IS IT TRUE WHAT THE SIGN SAYS? DOES THIS PLACE REALLY HAVE THE WORLD'S BEST FLAPJACKS?
'CAUSE I LOOOVE ME SOME FLAPJACKS.
SO HE TOLD YOU.
--GREAT--

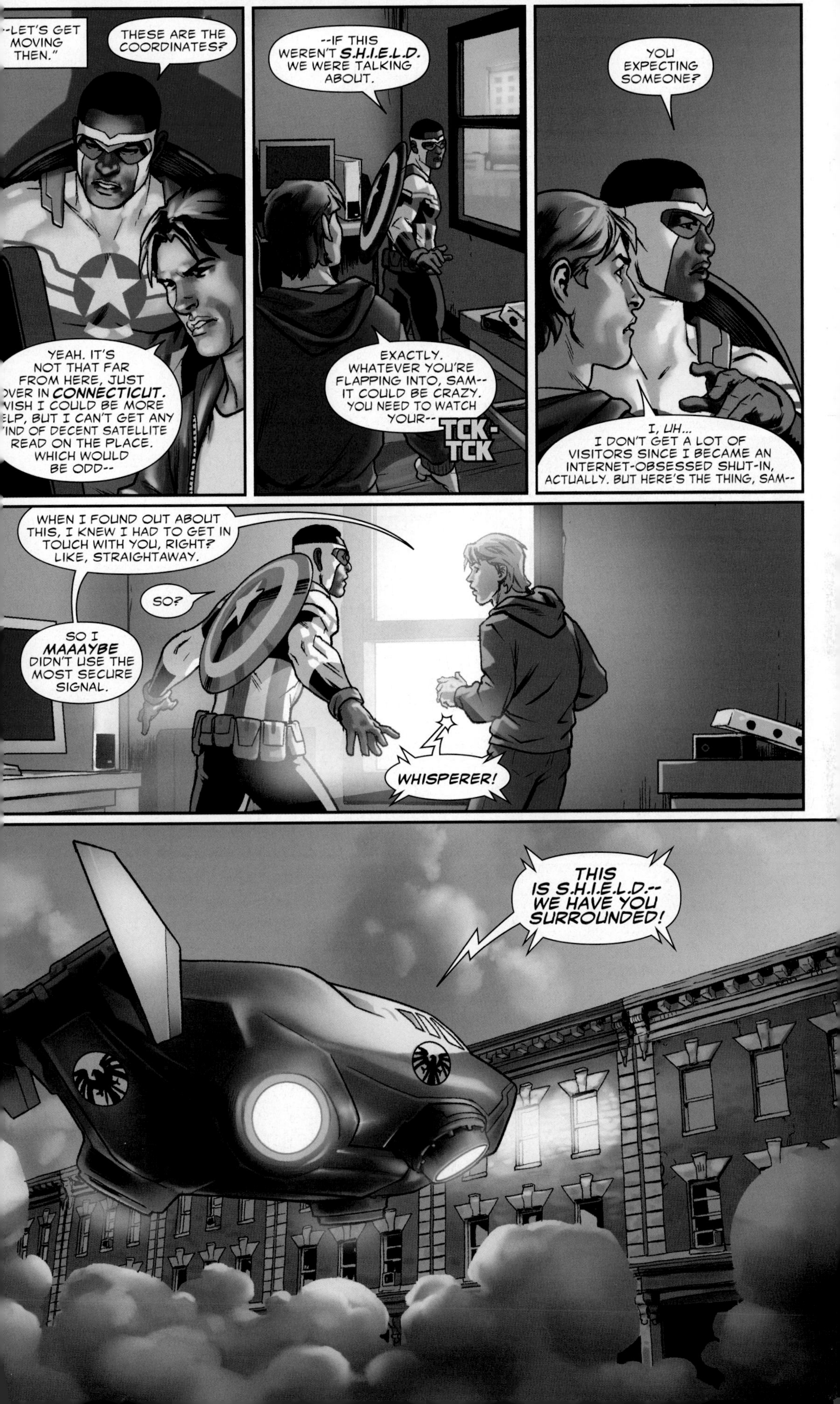

--LET'S GET MOVING THEN."
THESE ARE THE COORDINATES?
YEAH. IT'S NOT THAT FAR FROM HERE, JUST OVER IN CONNECTICUT. WISH I COULD BE MORE HELP, BUT I CAN'T GET ANY KIND OF DECENT SATELLITE READ ON THE PLACE. WHICH WOULD BE ODD--
--IF THIS WEREN'T S.H.I.E.L.D. WE WERE TALKING ABOUT.
EXACTLY. WHATEVER YOU'RE FLAPPING INTO, SAM-- IT COULD BE CRAZY. YOU NEED TO WATCH YOUR--
TCK-TCK
YOU EXPECTING SOMEONE?
I, UH... I DON'T GET A LOT OF VISITORS SINCE I BECAME AN INTERNET-OBSESSED SHUT-IN, ACTUALLY. BUT HERE'S THE THING, SAM--
WHEN I FOUND OUT ABOUT THIS, I KNEW I HAD TO GET IN TOUCH WITH YOU, RIGHT? LIKE, STRAIGHTAWAY.
SO?
SO I MAAAYBE DIDN'T USE THE MOST SECURE SIGNAL.
WHISPERER!
THIS IS S.H.I.E.L.D.-- WE HAVE YOU SURROUNDED!

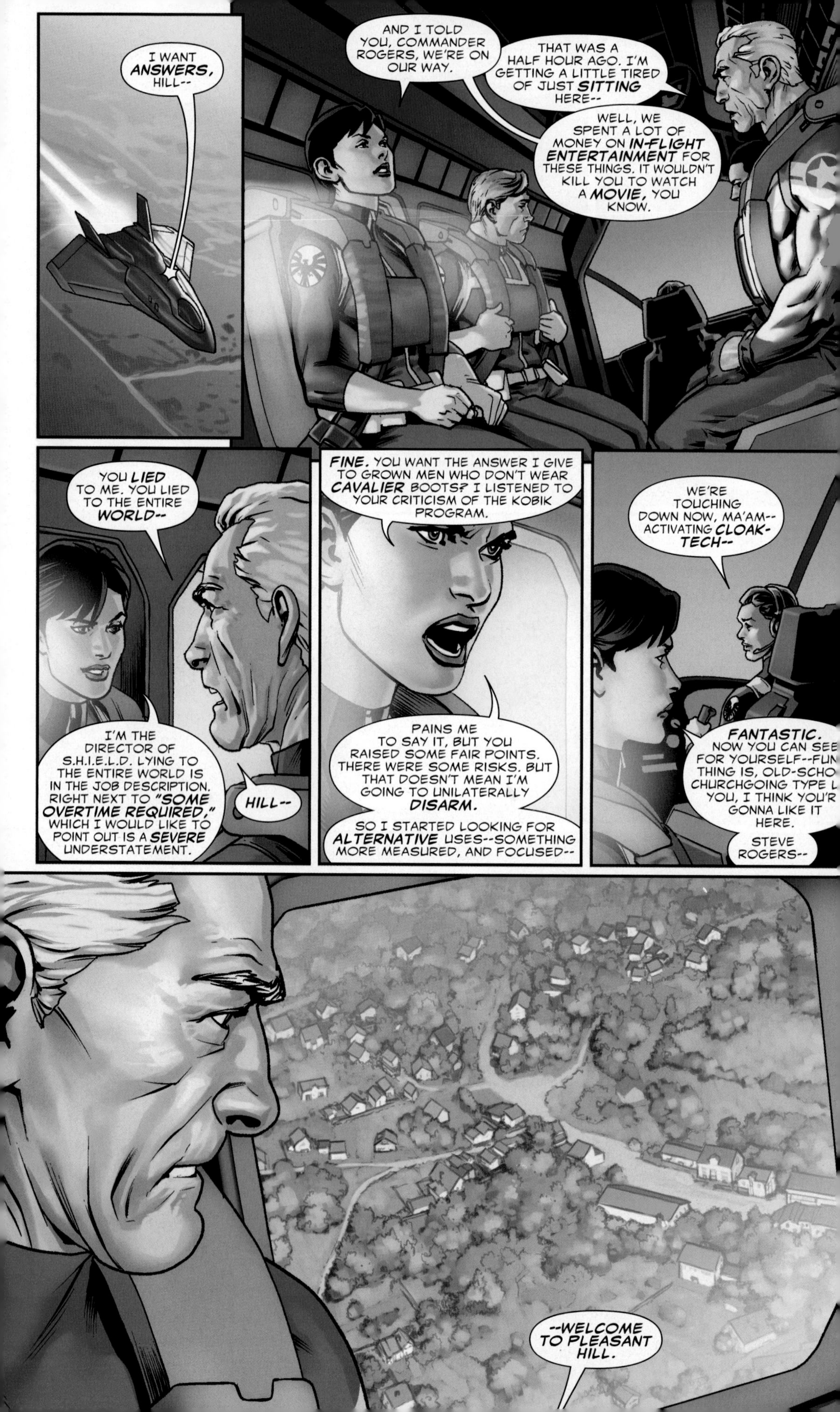

I WANT ANSWERS, HILL--
AND I TOLD YOU, COMMANDER ROGERS, WE'RE ON OUR WAY.
THAT WAS A HALF HOUR AGO. I'M GETTING A LITTLE TIRED OF JUST SITTING HERE--
WELL, WE SPENT A LOT OF MONEY ON IN-FLIGHT ENTERTAINMENT FOR THESE THINGS. IT WOULDN'T KILL YOU TO WATCH A MOVIE, YOU KNOW.
YOU LIED TO ME. YOU LIED TO THE ENTIRE WORLD--
I'M THE DIRECTOR OF S.H.I.E.L.D. LYING TO THE ENTIRE WORLD IS IN THE JOB DESCRIPTION. RIGHT NEXT TO "SOME OVERTIME REQUIRED," WHICH I WOULD LIKE TO POINT OUT IS A SEVERE UNDERSTATEMENT.
HILL--
FINE. YOU WANT THE ANSWER I GIVE TO GROWN MEN WHO DON'T WEAR CAVALIER BOOTS? I LISTENED TO YOUR CRITICISM OF THE KOBIK PROGRAM.
PAINS ME TO SAY IT, BUT YOU RAISED SOME FAIR POINTS. THERE WERE SOME RISKS. BUT THAT DOESN'T MEAN I'M GOING TO UNILATERALLY DISARM.
SO I STARTED LOOKING FOR ALTERNATIVE USES--SOMETHING MORE MEASURED, AND FOCUSED--
WE'RE TOUCHING DOWN NOW, MA'AM--ACTIVATING CLOAK-TECH--
FANTASTIC. NOW YOU CAN SEE FOR YOURSELF--FUN THING IS, OLD-SCHO CHURCHGOING TYPE L YOU, I THINK YOU'R GONNA LIKE IT HERE.
STEVE ROGERS--
--WELCOME TO PLEASANT HILL.

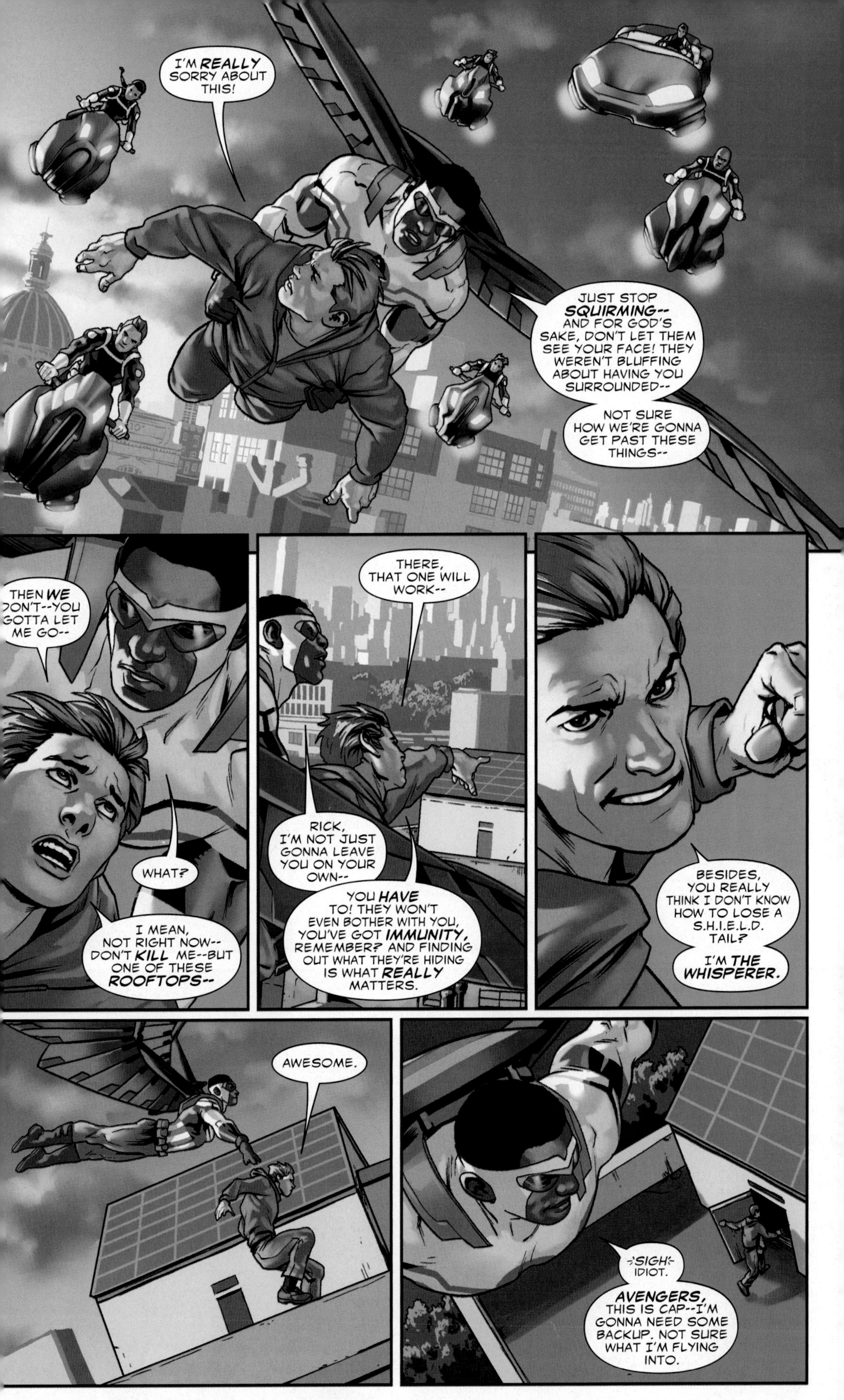

I'M REALLY SORRY ABOUT THIS!
JUST STOP SQUIRMING-- AND FOR GOD'S SAKE, DON'T LET THEM SEE YOUR FACE! THEY WEREN'T BLUFFING ABOUT HAVING YOU SURROUNDED--
NOT SURE HOW WE'RE GONNA GET PAST THESE THINGS--
THEN WE DON'T--YOU GOTTA LET ME GO--
WHAT?
I MEAN, NOT RIGHT NOW-- DON'T KILL ME--BUT ONE OF THESE ROOFTOPS--
THERE, THAT ONE WILL WORK--
RICK, I'M NOT JUST GONNA LEAVE YOU ON YOUR OWN--
YOU HAVE TO! THEY WON'T EVEN BOTHER WITH YOU, YOU'VE GOT IMMUNITY, REMEMBER? AND FINDING OUT WHAT THEY'RE HIDING IS WHAT REALLY MATTERS.
BESIDES, YOU REALLY THINK I DON'T KNOW HOW TO LOSE A S.H.I.E.L.D. TAIL?
I'M THE WHISPERER.
AWESOME.
-SIGH- IDIOT.
AVENGERS, THIS IS CAP--I'M GONNA NEED SOME BACKUP. NOT SURE WHAT I'M FLYING INTO.

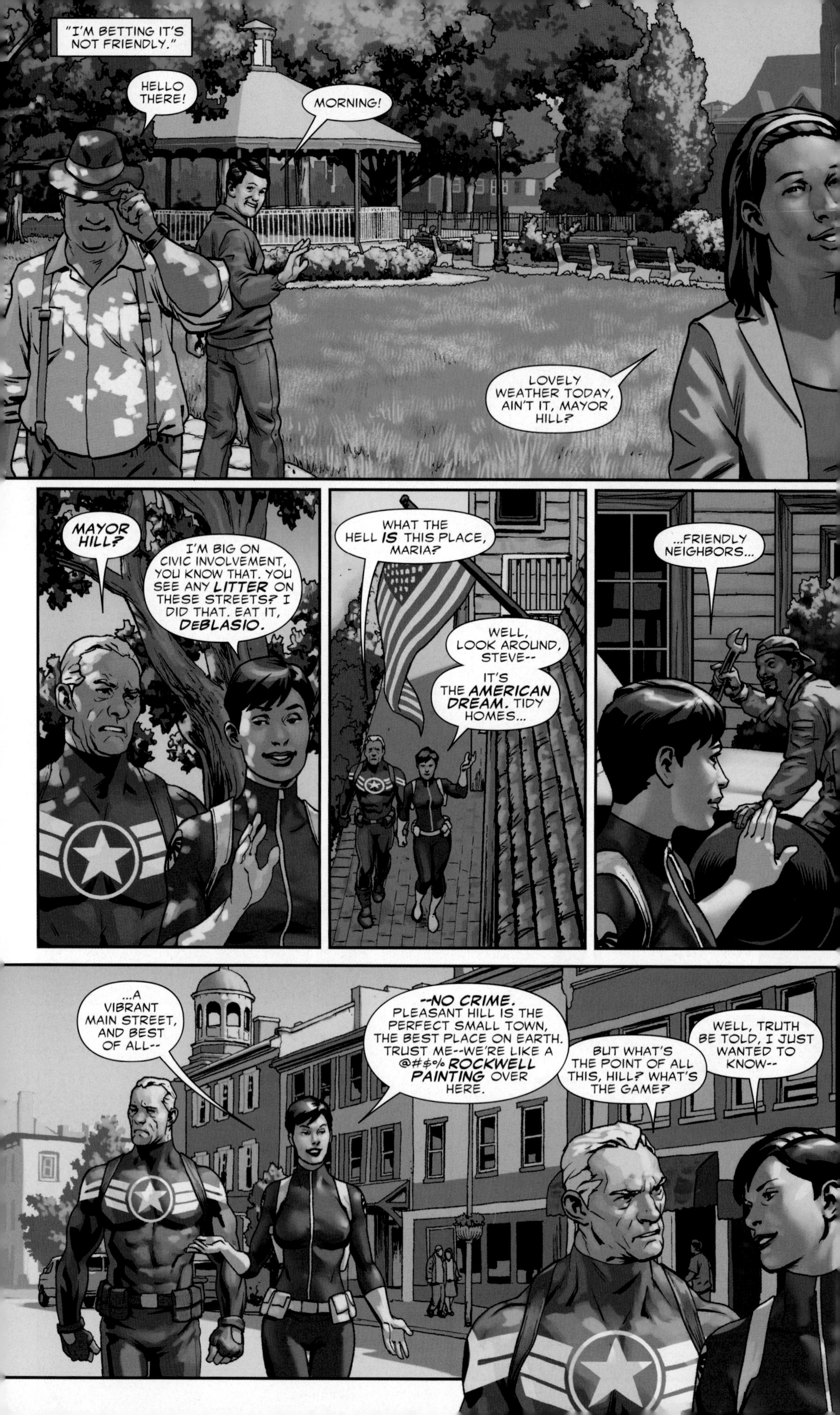
"I'M BETTING IT'S NOT FRIENDLY."
HELLO THERE!
MORNING!
LOVELY WEATHER TODAY, AIN'T IT, MAYOR HILL?
MAYOR HILL?
I'M BIG ON CIVIC INVOLVEMENT, YOU KNOW THAT. YOU SEE ANY LITTER ON THESE STREETS? I DID THAT. EAT IT, DEBLASIO.
WHAT THE HELL IS THIS PLACE, MARIA?
WELL, LOOK AROUND, STEVE--
IT'S THE AMERICAN DREAM. TIDY HOMES...
...FRIENDLY NEIGHBORS...
...A VIBRANT MAIN STREET, AND BEST OF ALL--
--NO CRIME. PLEASANT HILL IS THE PERFECT SMALL TOWN, THE BEST PLACE ON EARTH. TRUST ME--WE'RE LIKE A @#$% ROCKWELL PAINTING OVER HERE.
BUT WHAT'S THE POINT OF ALL THIS, HILL? WHAT'S THE GAME?
WELL, TRUTH BE TOLD, I JUST WANTED TO KNOW--

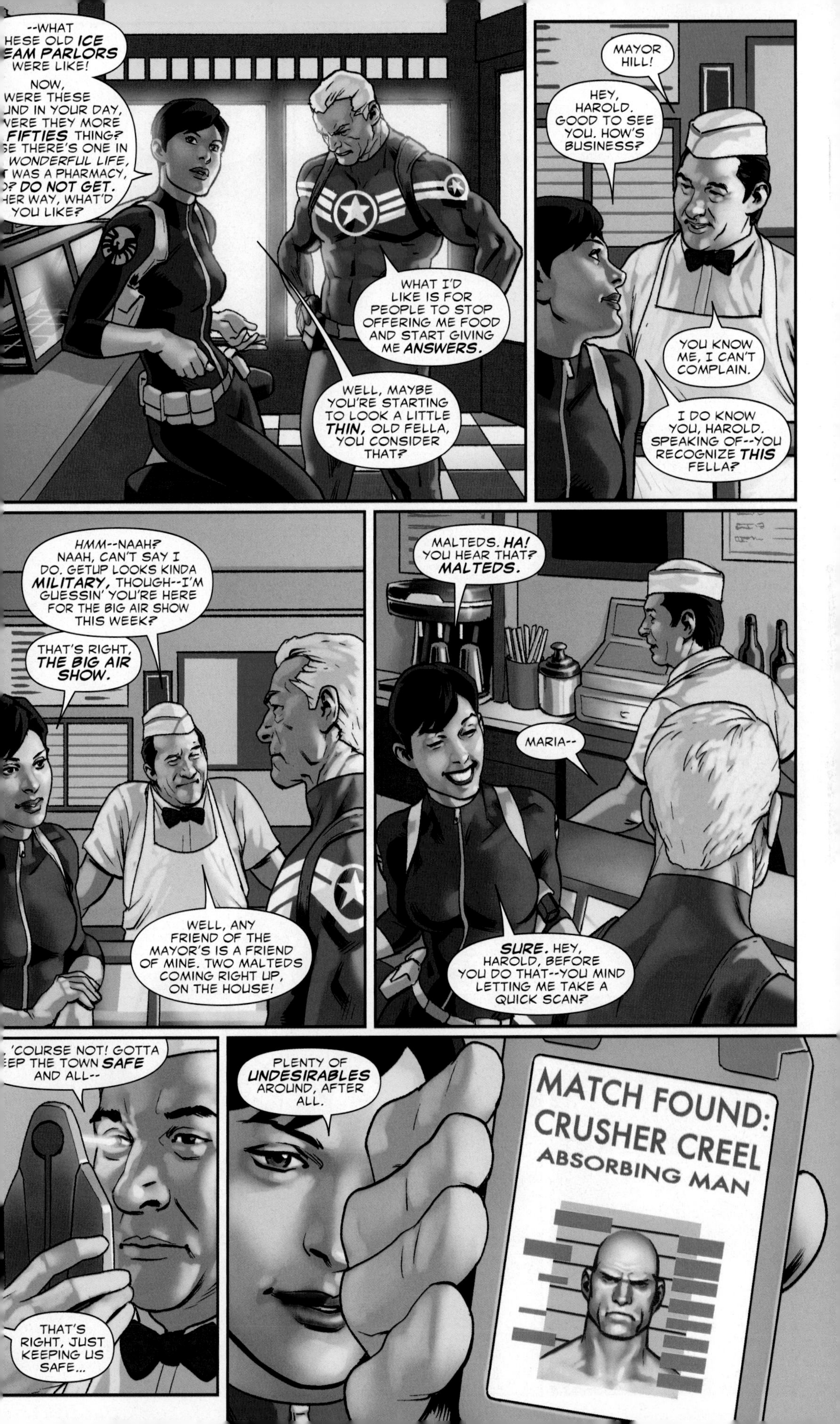
--WHAT
HESE OLD ICE
EAM PARLORS
WERE LIKE!
NOW,
WERE THESE
UND IN YOUR DAY,
VERE THEY MORE
FIFTIES THING?
E THERE'S ONE IN
WONDERFUL LIFE,
T WAS A PHARMACY,
? DO NOT GET.
HER WAY, WHAT'D
YOU LIKE?
WHAT I'D LIKE IS FOR PEOPLE TO STOP OFFERING ME FOOD AND START GIVING ME ANSWERS.
WELL, MAYBE YOU'RE STARTING TO LOOK A LITTLE THIN, OLD FELLA, YOU CONSIDER THAT?
MAYOR HILL!
HEY, HAROLD. GOOD TO SEE YOU. HOW'S BUSINESS?
YOU KNOW ME, I CAN'T COMPLAIN.
I DO KNOW YOU, HAROLD. SPEAKING OF--YOU RECOGNIZE THIS FELLA?
HMM--NAAH? NAAH, CAN'T SAY I DO. GETUP LOOKS KINDA MILITARY, THOUGH--I'M GUESSIN' YOU'RE HERE FOR THE BIG AIR SHOW THIS WEEK?
THAT'S RIGHT, THE BIG AIR SHOW.
WELL, ANY FRIEND OF THE MAYOR'S IS A FRIEND OF MINE. TWO MALTEDS COMING RIGHT UP, ON THE HOUSE!
MALTEDS. HA! YOU HEAR THAT? MALTEDS.
MARIA--
SURE. HEY, HAROLD, BEFORE YOU DO THAT--YOU MIND LETTING ME TAKE A QUICK SCAN?
'COURSE NOT! GOTTA
EEP THE TOWN SAFE AND ALL--
THAT'S RIGHT, JUST KEEPING US SAFE...
PLENTY OF UNDESIRABLES AROUND, AFTER ALL.
MATCH FOUND:
CRUSHER CREEL
ABSORBING MAN

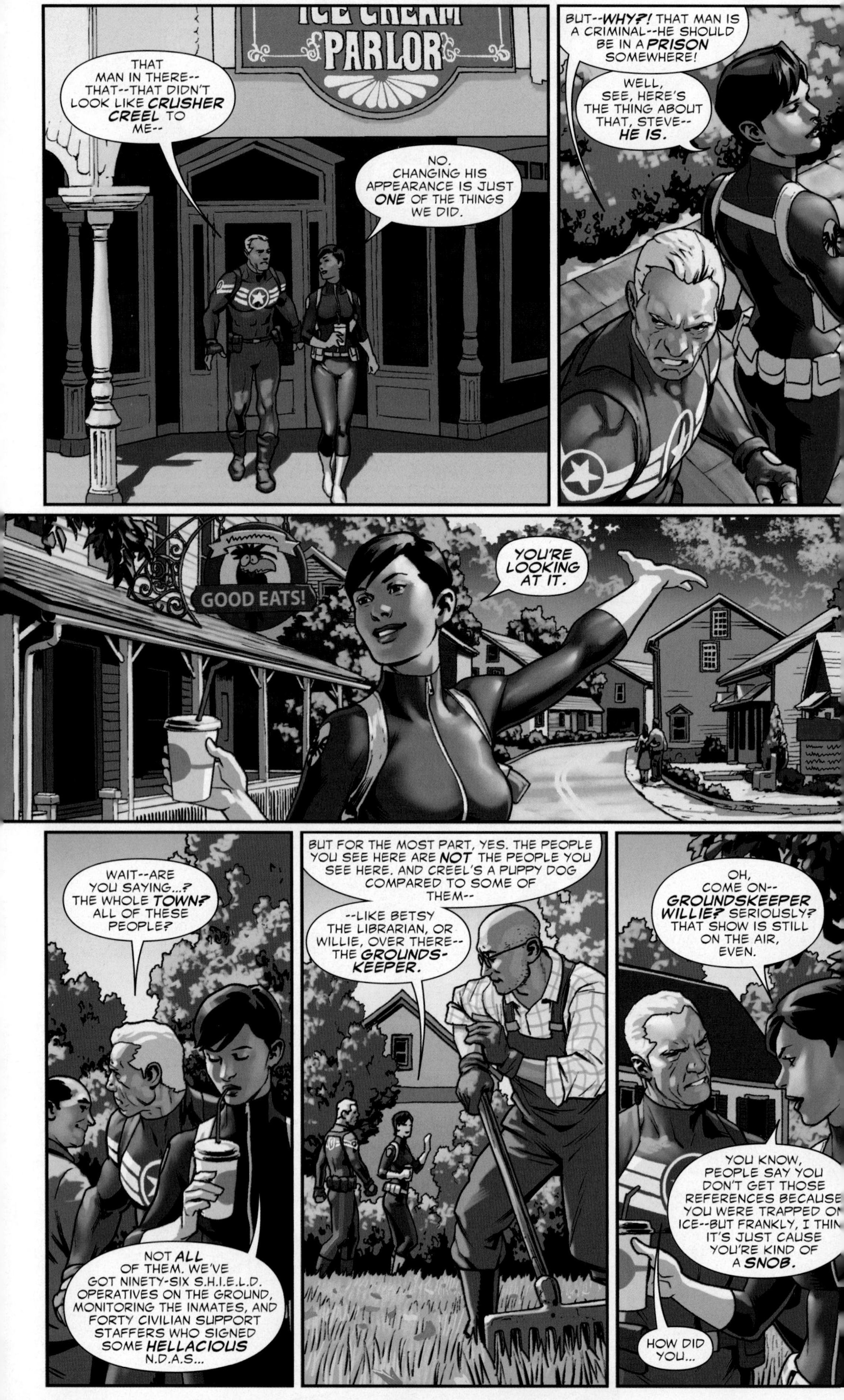
ICE CREAM PARLOR
THAT MAN IN THERE-- THAT--THAT DIDN'T LOOK LIKE CRUSHER CREEL TO ME--
NO. CHANGING HIS APPEARANCE IS JUST ONE OF THE THINGS WE DID.
BUT--WHY?! THAT MAN IS A CRIMINAL--HE SHOULD BE IN A PRISON SOMEWHERE!
WELL, SEE, HERE'S THE THING ABOUT THAT, STEVE-- HE IS.
GOOD EATS!
YOU'RE LOOKING AT IT.
WAIT--ARE YOU SAYING...? THE WHOLE TOWN? ALL OF THESE PEOPLE?
NOT ALL OF THEM. WE'VE GOT NINETY-SIX S.H.I.E.L.D. OPERATIVES ON THE GROUND, MONITORING THE INMATES, AND FORTY CIVILIAN SUPPORT STAFFERS WHO SIGNED SOME HELLACIOUS N.D.A.S...
BUT FOR THE MOST PART, YES. THE PEOPLE YOU SEE HERE ARE NOT THE PEOPLE YOU SEE HERE. AND CREEL'S A PUPPY DOG COMPARED TO SOME OF THEM--
--LIKE BETSY THE LIBRARIAN, OR WILLIE, OVER THERE-- THE GROUNDS-KEEPER.
OH, COME ON-- GROUNDSKEEPER WILLIE? SERIOUSLY? THAT SHOW IS STILL ON THE AIR, EVEN.
YOU KNOW, PEOPLE SAY YOU DON'T GET THOSE REFERENCES BECAUSE YOU WERE TRAPPED ON ICE--BUT FRANKLY, I THIN IT'S JUST CAUSE YOU'RE KIND OF A SNOB.
HOW DID YOU...

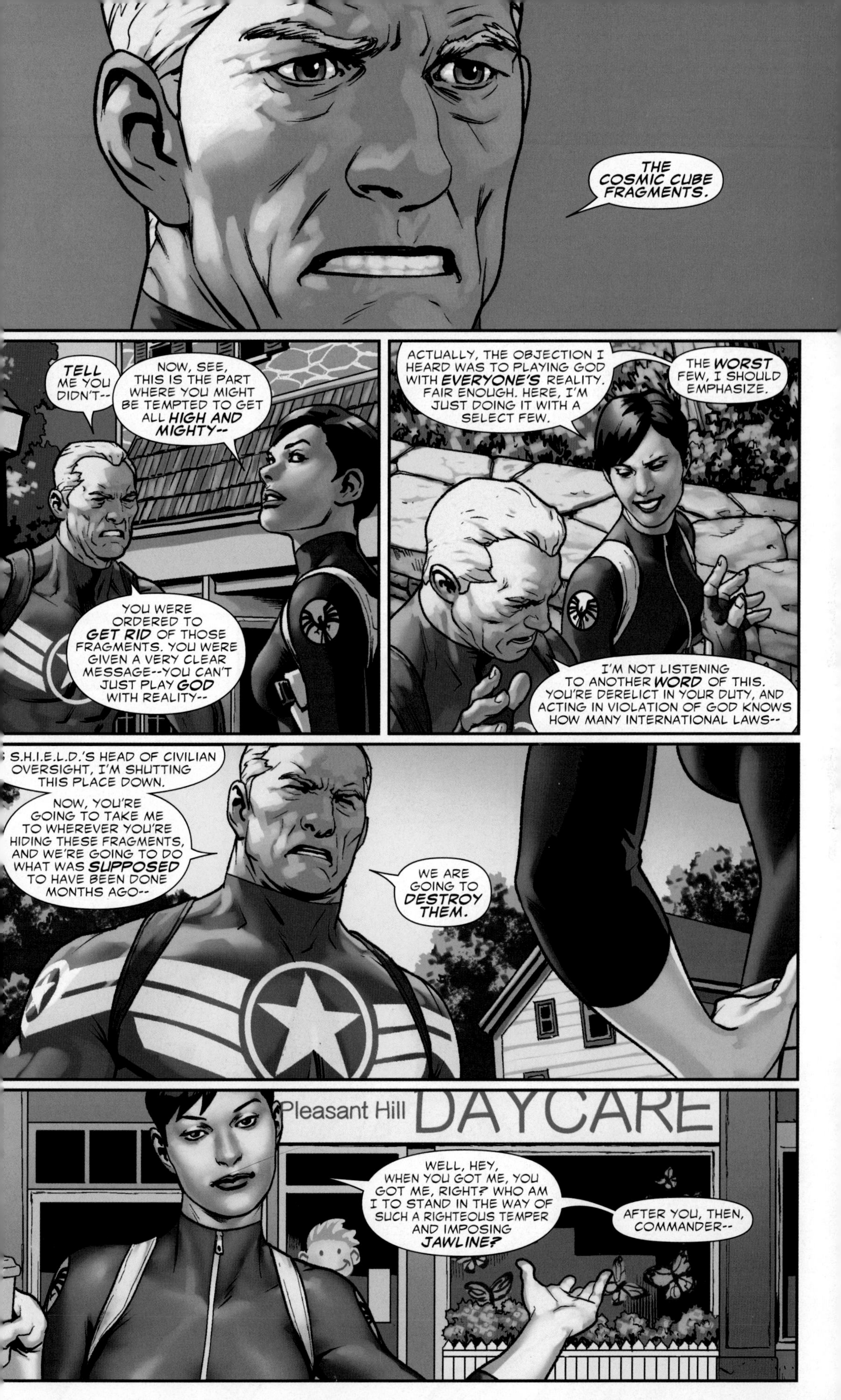
THE COSMIC CUBE FRAGMENTS.
TELL ME YOU DIDN'T--
NOW, SEE, THIS IS THE PART WHERE YOU MIGHT BE TEMPTED TO GET ALL HIGH AND MIGHTY--
YOU WERE ORDERED TO GET RID OF THOSE FRAGMENTS. YOU WERE GIVEN A VERY CLEAR MESSAGE--YOU CAN'T JUST PLAY GOD WITH REALITY--
ACTUALLY, THE OBJECTION I HEARD WAS TO PLAYING GOD WITH EVERYONE'S REALITY. FAIR ENOUGH. HERE, I'M JUST DOING IT WITH A SELECT FEW.
THE WORST FEW, I SHOULD EMPHASIZE.
I'M NOT LISTENING TO ANOTHER WORD OF THIS. YOU'RE DERELICT IN YOUR DUTY, AND ACTING IN VIOLATION OF GOD KNOWS HOW MANY INTERNATIONAL LAWS--
S.H.I.E.L.D.'S HEAD OF CIVILIAN OVERSIGHT, I'M SHUTTING THIS PLACE DOWN.
NOW, YOU'RE GOING TO TAKE ME TO WHEREVER YOU'RE HIDING THESE FRAGMENTS, AND WE'RE GOING TO DO WHAT WAS SUPPOSED TO HAVE BEEN DONE MONTHS AGO--
WE ARE GOING TO DESTROY THEM.
Pleasant Hill DAYCARE
WELL, HEY, WHEN YOU GOT ME, YOU GOT ME, RIGHT? WHO AM I TO STAND IN THE WAY OF SUCH A RIGHTEOUS TEMPER AND IMPOSING JAWLINE?
AFTER YOU, THEN, COMMANDER--

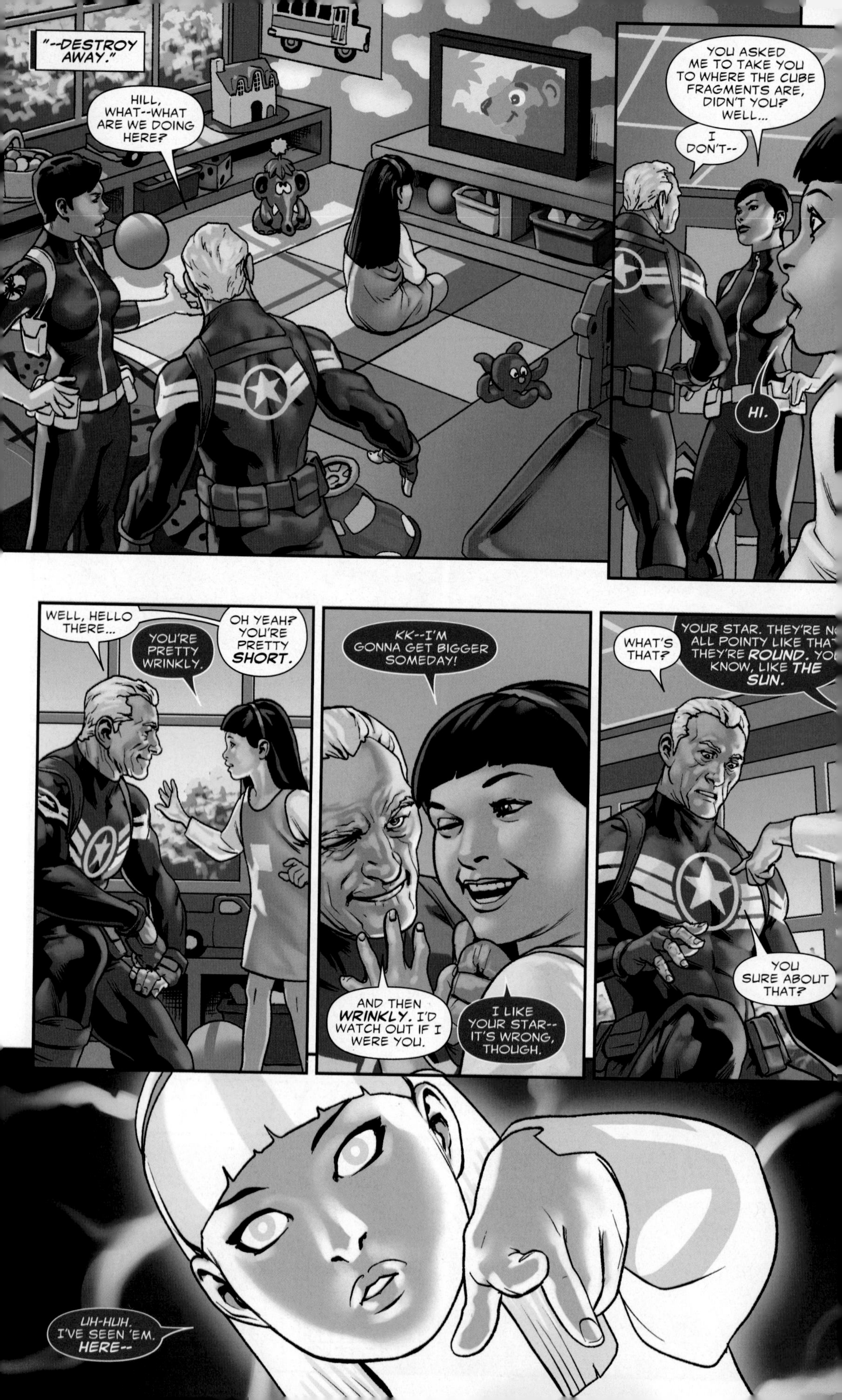
"--DESTROY AWAY."
HILL, WHAT--WHAT ARE WE DOING HERE?
YOU ASKED ME TO TAKE YOU TO WHERE THE CUBE FRAGMENTS ARE, DIDN'T YOU? WELL...
I DON'T--
HI.
WELL, HELLO THERE...
YOU'RE PRETTY WRINKLY.
OH YEAH? YOU'RE PRETTY SHORT.
KK--I'M GONNA GET BIGGER SOMEDAY!
AND THEN WRINKLY. I'D WATCH OUT IF I WERE YOU.
I LIKE YOUR STAR-- IT'S WRONG, THOUGH.
WHAT'S THAT?
YOUR STAR. THEY'RE N ALL POINTY LIKE THAT THEY'RE ROUND. YO KNOW, LIKE THE SUN.
YOU SURE ABOUT THAT?
UH-HUH. I'VE SEEN 'EM. HERE--

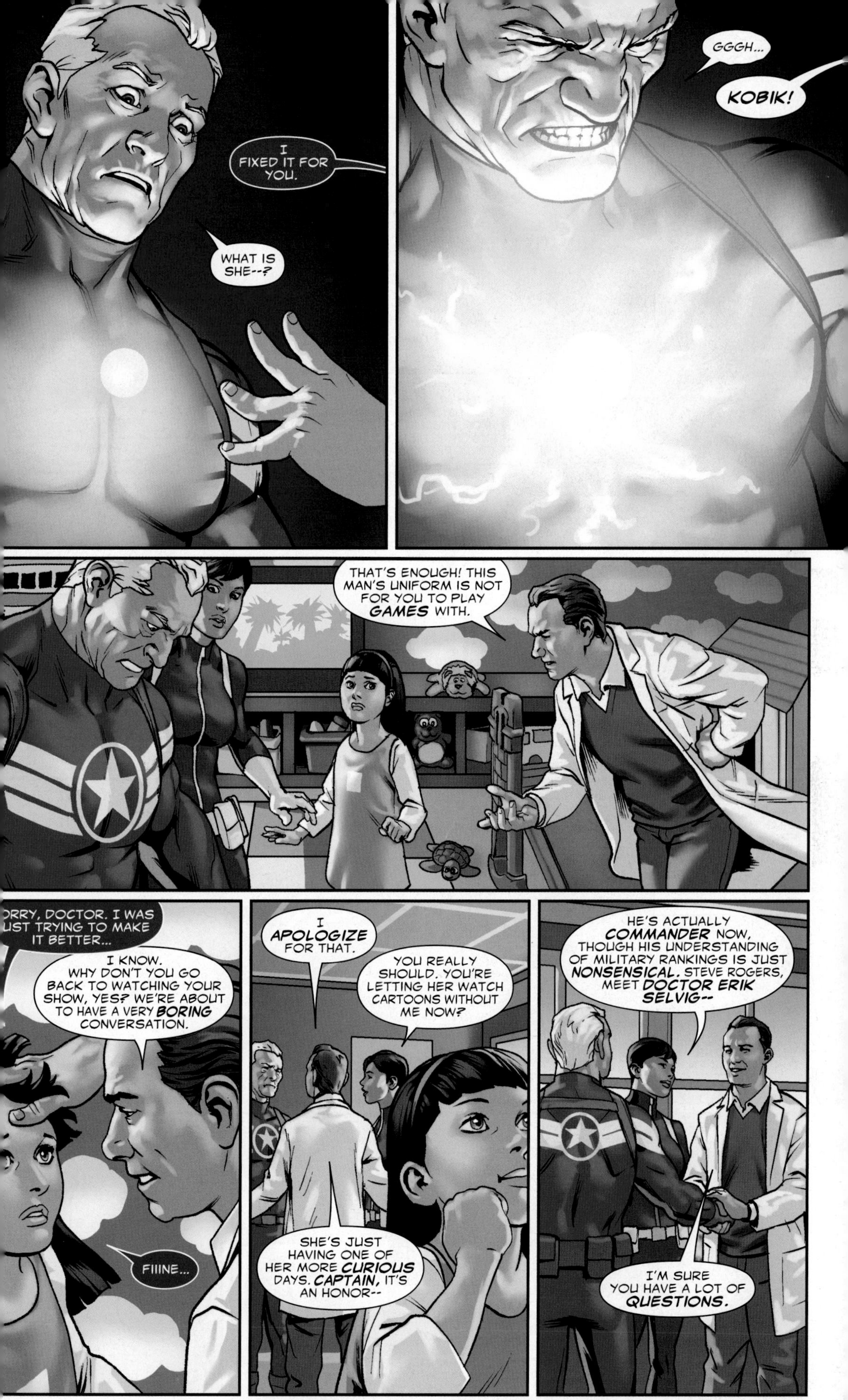
I FIXED IT FOR YOU.
WHAT IS SHE--?
GGGH...
KOBIK!
THAT'S ENOUGH! THIS MAN'S UNIFORM IS NOT FOR YOU TO PLAY GAMES WITH.
ORRY, DOCTOR. I WAS JUST TRYING TO MAKE IT BETTER...
I KNOW. WHY DON'T YOU GO BACK TO WATCHING YOUR SHOW, YES? WE'RE ABOUT TO HAVE A VERY BORING CONVERSATION.
FIIINE...
I APOLOGIZE FOR THAT.
YOU REALLY SHOULD. YOU'RE LETTING HER WATCH CARTOONS WITHOUT ME NOW?
SHE'S JUST HAVING ONE OF HER MORE CURIOUS DAYS. CAPTAIN, IT'S AN HONOR--
HE'S ACTUALLY COMMANDER NOW, THOUGH HIS UNDERSTANDING OF MILITARY RANKINGS IS JUST NONSENSICAL. STEVE ROGERS, MEET DOCTOR ERIK SELVIG--
I'M SURE YOU HAVE A LOT OF QUESTIONS.

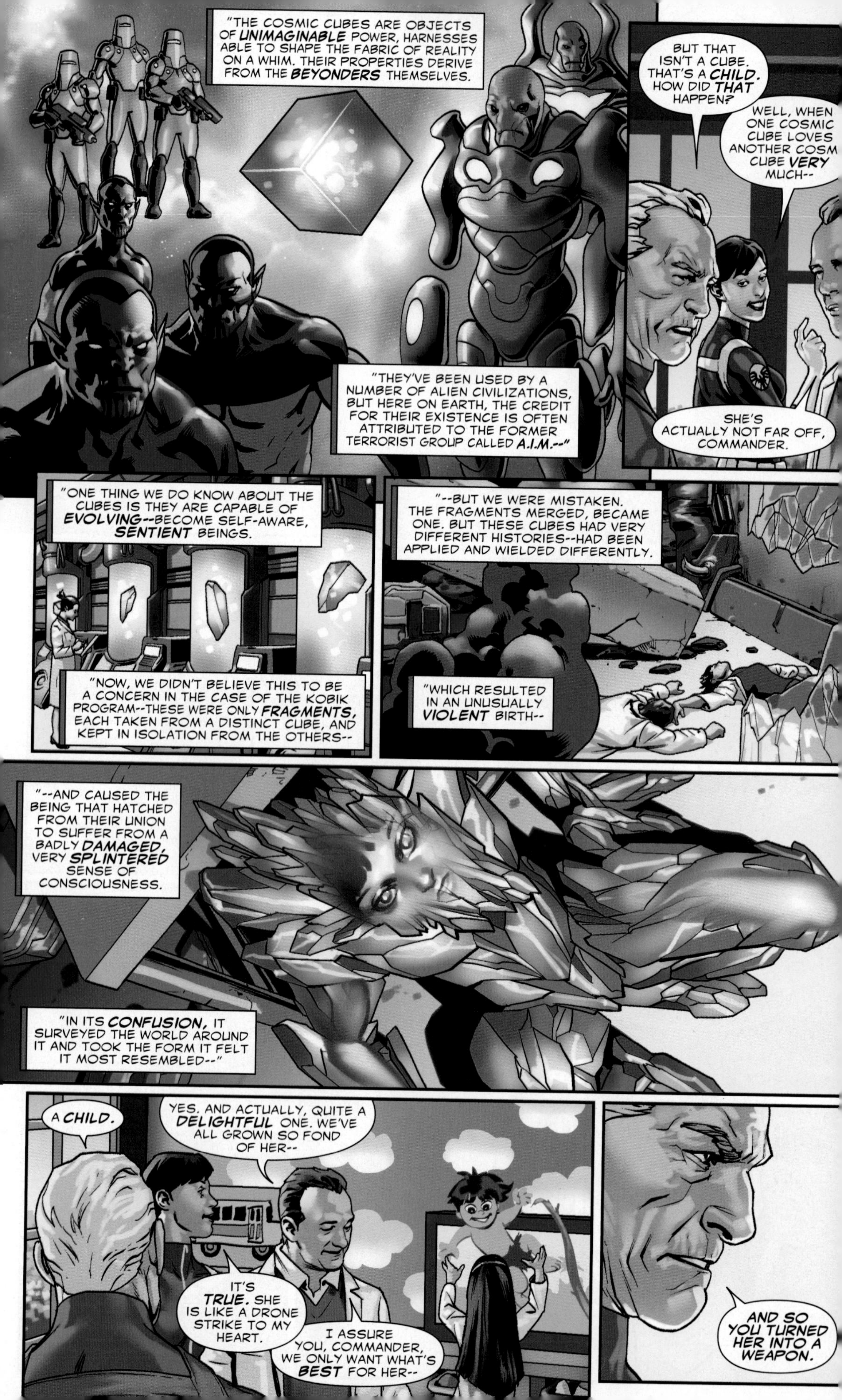

"THE COSMIC CUBES ARE OBJECTS OF UNIMAGINABLE POWER, HARNESSES ABLE TO SHAPE THE FABRIC OF REALITY ON A WHIM. THEIR PROPERTIES DERIVE FROM THE BEYONDERS THEMSELVES.
"THEY'VE BEEN USED BY A NUMBER OF ALIEN CIVILIZATIONS, BUT HERE ON EARTH, THE CREDIT FOR THEIR EXISTENCE IS OFTEN ATTRIBUTED TO THE FORMER TERRORIST GROUP CALLED A.I.M.--"
BUT THAT ISN'T A CUBE. THAT'S A CHILD. HOW DID THAT HAPPEN?
WELL, WHEN ONE COSMIC CUBE LOVES ANOTHER COSM CUBE VERY MUCH--
SHE'S ACTUALLY NOT FAR OFF, COMMANDER.
"ONE THING WE DO KNOW ABOUT THE CUBES IS THEY ARE CAPABLE OF EVOLVING--BECOME SELF-AWARE, SENTIENT BEINGS.
"NOW, WE DIDN'T BELIEVE THIS TO BE A CONCERN IN THE CASE OF THE KOBIK PROGRAM--THESE WERE ONLY FRAGMENTS, EACH TAKEN FROM A DISTINCT CUBE, AND KEPT IN ISOLATION FROM THE OTHERS--
"--BUT WE WERE MISTAKEN. THE FRAGMENTS MERGED, BECAME ONE. BUT THESE CUBES HAD VERY DIFFERENT HISTORIES--HAD BEEN APPLIED AND WIELDED DIFFERENTLY.
"WHICH RESULTED IN AN UNUSUALLY VIOLENT BIRTH--
"--AND CAUSED THE BEING THAT HATCHED FROM THEIR UNION TO SUFFER FROM A BADLY DAMAGED, VERY SPLINTERED SENSE OF CONSCIOUSNESS.
"IN ITS CONFUSION, IT SURVEYED THE WORLD AROUND IT AND TOOK THE FORM IT FELT IT MOST RESEMBLED--"
A CHILD.
YES. AND ACTUALLY, QUITE A DELIGHTFUL ONE. WE'VE ALL GROWN SO FOND OF HER--
IT'S TRUE. SHE IS LIKE A DRONE STRIKE TO MY HEART.
I ASSURE YOU, COMMANDER, WE ONLY WANT WHAT'S BEST FOR HER--
AND SO YOU TURNED HER INTO A WEAPON.

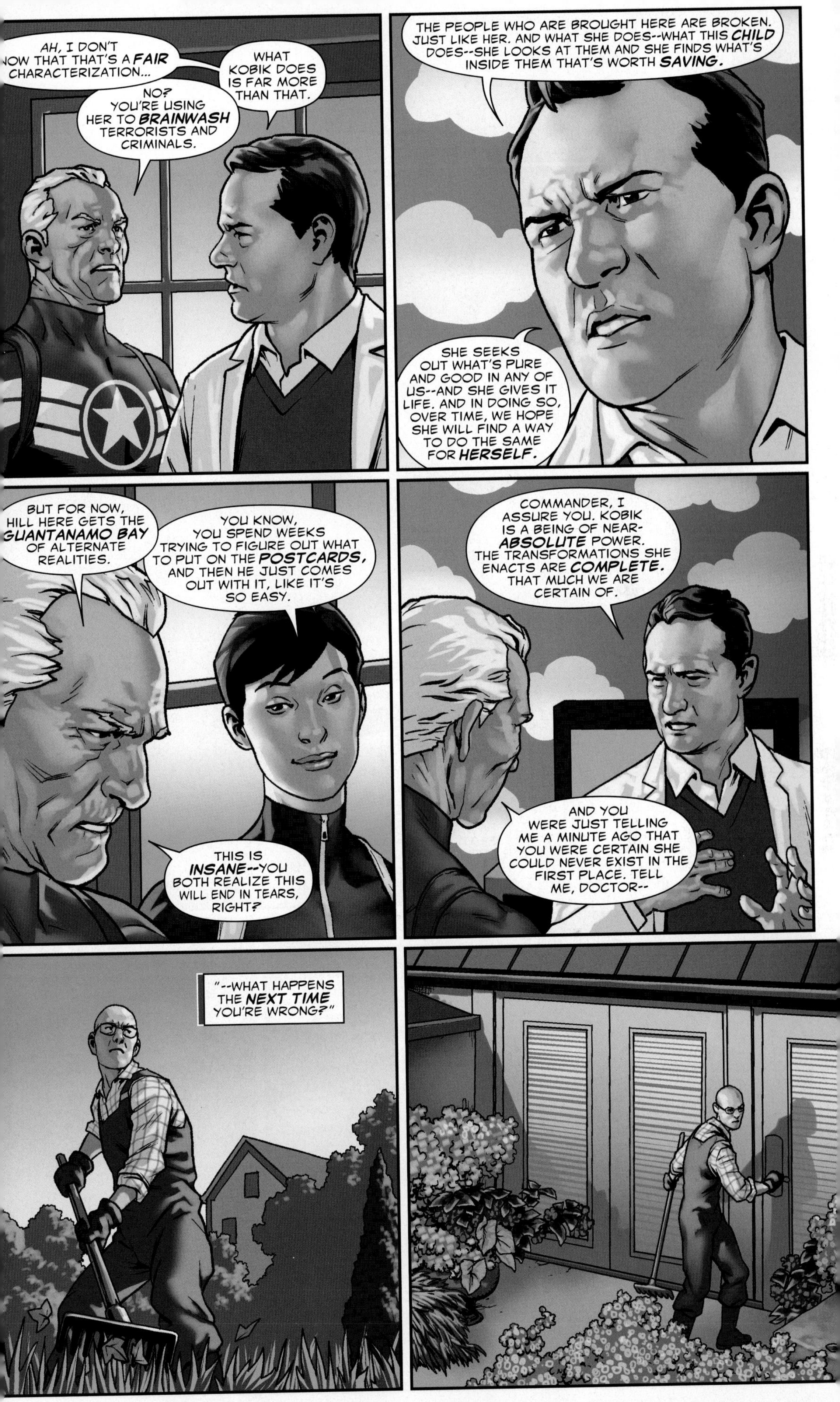
AH, I DON'T
NOW THAT THAT'S A FAIR CHARACTERIZATION...
WHAT KOBIK DOES IS FAR MORE THAN THAT.
NO? YOU'RE USING HER TO BRAINWASH TERRORISTS AND CRIMINALS.
THE PEOPLE WHO ARE BROUGHT HERE ARE BROKEN. JUST LIKE HER. AND WHAT SHE DOES--WHAT THIS CHILD DOES--SHE LOOKS AT THEM AND SHE FINDS WHAT'S INSIDE THEM THAT'S WORTH SAVING.
SHE SEEKS OUT WHAT'S PURE AND GOOD IN ANY OF US--AND SHE GIVES IT LIFE. AND IN DOING SO, OVER TIME, WE HOPE SHE WILL FIND A WAY TO DO THE SAME FOR HERSELF.
BUT FOR NOW, HILL HERE GETS THE GUANTANAMO BAY OF ALTERNATE REALITIES.
YOU KNOW, YOU SPEND WEEKS TRYING TO FIGURE OUT WHAT TO PUT ON THE POSTCARDS, AND THEN HE JUST COMES OUT WITH IT, LIKE IT'S SO EASY.
THIS IS INSANE--YOU BOTH REALIZE THIS WILL END IN TEARS, RIGHT?
COMMANDER, I ASSURE YOU. KOBIK IS A BEING OF NEAR-ABSOLUTE POWER. THE TRANSFORMATIONS SHE ENACTS ARE COMPLETE. THAT MUCH WE ARE CERTAIN OF.
AND YOU WERE JUST TELLING ME A MINUTE AGO THAT YOU WERE CERTAIN SHE COULD NEVER EXIST IN THE FIRST PLACE. TELL ME, DOCTOR--
"--WHAT HAPPENS THE NEXT TIME YOU'RE WRONG?"

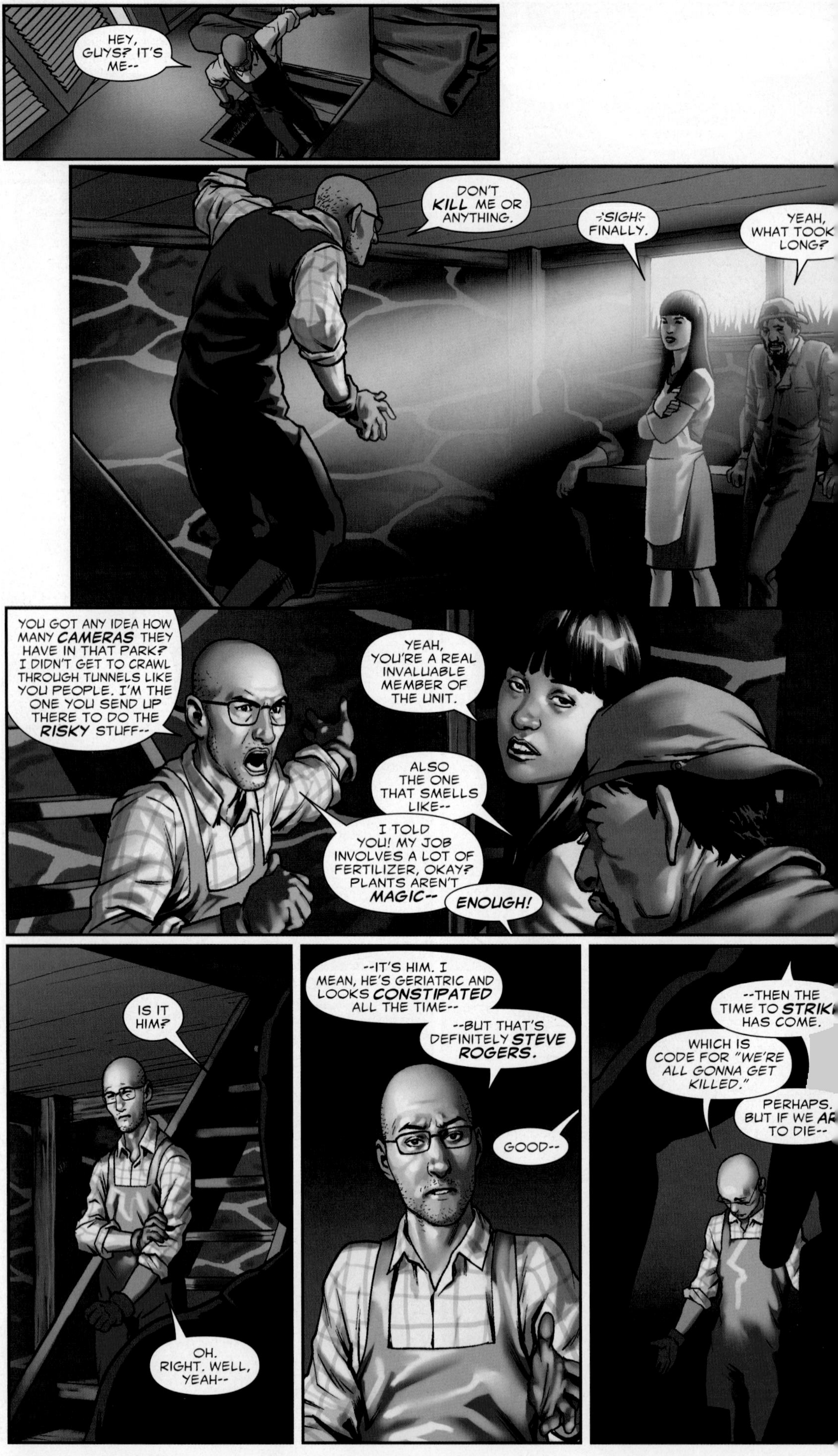
HEY, GUYS? IT'S ME--
DON'T KILL ME OR ANYTHING.
SIGH FINALLY.
YEAH, WHAT TOOK LONG?
YOU GOT ANY IDEA HOW MANY CAMERAS THEY HAVE IN THAT PARK? I DIDN'T GET TO CRAWL THROUGH TUNNELS LIKE YOU PEOPLE. I'M THE ONE YOU SEND UP THERE TO DO THE RISKY STUFF--
YEAH, YOU'RE A REAL INVALUABLE MEMBER OF THE UNIT.
ALSO THE ONE THAT SMELLS LIKE--
I TOLD YOU! MY JOB INVOLVES A LOT OF FERTILIZER, OKAY? PLANTS AREN'T MAGIC--
ENOUGH!
IS IT HIM?
OH. RIGHT. WELL, YEAH--
--IT'S HIM. I MEAN, HE'S GERIATRIC AND LOOKS CONSTIPATED ALL THE TIME--
--BUT THAT'S DEFINITELY STEVE ROGERS.
GOOD--
--THEN THE TIME TO STRIK
HAS COME.
WHICH IS CODE FOR "WE'RE ALL GONNA GET KILLED."
PERHAPS. BUT IF WE AR
TO DIE--

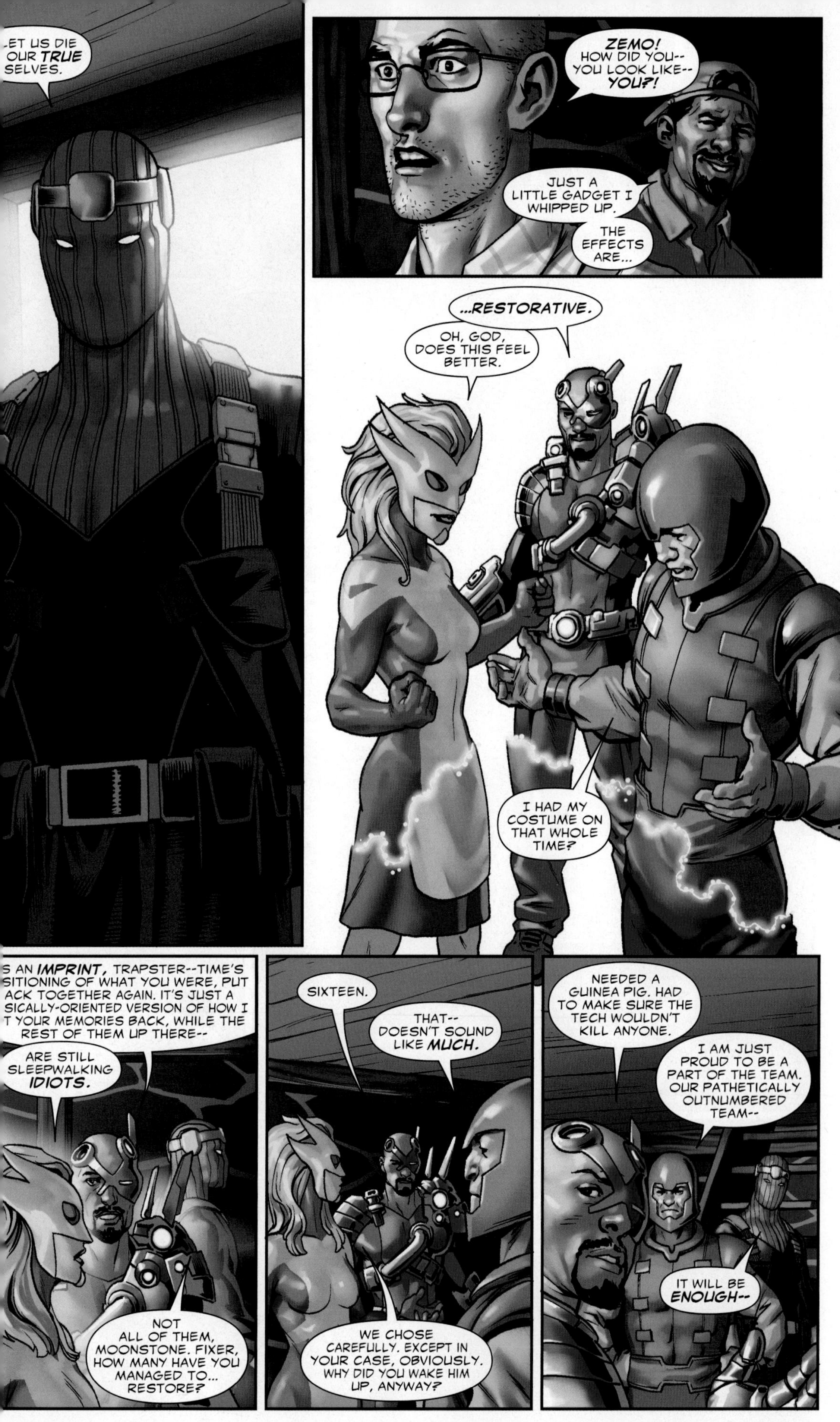

-ET US DIE OUR TRUE SELVES.
ZEMO! HOW DID YOU-- YOU LOOK LIKE-- YOU?!
JUST A LITTLE GADGET I WHIPPED UP.
THE EFFECTS ARE...
...RESTORATIVE.
OH, GOD, DOES THIS FEEL BETTER.
I HAD MY COSTUME ON THAT WHOLE TIME?
S AN IMPRINT, TRAPSTER--TIME'S SITIONING OF WHAT YOU WERE, PUT ACK TOGETHER AGAIN. IT'S JUST A SICALLY-ORIENTED VERSION OF HOW I T YOUR MEMORIES BACK, WHILE THE REST OF THEM UP THERE--
ARE STILL SLEEPWALKING IDIOTS.
NOT ALL OF THEM, MOONSTONE. FIXER, HOW MANY HAVE YOU MANAGED TO... RESTORE?
SIXTEEN.
THAT-- DOESN'T SOUND LIKE MUCH.
WE CHOSE CAREFULLY. EXCEPT IN YOUR CASE, OBVIOUSLY. WHY DID YOU WAKE HIM UP, ANYWAY?
NEEDED A GUINEA PIG. HAD TO MAKE SURE THE TECH WOULDN'T KILL ANYONE.
I AM JUST PROUD TO BE A PART OF THE TEAM. OUR PATHETICALLY OUTNUMBERED TEAM--
IT WILL BE ENOUGH--

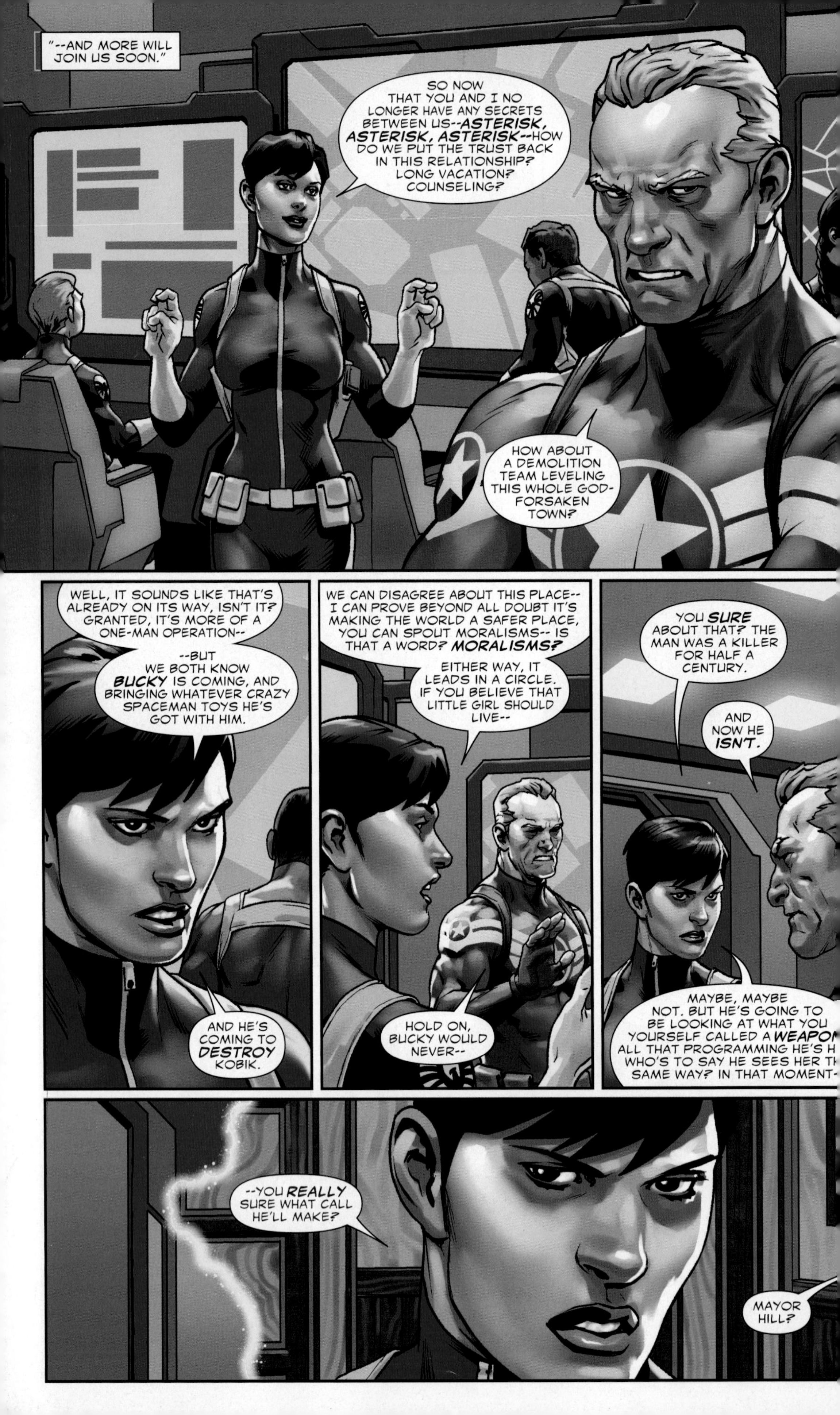
"--AND MORE WILL JOIN US SOON."
SO NOW THAT YOU AND I NO LONGER HAVE ANY SECRETS BETWEEN US--*ASTERISK, ASTERISK, ASTERISK*--HOW DO WE PUT THE TRUST BACK IN THIS RELATIONSHIP? LONG VACATION? COUNSELING?
HOW ABOUT A DEMOLITION TEAM LEVELING THIS WHOLE GOD-FORSAKEN TOWN?
WELL, IT SOUNDS LIKE THAT'S ALREADY ON ITS WAY, ISN'T IT? GRANTED, IT'S MORE OF A ONE-MAN OPERATION--
--BUT WE BOTH KNOW *BUCKY* IS COMING, AND BRINGING WHATEVER CRAZY SPACEMAN TOYS HE'S GOT WITH HIM.
AND HE'S COMING TO *DESTROY* KOBIK.
WE CAN DISAGREE ABOUT THIS PLACE-- I CAN PROVE BEYOND ALL DOUBT IT'S MAKING THE WORLD A SAFER PLACE, YOU CAN SPOUT MORALISMS-- IS THAT A WORD? *MORALISMS?*
EITHER WAY, IT LEADS IN A CIRCLE. IF YOU BELIEVE THAT LITTLE GIRL SHOULD LIVE--
HOLD ON, BUCKY WOULD NEVER--
YOU *SURE* ABOUT THAT? THE MAN WAS A KILLER FOR HALF A CENTURY.
AND NOW HE *ISN'T*.
MAYBE, MAYBE NOT. BUT HE'S GOING TO BE LOOKING AT WHAT YOU YOURSELF CALLED A *WEAPO*
ALL THAT PROGRAMMING HE'S H
WHO'S TO SAY HE SEES HER T
SAME WAY? IN THAT MOMENT-
--YOU *REALLY* SURE WHAT CALL HE'LL MAKE?
MAYOR HILL?

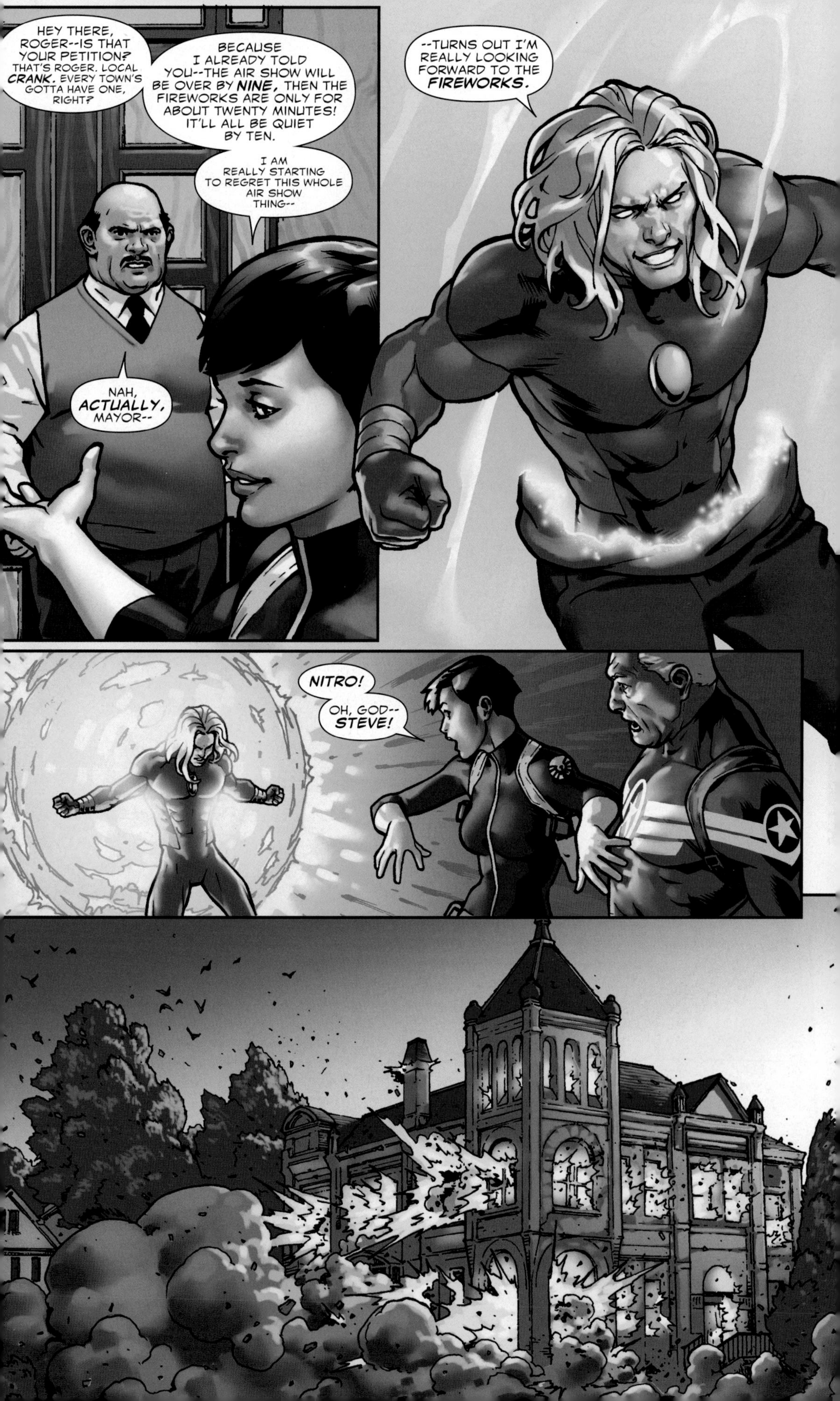
HEY THERE, ROGER--IS THAT YOUR PETITION? THAT'S ROGER. LOCAL CRANK. EVERY TOWN'S GOTTA HAVE ONE, RIGHT?
BECAUSE I ALREADY TOLD YOU--THE AIR SHOW WILL BE OVER BY NINE, THEN THE FIREWORKS ARE ONLY FOR ABOUT TWENTY MINUTES! IT'LL ALL BE QUIET BY TEN.
I AM REALLY STARTING TO REGRET THIS WHOLE AIR SHOW THING--
NAH, ACTUALLY, MAYOR--
--TURNS OUT I'M REALLY LOOKING FORWARD TO THE FIREWORKS.
NITRO!
OH, GOD--STEVE!

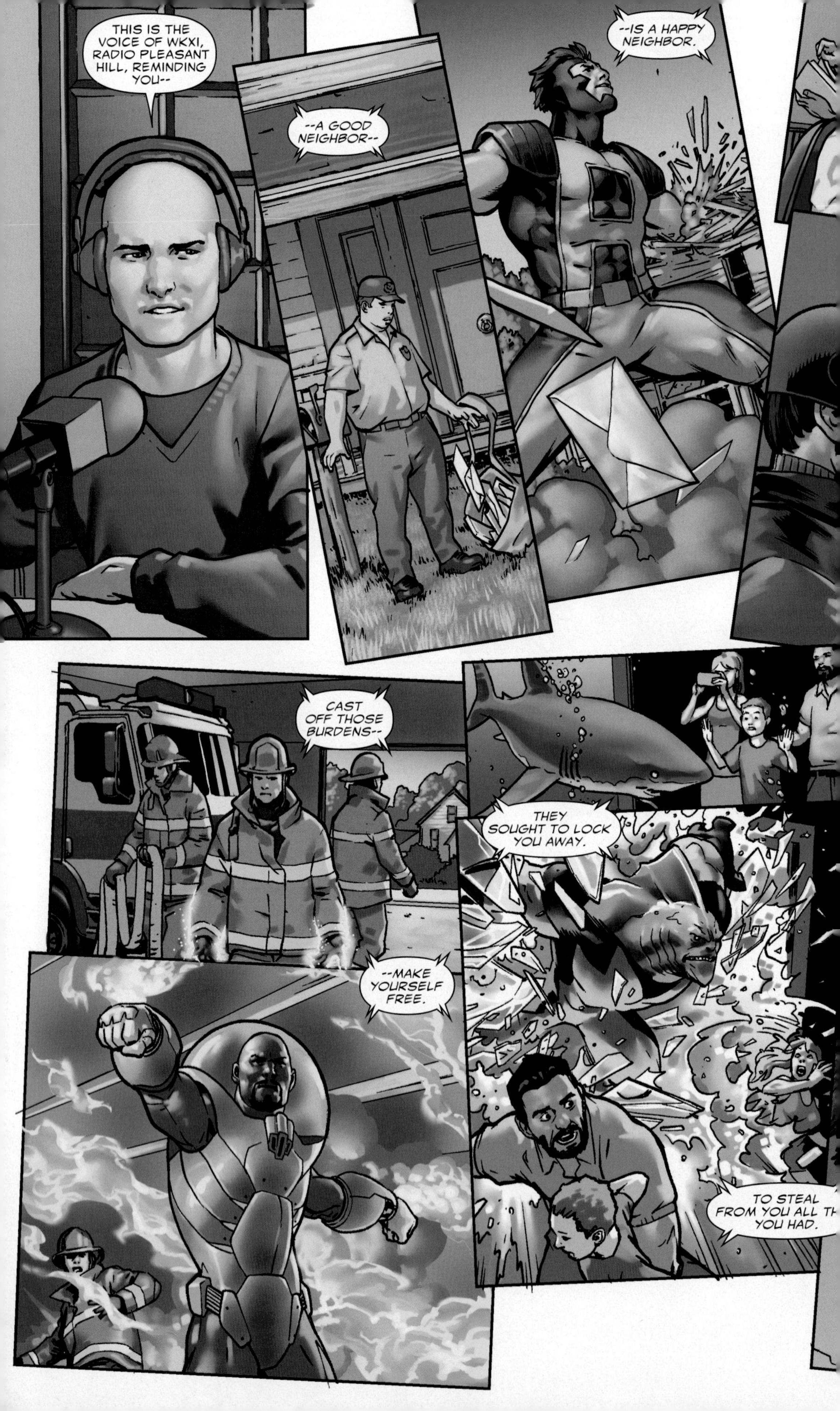
THIS IS THE VOICE OF WKXI, RADIO PLEASANT HILL, REMINDING YOU--
--A GOOD NEIGHBOR--
--IS A HAPPY NEIGHBOR.
CAST OFF THOSE BURDENS--
--MAKE YOURSELF FREE.
THEY SOUGHT TO LOCK YOU AWAY.
TO STEAL FROM YOU ALL TH
YOU HAD.

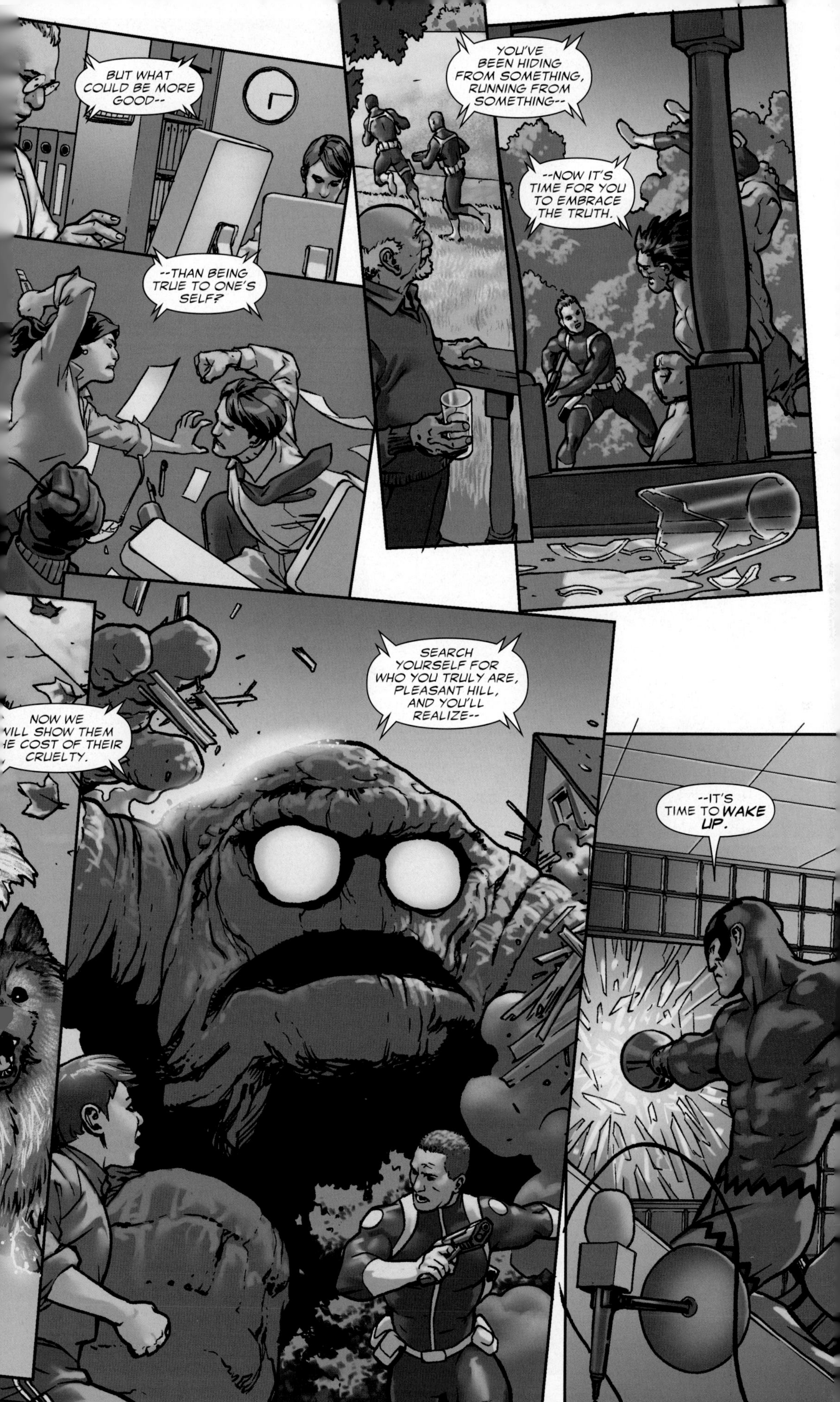
BUT WHAT COULD BE MORE GOOD--
--THAN BEING TRUE TO ONE'S SELF?
YOU'VE BEEN HIDING FROM SOMETHING, RUNNING FROM SOMETHING--
--NOW IT'S TIME FOR YOU TO EMBRACE THE TRUTH.
NOW WE ILL SHOW THEM HE COST OF THEIR CRUELTY.
SEARCH YOURSELF FOR WHO YOU TRULY ARE, PLEASANT HILL, AND YOU'LL REALIZE--
--IT'S TIME TO WAKE UP.

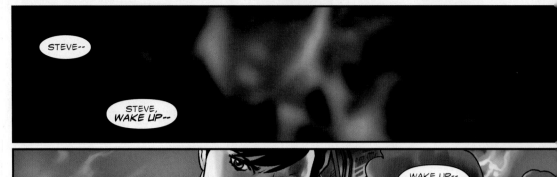

STEVE--

STEVE, *WAKE UP*--

WAKE UP-- COME ON...WE HAVE TO GET YOU OUT OF HERE...

W-WHAT HAPPENED?

I'M GONNA GO WITH--*UHN*-- YOU TOTALLY *JINXED* US.

YOU'RE HURT...

YEAH, WELL, LEAST I DIDN'T GET CAPTAIN AMERICA KILLED ON MY SHIFT. WE'RE UNDER ATTACK-- FIRST THING I GOTTA MAKE SURE OF--

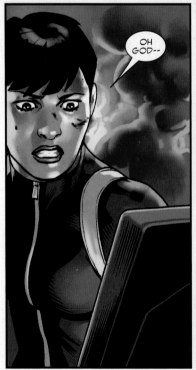

OH GOD--

KOBIK...

I'M CALLING FOR BACKUP-- *UNITY SQUAD*, THIS IS COMMAND ROGERS--REPEAT, THIS IS COMMAND ROGERS, REQUESTING EMERGENC AVENGERS RESPONSE--

YES, CALL THE CAPTAIN

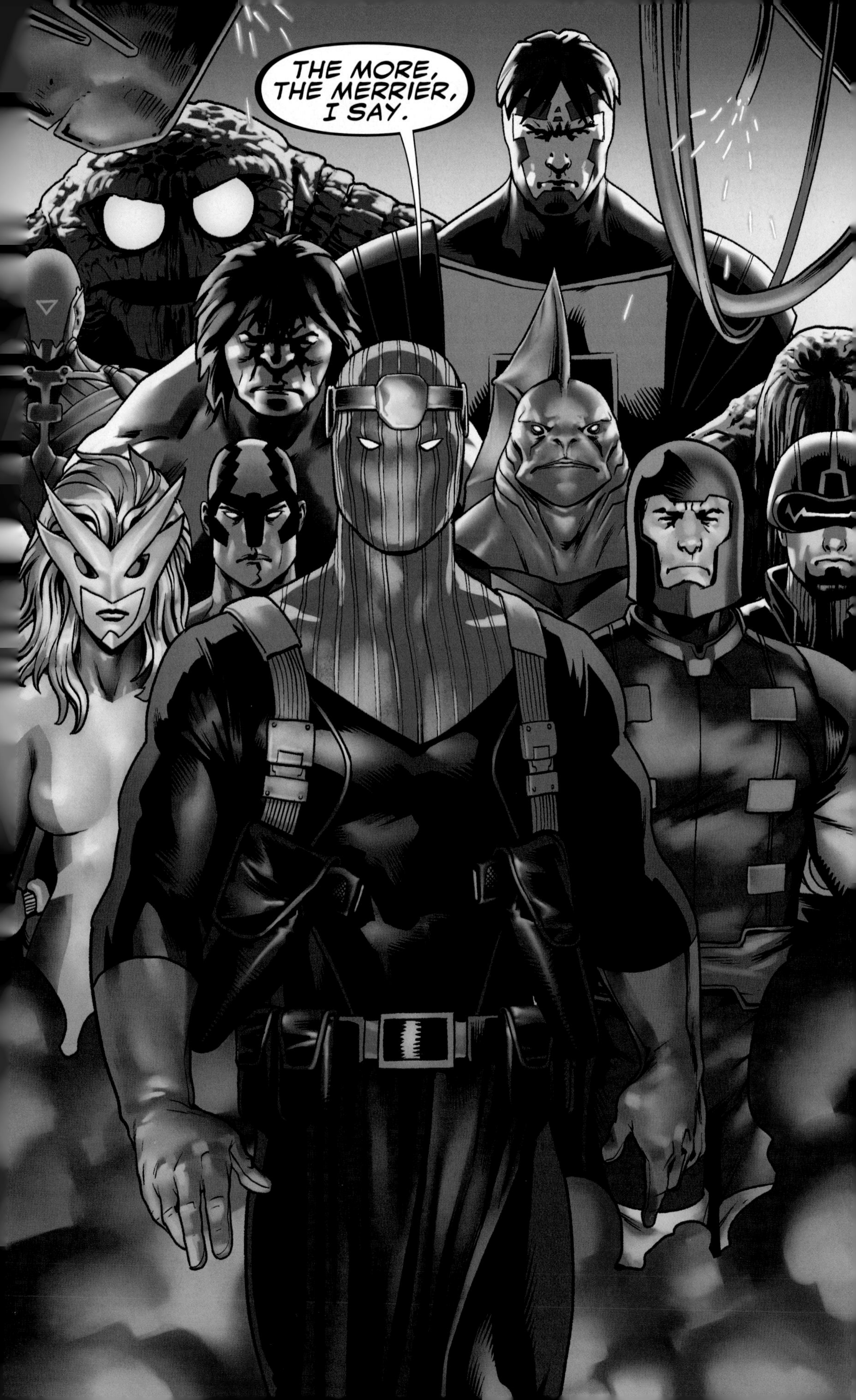
THE MORE, THE MERRIER, I SAY.

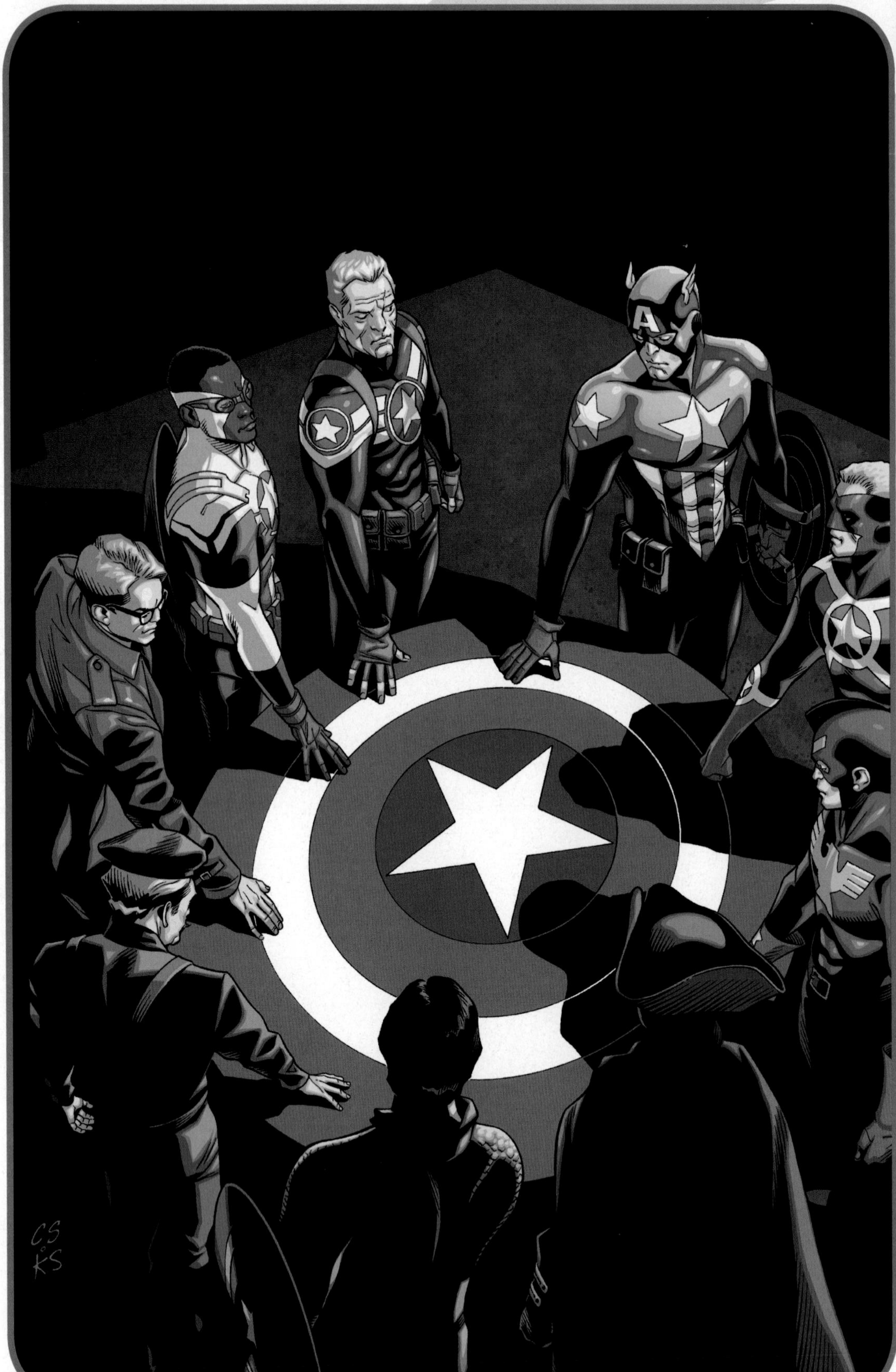
CS
KS

#7 All Eras variant by
CHRIS SPROUSE, KARL STORY & DAVE MCCAIG

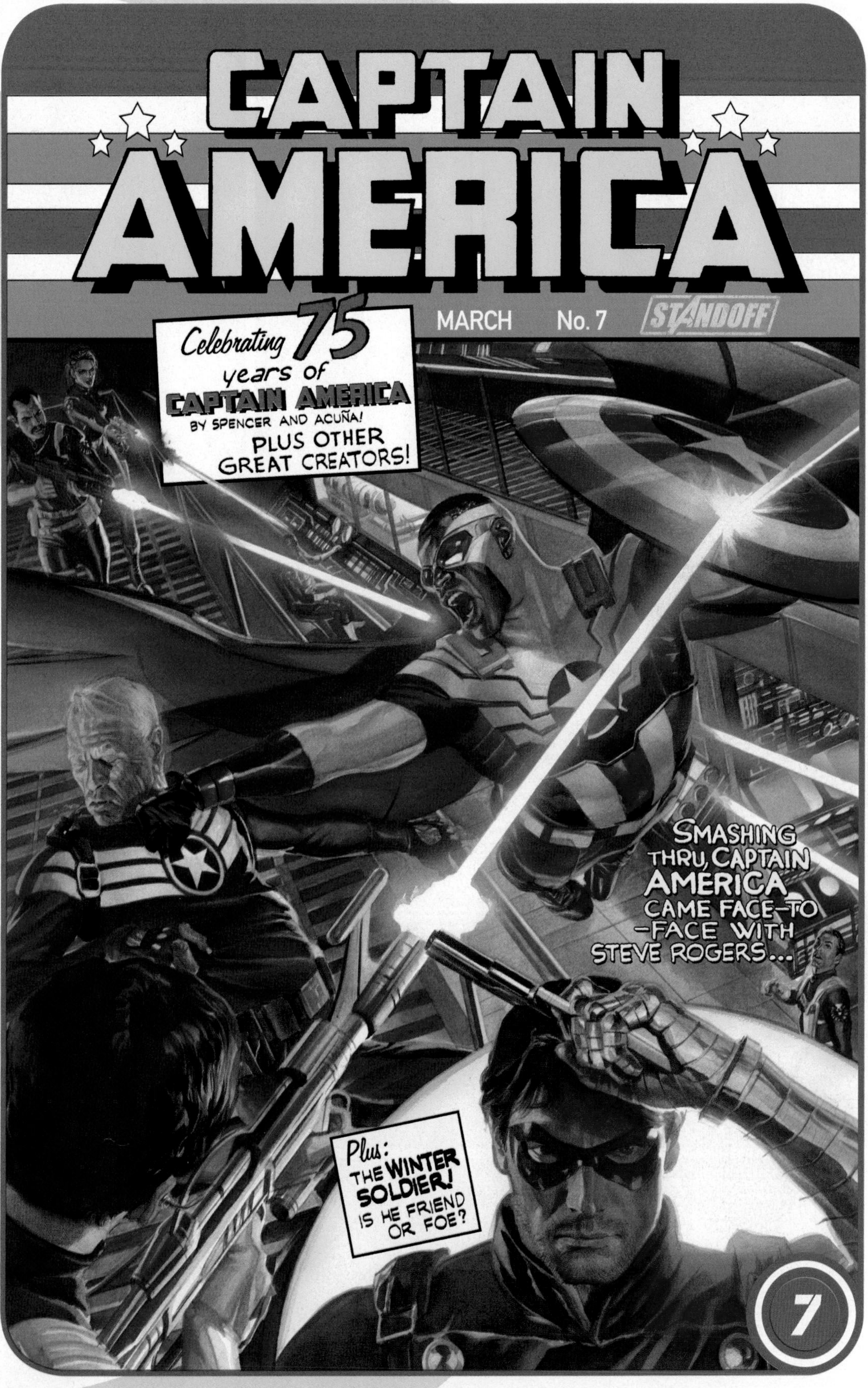
CAPTAIN AMERICA
MARCH No. 7 STANDOFF
Celebrating 75 years of CAPTAIN AMERICA BY SPENCER AND ACUÑA! PLUS OTHER GREAT CREATORS!
SMASHING THRU, CAPTAIN AMERICA CAME FACE-TO-FACE WITH STEVE ROGERS...
Plus: THE WINTER SOLDIER! IS HE FRIEND OR FOE?
7

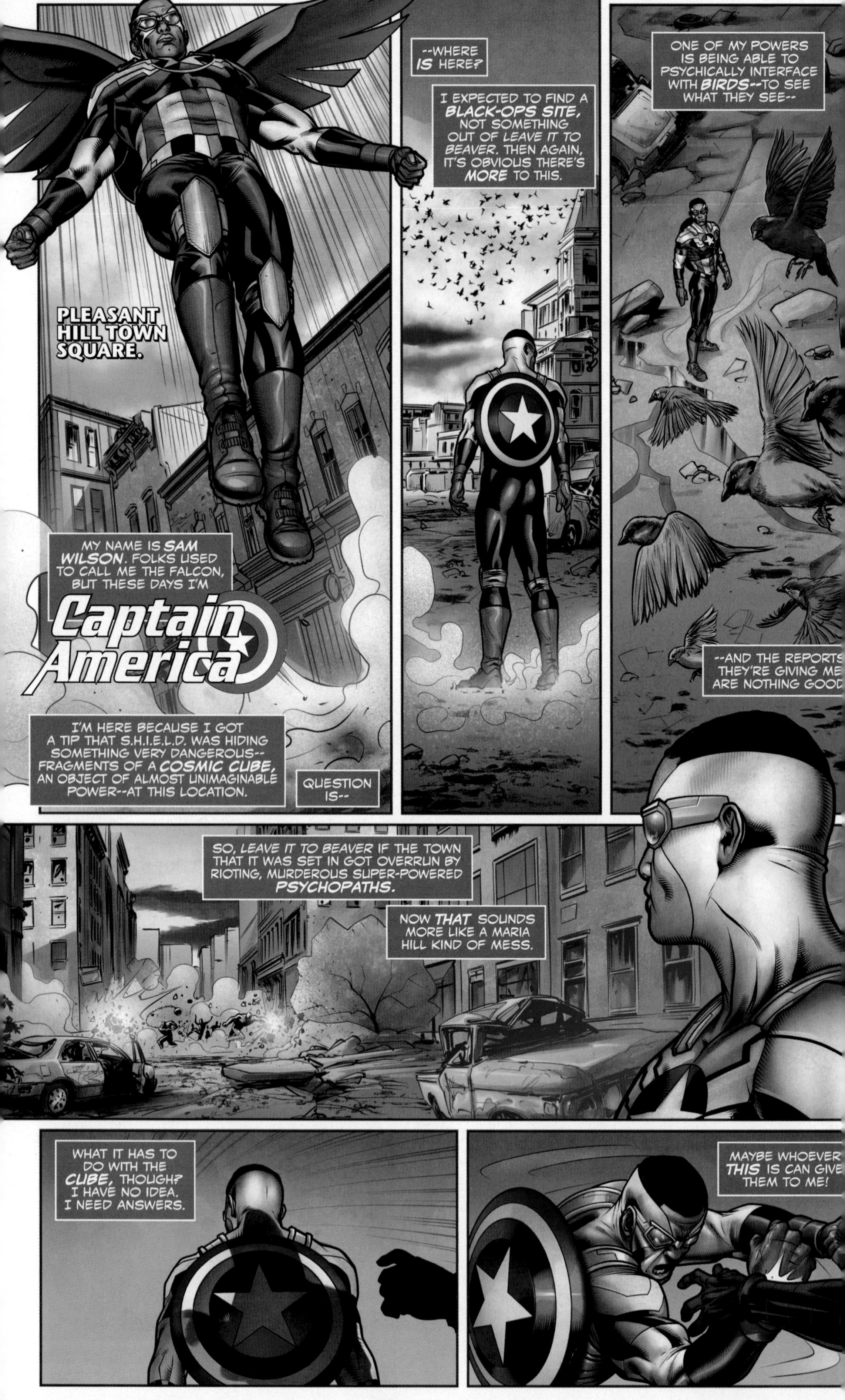
PLEASANT HILL TOWN SQUARE.
MY NAME IS SAM WILSON. FOLKS USED TO CALL ME THE FALCON, BUT THESE DAYS I'M
Captain America
I'M HERE BECAUSE I GOT A TIP THAT S.H.I.E.L.D. WAS HIDING SOMETHING VERY DANGEROUS--FRAGMENTS OF A COSMIC CUBE, AN OBJECT OF ALMOST UNIMAGINABLE POWER--AT THIS LOCATION.
QUESTION IS--
--WHERE IS HERE?
I EXPECTED TO FIND A BLACK-OPS SITE, NOT SOMETHING OUT OF LEAVE IT TO BEAVER. THEN AGAIN, IT'S OBVIOUS THERE'S MORE TO THIS.
ONE OF MY POWERS IS BEING ABLE TO PSYCHICALLY INTERFACE WITH BIRDS--TO SEE WHAT THEY SEE--
--AND THE REPORTS THEY'RE GIVING ME ARE NOTHING GOOD
SO, LEAVE IT TO BEAVER IF THE TOWN THAT IT WAS SET IN GOT OVERRUN BY RIOTING, MURDEROUS SUPER-POWERED PSYCHOPATHS.
NOW THAT SOUNDS MORE LIKE A MARIA HILL KIND OF MESS.
WHAT IT HAS TO DO WITH THE CUBE, THOUGH? I HAVE NO IDEA. I NEED ANSWERS.
MAYBE WHOEVER THIS IS CAN GIVE THEM TO ME!

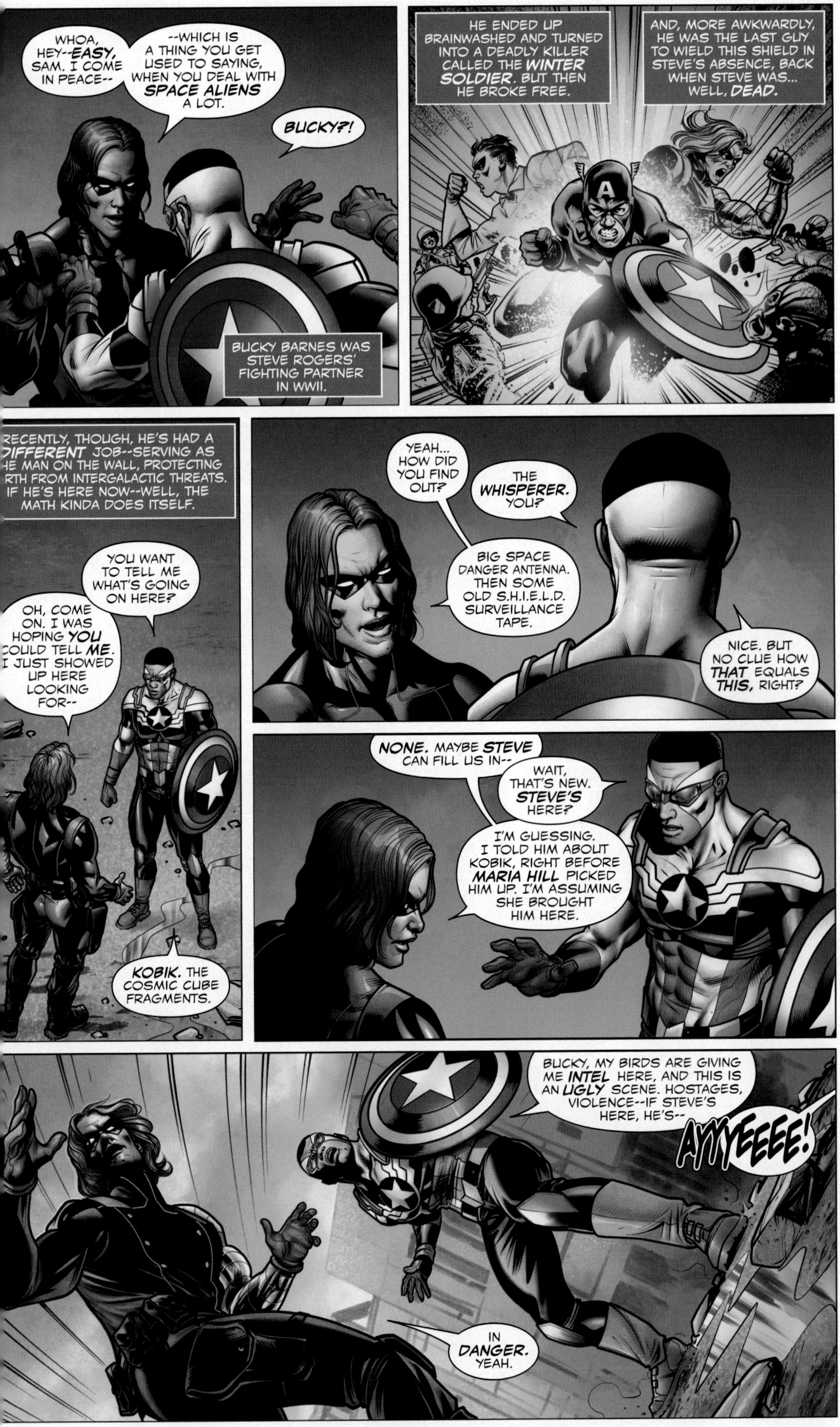
WHOA, HEY--**EASY,** SAM. I COME IN PEACE--
--WHICH IS A THING YOU GET USED TO SAYING, WHEN YOU DEAL WITH **SPACE ALIENS** A LOT.
BUCKY?!
BUCKY BARNES WAS STEVE ROGERS' FIGHTING PARTNER IN WWII.
HE ENDED UP BRAINWASHED AND TURNED INTO A DEADLY KILLER CALLED THE **WINTER SOLDIER**. BUT THEN HE BROKE FREE.
AND, MORE AWKWARDLY, HE WAS THE LAST GUY TO WIELD THIS SHIELD IN STEVE'S ABSENCE, BACK WHEN STEVE WAS... WELL, **DEAD.**
RECENTLY, THOUGH, HE'S HAD A **DIFFERENT** JOB--SERVING AS HE MAN ON THE WALL, PROTECTING RTH FROM INTERGALACTIC THREATS. IF HE'S HERE NOW--WELL, THE MATH KINDA DOES ITSELF.
YOU WANT TO TELL ME WHAT'S GOING ON HERE?
OH, COME ON. I WAS HOPING **YOU** COULD TELL **ME**. I JUST SHOWED UP HERE LOOKING FOR--
KOBIK. THE COSMIC CUBE FRAGMENTS.
YEAH... HOW DID YOU FIND OUT?
THE **WHISPERER.** YOU?
BIG SPACE DANGER ANTENNA. THEN SOME OLD S.H.I.E.L.D. SURVEILLANCE TAPE.
NICE. BUT NO CLUE HOW **THAT** EQUALS **THIS,** RIGHT?
NONE. MAYBE **STEVE** CAN FILL US IN--
WAIT, THAT'S NEW. **STEVE'S** HERE?
I'M GUESSING. I TOLD HIM ABOUT KOBIK, RIGHT BEFORE **MARIA HILL** PICKED HIM UP. I'M ASSUMING SHE BROUGHT HIM HERE.
BUCKY, MY BIRDS ARE GIVING ME **INTEL** HERE, AND THIS IS AN **UGLY** SCENE. HOSTAGES, VIOLENCE--IF STEVE'S HERE, HE'S--
AYYYEEEE!
IN **DANGER.** YEAH.

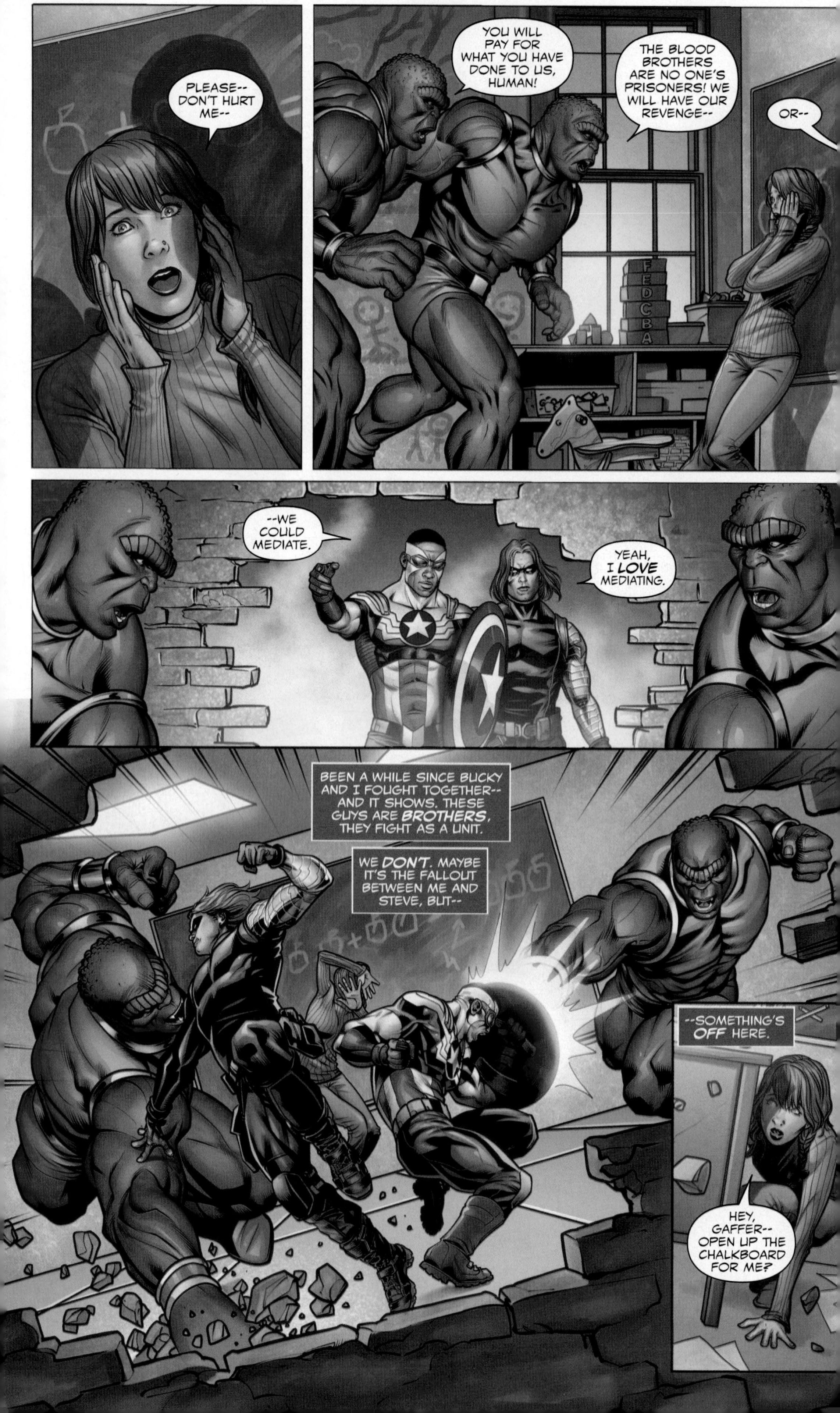
PLEASE-- DON'T HURT ME--
YOU WILL PAY FOR WHAT YOU HAVE DONE TO US, HUMAN!
THE BLOOD BROTHERS ARE NO ONE'S PRISONERS! WE WILL HAVE OUR REVENGE--
OR--
--WE COULD MEDIATE.
YEAH, I LOVE MEDIATING.
BEEN A WHILE SINCE BUCKY AND I FOUGHT TOGETHER-- AND IT SHOWS. THESE GUYS ARE BROTHERS, THEY FIGHT AS A UNIT.
WE DON'T. MAYBE IT'S THE FALLOUT BETWEEN ME AND STEVE, BUT--
--SOMETHING'S OFF HERE.
HEY, GAFFER-- OPEN UP THE CHALKBOARD FOR ME?

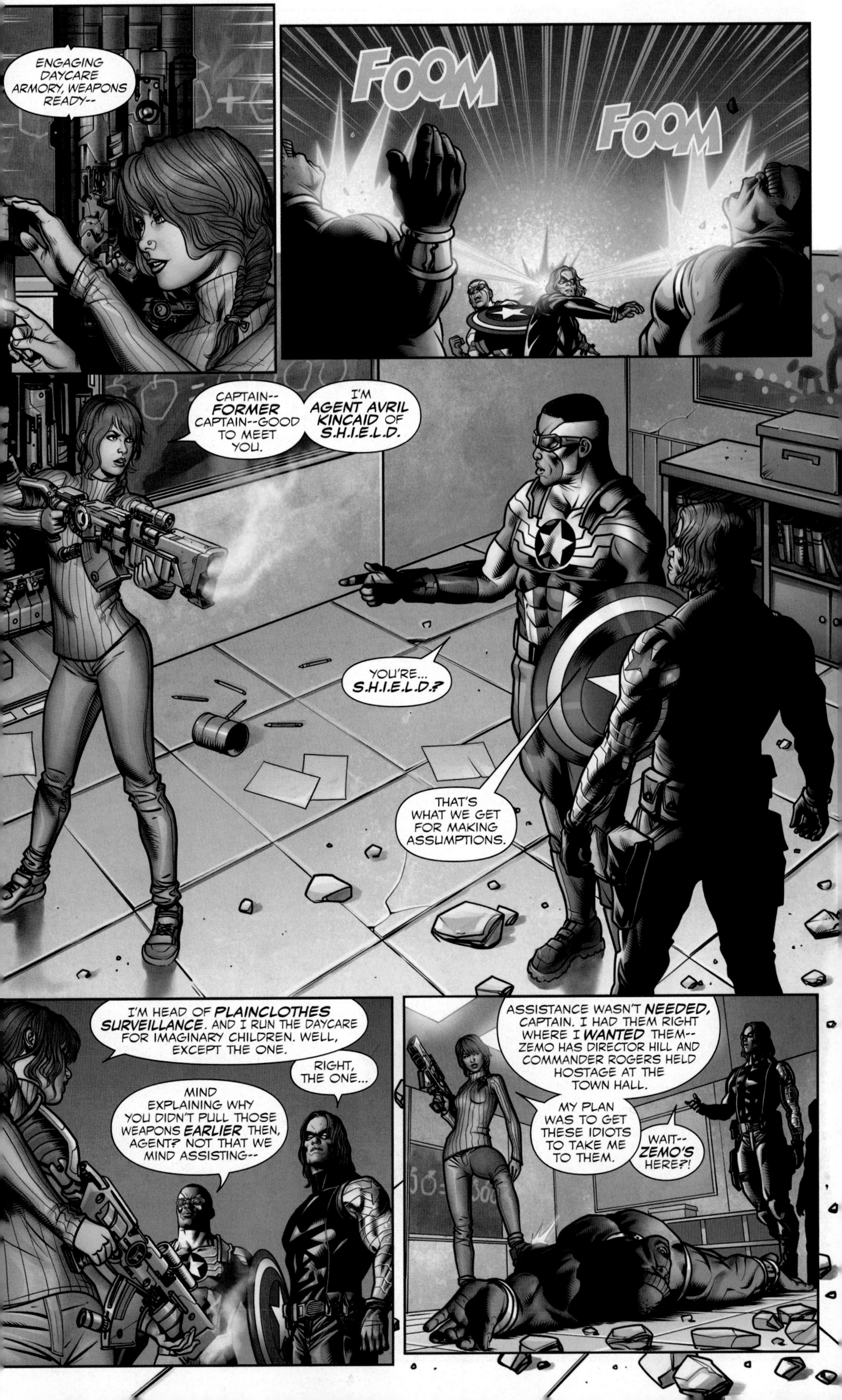
ENGAGING DAYCARE ARMORY, WEAPONS READY--
FOOM
FOOM
CAPTAIN-- FORMER CAPTAIN--GOOD TO MEET YOU.
I'M AGENT AVRIL KINCAID OF S.H.I.E.L.D.
YOU'RE... S.H.I.E.L.D.?
THAT'S WHAT WE GET FOR MAKING ASSUMPTIONS.
I'M HEAD OF PLAINCLOTHES SURVEILLANCE. AND I RUN THE DAYCARE FOR IMAGINARY CHILDREN. WELL, EXCEPT THE ONE.
RIGHT, THE ONE...
MIND EXPLAINING WHY YOU DIDN'T PULL THOSE WEAPONS EARLIER THEN, AGENT? NOT THAT WE MIND ASSISTING--
ASSISTANCE WASN'T NEEDED, CAPTAIN. I HAD THEM RIGHT WHERE I WANTED THEM-- ZEMO HAS DIRECTOR HILL AND COMMANDER ROGERS HELD HOSTAGE AT THE TOWN HALL.
MY PLAN WAS TO GET THESE IDIOTS TO TAKE ME TO THEM.
WAIT-- ZEMO'S HERE?!

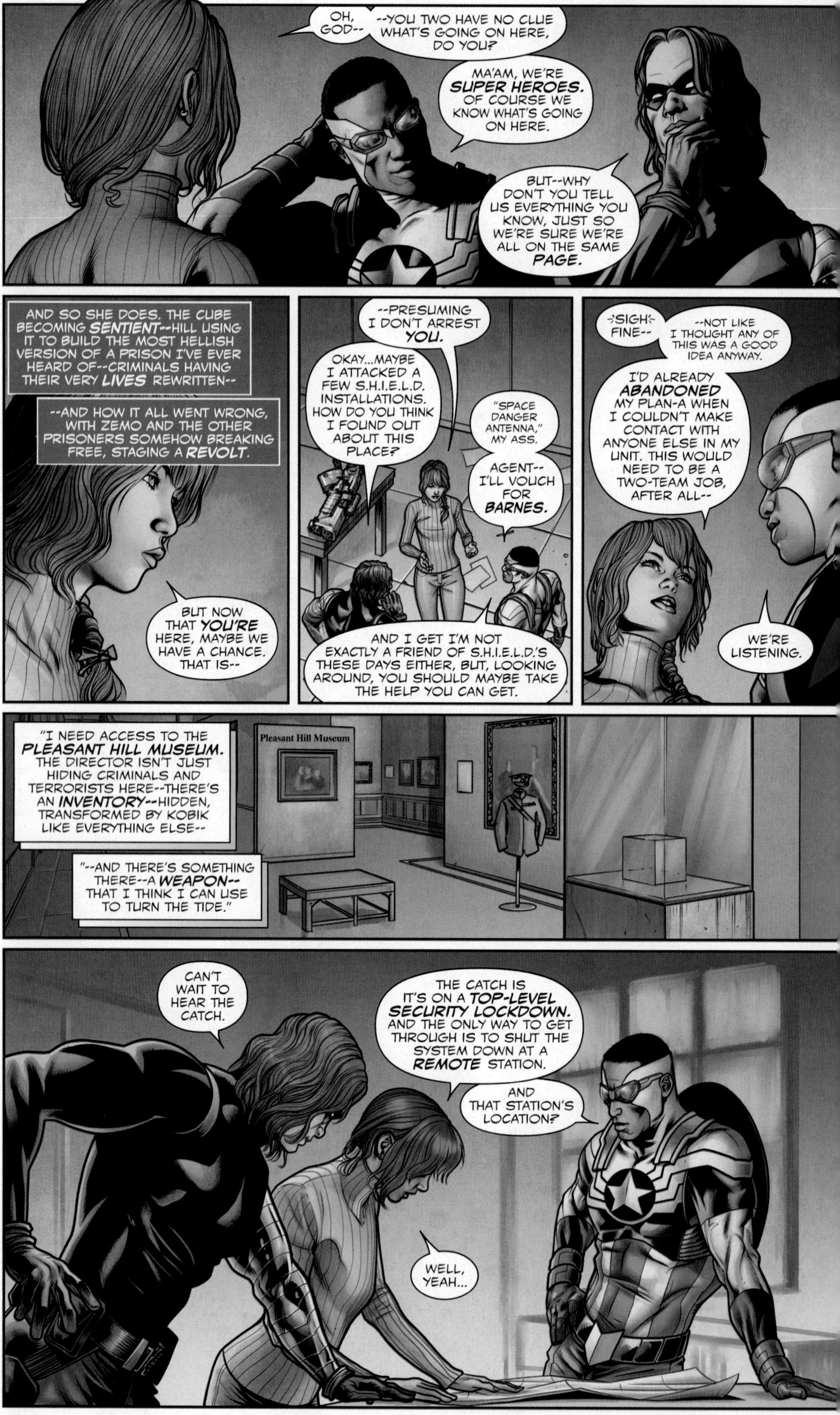
OH, GOD--
--YOU TWO HAVE NO CLUE WHAT'S GOING ON HERE, DO YOU?
MA'AM, WE'RE SUPER HEROES. OF COURSE WE KNOW WHAT'S GOING ON HERE.
BUT--WHY DON'T YOU TELL US EVERYTHING YOU KNOW, JUST SO WE'RE SURE WE'RE ALL ON THE SAME PAGE.
AND SO SHE DOES. THE CUBE BECOMING SENTIENT--HILL USING IT TO BUILD THE MOST HELLISH VERSION OF A PRISON I'VE EVER HEARD OF--CRIMINALS HAVING THEIR VERY LIVES REWRITTEN--
--AND HOW IT ALL WENT WRONG, WITH ZEMO AND THE OTHER PRISONERS SOMEHOW BREAKING FREE, STAGING A REVOLT.
BUT NOW THAT YOU'RE HERE, MAYBE WE HAVE A CHANCE. THAT IS--
--PRESUMING I DON'T ARREST YOU.
OKAY...MAYBE I ATTACKED A FEW S.H.I.E.L.D. INSTALLATIONS. HOW DO YOU THINK I FOUND OUT ABOUT THIS PLACE?
"SPACE DANGER ANTENNA," MY ASS.
AGENT-- I'LL VOUCH FOR BARNES.
AND I GET I'M NOT EXACTLY A FRIEND OF S.H.I.E.L.D.'S THESE DAYS EITHER, BUT, LOOKING AROUND, YOU SHOULD MAYBE TAKE THE HELP YOU CAN GET.
SIGH FINE--
--NOT LIKE I THOUGHT ANY OF THIS WAS A GOOD IDEA ANYWAY.
I'D ALREADY ABANDONED MY PLAN-A WHEN I COULDN'T MAKE CONTACT WITH ANYONE ELSE IN MY UNIT. THIS WOULD NEED TO BE A TWO-TEAM JOB, AFTER ALL--
WE'RE LISTENING.
"I NEED ACCESS TO THE PLEASANT HILL MUSEUM. THE DIRECTOR ISN'T JUST HIDING CRIMINALS AND TERRORISTS HERE--THERE'S AN INVENTORY--HIDDEN, TRANSFORMED BY KOBIK LIKE EVERYTHING ELSE--
Pleasant Hill Museum
"--AND THERE'S SOMETHING THERE--A WEAPON--THAT I THINK I CAN USE TO TURN THE TIDE."
CAN'T WAIT TO HEAR THE CATCH.
THE CATCH IS IT'S ON A TOP-LEVEL SECURITY LOCKDOWN. AND THE ONLY WAY TO GET THROUGH IS TO SHUT THE SYSTEM DOWN AT A REMOTE STATION.
AND THAT STATION'S LOCATION?
WELL, YEAH...

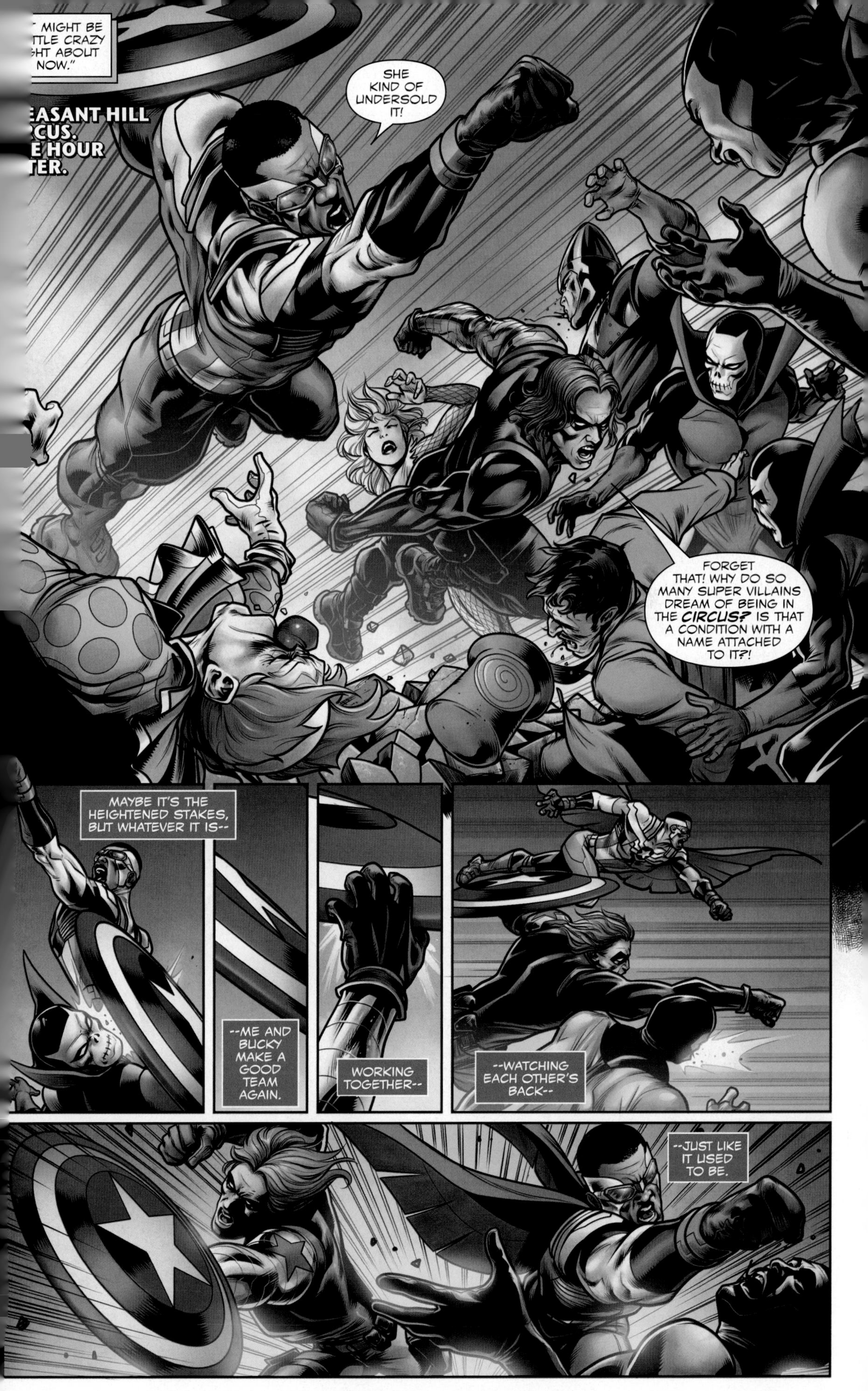
T MIGHT BE TTLE CRAZY GHT ABOUT NOW."
EASANT HILL RCUS. E HOUR TER.
SHE KIND OF UNDERSOLD IT!
FORGET THAT! WHY DO SO MANY SUPER VILLAINS DREAM OF BEING IN THE CIRCUS? IS THAT A CONDITION WITH A NAME ATTACHED TO IT?!
MAYBE IT'S THE HEIGHTENED STAKES, BUT WHATEVER IT IS--
--ME AND BUCKY MAKE A GOOD TEAM AGAIN.
WORKING TOGETHER--
--WATCHING EACH OTHER'S BACK--
--JUST LIKE IT USED TO BE.

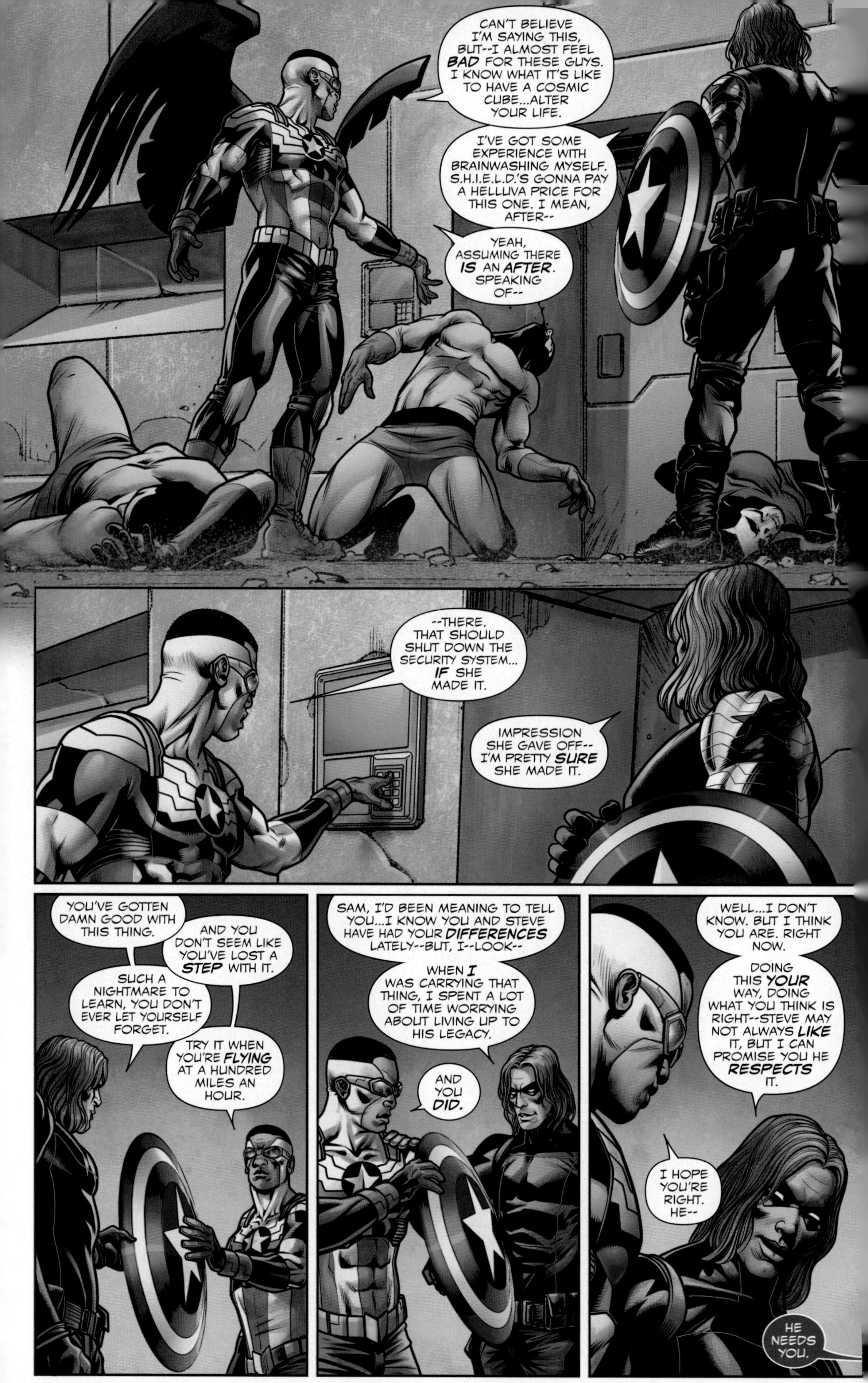
CAN'T BELIEVE I'M SAYING THIS, BUT--I ALMOST FEEL BAD FOR THESE GUYS. I KNOW WHAT IT'S LIKE TO HAVE A COSMIC CUBE...ALTER YOUR LIFE.
I'VE GOT SOME EXPERIENCE WITH BRAINWASHING MYSELF. S.H.I.E.L.D.'S GONNA PAY A HELLUVA PRICE FOR THIS ONE. I MEAN, AFTER--
YEAH, ASSUMING THERE IS AN AFTER. SPEAKING OF--
--THERE. THAT SHOULD SHUT DOWN THE SECURITY SYSTEM... IF SHE MADE IT.
IMPRESSION SHE GAVE OFF-- I'M PRETTY SURE SHE MADE IT.
YOU'VE GOTTEN DAMN GOOD WITH THIS THING.
AND YOU DON'T SEEM LIKE YOU'VE LOST A STEP WITH IT.
SUCH A NIGHTMARE TO LEARN, YOU DON'T EVER LET YOURSELF FORGET.
TRY IT WHEN YOU'RE FLYING AT A HUNDRED MILES AN HOUR.
SAM, I'D BEEN MEANING TO TELL YOU...I KNOW YOU AND STEVE HAVE HAD YOUR DIFFERENCES LATELY--BUT, I--LOOK--
WHEN I WAS CARRYING THAT THING, I SPENT A LOT OF TIME WORRYING ABOUT LIVING UP TO HIS LEGACY.
AND YOU DID.
WELL...I DON'T KNOW. BUT I THINK YOU ARE. RIGHT NOW.
DOING THIS YOUR WAY, DOING WHAT YOU THINK IS RIGHT--STEVE MAY NOT ALWAYS LIKE IT, BUT I CAN PROMISE YOU HE RESPECTS IT.
I HOPE YOU'RE RIGHT. HE--
HE NEEDS YOU.

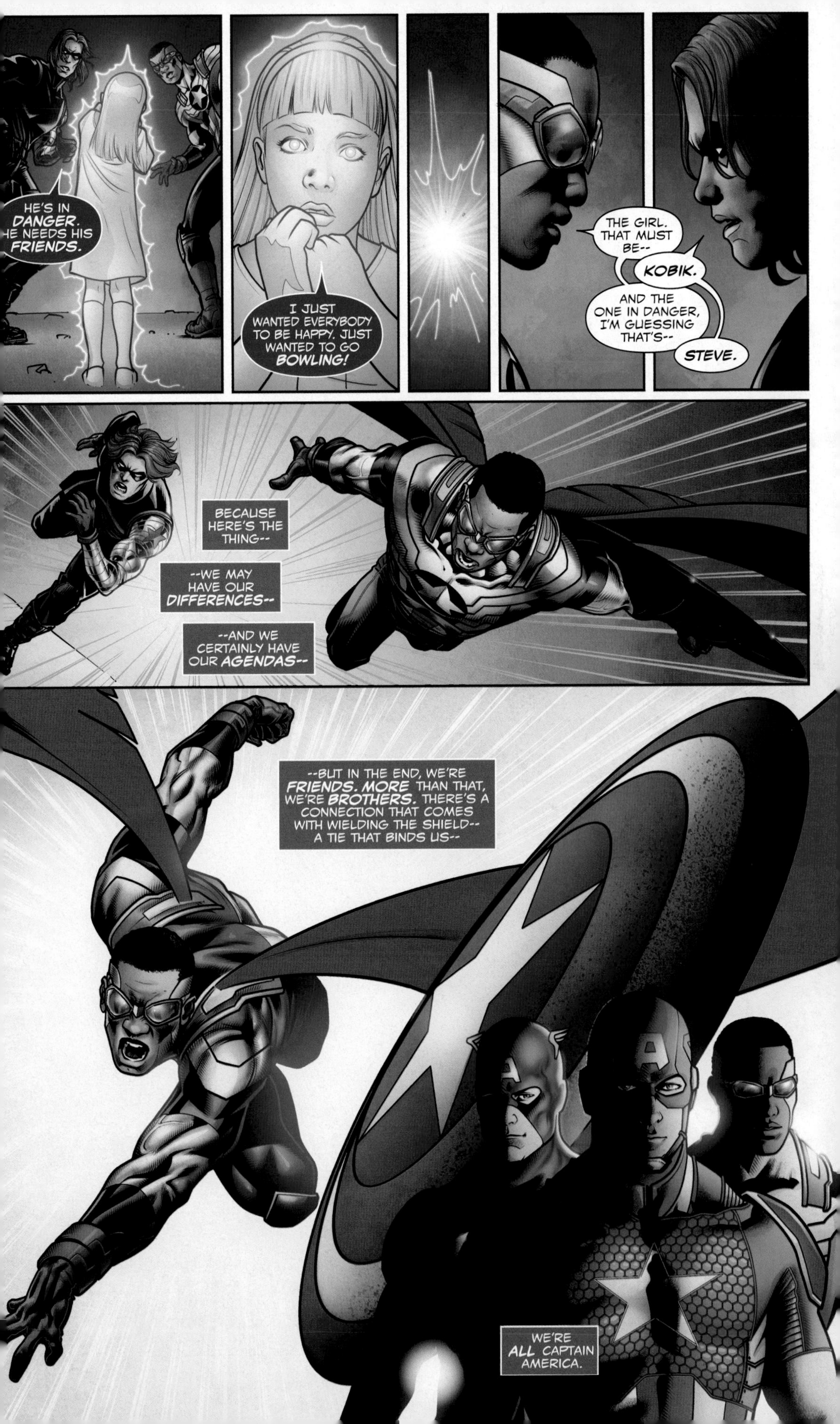
HE'S IN DANGER. HE NEEDS HIS FRIENDS.
I JUST WANTED EVERYBODY TO BE HAPPY. JUST WANTED TO GO BOWLING!
THE GIRL. THAT MUST BE--
KOBIK.
AND THE ONE IN DANGER, I'M GUESSING THAT'S--
STEVE.
BECAUSE HERE'S THE THING--
--WE MAY HAVE OUR DIFFERENCES--
--AND WE CERTAINLY HAVE OUR AGENDAS--
--BUT IN THE END, WE'RE FRIENDS. MORE THAN THAT, WE'RE BROTHERS. THERE'S A CONNECTION THAT COMES WITH WIELDING THE SHIELD-- A TIE THAT BINDS US--
WE'RE ALL CAPTAIN AMERICA.

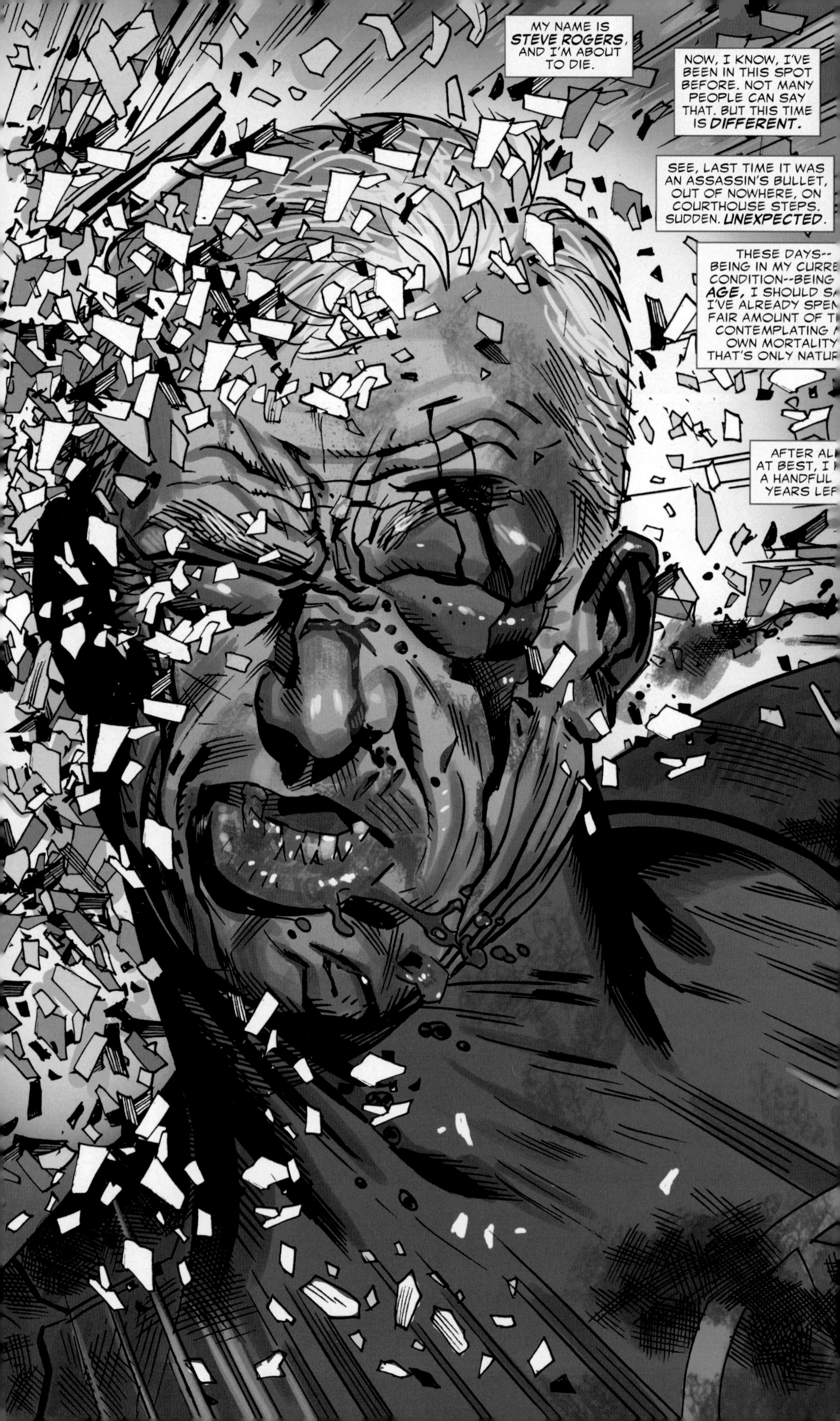
MY NAME IS **STEVE ROGERS**, AND I'M ABOUT TO DIE.
NOW, I KNOW, I'VE BEEN IN THIS SPOT BEFORE. NOT MANY PEOPLE CAN SAY THAT. BUT THIS TIME IS ***DIFFERENT.***
SEE, LAST TIME IT WAS AN ASSASSIN'S BULLET, OUT OF NOWHERE, ON COURTHOUSE STEPS. SUDDEN. ***UNEXPECTED.***
THESE DAYS-- BEING IN MY CURRE CONDITION--BEING **AGE,** I SHOULD SA I'VE ALREADY SPEN FAIR AMOUNT OF T CONTEMPLATING OWN MORTALITY THAT'S ONLY NATUR
AFTER AL AT BEST, I A HANDFUL YEARS LEF

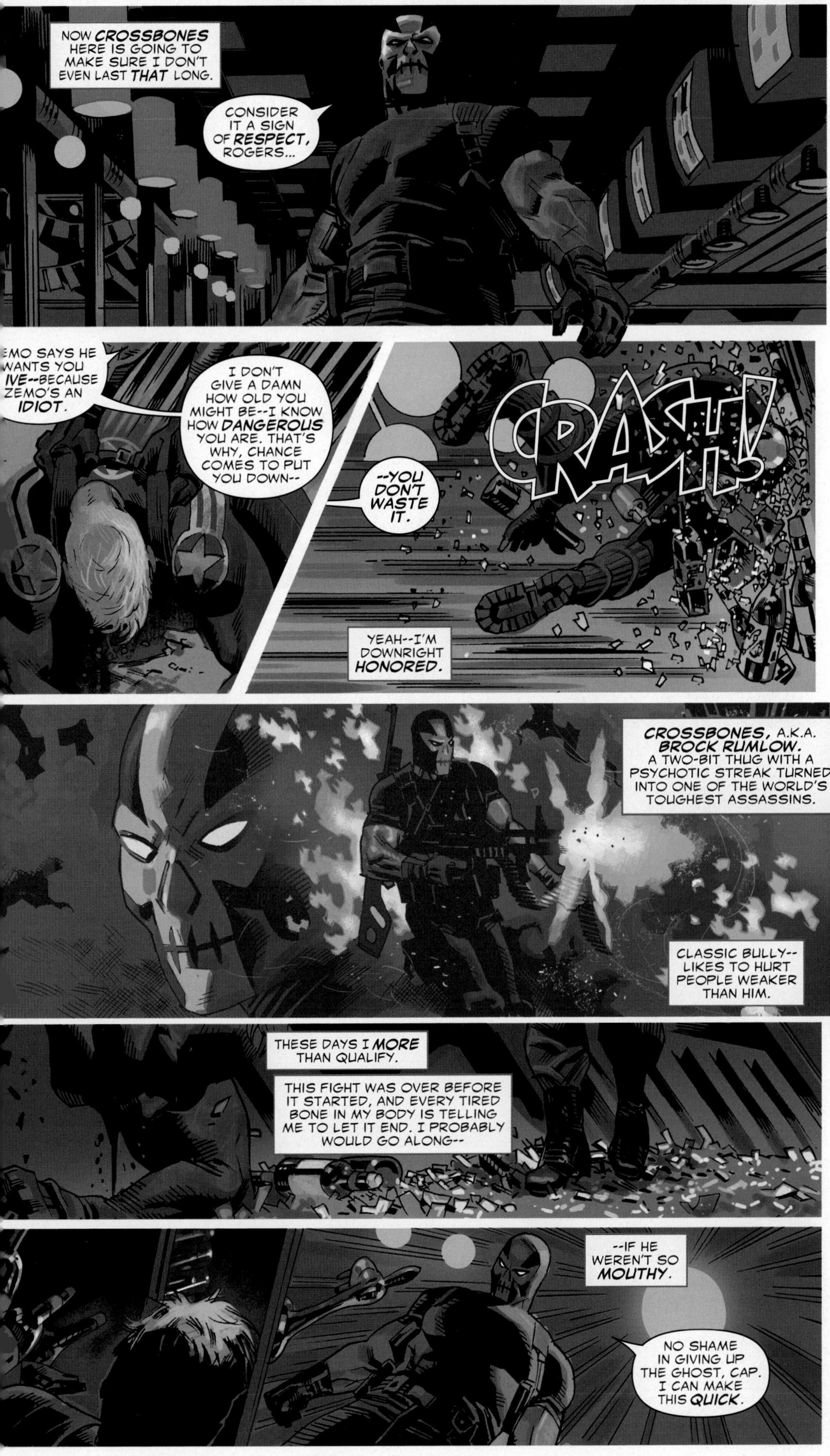
NOW CROSSBONES HERE IS GOING TO MAKE SURE I DON'T EVEN LAST THAT LONG.
CONSIDER IT A SIGN OF RESPECT, ROGERS...
EMO SAYS HE WANTS YOU IVE--BECAUSE ZEMO'S AN IDIOT.
I DON'T GIVE A DAMN HOW OLD YOU MIGHT BE--I KNOW HOW DANGEROUS YOU ARE. THAT'S WHY, CHANCE COMES TO PUT YOU DOWN--
--YOU DON'T WASTE IT.
CRASH!
YEAH--I'M DOWNRIGHT HONORED.
CROSSBONES, A.K.A. BROCK RUMLOW. A TWO-BIT THUG WITH A PSYCHOTIC STREAK TURNED INTO ONE OF THE WORLD'S TOUGHEST ASSASSINS.
CLASSIC BULLY--LIKES TO HURT PEOPLE WEAKER THAN HIM.
THESE DAYS I MORE THAN QUALIFY.
THIS FIGHT WAS OVER BEFORE IT STARTED, AND EVERY TIRED BONE IN MY BODY IS TELLING ME TO LET IT END. I PROBABLY WOULD GO ALONG--
--IF HE WEREN'T SO MOUTHY.
NO SHAME IN GIVING UP THE GHOST, CAP. I CAN MAKE THIS QUICK.

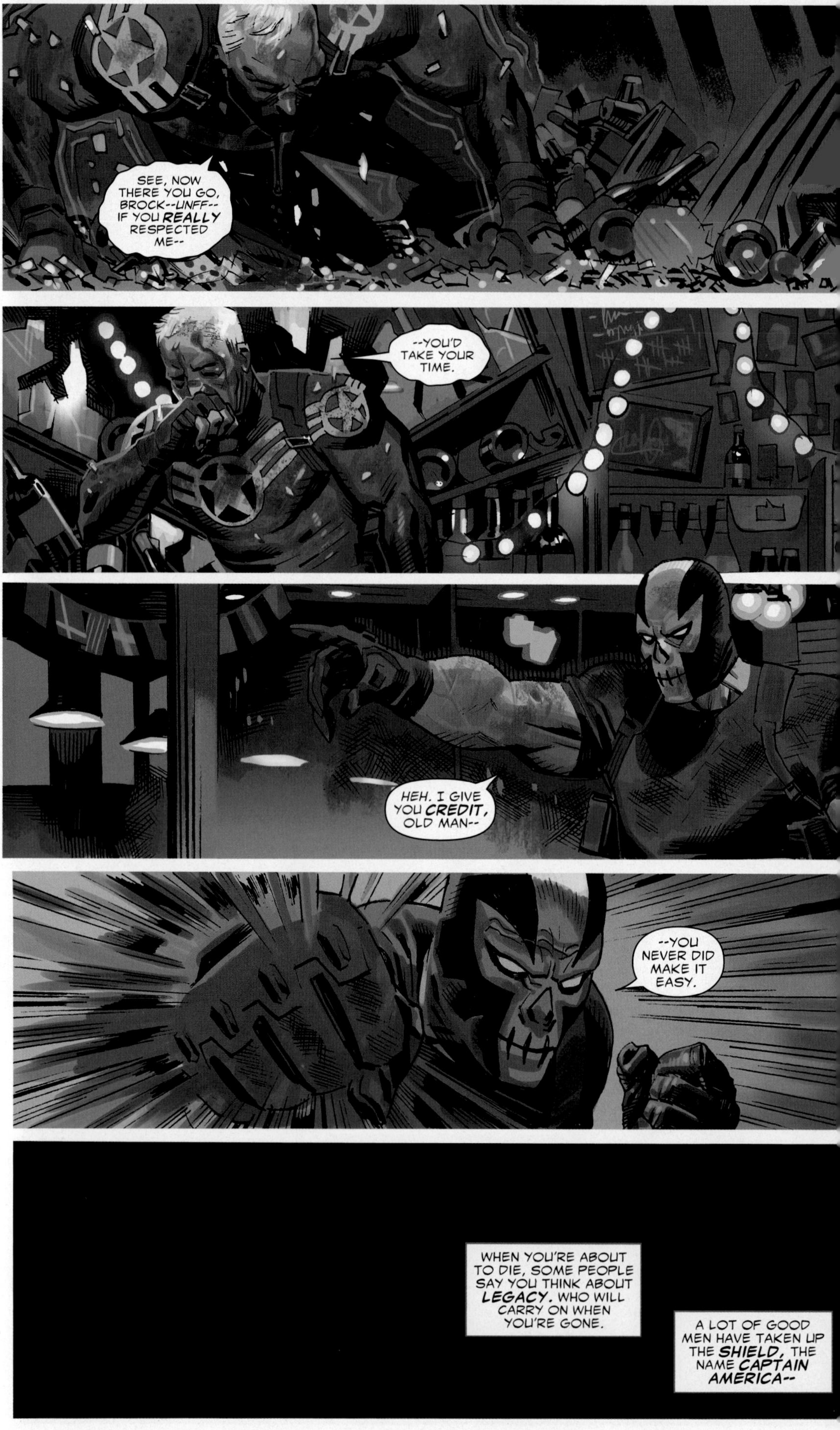
SEE, NOW THERE YOU GO, BROCK--UNFF-- IF YOU REALLY RESPECTED ME--
--YOU'D TAKE YOUR TIME.
HEH. I GIVE YOU CREDIT, OLD MAN--
--YOU NEVER DID MAKE IT EASY.
WHEN YOU'RE ABOUT TO DIE, SOME PEOPLE SAY YOU THINK ABOUT LEGACY. WHO WILL CARRY ON WHEN YOU'RE GONE.
A LOT OF GOOD MEN HAVE TAKEN UP THE SHIELD, THE NAME CAPTAIN AMERICA--

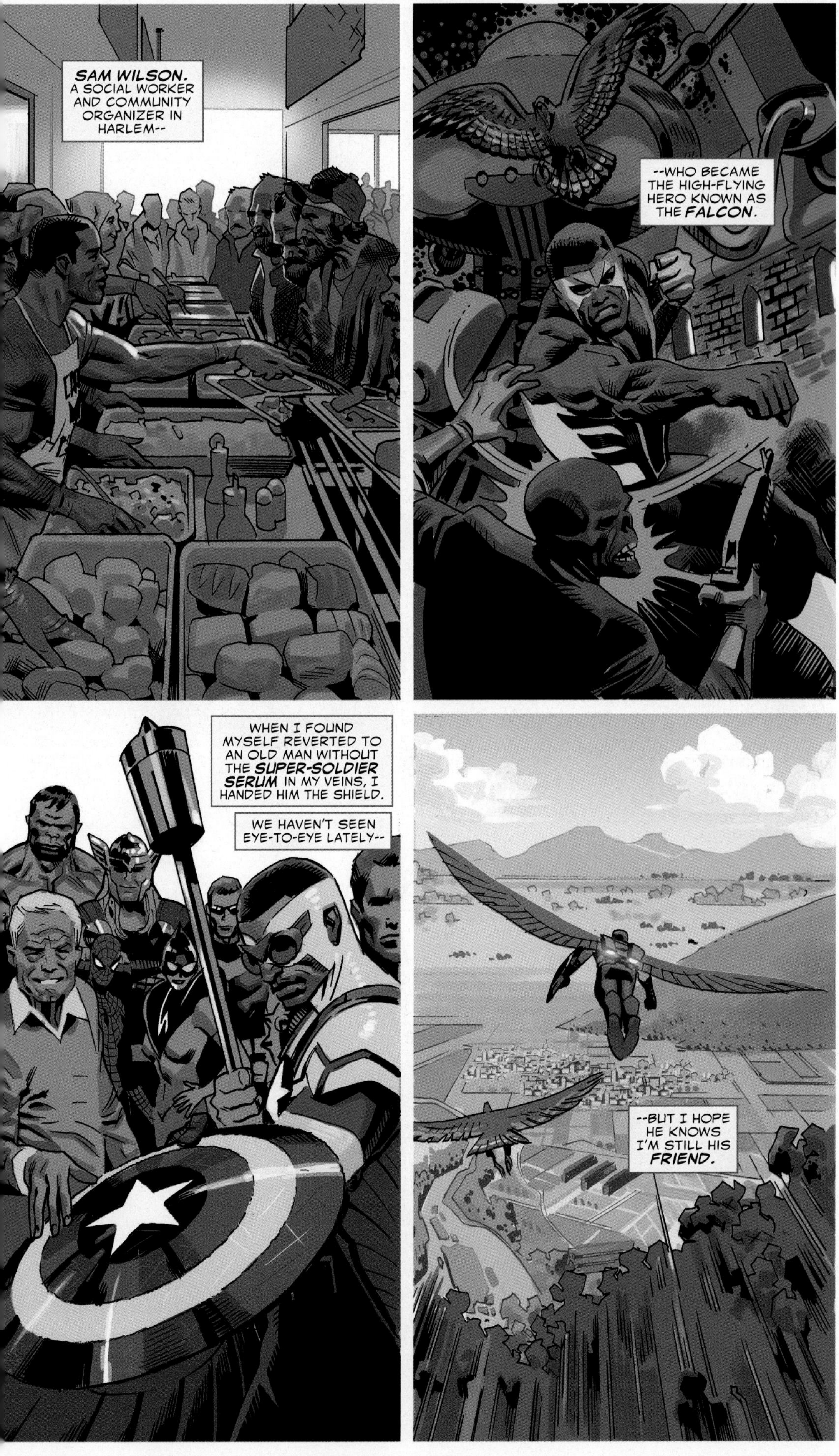
SAM WILSON. A SOCIAL WORKER AND COMMUNITY ORGANIZER IN HARLEM--
--WHO BECAME THE HIGH-FLYING HERO KNOWN AS THE FALCON.
WHEN I FOUND MYSELF REVERTED TO AN OLD MAN WITHOUT THE SUPER-SOLDIER SERUM IN MY VEINS, I HANDED HIM THE SHIELD.
WE HAVEN'T SEEN EYE-TO-EYE LATELY--
--BUT I HOPE HE KNOWS I'M STILL HIS FRIEND.

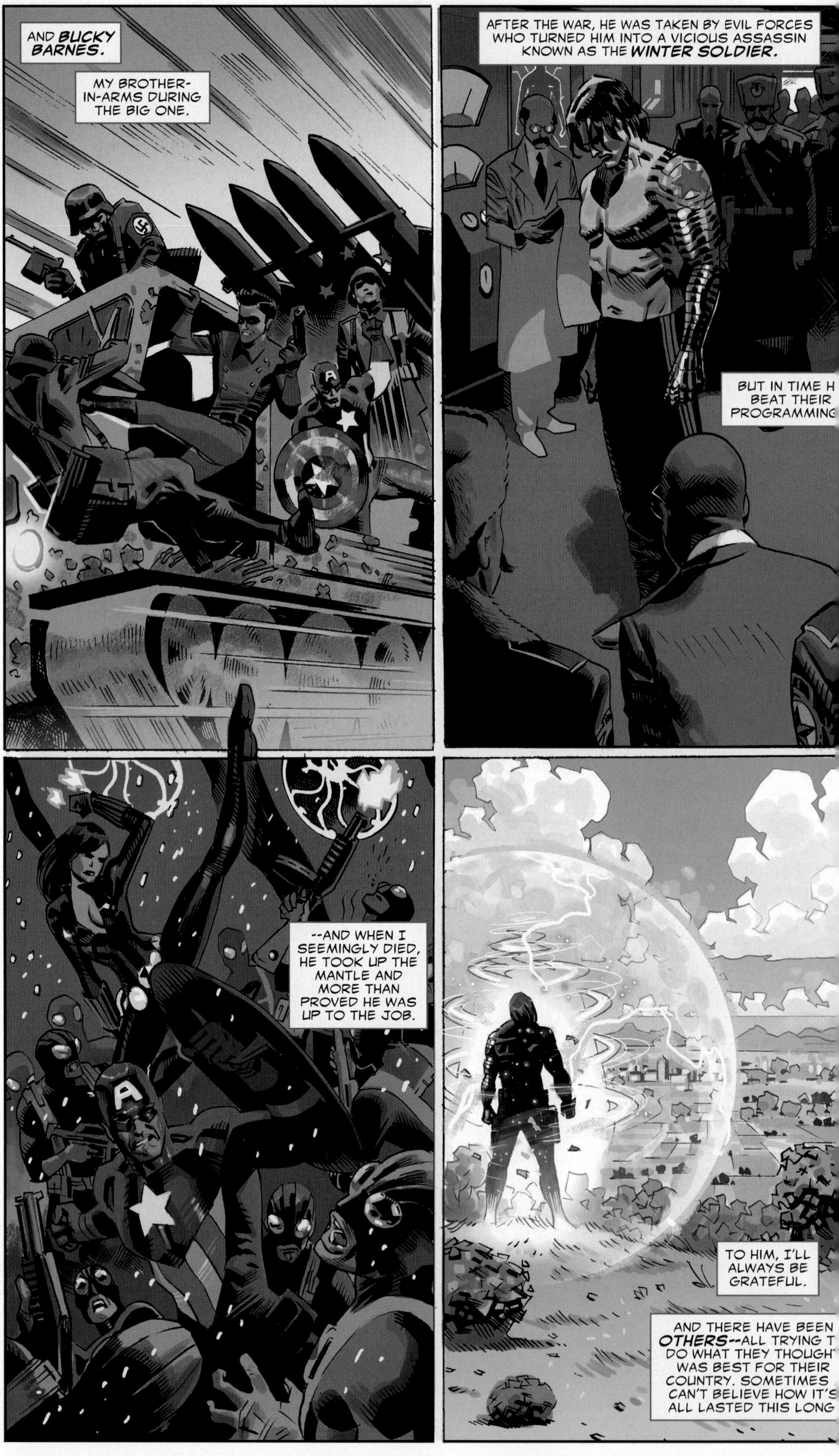
AND BUCKY BARNES.
MY BROTHER-IN-ARMS DURING THE BIG ONE.
AFTER THE WAR, HE WAS TAKEN BY EVIL FORCES WHO TURNED HIM INTO A VICIOUS ASSASSIN KNOWN AS THE WINTER SOLDIER.
BUT IN TIME H
BEAT THEIR
PROGRAMMING
--AND WHEN I SEEMINGLY DIED, HE TOOK UP THE MANTLE AND MORE THAN PROVED HE WAS UP TO THE JOB.
TO HIM, I'LL ALWAYS BE GRATEFUL.
AND THERE HAVE BEEN OTHERS--ALL TRYING T DO WHAT THEY THOUGHT WAS BEST FOR THEIR COUNTRY. SOMETIMES CAN'T BELIEVE HOW IT'S ALL LASTED THIS LONG

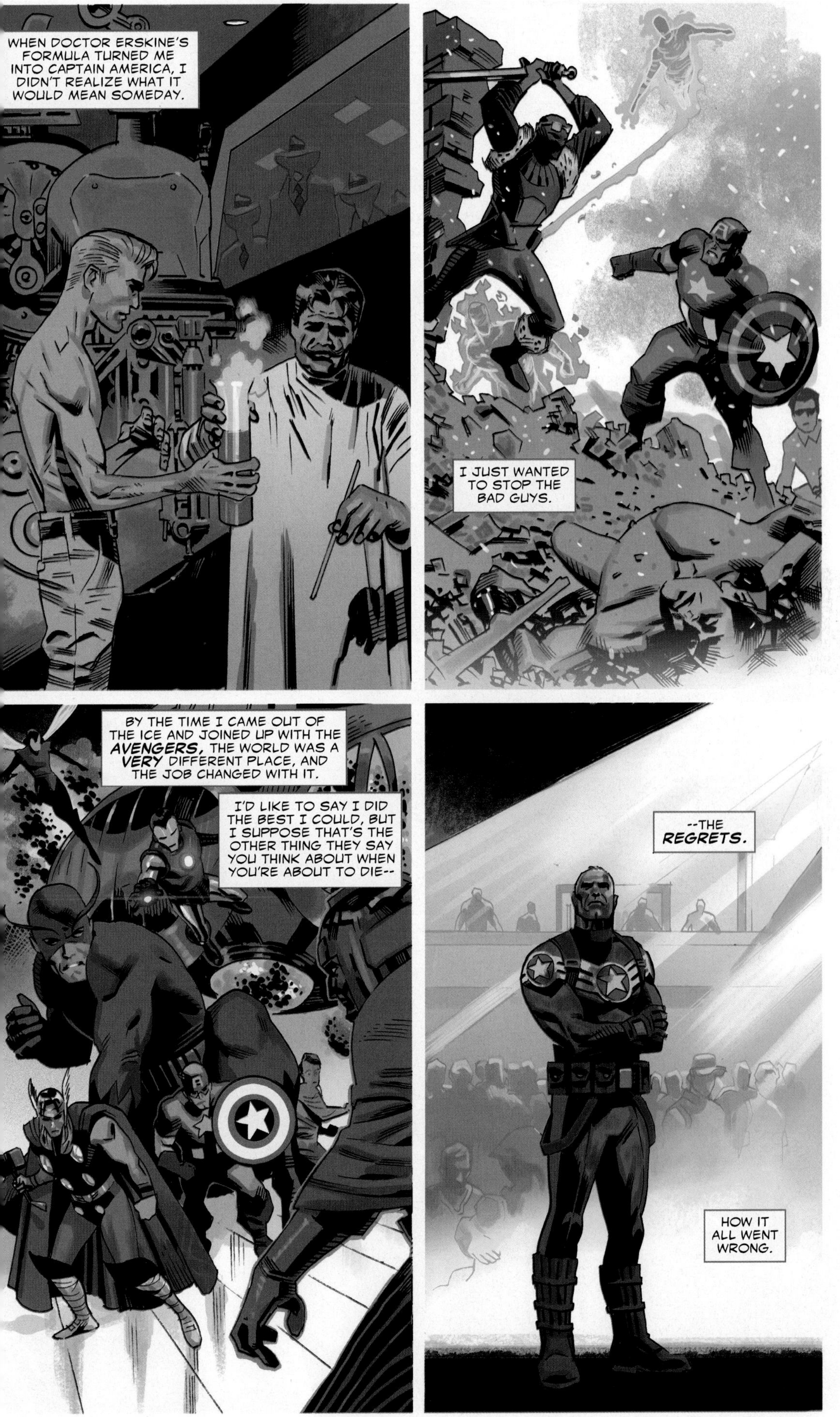
WHEN DOCTOR ERSKINE'S FORMULA TURNED ME INTO CAPTAIN AMERICA, I DIDN'T REALIZE WHAT IT WOULD MEAN SOMEDAY.
I JUST WANTED TO STOP THE BAD GUYS.
BY THE TIME I CAME OUT OF THE ICE AND JOINED UP WITH THE AVENGERS, THE WORLD WAS A VERY DIFFERENT PLACE, AND THE JOB CHANGED WITH IT.
I'D LIKE TO SAY I DID THE BEST I COULD, BUT I SUPPOSE THAT'S THE OTHER THING THEY SAY YOU THINK ABOUT WHEN YOU'RE ABOUT TO DIE--
--THE REGRETS.
HOW IT ALL WENT WRONG.

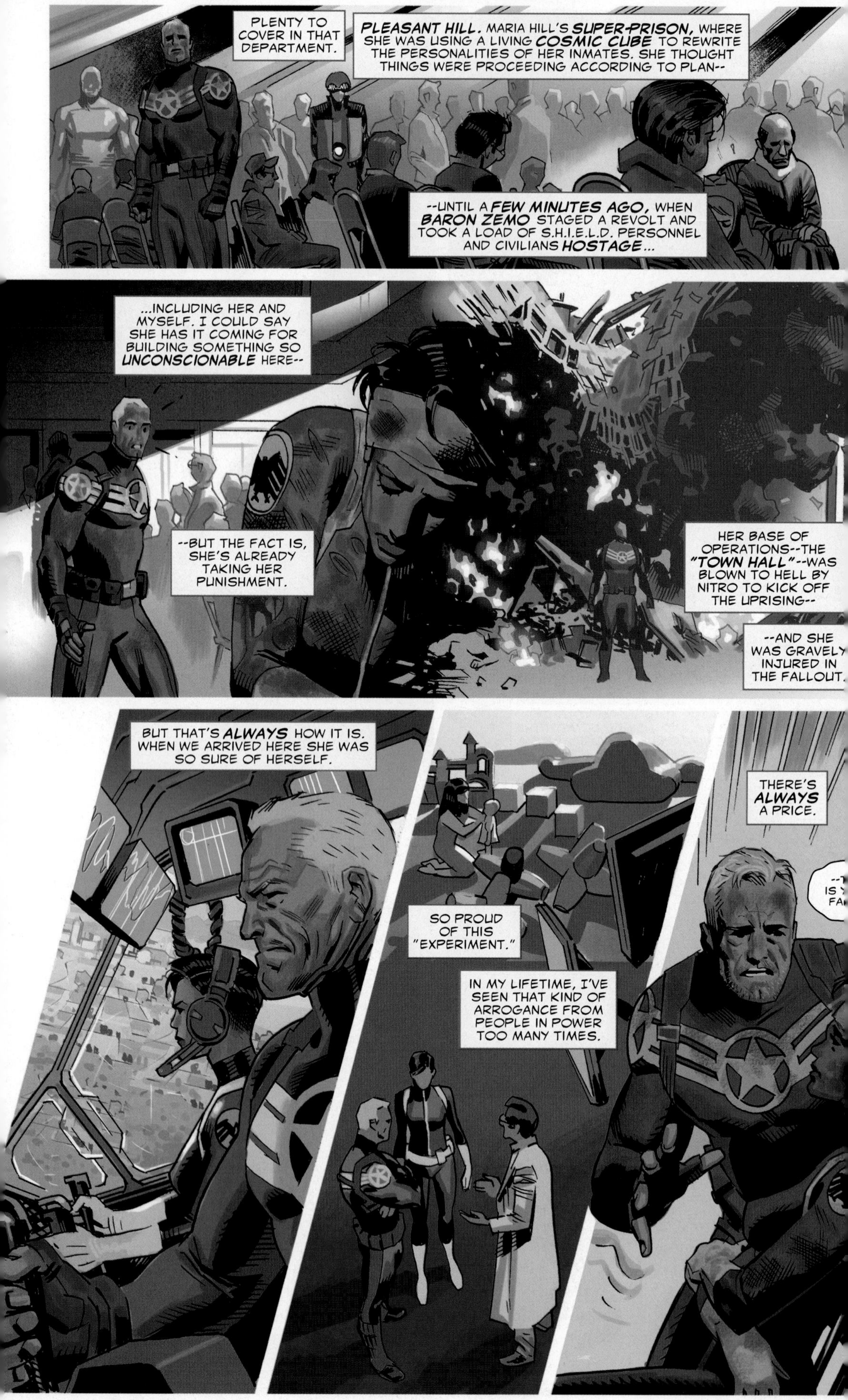
PLENTY TO COVER IN THAT DEPARTMENT.
PLEASANT HILL. MARIA HILL'S SUPER-PRISON, WHERE SHE WAS USING A LIVING COSMIC CUBE TO REWRITE THE PERSONALITIES OF HER INMATES. SHE THOUGHT THINGS WERE PROCEEDING ACCORDING TO PLAN--
--UNTIL A FEW MINUTES AGO, WHEN BARON ZEMO STAGED A REVOLT AND TOOK A LOAD OF S.H.I.E.L.D. PERSONNEL AND CIVILIANS HOSTAGE...
...INCLUDING HER AND MYSELF. I COULD SAY SHE HAS IT COMING FOR BUILDING SOMETHING SO UNCONSCIONABLE HERE--
--BUT THE FACT IS, SHE'S ALREADY TAKING HER PUNISHMENT.
HER BASE OF OPERATIONS--THE "TOWN HALL"--WAS BLOWN TO HELL BY NITRO TO KICK OFF THE UPRISING--
--AND SHE WAS GRAVELY INJURED IN THE FALLOUT.
BUT THAT'S ALWAYS HOW IT IS. WHEN WE ARRIVED HERE SHE WAS SO SURE OF HERSELF.
SO PROUD OF THIS "EXPERIMENT."
IN MY LIFETIME, I'VE SEEN THAT KIND OF ARROGANCE FROM PEOPLE IN POWER TOO MANY TIMES.
THERE'S ALWAYS A PRICE.

THAT RIGHT?

YUP. WE'VE HAD THIS PLACE UP AND--*UNFF*--RUNNING FOR MONTHS, NOT SO MUCH AS THE CABLE GOING OUT. *YOU* SHOW UP, NOW--HRR--

EASY-- DON'T TRY TO MOVE--

NN--I KNOW YOU THINK WE HAVE THIS COMING--

I NEVER SAID THAT.

DIDN'T HAVE TO. *NONVERBAL SANCTIMONY* IS YOUR MUTANT SUPER-POWER, BUT YOU KNOW WHAT PISSES ME OFF ABOUT THIS THE *MOST?*

I'M NEVER GONNA GET TO MOVE IN.

WHAT IS THIS?

IT'S OVER ON APPLEWOOD LANE. NICEST HOUSE ON THE STREET. FELL IN LOVE WITH THAT FRONT PORCH THE SECOND I SAW IT.

KOBIK-- YOU WERE GOING TO TURN IT ON *YOURSELF*...

...IT'D FEEL SO GOOD, 'T YOU THINK? ORGET ALL THIS. T WHO YOU *ARE*... YOU'VE *DONE*... ME THE *BEST PART* OF OURSELF...

SEE, ROGERS-- NEW. I KNEW HAT I WAS OING WAS 'RIMINAL--

I JUST THOUGHT IT WAS... NECESSARY...

HILL?! *HILL?!* MARIA, STAY WITH ME--

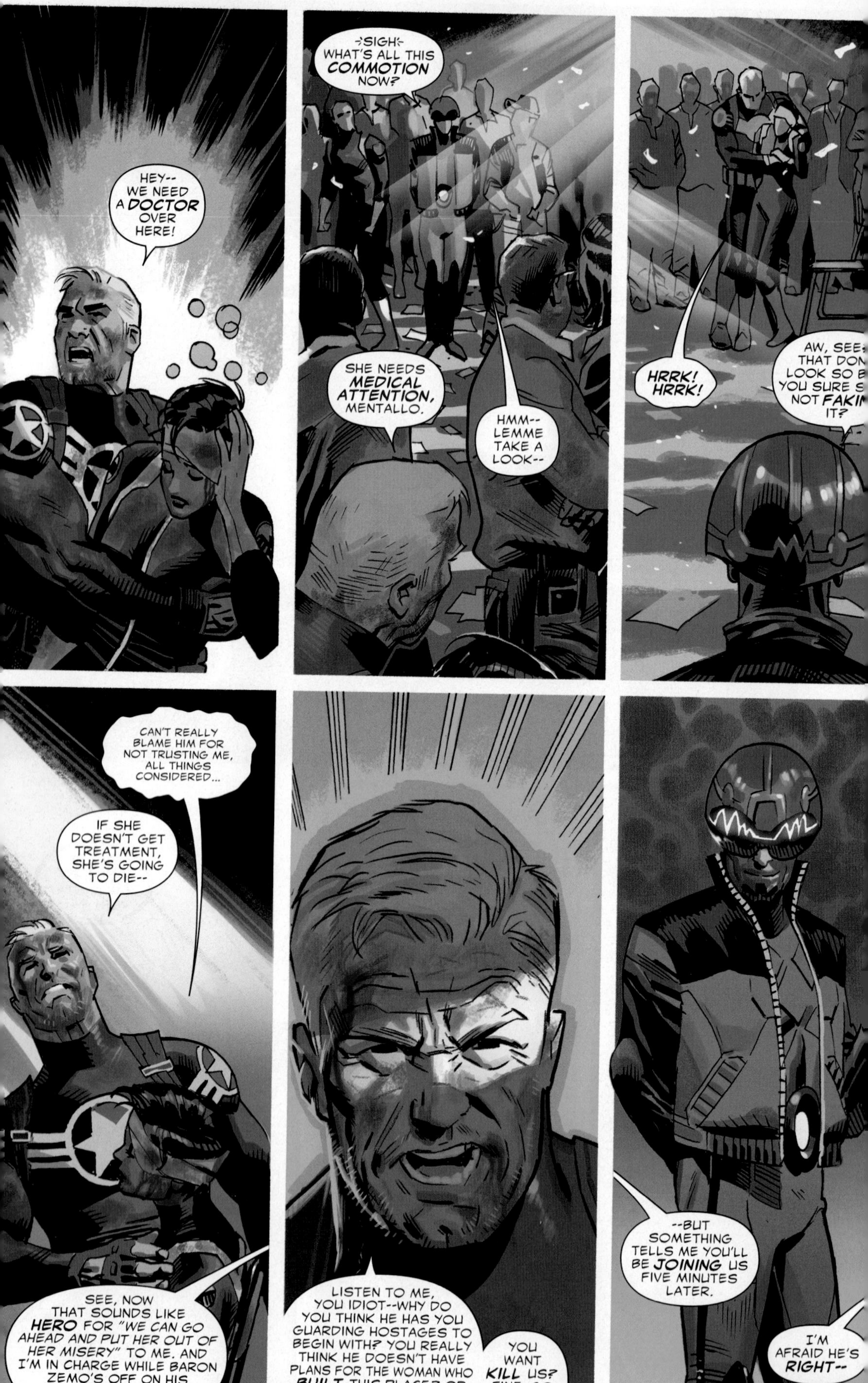
HEY-- WE NEED A DOCTOR OVER HERE!
-SIGH- WHAT'S ALL THIS COMMOTION NOW?
SHE NEEDS MEDICAL ATTENTION, MENTALLO.
HMM-- LEMME TAKE A LOOK--
HRRK! HRRK!
AW, SEE; THAT DON LOOK SO B YOU SURE S NOT FAKI IT?
CAN'T REALLY BLAME HIM FOR NOT TRUSTING ME, ALL THINGS CONSIDERED...
IF SHE DOESN'T GET TREATMENT, SHE'S GOING TO DIE--
SEE, NOW THAT SOUNDS LIKE HERO FOR "WE CAN GO AHEAD AND PUT HER OUT OF HER MISERY" TO ME. AND I'M IN CHARGE WHILE BARON ZEMO'S OFF ON HIS SCAVENGER HUNT.
LISTEN TO ME, YOU IDIOT--WHY DO YOU THINK HE HAS YOU GUARDING HOSTAGES TO BEGIN WITH? YOU REALLY THINK HE DOESN'T HAVE PLANS FOR THE WOMAN WHO BUILT THIS PLACE? OR ME, FOR THAT MATTER?
YOU WANT KILL US? FINE, GO AHEAD--
--BUT SOMETHING TELLS ME YOU'LL BE JOINING US FIVE MINUTES LATER.
I'M AFRAID HE'S RIGHT--

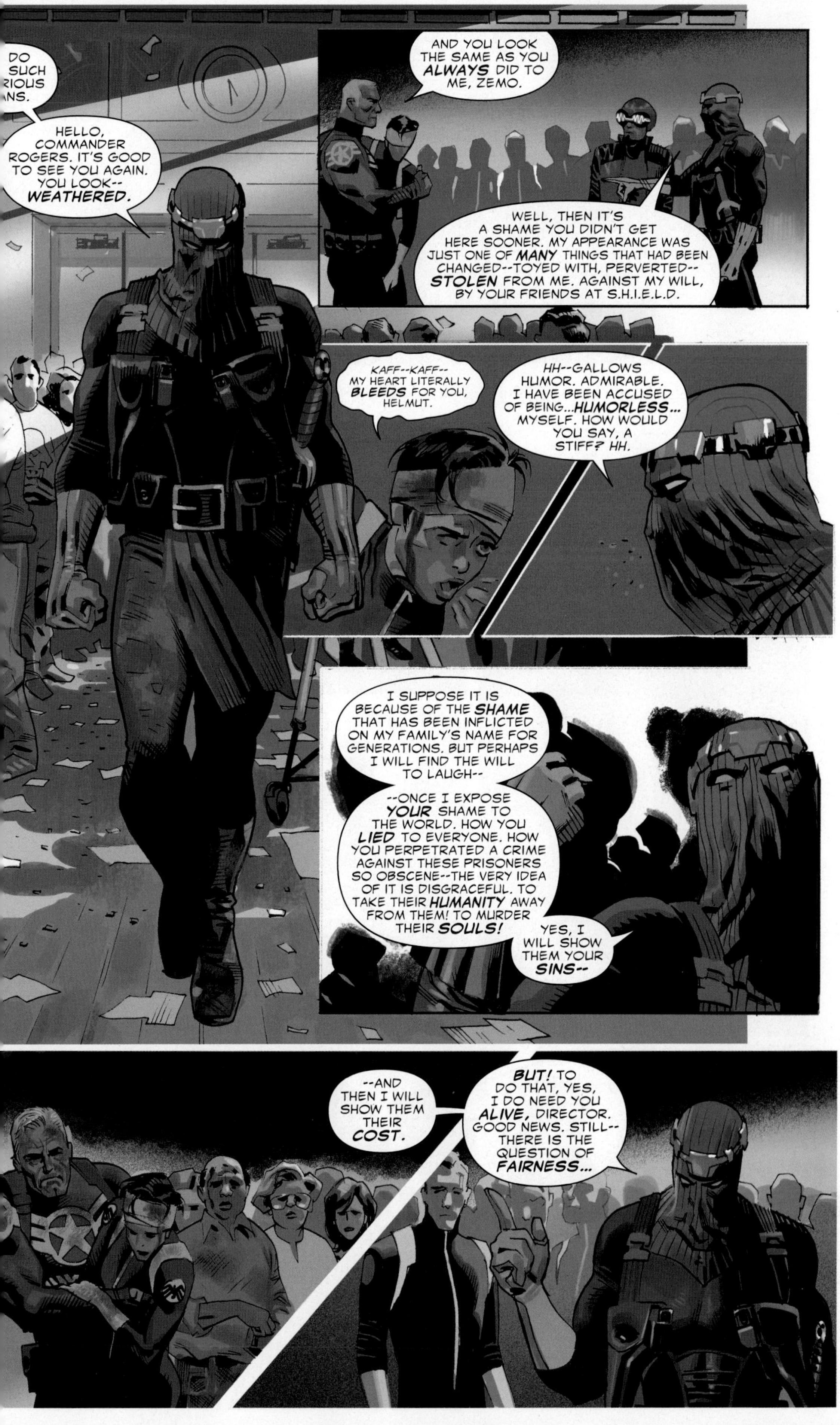

DO SUCH RIOUS ANS.
HELLO, COMMANDER ROGERS. IT'S GOOD TO SEE YOU AGAIN. YOU LOOK-- WEATHERED.
AND YOU LOOK THE SAME AS YOU ALWAYS DID TO ME, ZEMO.
WELL, THEN IT'S A SHAME YOU DIDN'T GET HERE SOONER. MY APPEARANCE WAS JUST ONE OF MANY THINGS THAT HAD BEEN CHANGED--TOYED WITH, PERVERTED-- STOLEN FROM ME. AGAINST MY WILL, BY YOUR FRIENDS AT S.H.I.E.L.D.
KAFF--KAFF-- MY HEART LITERALLY BLEEDS FOR YOU, HELMUT.
HH--GALLOWS HUMOR. ADMIRABLE. I HAVE BEEN ACCUSED OF BEING...HUMORLESS... MYSELF. HOW WOULD YOU SAY, A STIFF? HH.
I SUPPOSE IT IS BECAUSE OF THE SHAME THAT HAS BEEN INFLICTED ON MY FAMILY'S NAME FOR GENERATIONS. BUT PERHAPS I WILL FIND THE WILL TO LAUGH--
--ONCE I EXPOSE YOUR SHAME TO THE WORLD. HOW YOU LIED TO EVERYONE. HOW YOU PERPETRATED A CRIME AGAINST THESE PRISONERS SO OBSCENE--THE VERY IDEA OF IT IS DISGRACEFUL. TO TAKE THEIR HUMANITY AWAY FROM THEM! TO MURDER THEIR SOULS!
YES, I WILL SHOW THEM YOUR SINS--
--AND THEN I WILL SHOW THEM THEIR COST.
BUT! TO DO THAT, YES, I DO NEED YOU ALIVE, DIRECTOR. GOOD NEWS. STILL-- THERE IS THE QUESTION OF FAIRNESS...

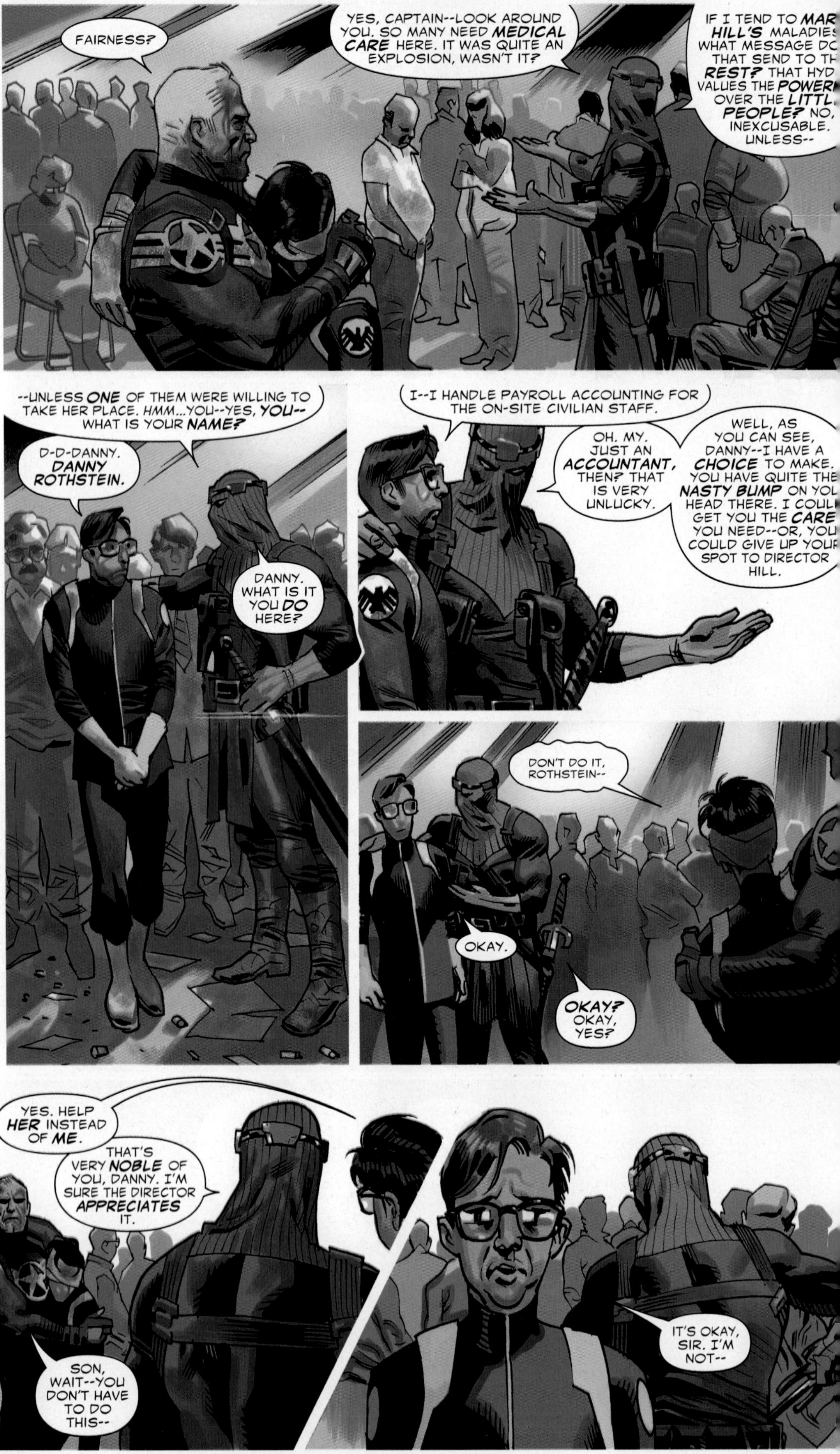
FAIRNESS?
YES, CAPTAIN--LOOK AROUND YOU. SO MANY NEED MEDICAL CARE HERE. IT WAS QUITE AN EXPLOSION, WASN'T IT?
IF I TEND TO MAR HILL'S MALADIE WHAT MESSAGE DO THAT SEND TO TH REST? THAT HYD VALUES THE POWER OVER THE LITTL PEOPLE? NO, INEXCUSABLE. UNLESS--
--UNLESS ONE OF THEM WERE WILLING TO TAKE HER PLACE. HMM...YOU--YES, YOU-- WHAT IS YOUR NAME?
D-D-DANNY. DANNY ROTHSTEIN.
DANNY. WHAT IS IT YOU DO HERE?
I--I HANDLE PAYROLL ACCOUNTING FOR THE ON-SITE CIVILIAN STAFF.
OH. MY. JUST AN ACCOUNTANT, THEN? THAT IS VERY UNLUCKY.
WELL, AS YOU CAN SEE, DANNY--I HAVE A CHOICE TO MAKE. YOU HAVE QUITE THE NASTY BUMP ON YOU HEAD THERE. I COUL GET YOU THE CARE YOU NEED--OR, YOU COULD GIVE UP YOUR SPOT TO DIRECTOR HILL.
DON'T DO IT, ROTHSTEIN--
OKAY.
OKAY? OKAY, YES?
YES. HELP HER INSTEAD OF ME.
THAT'S VERY NOBLE OF YOU, DANNY. I'M SURE THE DIRECTOR APPRECIATES IT.
SON, WAIT--YOU DON'T HAVE TO DO THIS--
IT'S OKAY, SIR. I'M NOT--

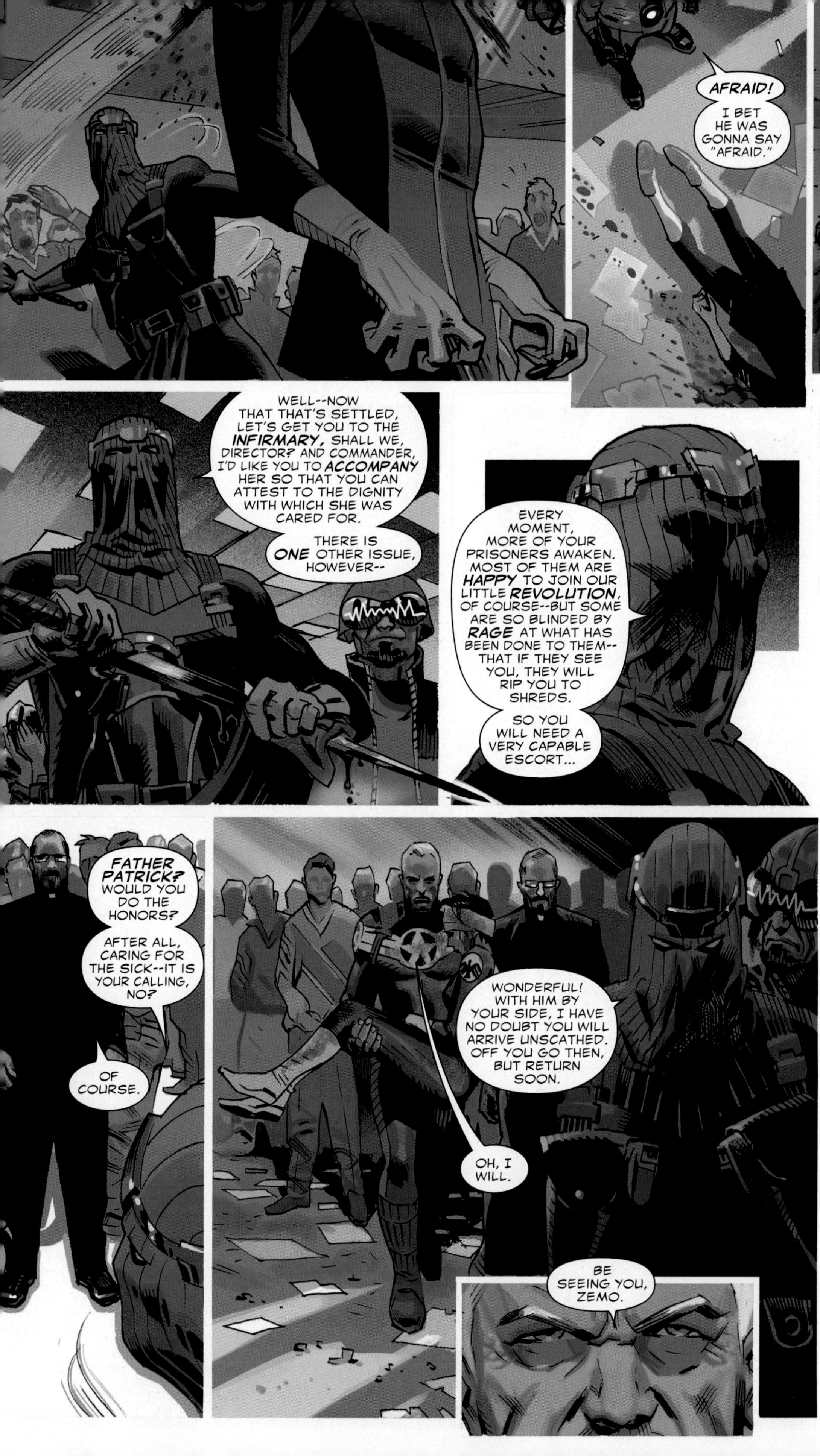
AFRAID! I BET HE WAS GONNA SAY "AFRAID."
WELL--NOW THAT THAT'S SETTLED, LET'S GET YOU TO THE INFIRMARY, SHALL WE, DIRECTOR? AND COMMANDER, I'D LIKE YOU TO ACCOMPANY HER SO THAT YOU CAN ATTEST TO THE DIGNITY WITH WHICH SHE WAS CARED FOR.
THERE IS ONE OTHER ISSUE, HOWEVER--
EVERY MOMENT, MORE OF YOUR PRISONERS AWAKEN. MOST OF THEM ARE HAPPY TO JOIN OUR LITTLE REVOLUTION, OF COURSE--BUT SOME ARE SO BLINDED BY RAGE AT WHAT HAS BEEN DONE TO THEM--THAT IF THEY SEE YOU, THEY WILL RIP YOU TO SHREDS.
SO YOU WILL NEED A VERY CAPABLE ESCORT...
FATHER PATRICK? WOULD YOU DO THE HONORS?
AFTER ALL, CARING FOR THE SICK--IT IS YOUR CALLING, NO?
OF COURSE.
WONDERFUL! WITH HIM BY YOUR SIDE, I HAVE NO DOUBT YOU WILL ARRIVE UNSCATHED. OFF YOU GO THEN, BUT RETURN SOON.
OH, I WILL.
BE SEEING YOU, ZEMO.

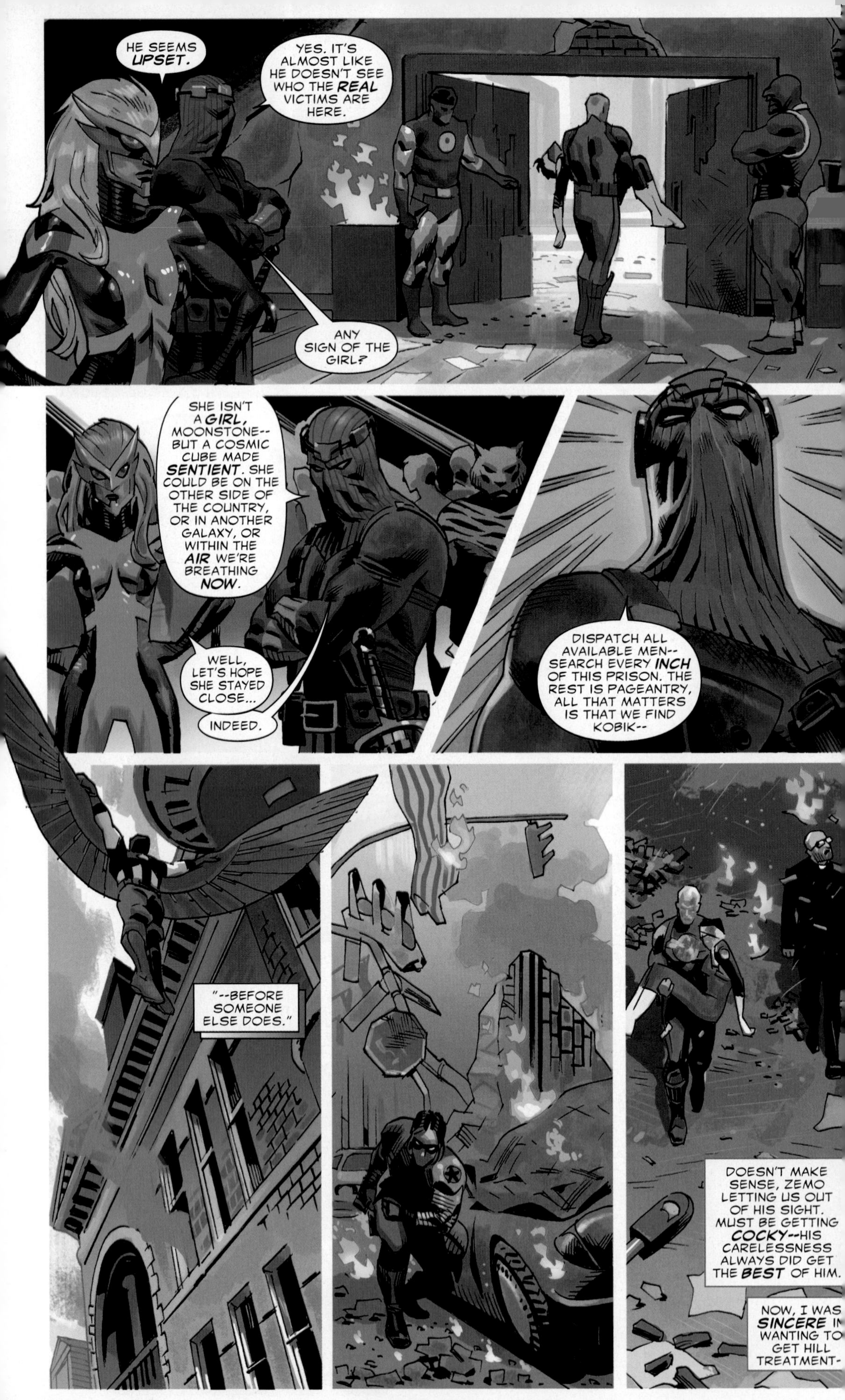
HE SEEMS UPSET.
YES. IT'S ALMOST LIKE HE DOESN'T SEE WHO THE REAL VICTIMS ARE HERE.
ANY SIGN OF THE GIRL?
SHE ISN'T A GIRL, MOONSTONE-- BUT A COSMIC CUBE MADE SENTIENT. SHE COULD BE ON THE OTHER SIDE OF THE COUNTRY, OR IN ANOTHER GALAXY, OR WITHIN THE AIR WE'RE BREATHING NOW.
WELL, LET'S HOPE SHE STAYED CLOSE...
INDEED.
DISPATCH ALL AVAILABLE MEN-- SEARCH EVERY INCH OF THIS PRISON. THE REST IS PAGEANTRY, ALL THAT MATTERS IS THAT WE FIND KOBIK--
"--BEFORE SOMEONE ELSE DOES."
DOESN'T MAKE SENSE, ZEMO LETTING US OUT OF HIS SIGHT. MUST BE GETTING COCKY--HIS CARELESSNESS ALWAYS DID GET THE BEST OF HIM.
NOW, I WAS SINCERE IN WANTING TO GET HILL TREATMENT-

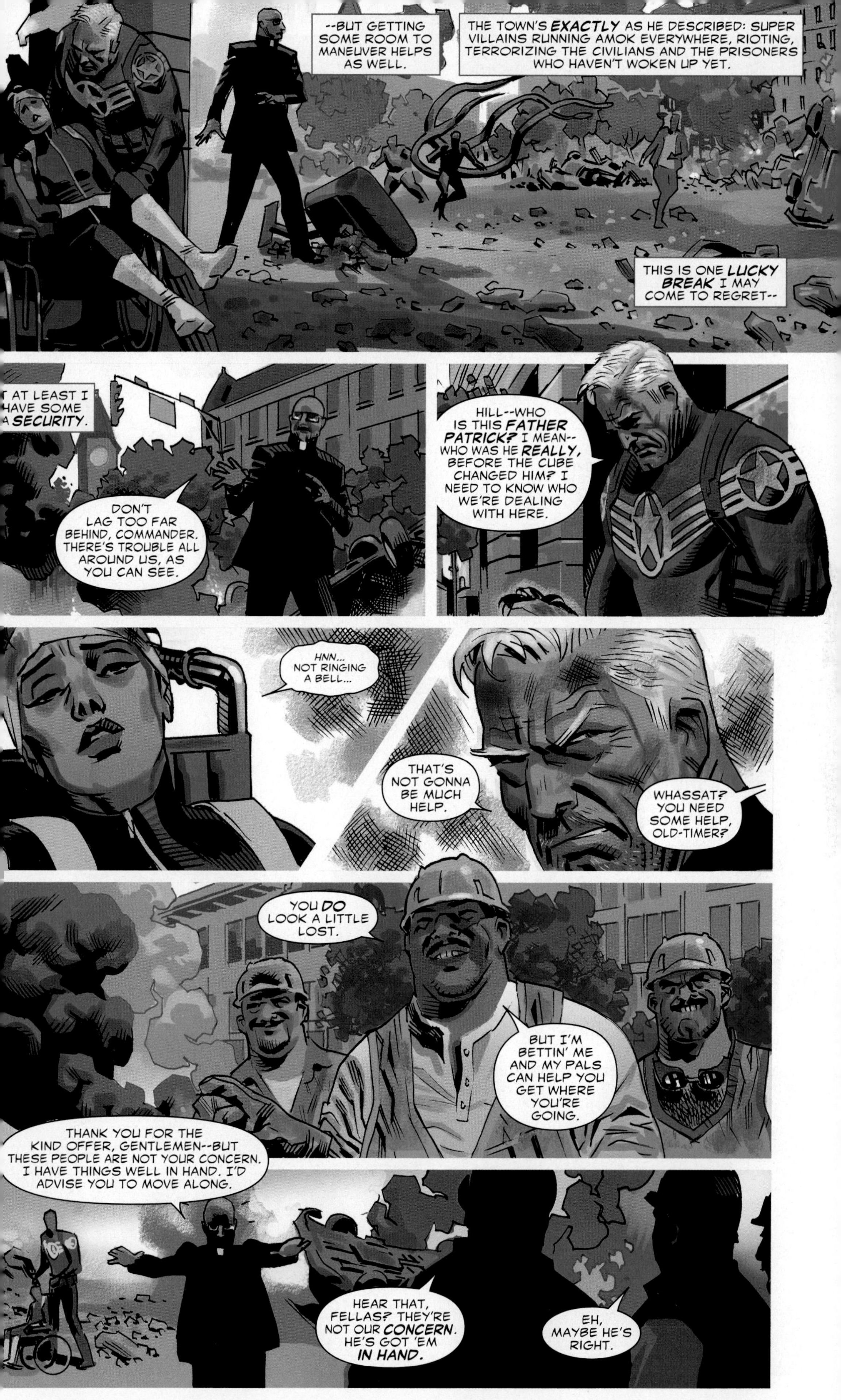
--BUT GETTING SOME ROOM TO MANEUVER HELPS AS WELL.
THE TOWN'S EXACTLY AS HE DESCRIBED: SUPER VILLAINS RUNNING AMOK EVERYWHERE, RIOTING, TERRORIZING THE CIVILIANS AND THE PRISONERS WHO HAVEN'T WOKEN UP YET.
THIS IS ONE LUCKY BREAK I MAY COME TO REGRET--
T AT LEAST I HAVE SOME A SECURITY.
DON'T LAG TOO FAR BEHIND, COMMANDER. THERE'S TROUBLE ALL AROUND US, AS YOU CAN SEE.
HILL--WHO IS THIS FATHER PATRICK? I MEAN--WHO WAS HE REALLY, BEFORE THE CUBE CHANGED HIM? I NEED TO KNOW WHO WE'RE DEALING WITH HERE.
HNN... NOT RINGING A BELL...
THAT'S NOT GONNA BE MUCH HELP.
WHASSAT? YOU NEED SOME HELP, OLD-TIMER?
YOU DO LOOK A LITTLE LOST.
BUT I'M BETTIN' ME AND MY PALS CAN HELP YOU GET WHERE YOU'RE GOING.
THANK YOU FOR THE KIND OFFER, GENTLEMEN--BUT THESE PEOPLE ARE NOT YOUR CONCERN. I HAVE THINGS WELL IN HAND. I'D ADVISE YOU TO MOVE ALONG.
HEAR THAT, FELLAS? THEY'RE NOT OUR CONCERN. HE'S GOT 'EM IN HAND.
EH, MAYBE HE'S RIGHT.

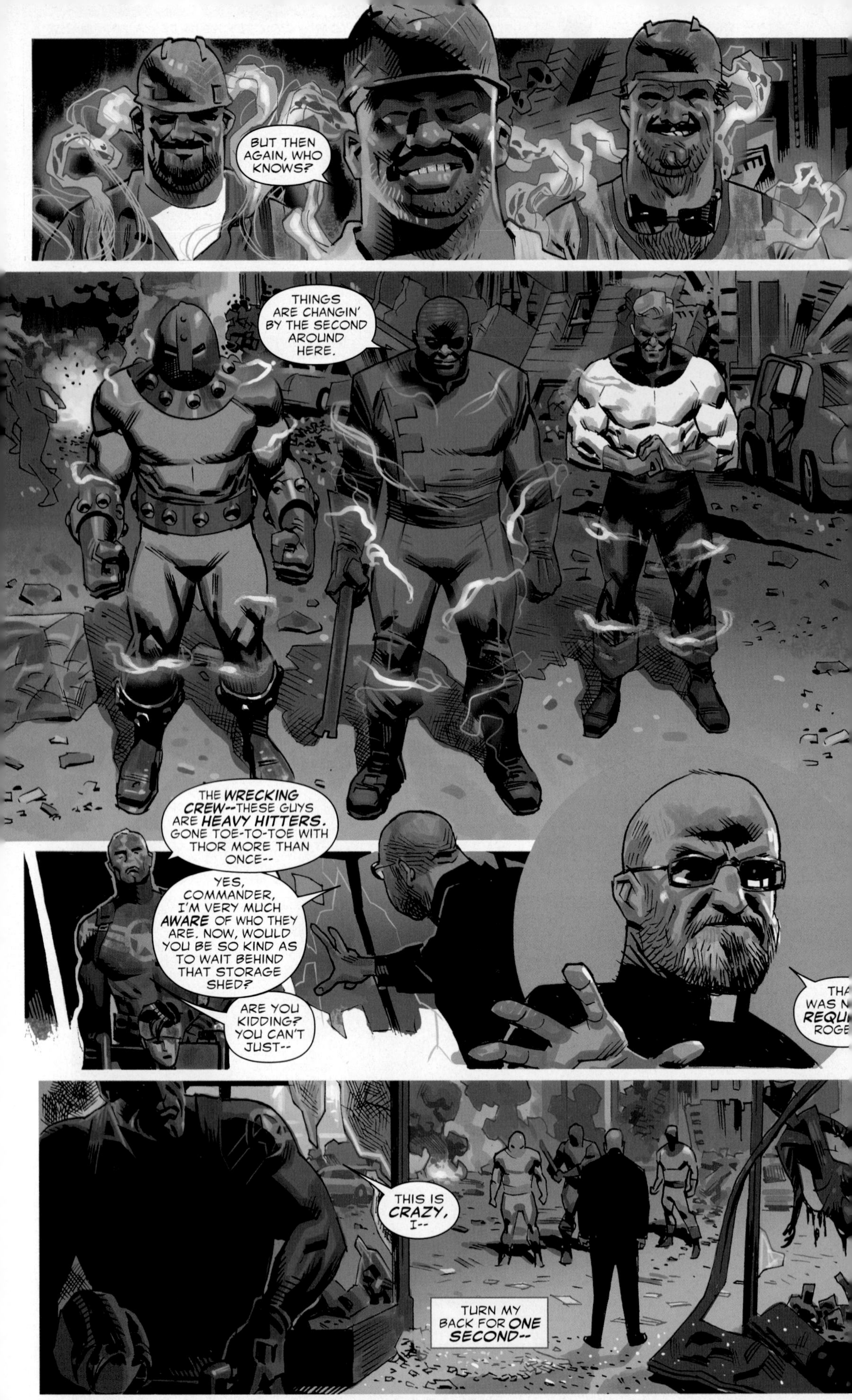
BUT THEN AGAIN, WHO KNOWS?
THINGS ARE CHANGIN' BY THE SECOND AROUND HERE.
THE WRECKING CREW--THESE GUYS ARE HEAVY HITTERS. GONE TOE-TO-TOE WITH THOR MORE THAN ONCE--
YES, COMMANDER, I'M VERY MUCH AWARE OF WHO THEY ARE. NOW, WOULD YOU BE SO KIND AS TO WAIT BEHIND THAT STORAGE SHED?
ARE YOU KIDDING? YOU CAN'T JUST--
THIS IS CRAZY, I--
TURN MY BACK FOR ONE SECOND--

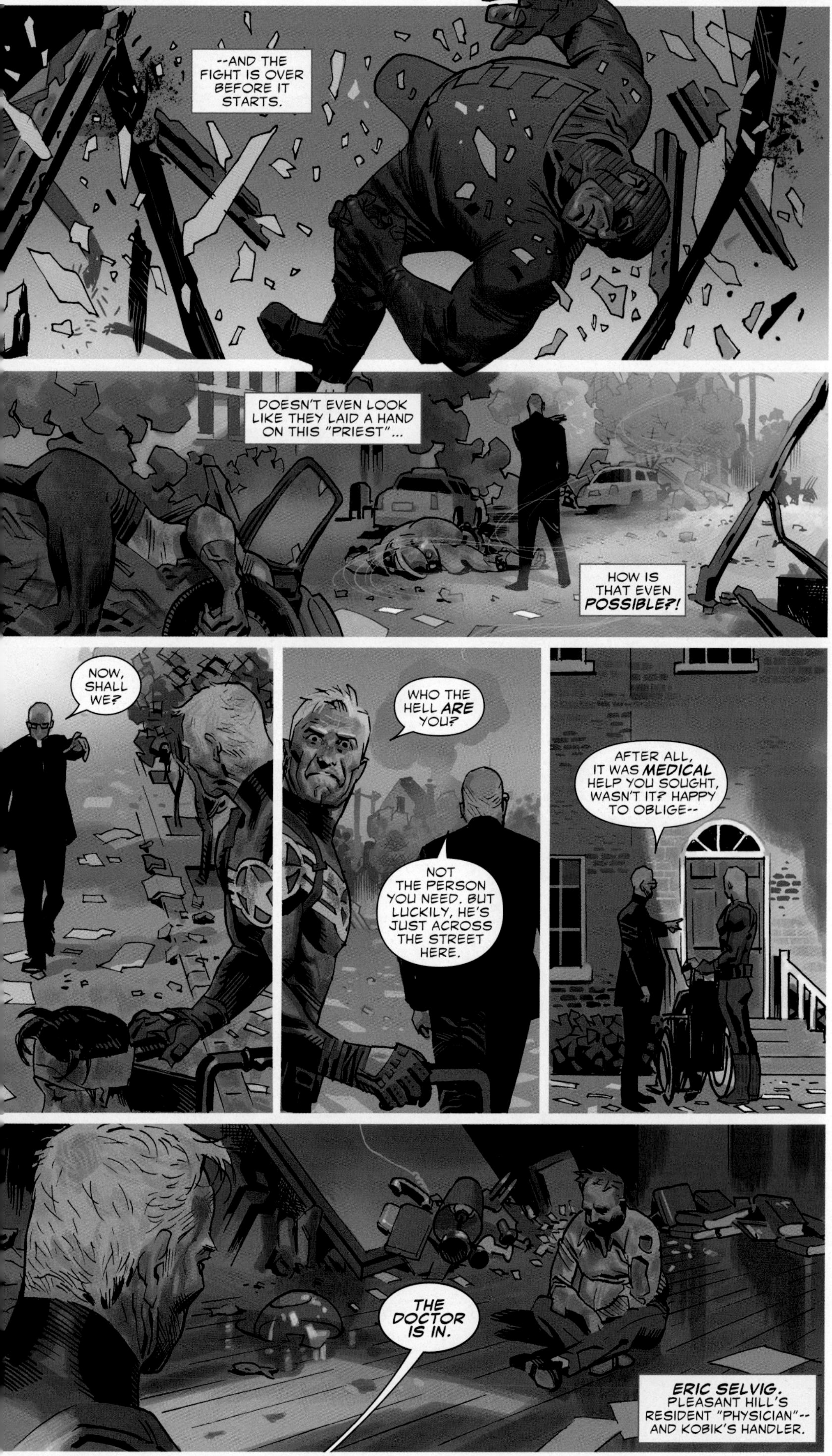
--AND THE FIGHT IS OVER BEFORE IT STARTS.
DOESN'T EVEN LOOK LIKE THEY LAID A HAND ON THIS "PRIEST"...
HOW IS THAT EVEN POSSIBLE?!
NOW, SHALL WE?
WHO THE HELL ARE YOU?
NOT THE PERSON YOU NEED. BUT LUCKILY, HE'S JUST ACROSS THE STREET HERE.
AFTER ALL, IT WAS MEDICAL HELP YOU SOUGHT, WASN'T IT? HAPPY TO OBLIGE--
THE DOCTOR IS IN.
ERIC SELVIG. PLEASANT HILL'S RESIDENT "PHYSICIAN"-- AND KOBIK'S HANDLER.

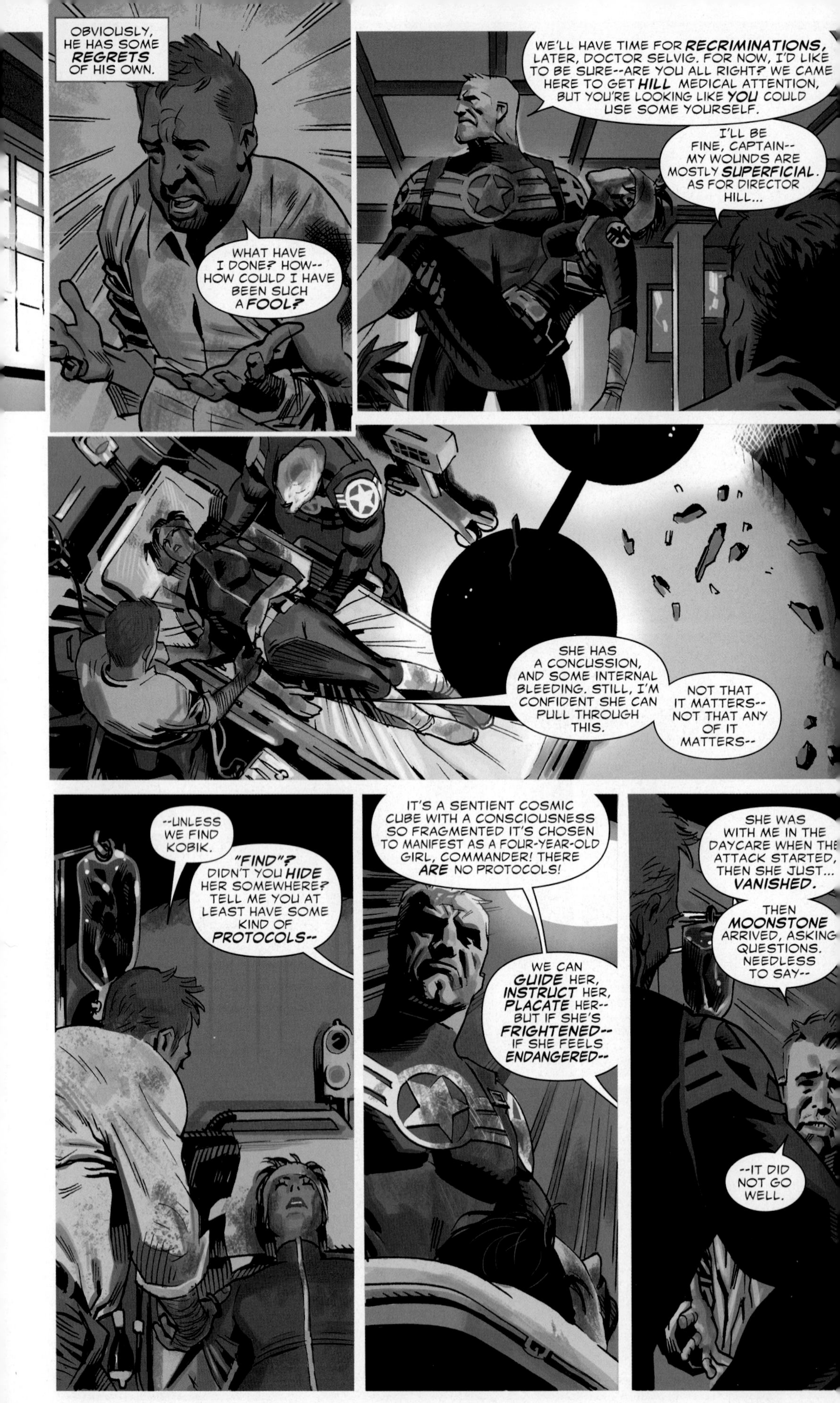
OBVIOUSLY, HE HAS SOME REGRETS OF HIS OWN.
WHAT HAVE I DONE? HOW-- HOW COULD I HAVE BEEN SUCH A FOOL?
WE'LL HAVE TIME FOR RECRIMINATIONS, LATER, DOCTOR SELVIG. FOR NOW, I'D LIKE TO BE SURE--ARE YOU ALL RIGHT? WE CAME HERE TO GET HILL MEDICAL ATTENTION, BUT YOU'RE LOOKING LIKE YOU COULD USE SOME YOURSELF.
I'LL BE FINE, CAPTAIN-- MY WOUNDS ARE MOSTLY SUPERFICIAL. AS FOR DIRECTOR HILL...
SHE HAS A CONCUSSION, AND SOME INTERNAL BLEEDING. STILL, I'M CONFIDENT SHE CAN PULL THROUGH THIS.
NOT THAT IT MATTERS-- NOT THAT ANY OF IT MATTERS--
--UNLESS WE FIND KOBIK.
"FIND"? DIDN'T YOU HIDE HER SOMEWHERE? TELL ME YOU AT LEAST HAVE SOME KIND OF PROTOCOLS--
IT'S A SENTIENT COSMIC CUBE WITH A CONSCIOUSNESS SO FRAGMENTED IT'S CHOSEN TO MANIFEST AS A FOUR-YEAR-OLD GIRL, COMMANDER! THERE ARE NO PROTOCOLS!
WE CAN GUIDE HER, INSTRUCT HER, PLACATE HER-- BUT IF SHE'S FRIGHTENED-- IF SHE FEELS ENDANGERED--
SHE WAS WITH ME IN THE DAYCARE WHEN THE ATTACK STARTED, THEN SHE JUST... VANISHED.
THEN MOONSTONE ARRIVED, ASKING QUESTIONS. NEEDLESS TO SAY--
--IT DID NOT GO WELL.

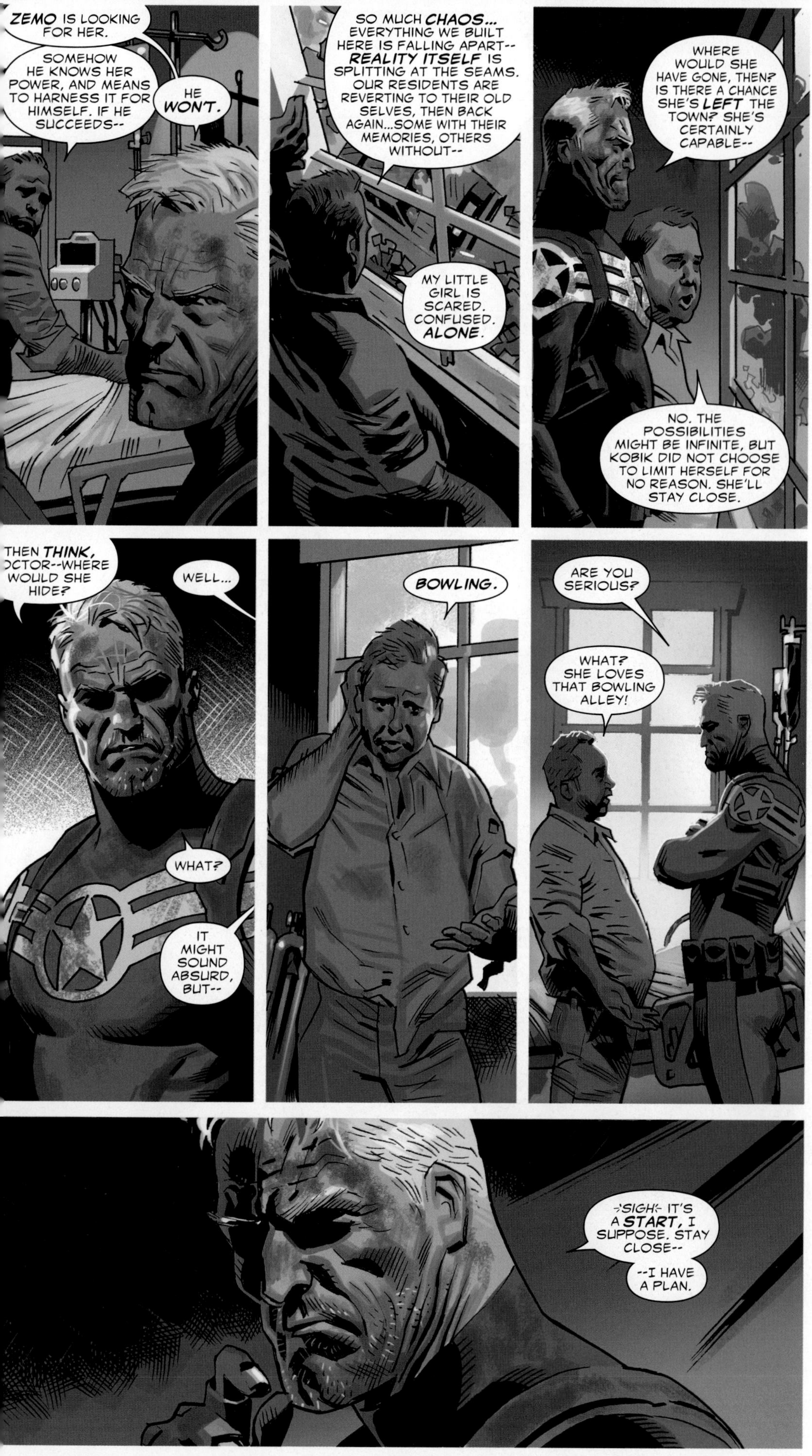
ZEMO IS LOOKING FOR HER.
SOMEHOW HE KNOWS HER POWER, AND MEANS TO HARNESS IT FOR HIMSELF. IF HE SUCCEEDS--
HE WON'T.
SO MUCH CHAOS... EVERYTHING WE BUILT HERE IS FALLING APART-- REALITY ITSELF IS SPLITTING AT THE SEAMS. OUR RESIDENTS ARE REVERTING TO THEIR OLD SELVES, THEN BACK AGAIN...SOME WITH THEIR MEMORIES, OTHERS WITHOUT--
MY LITTLE GIRL IS SCARED. CONFUSED. ALONE.
WHERE WOULD SHE HAVE GONE, THEN? IS THERE A CHANCE SHE'S LEFT THE TOWN? SHE'S CERTAINLY CAPABLE--
NO. THE POSSIBILITIES MIGHT BE INFINITE, BUT KOBIK DID NOT CHOOSE TO LIMIT HERSELF FOR NO REASON. SHE'LL STAY CLOSE.
THEN THINK, DOCTOR--WHERE WOULD SHE HIDE?
WELL...
WHAT?
IT MIGHT SOUND ABSURD, BUT--
BOWLING.
ARE YOU SERIOUS?
WHAT? SHE LOVES THAT BOWLING ALLEY!
SIGH IT'S A START, I SUPPOSE. STAY CLOSE--
--I HAVE A PLAN.

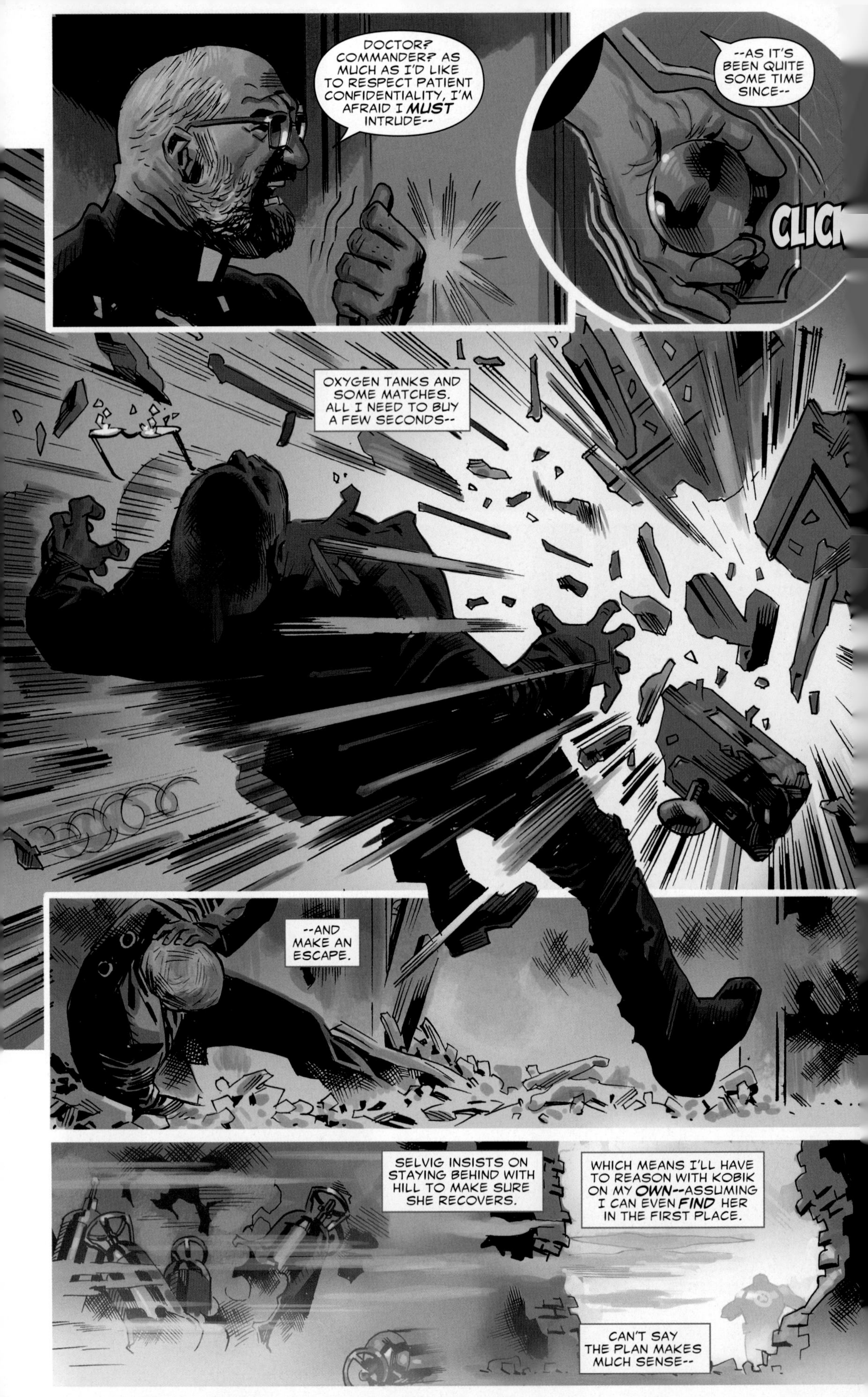
DOCTOR? COMMANDER? AS MUCH AS I'D LIKE TO RESPECT PATIENT CONFIDENTIALITY, I'M AFRAID I MUST INTRUDE--
--AS IT'S BEEN QUITE SOME TIME SINCE--
CLICK
OXYGEN TANKS AND SOME MATCHES. ALL I NEED TO BUY A FEW SECONDS--
--AND MAKE AN ESCAPE.
SELVIG INSISTS ON STAYING BEHIND WITH HILL TO MAKE SURE SHE RECOVERS.
WHICH MEANS I'LL HAVE TO REASON WITH KOBIK ON MY OWN--ASSUMING I CAN EVEN FIND HER IN THE FIRST PLACE.
CAN'T SAY THE PLAN MAKES MUCH SENSE--

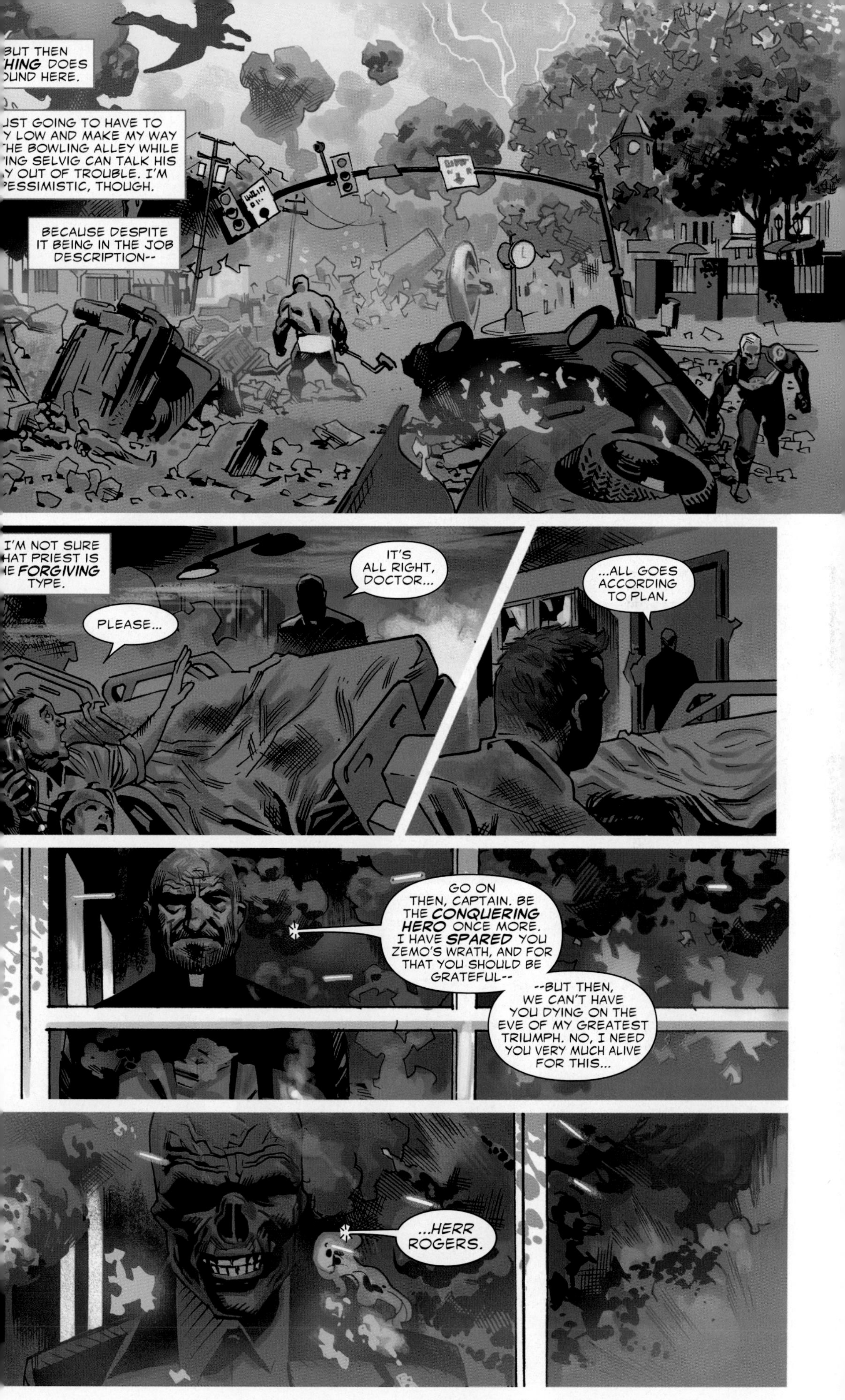

BUT THEN
THING DOES
OUND HERE.
UST GOING TO HAVE TO
Y LOW AND MAKE MY WAY
THE BOWLING ALLEY WHILE
ING SELVIG CAN TALK HIS
Y OUT OF TROUBLE. I'M
PESSIMISTIC, THOUGH.
BECAUSE DESPITE IT BEING IN THE JOB DESCRIPTION--
I'M NOT SURE
HAT PRIEST IS
E FORGIVING
TYPE.
PLEASE...
IT'S ALL RIGHT, DOCTOR...
...ALL GOES ACCORDING TO PLAN.
GO ON THEN, CAPTAIN. BE THE CONQUERING HERO ONCE MORE. I HAVE SPARED YOU ZEMO'S WRATH, AND FOR THAT YOU SHOULD BE GRATEFUL--
--BUT THEN, WE CAN'T HAVE YOU DYING ON THE EVE OF MY GREATEST TRIUMPH. NO, I NEED YOU VERY MUCH ALIVE FOR THIS...
...HERR ROGERS.

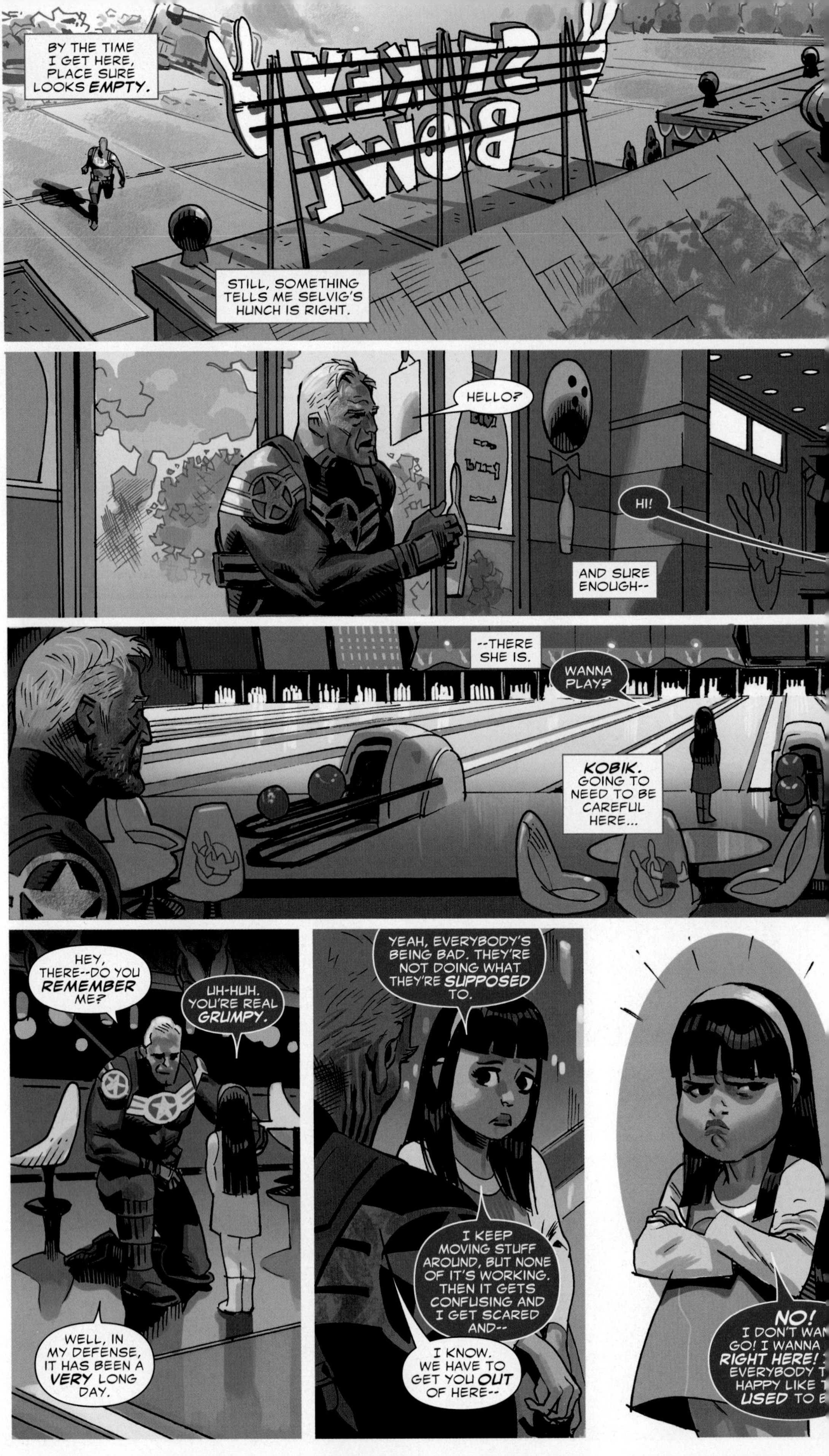

BY THE TIME I GET HERE, PLACE SURE LOOKS EMPTY.
STILL, SOMETHING TELLS ME SELVIG'S HUNCH IS RIGHT.
HELLO?
HI!
AND SURE ENOUGH--
--THERE SHE IS.
WANNA PLAY?
KOBIK. GOING TO NEED TO BE CAREFUL HERE...
HEY, THERE--DO YOU REMEMBER ME?
UH-HUH. YOU'RE REAL GRUMPY.
WELL, IN MY DEFENSE, IT HAS BEEN A VERY LONG DAY.
YEAH, EVERYBODY'S BEING BAD. THEY'RE NOT DOING WHAT THEY'RE SUPPOSED TO.
I KEEP MOVING STUFF AROUND, BUT NONE OF IT'S WORKING. THEN IT GETS CONFUSING AND I GET SCARED AND--
I KNOW. WE HAVE TO GET YOU OUT OF HERE--
NO! I DON'T WAN GO! I WANNA RIGHT HERE! EVERYBODY HAPPY LIKE USED TO B

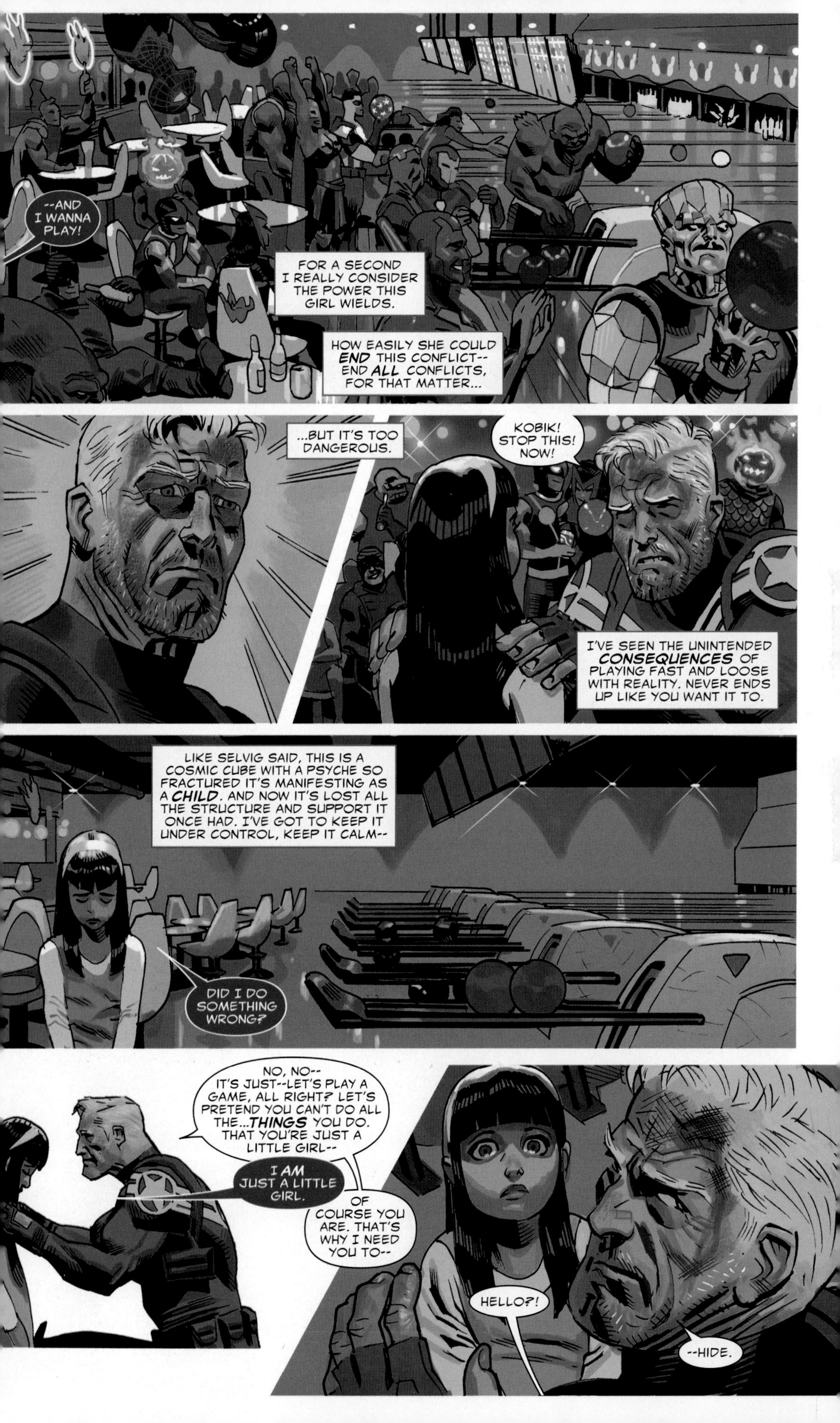

--AND I WANNA PLAY!
FOR A SECOND I REALLY CONSIDER THE POWER THIS GIRL WIELDS.
HOW EASILY SHE COULD END THIS CONFLICT-- END ALL CONFLICTS, FOR THAT MATTER...
...BUT IT'S TOO DANGEROUS.
KOBIK! STOP THIS! NOW!
I'VE SEEN THE UNINTENDED CONSEQUENCES OF PLAYING FAST AND LOOSE WITH REALITY. NEVER ENDS UP LIKE YOU WANT IT TO.
LIKE SELVIG SAID, THIS IS A COSMIC CUBE WITH A PSYCHE SO FRACTURED IT'S MANIFESTING AS A CHILD. AND NOW IT'S LOST ALL THE STRUCTURE AND SUPPORT IT ONCE HAD. I'VE GOT TO KEEP IT UNDER CONTROL, KEEP IT CALM--
DID I DO SOMETHING WRONG?
NO, NO-- IT'S JUST--LET'S PLAY A GAME, ALL RIGHT? LET'S PRETEND YOU CAN'T DO ALL THE...THINGS YOU DO. THAT YOU'RE JUST A LITTLE GIRL--
I AM JUST A LITTLE GIRL.
OF COURSE YOU ARE. THAT'S WHY I NEED YOU TO--
HELLO?!
--HIDE.

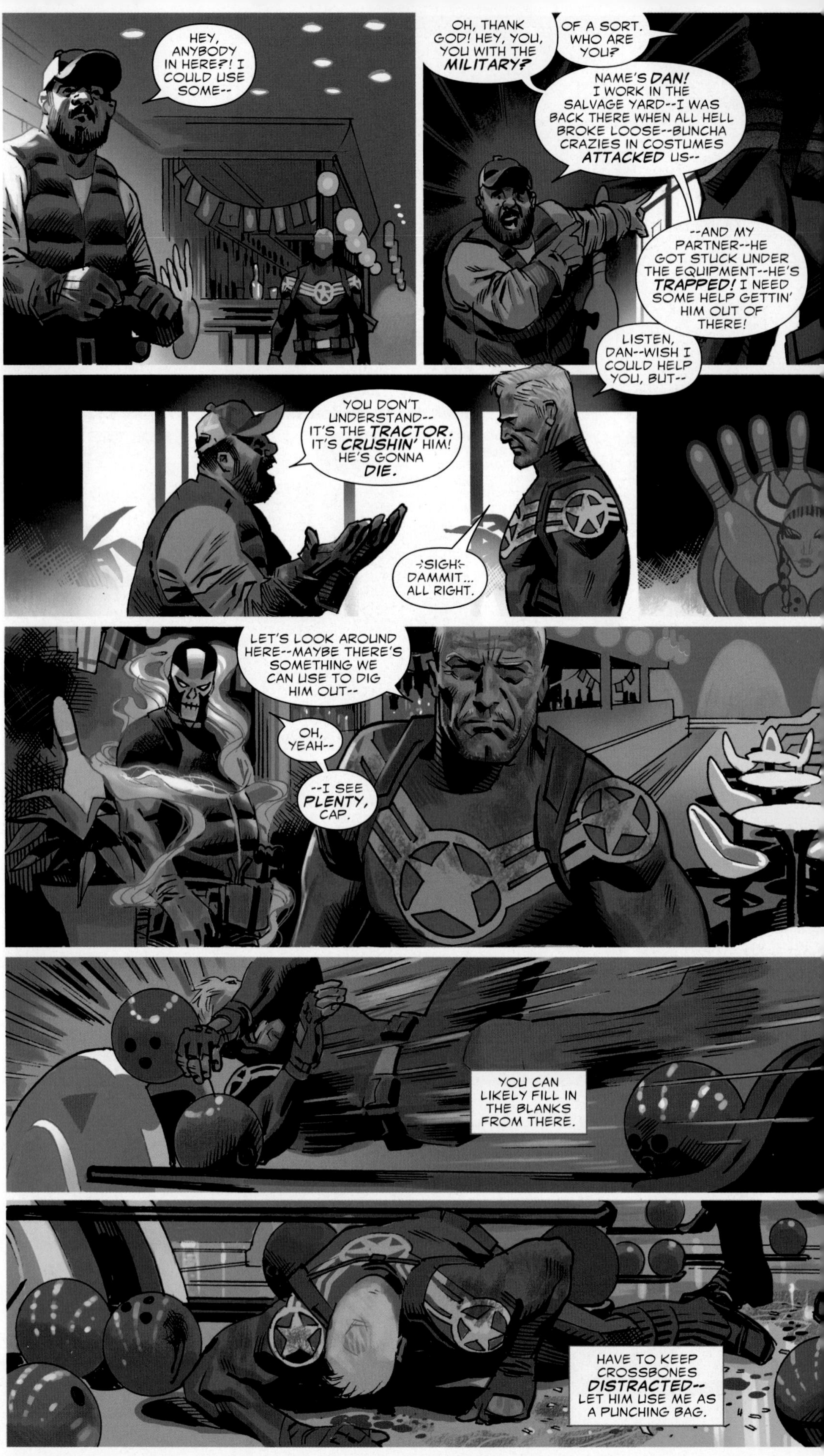
HEY, ANYBODY IN HERE?! I COULD USE SOME--
OH, THANK GOD! HEY, YOU, YOU WITH THE MILITARY?
OF A SORT. WHO ARE YOU?
NAME'S DAN! I WORK IN THE SALVAGE YARD--I WAS BACK THERE WHEN ALL HELL BROKE LOOSE--BUNCHA CRAZIES IN COSTUMES ATTACKED US--
--AND MY PARTNER--HE GOT STUCK UNDER THE EQUIPMENT--HE'S TRAPPED! I NEED SOME HELP GETTIN' HIM OUT OF THERE!
LISTEN, DAN--WISH I COULD HELP YOU, BUT--
YOU DON'T UNDERSTAND-- IT'S THE TRACTOR. IT'S CRUSHIN' HIM! HE'S GONNA DIE.
-SIGH- DAMMIT... ALL RIGHT.
LET'S LOOK AROUND HERE--MAYBE THERE'S SOMETHING WE CAN USE TO DIG HIM OUT--
OH, YEAH--
--I SEE PLENTY, CAP.
YOU CAN LIKELY FILL IN THE BLANKS FROM THERE.
HAVE TO KEEP CROSSBONES DISTRACTED-- LET HIM USE ME AS A PUNCHING BAG.

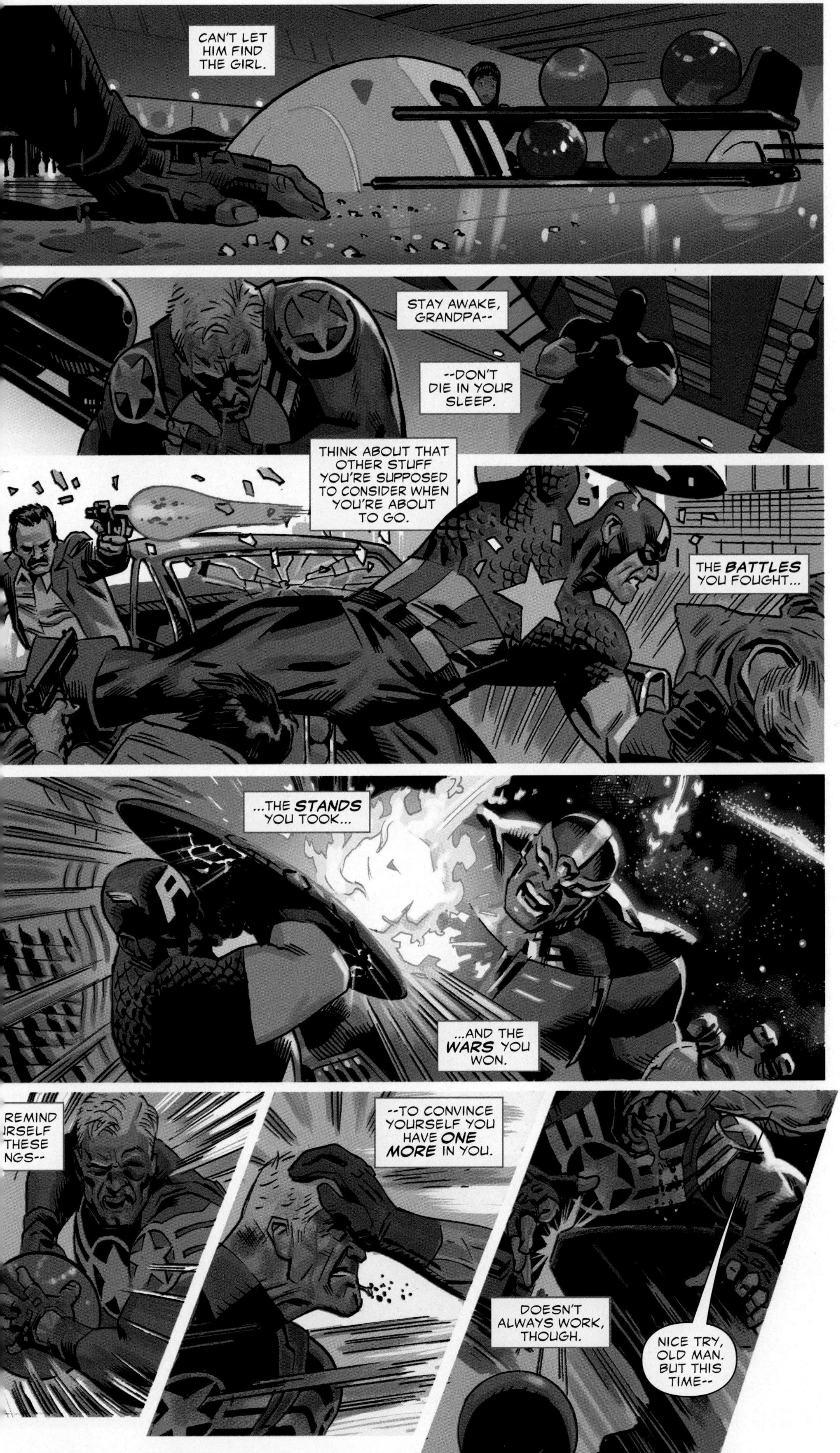
CAN'T LET HIM FIND THE GIRL.
STAY AWAKE, GRANDPA--
--DON'T DIE IN YOUR SLEEP.
THINK ABOUT THAT OTHER STUFF YOU'RE SUPPOSED TO CONSIDER WHEN YOU'RE ABOUT TO GO.
THE BATTLES YOU FOUGHT...
...THE STANDS YOU TOOK...
...AND THE WARS YOU WON.
REMIND
RSELF
THESE
NGS--
--TO CONVINCE YOURSELF YOU HAVE ONE MORE IN YOU.
DOESN'T ALWAYS WORK, THOUGH.
NICE TRY, OLD MAN. BUT THIS TIME--

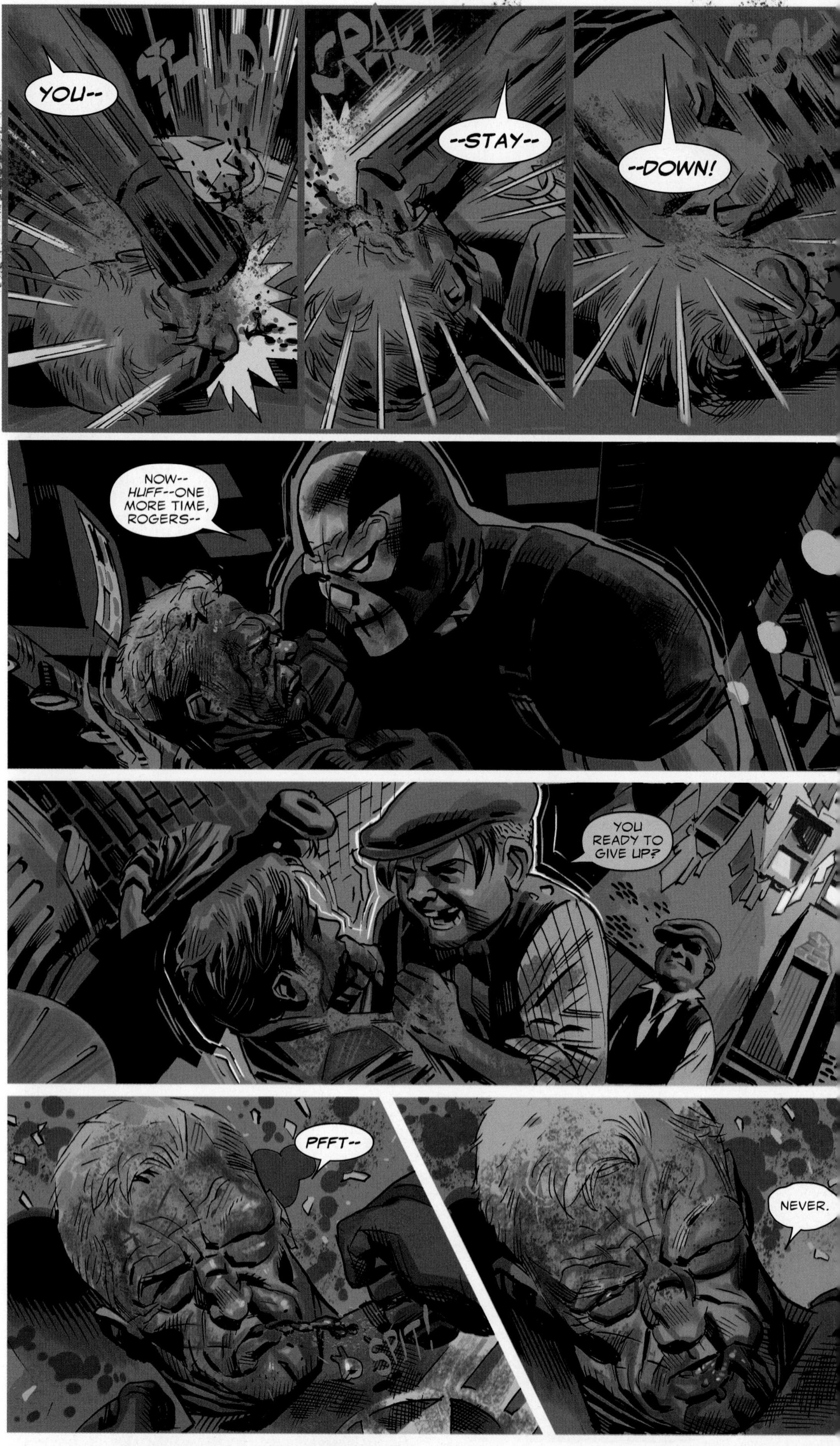
YOU--
--STAY--
--DOWN!
NOW-- HUFF--ONE MORE TIME, ROGERS--
YOU READY TO GIVE UP?
PFFT--
NEVER.

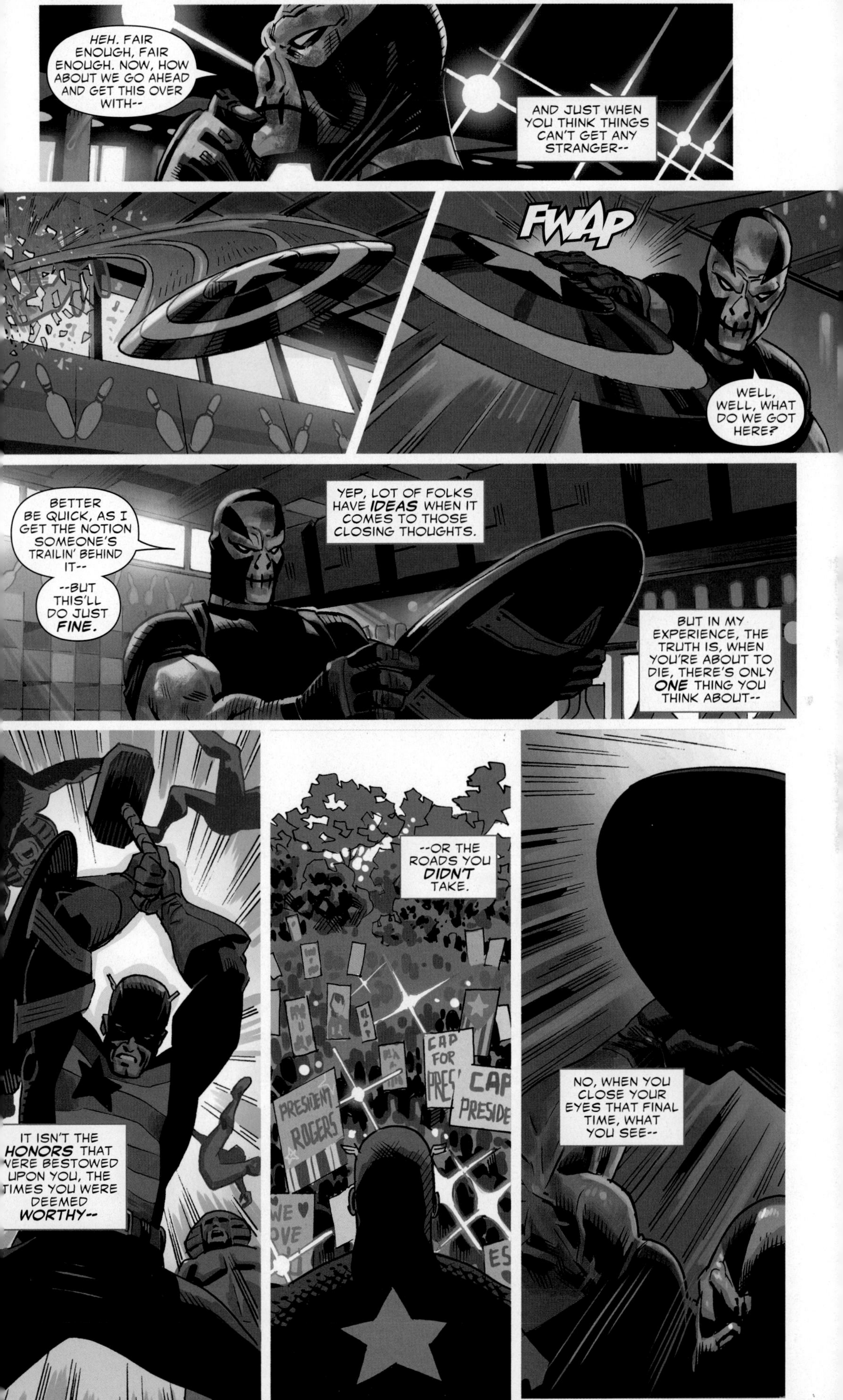
HEH. FAIR ENOUGH, FAIR ENOUGH. NOW, HOW ABOUT WE GO AHEAD AND GET THIS OVER WITH--
AND JUST WHEN YOU THINK THINGS CAN'T GET ANY STRANGER--
FWAP
WELL, WELL, WHAT DO WE GOT HERE?
BETTER BE QUICK, AS I GET THE NOTION SOMEONE'S TRAILIN' BEHIND IT--
YEP, LOT OF FOLKS HAVE IDEAS WHEN IT COMES TO THOSE CLOSING THOUGHTS.
--BUT THIS'LL DO JUST FINE.
BUT IN MY EXPERIENCE, THE TRUTH IS, WHEN YOU'RE ABOUT TO DIE, THERE'S ONLY ONE THING YOU THINK ABOUT--
IT ISN'T THE HONORS THAT WERE BESTOWED UPON YOU, THE TIMES YOU WERE DEEMED WORTHY--
--OR THE ROADS YOU DIDN'T TAKE.
CAP FOR PRES
CAP PRESIDE
PRESIDENT ROGERS
WE OVE
NO, WHEN YOU CLOSE YOUR EYES THAT FINAL TIME, WHAT YOU SEE--

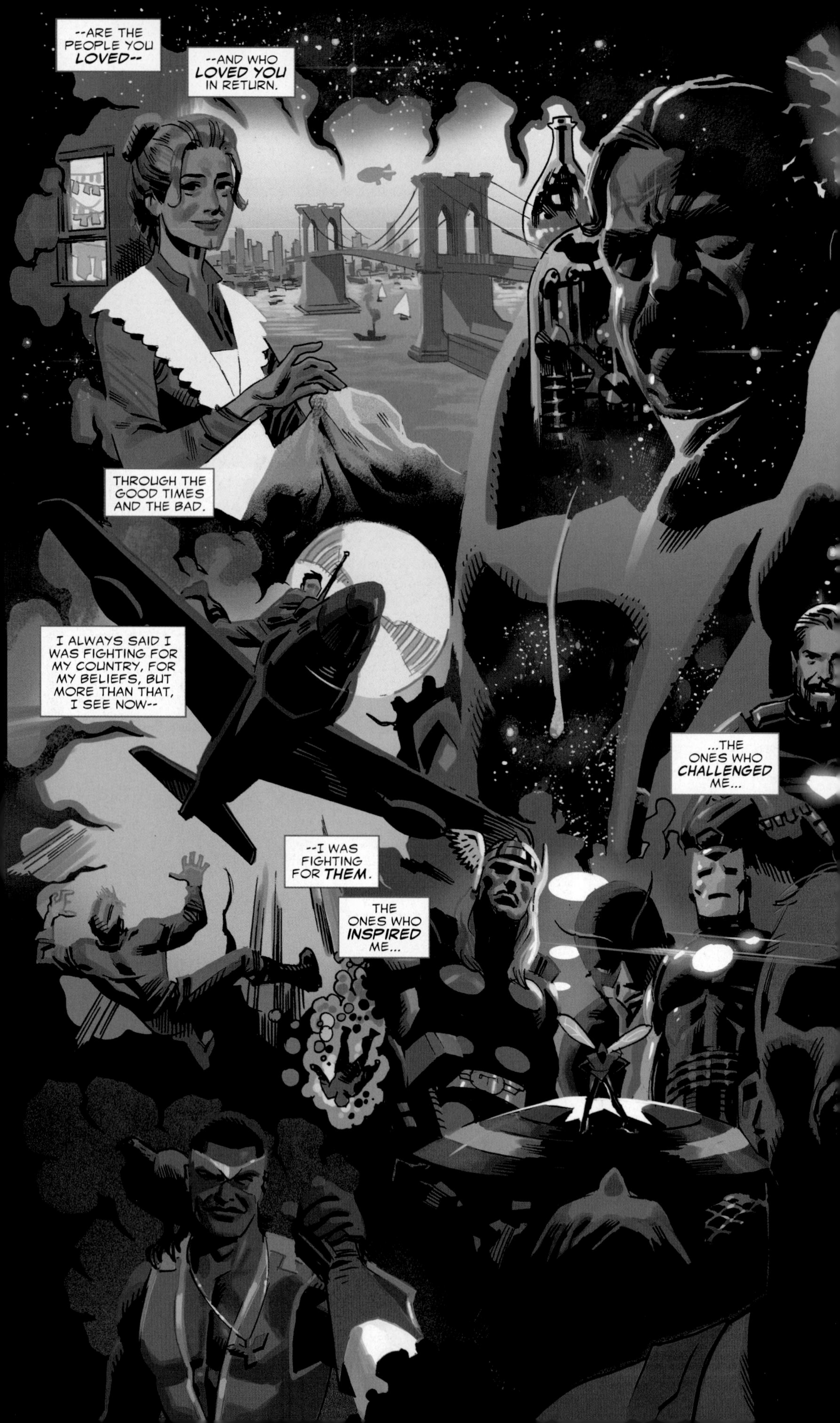
--ARE THE PEOPLE YOU LOVED--
--AND WHO LOVED YOU IN RETURN.
THROUGH THE GOOD TIMES AND THE BAD.
I ALWAYS SAID I WAS FIGHTING FOR MY COUNTRY, FOR MY BELIEFS, BUT MORE THAN THAT, I SEE NOW--
--I WAS FIGHTING FOR THEM.
THE ONES WHO INSPIRED ME...
...THE ONES WHO CHALLENGED ME...

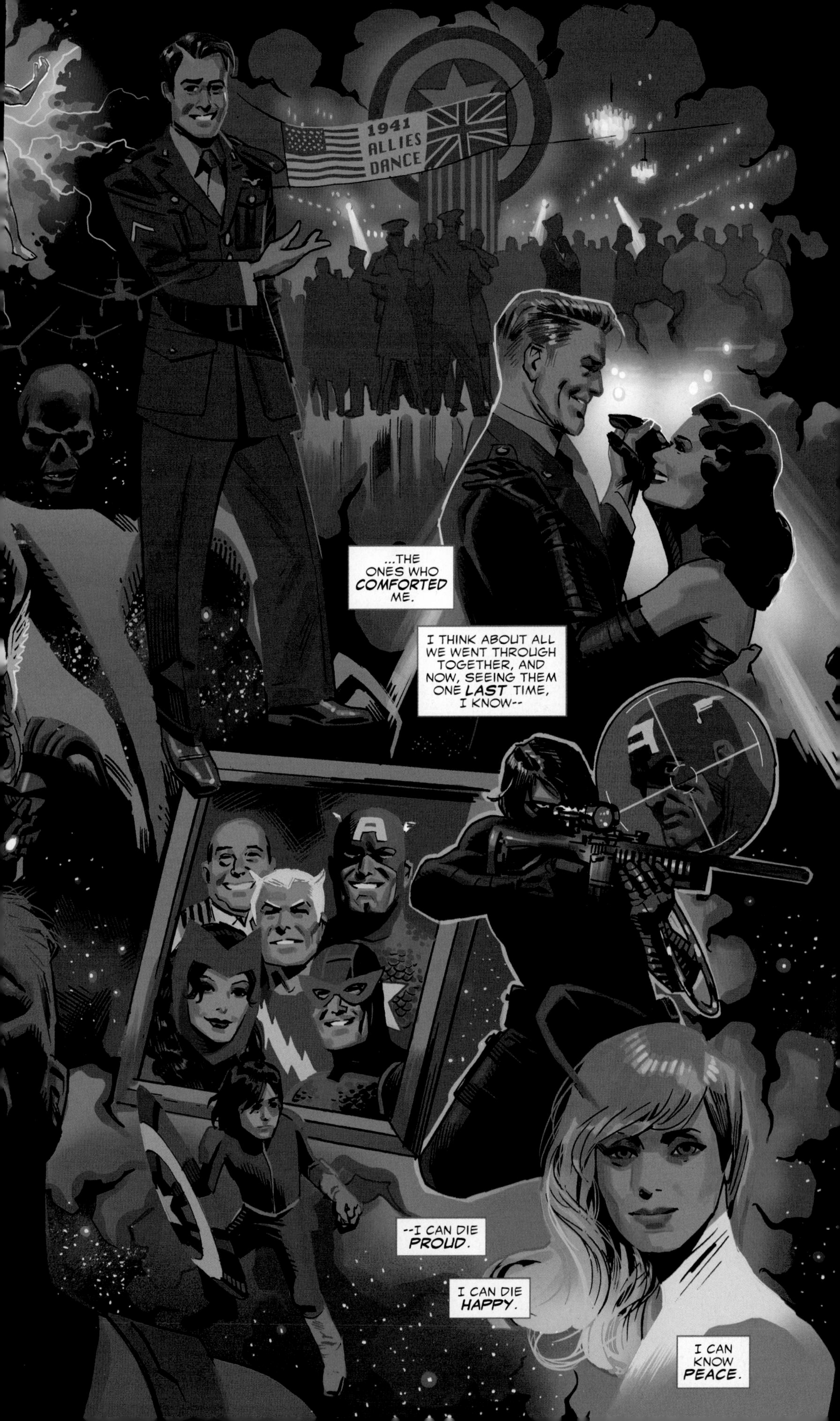
1941
ALLIES
DANCE
...THE ONES WHO COMFORTED ME.
I THINK ABOUT ALL WE WENT THROUGH TOGETHER, AND NOW, SEEING THEM ONE LAST TIME, I KNOW--
--I CAN DIE PROUD.
I CAN DIE HAPPY.
I CAN KNOW PEACE.

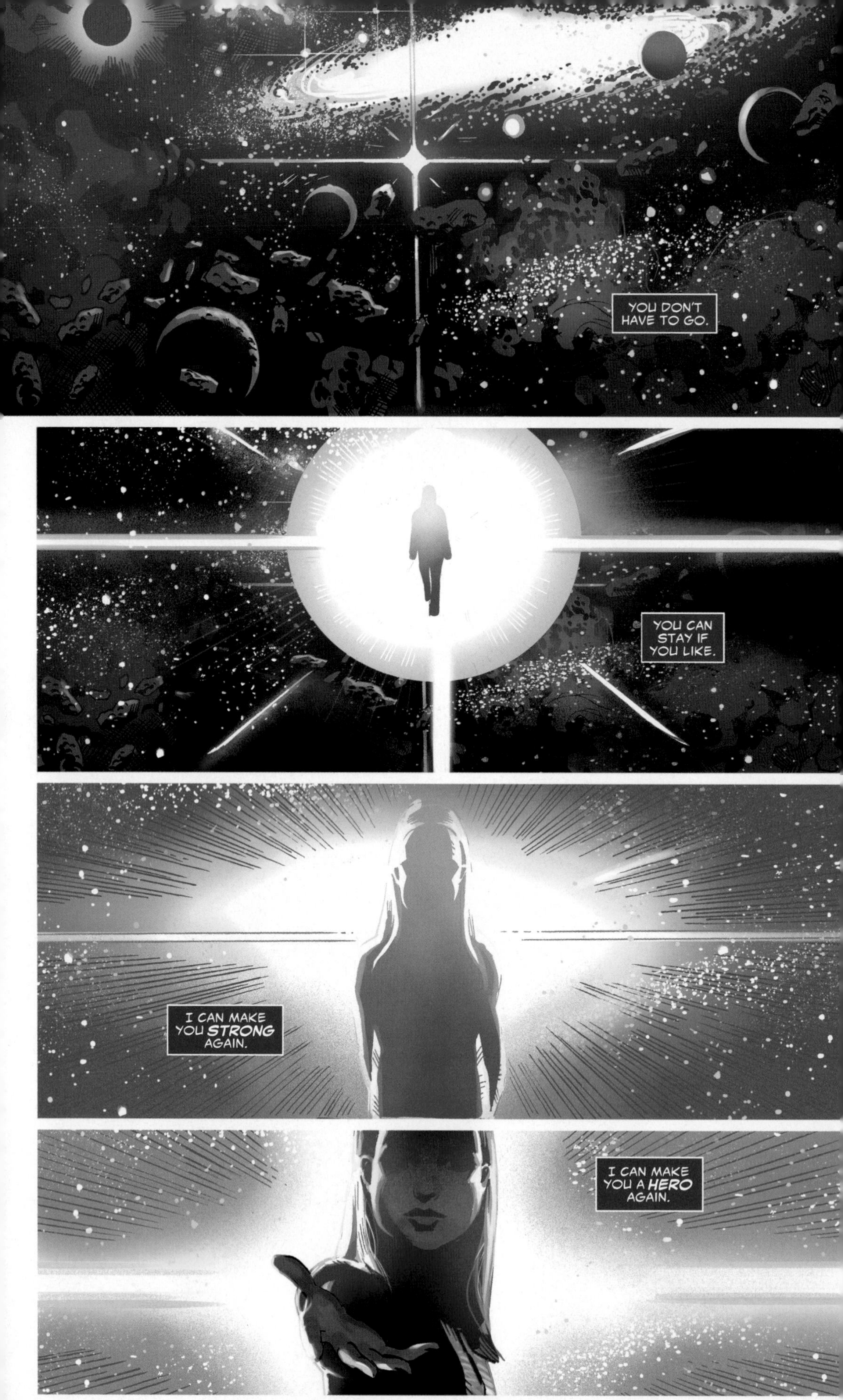
YOU DON'T HAVE TO GO.
YOU CAN STAY IF YOU LIKE.
I CAN MAKE YOU STRONG AGAIN.
I CAN MAKE YOU A HERO AGAIN.

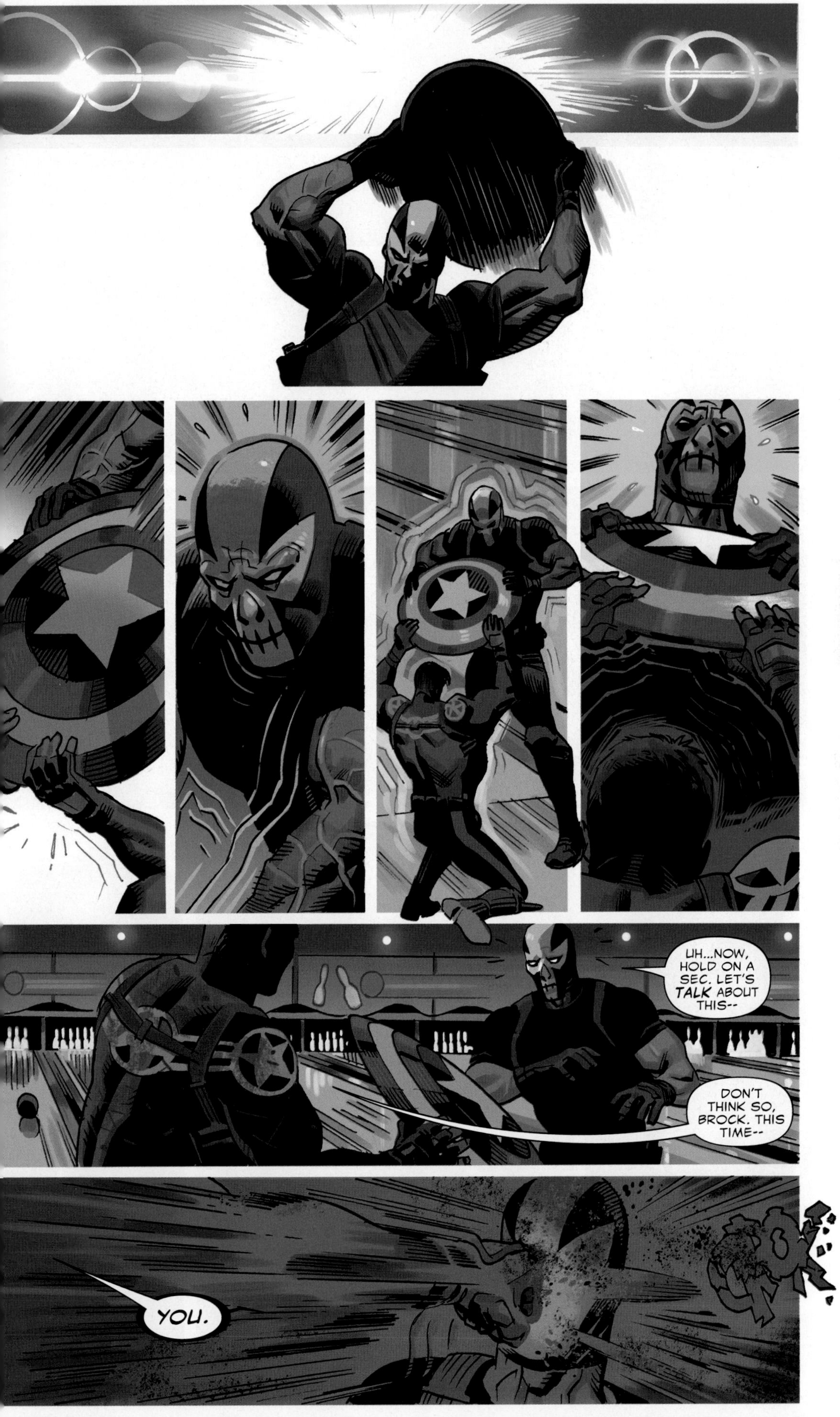
UH...NOW, HOLD ON A SEC. LET'S TALK ABOUT THIS--
DON'T THINK SO, BROCK. THIS TIME--
YOU.

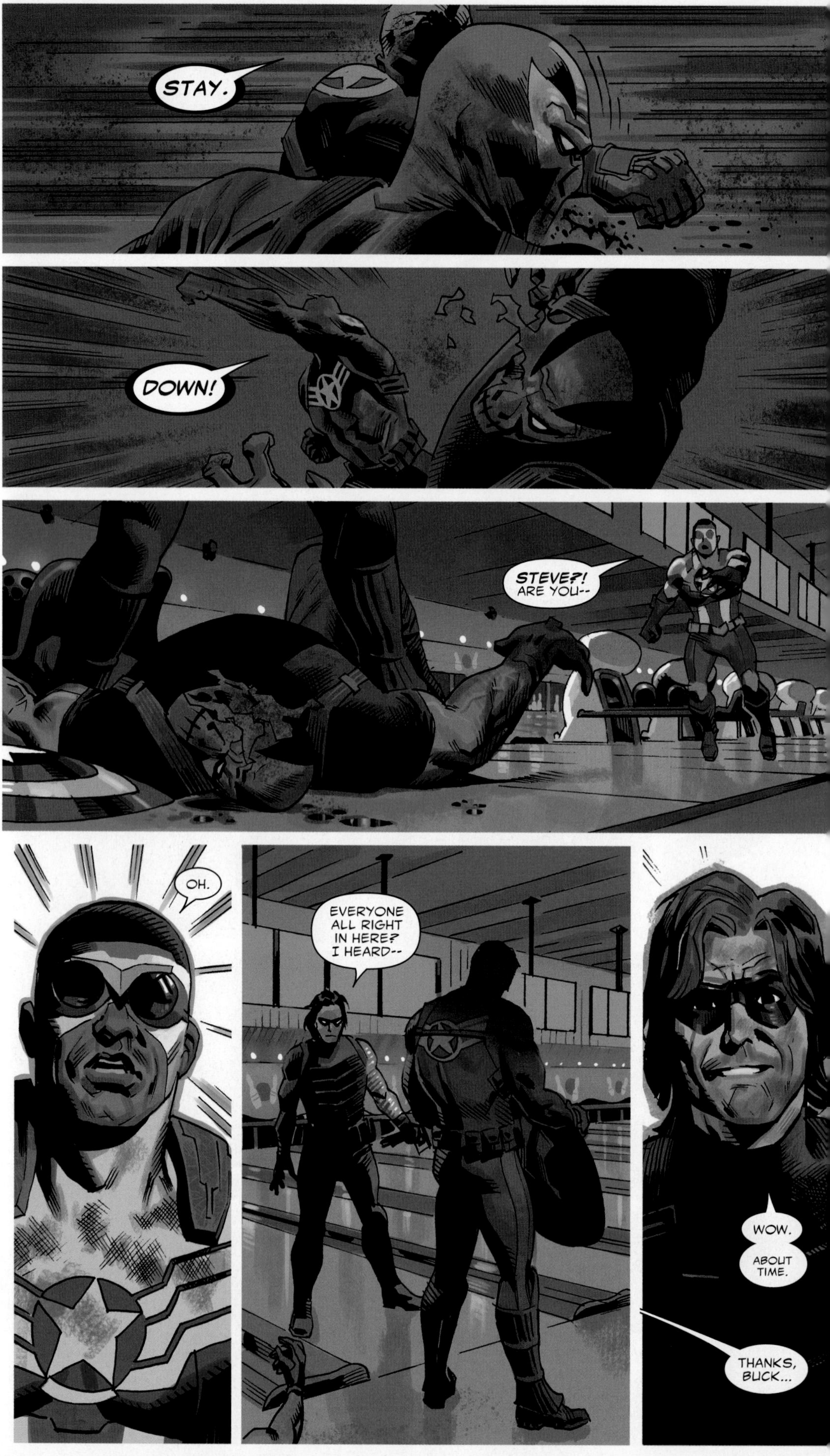
STAY.
DOWN!
STEVE?! ARE YOU--
OH.
EVERYONE ALL RIGHT IN HERE? I HEARD--
WOW.
ABOUT TIME.
THANKS, BUCK...

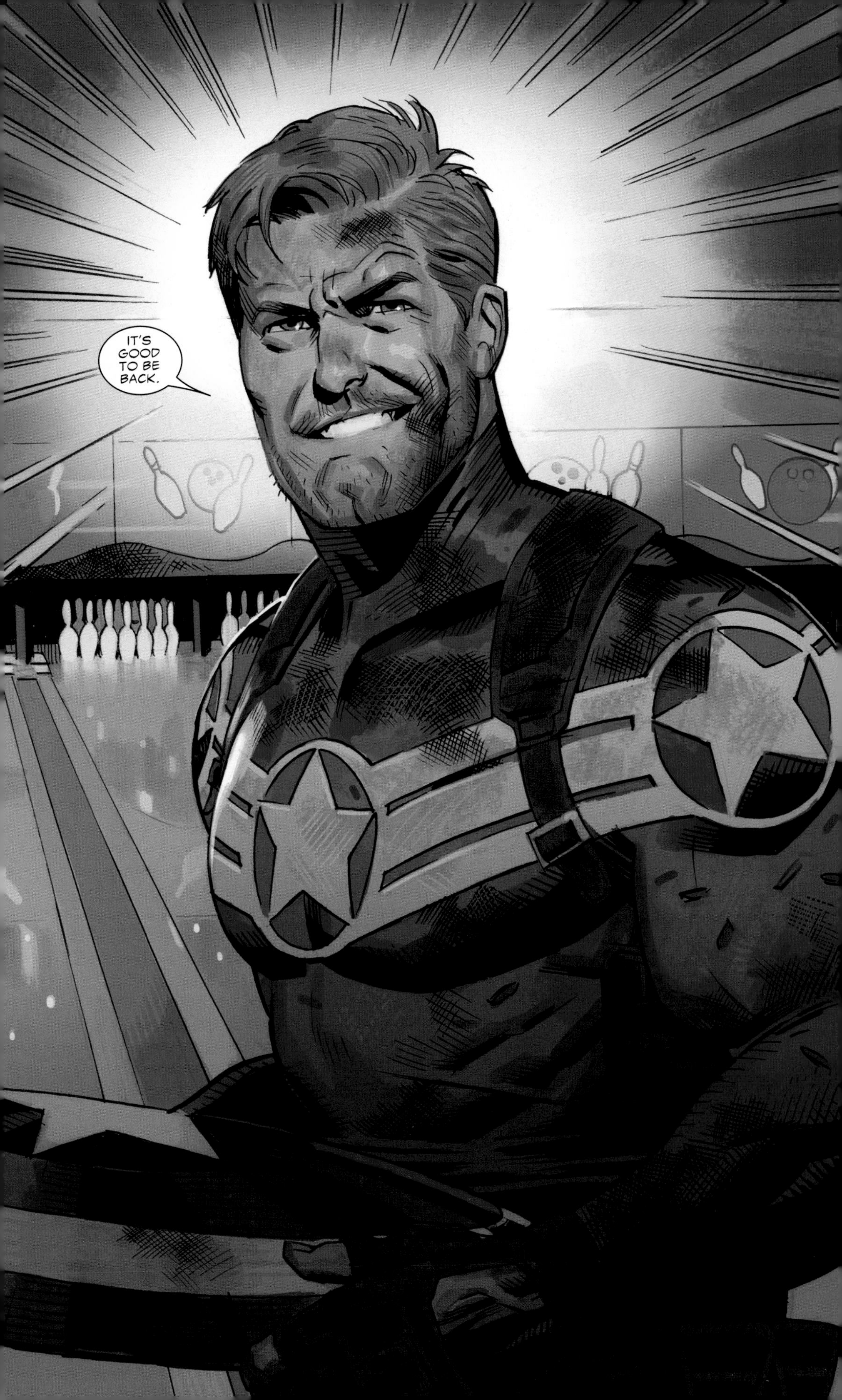
IT'S GOOD TO BE BACK.

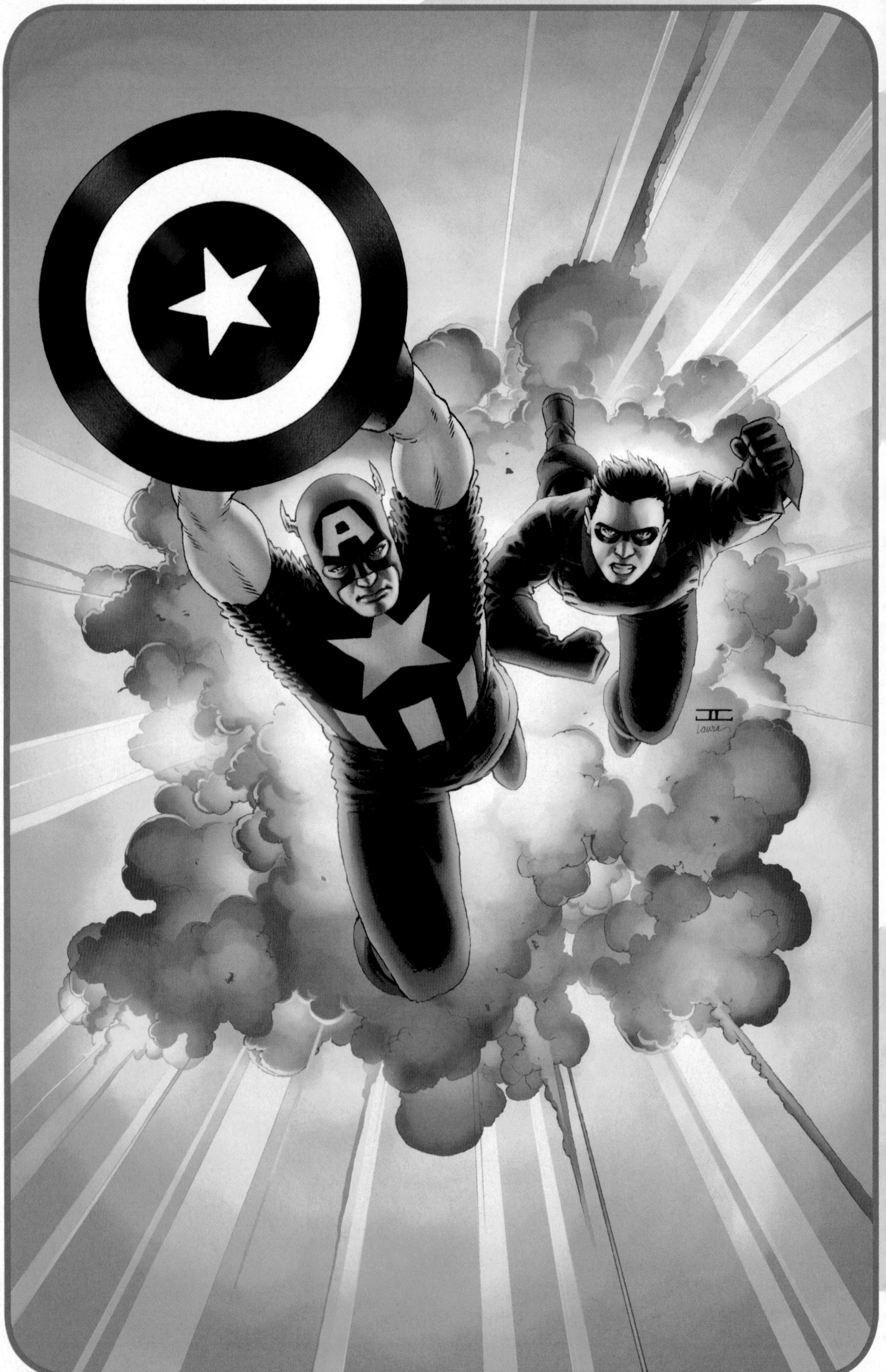

#7 variant by
JOHN CASSADAY & LAURA MARTIN

CAPTAIN AMERICA

Celebrating 75 years of CAPTAIN AMERICA

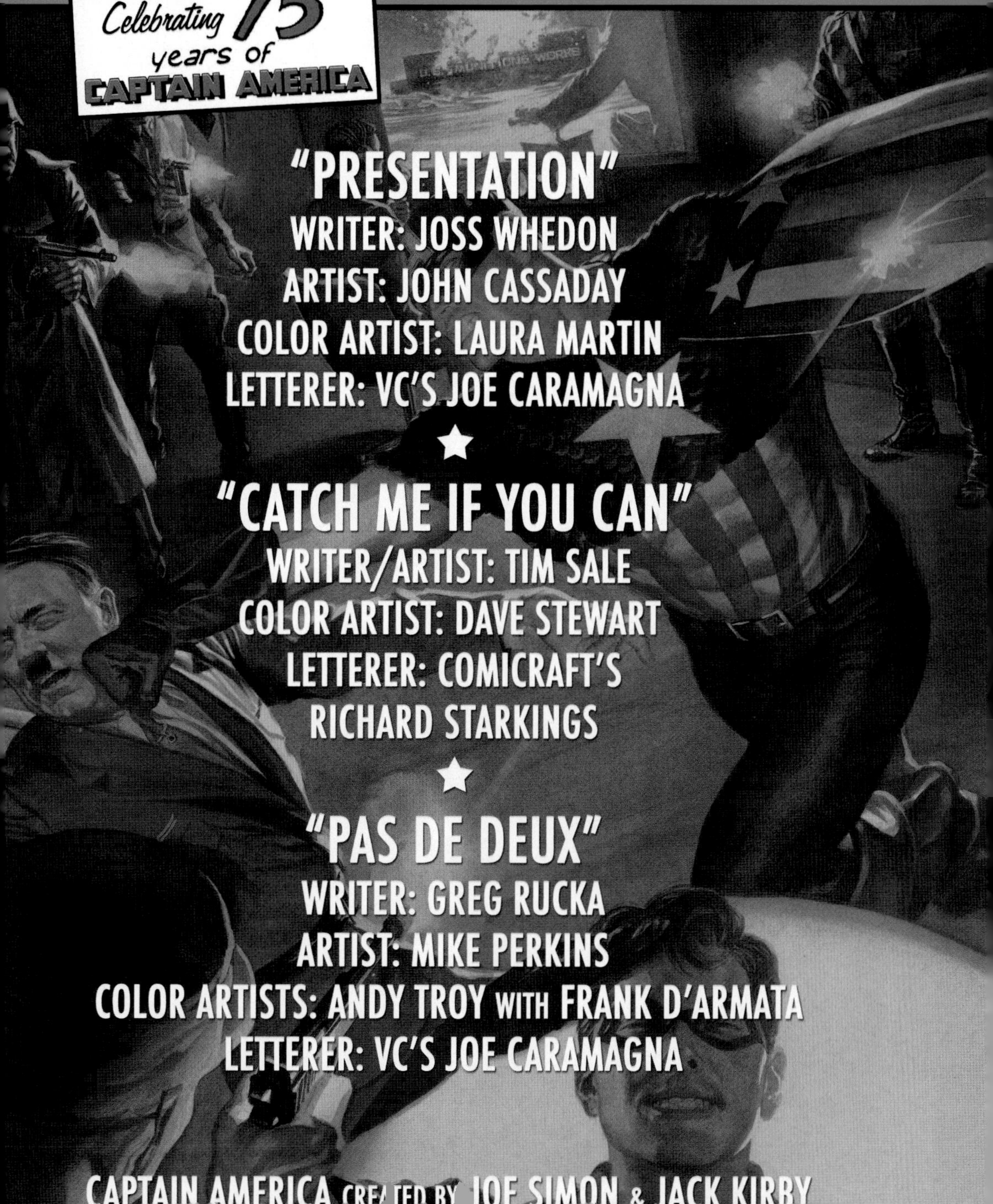

"PRESENTATION"

WRITER: JOSS WHEDON
ARTIST: JOHN CASSADAY
COLOR ARTIST: LAURA MARTIN
LETTERER: VC'S JOE CARAMAGNA

★

"CATCH ME IF YOU CAN"

WRITER/ARTIST: TIM SALE
COLOR ARTIST: DAVE STEWART
LETTERER: COMICRAFT'S RICHARD STARKINGS

★

"PAS DE DEUX"

WRITER: GREG RUCKA
ARTIST: MIKE PERKINS
COLOR ARTISTS: ANDY TROY WITH FRANK D'ARMATA
LETTERER: VC'S JOE CARAMAGNA

CAPTAIN AMERICA CREATED BY JOE SIMON & JACK KIRBY

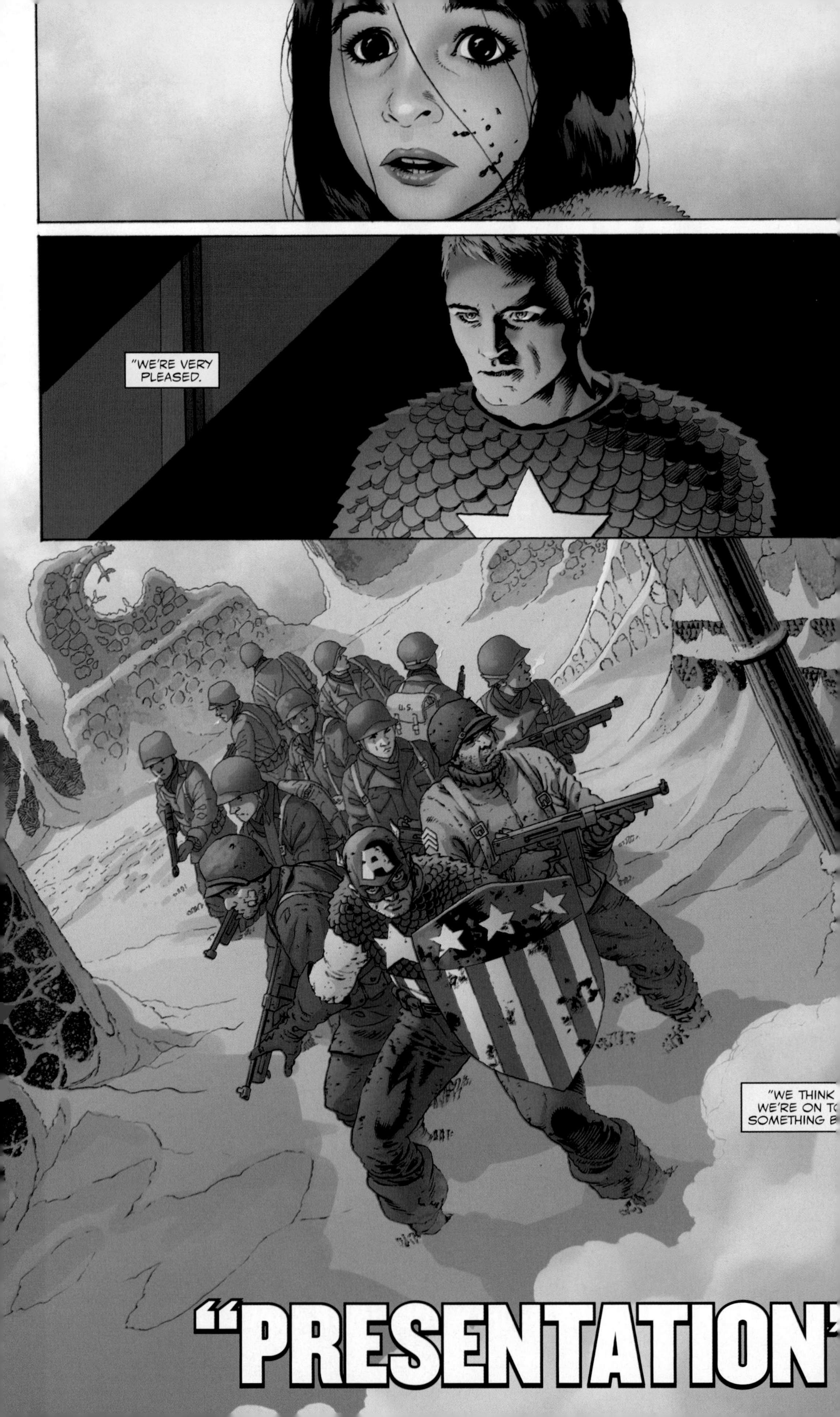
"WE'RE VERY PLEASED.
"WE THINK WE'RE ON T SOMETHING B
"PRESENTATION"

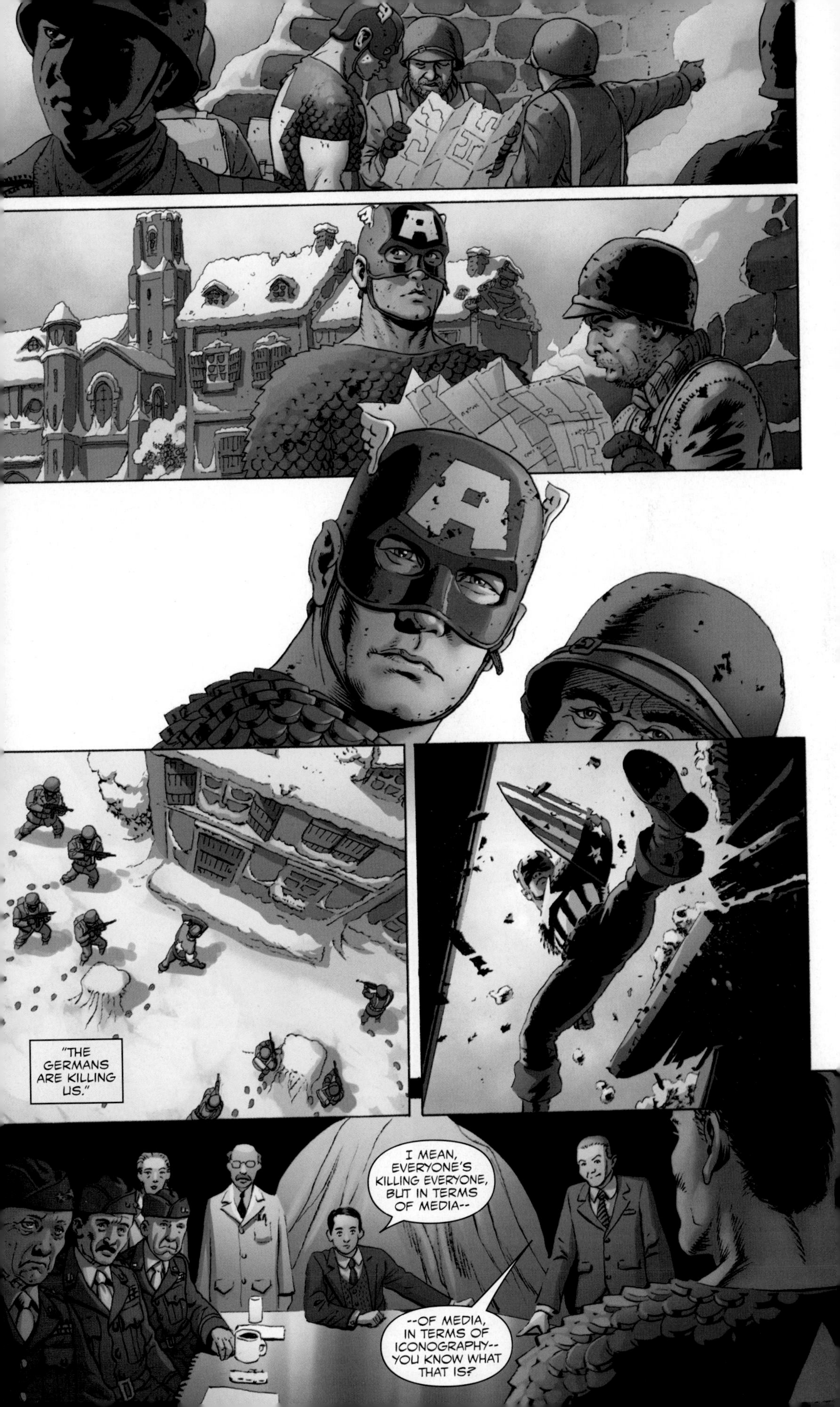
"THE GERMANS ARE KILLING US."
I MEAN, EVERYONE'S KILLING EVERYONE, BUT IN TERMS OF MEDIA--
--OF MEDIA, IN TERMS OF ICONOGRAPHY-- YOU KNOW WHAT THAT IS?

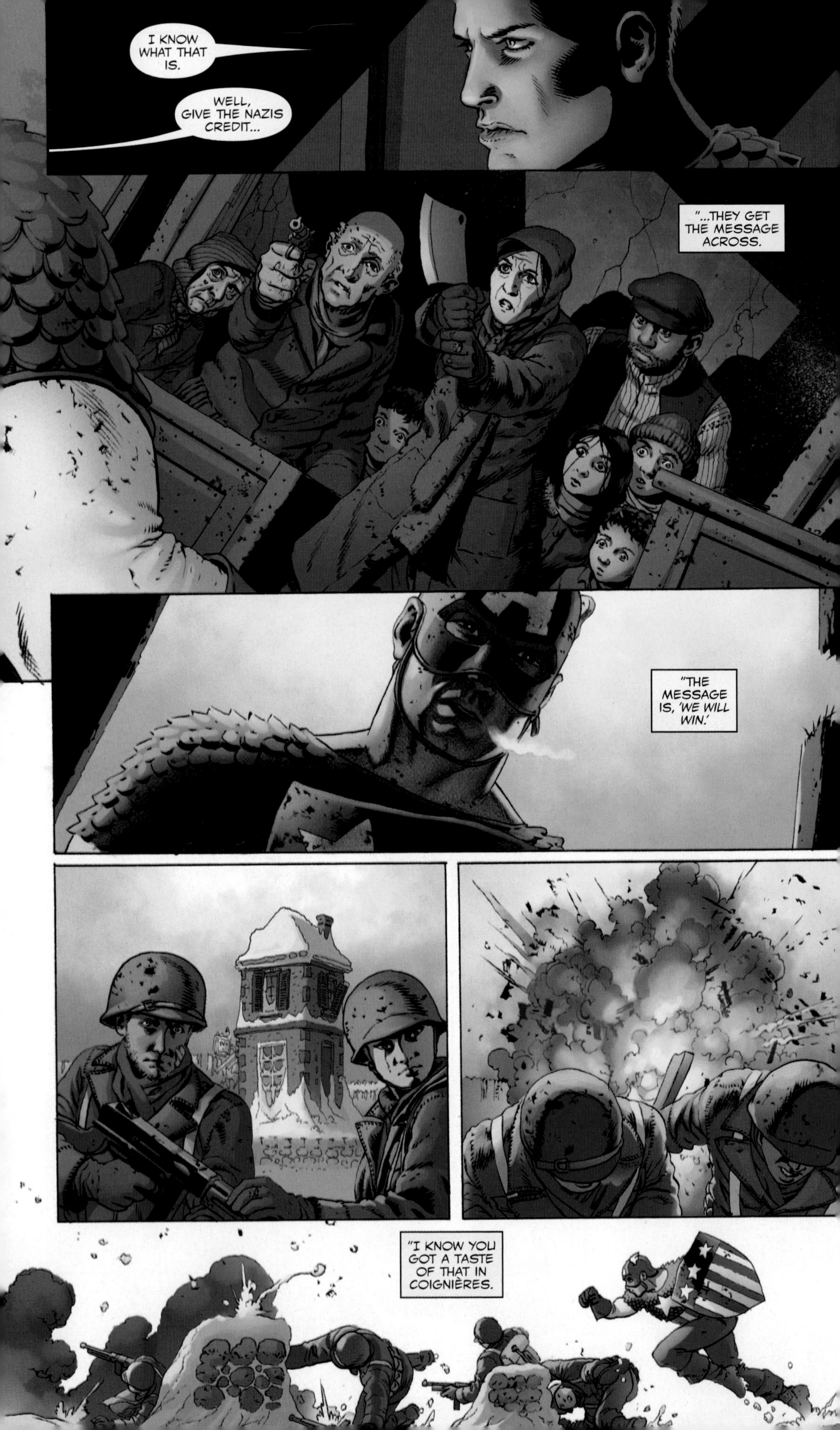
I KNOW WHAT THAT IS.
WELL, GIVE THE NAZIS CREDIT...
"...THEY GET THE MESSAGE ACROSS.
"THE MESSAGE IS, 'WE WILL WIN.'
"I KNOW YOU GOT A TASTE OF THAT IN COIGNIÈRES.

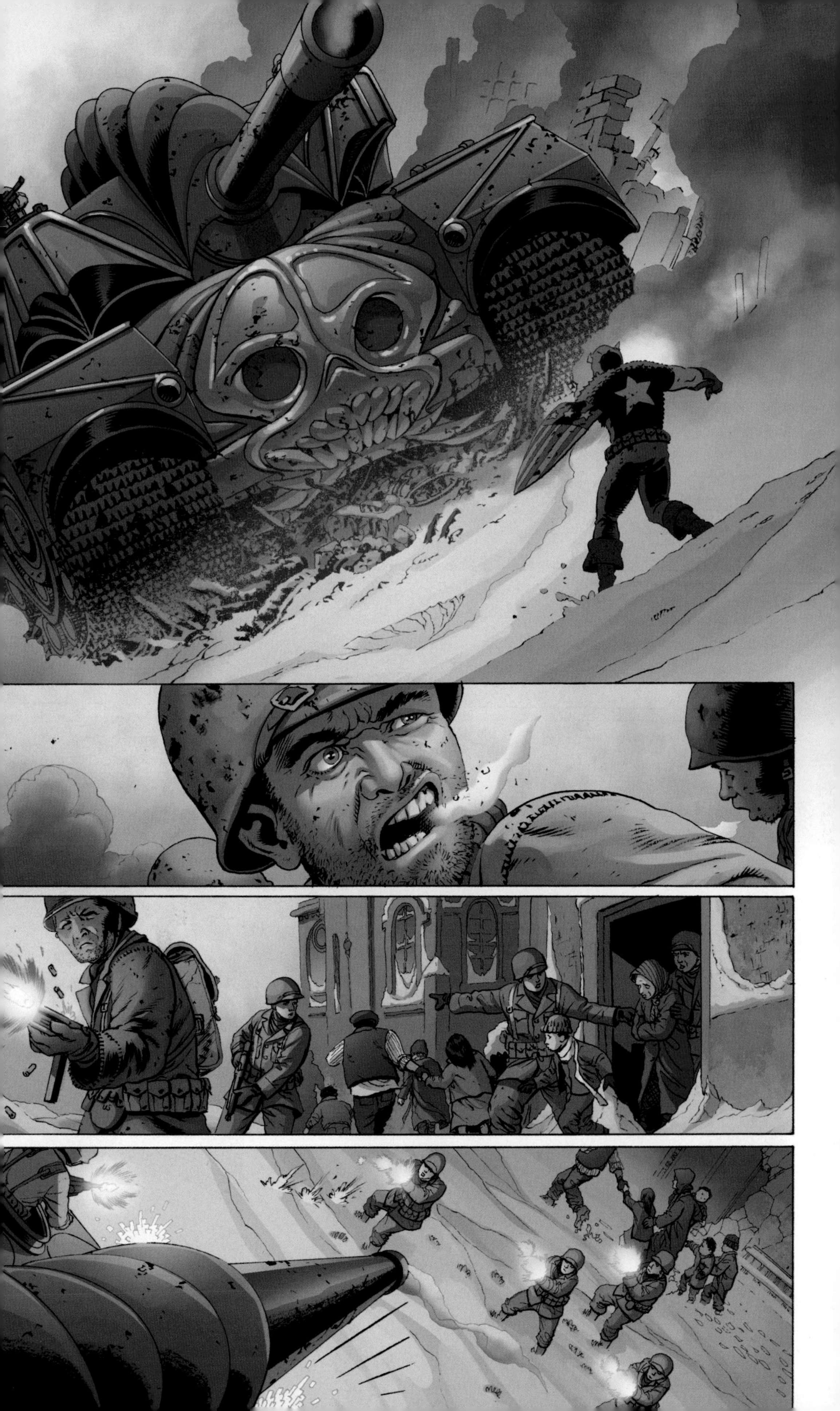

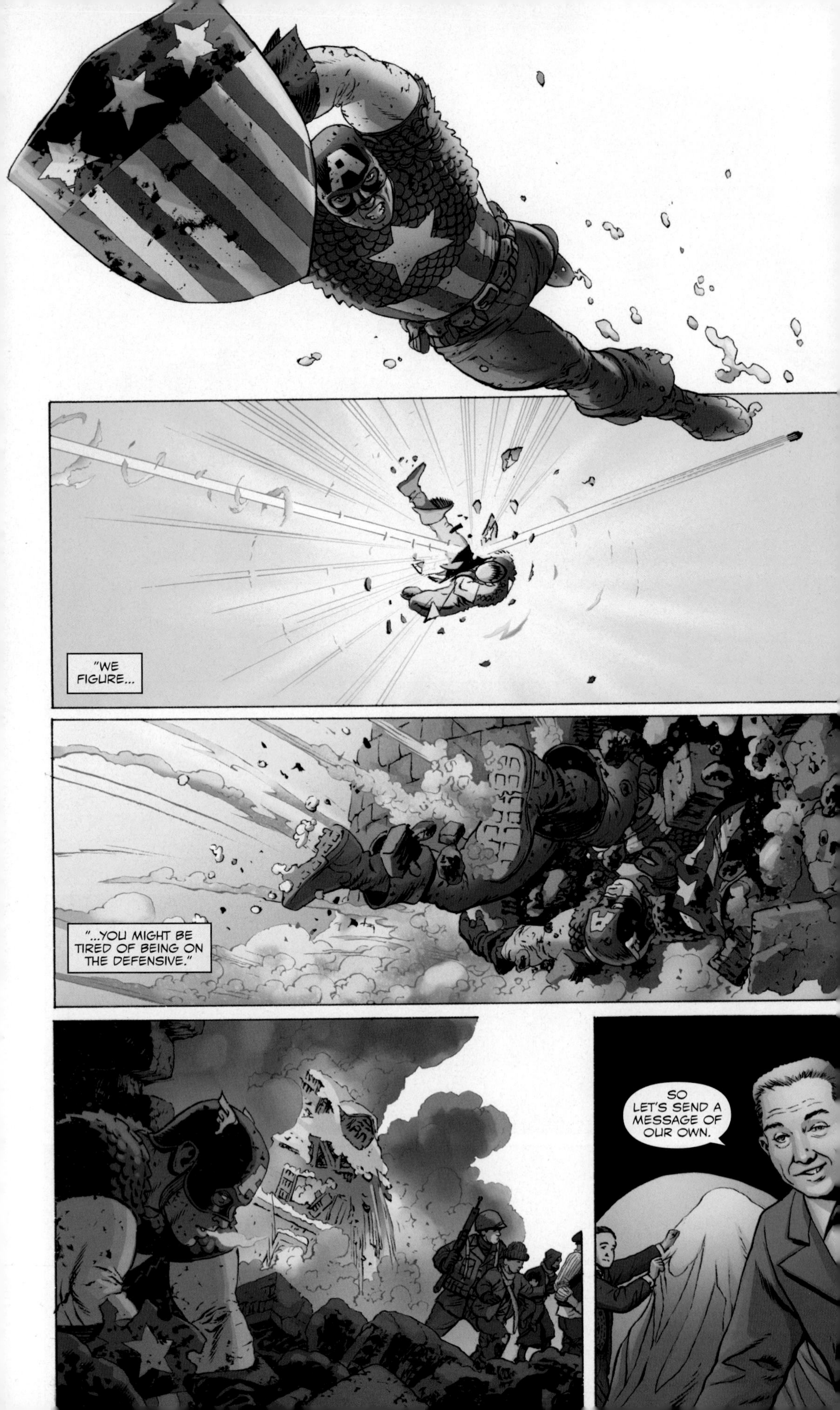
"WE FIGURE...
"...YOU MIGHT BE TIRED OF BEING ON THE DEFENSIVE."
SO LET'S SEND A MESSAGE OF OUR OWN.

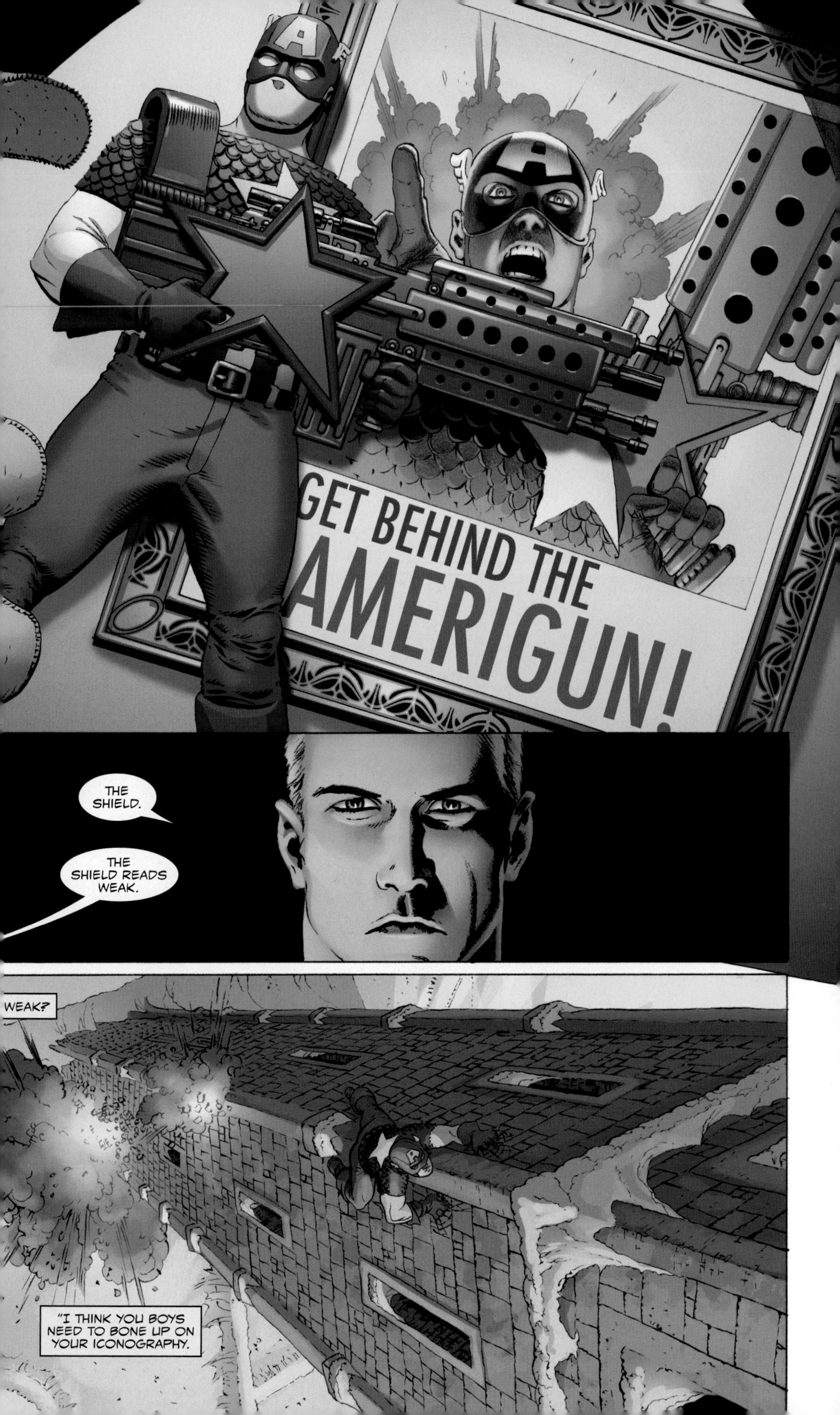
GET BEHIND THE AMERIGUN!
THE SHIELD.
THE SHIELD READS WEAK.
WEAK?
"I THINK YOU BOYS NEED TO BONE UP ON YOUR ICONOGRAPHY.

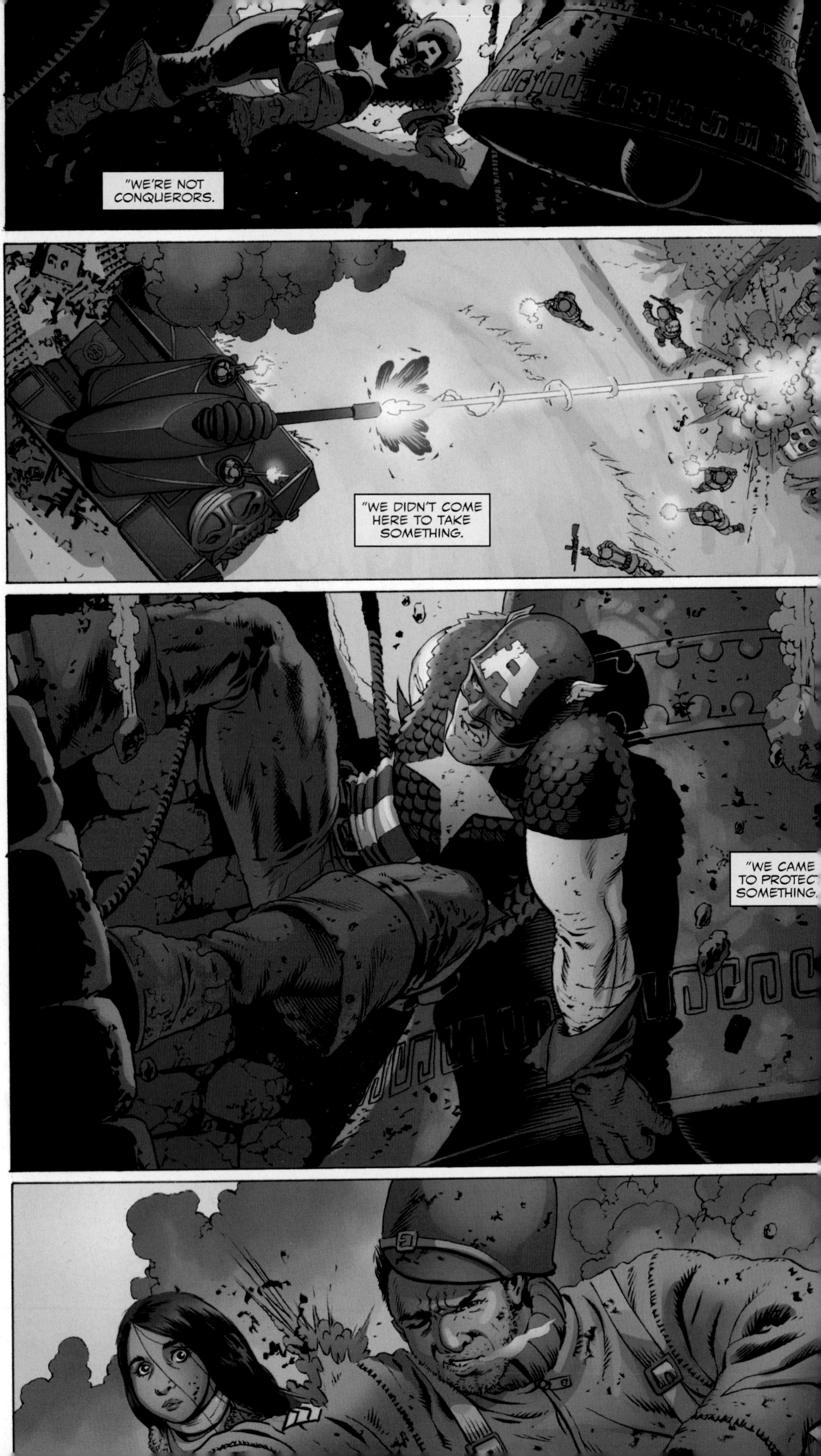

"WE'RE NOT CONQUERORS.
"WE DIDN'T COME HERE TO TAKE SOMETHING.
"WE CAME TO PROTECT SOMETHING.

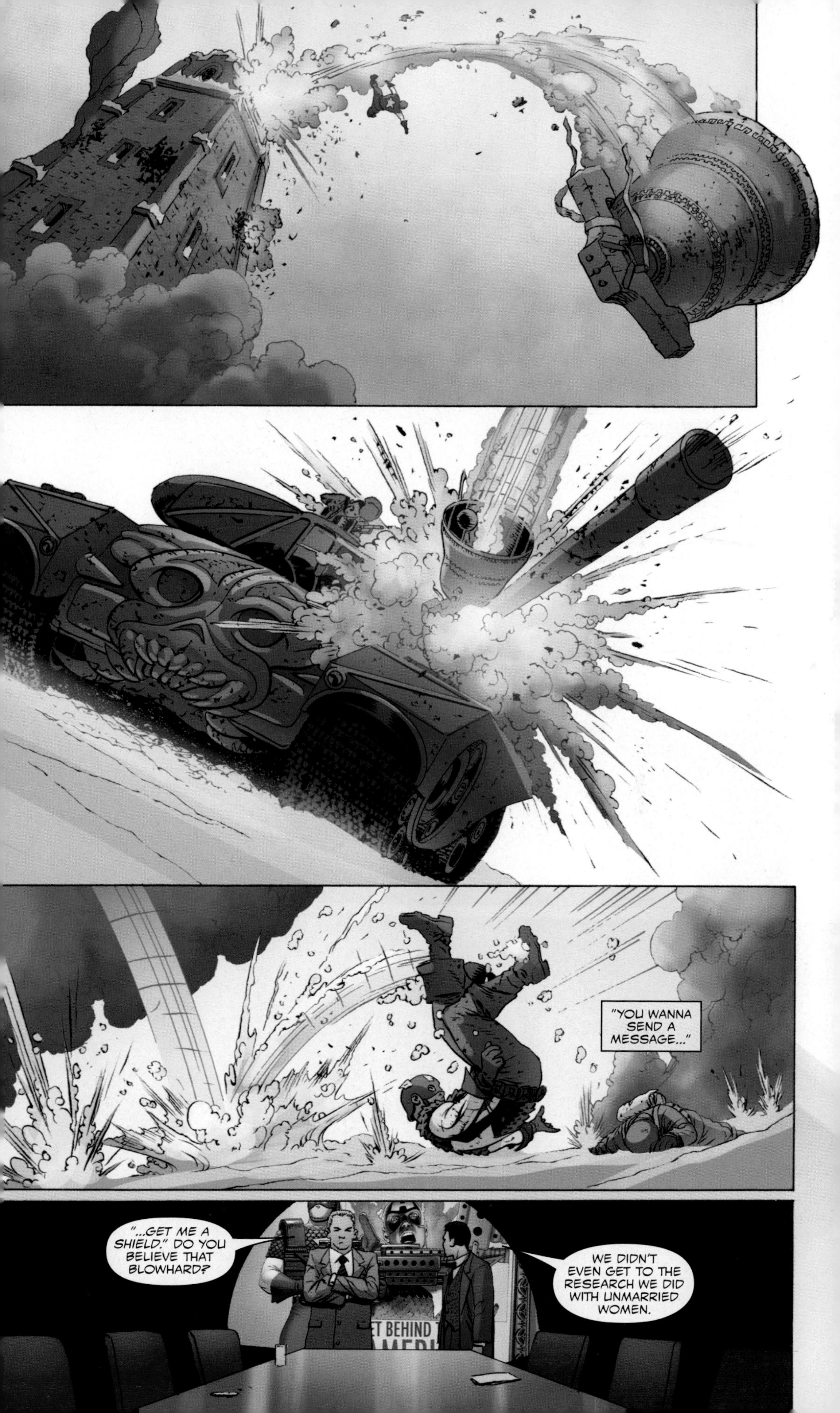
"YOU WANNA SEND A MESSAGE..."
"...GET ME A SHIELD." DO YOU BELIEVE THAT BLOWHARD?
WE DIDN'T EVEN GET TO THE RESEARCH WE DID WITH UNMARRIED WOMEN.

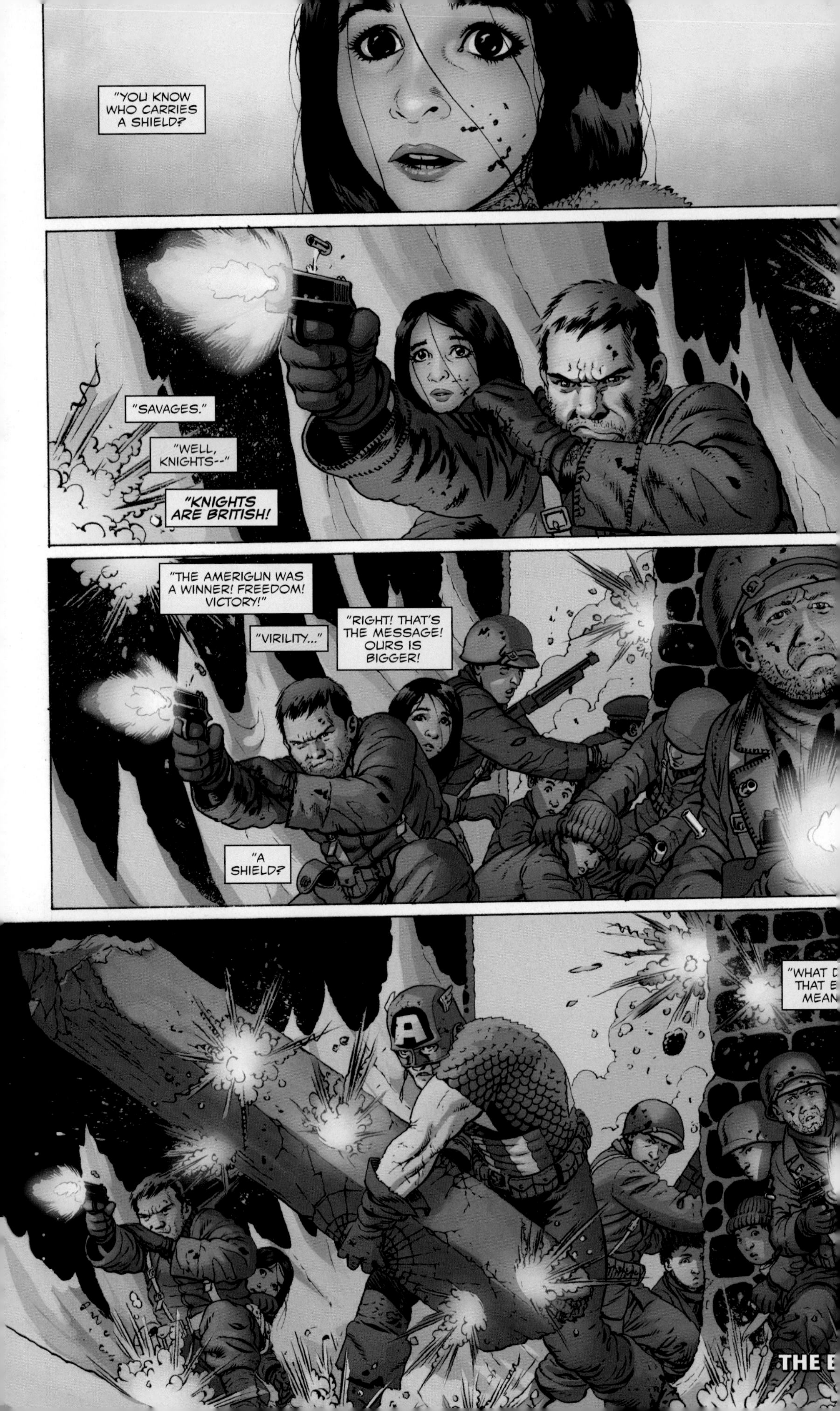
"YOU KNOW WHO CARRIES A SHIELD?
"SAVAGES."
"WELL, KNIGHTS--"
"KNIGHTS ARE BRITISH!
"THE AMERIGUN WAS A WINNER! FREEDOM! VICTORY!"
"VIRILITY..."
"RIGHT! THAT'S THE MESSAGE! OURS IS BIGGER!
"A SHIELD?

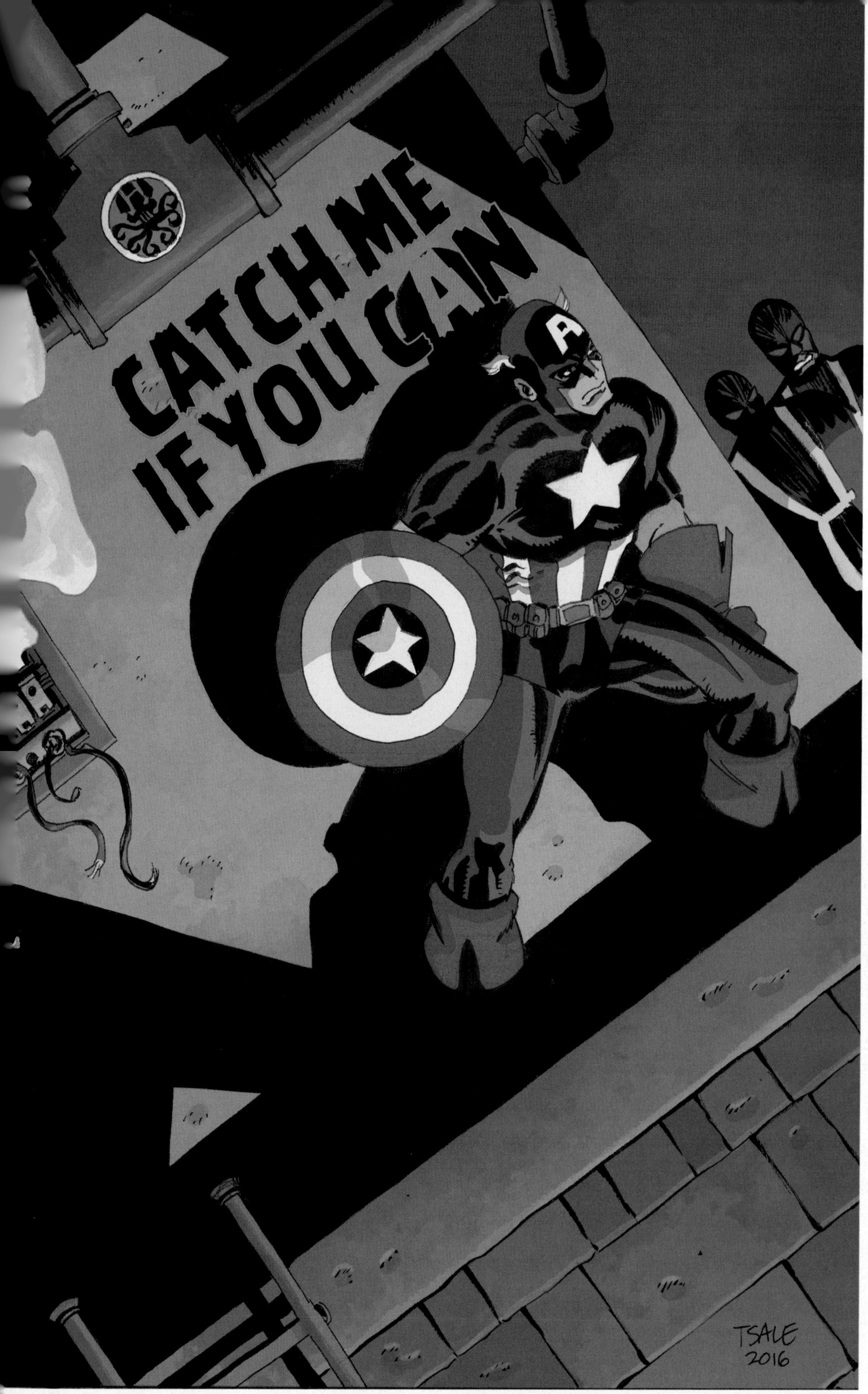
CATCH ME
IF YOU CAN
TSALE
2016

TIM SALE STORY & ART • DAVE STEWART COLOR • RICHARD STARKINGS LETTERS

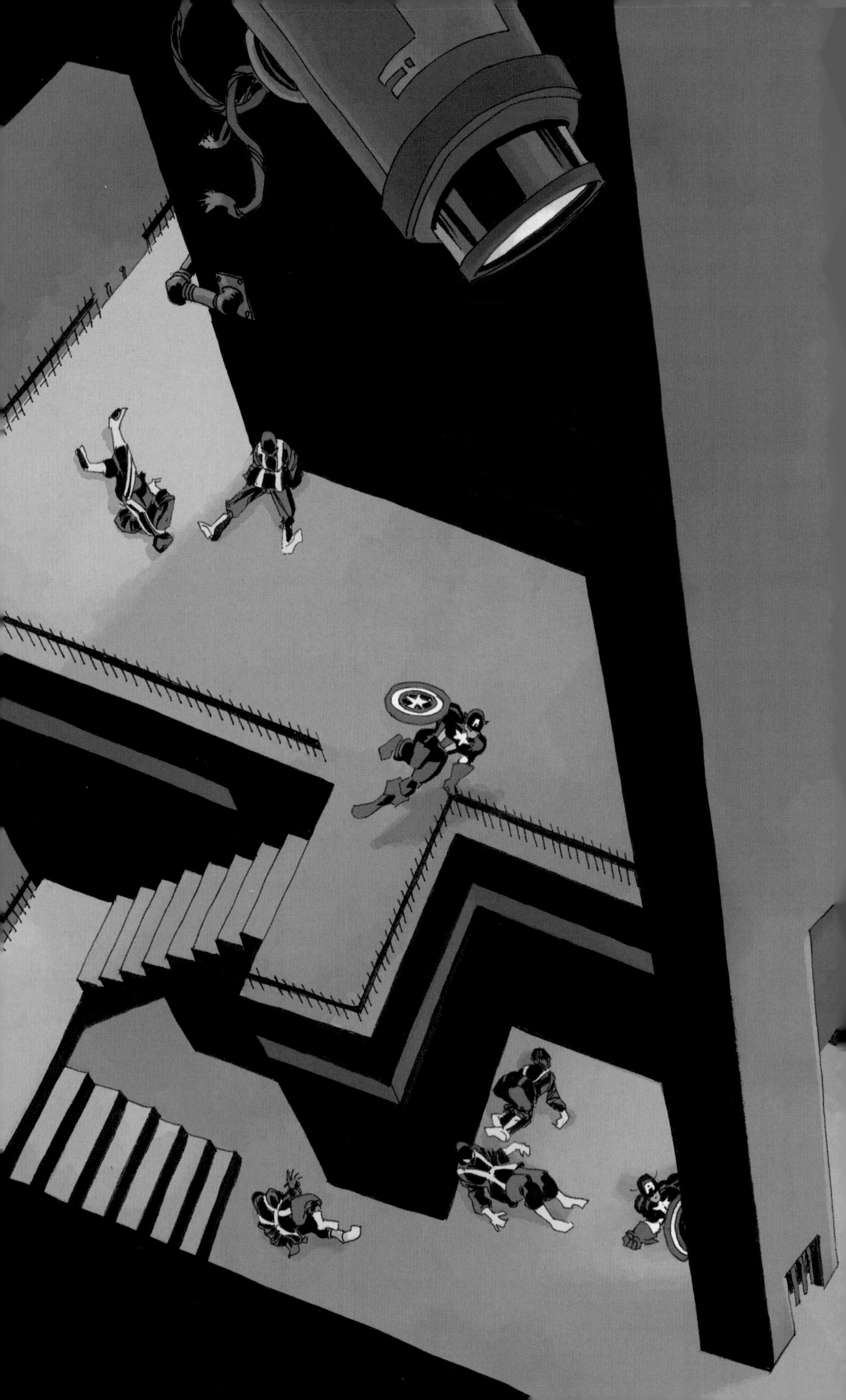

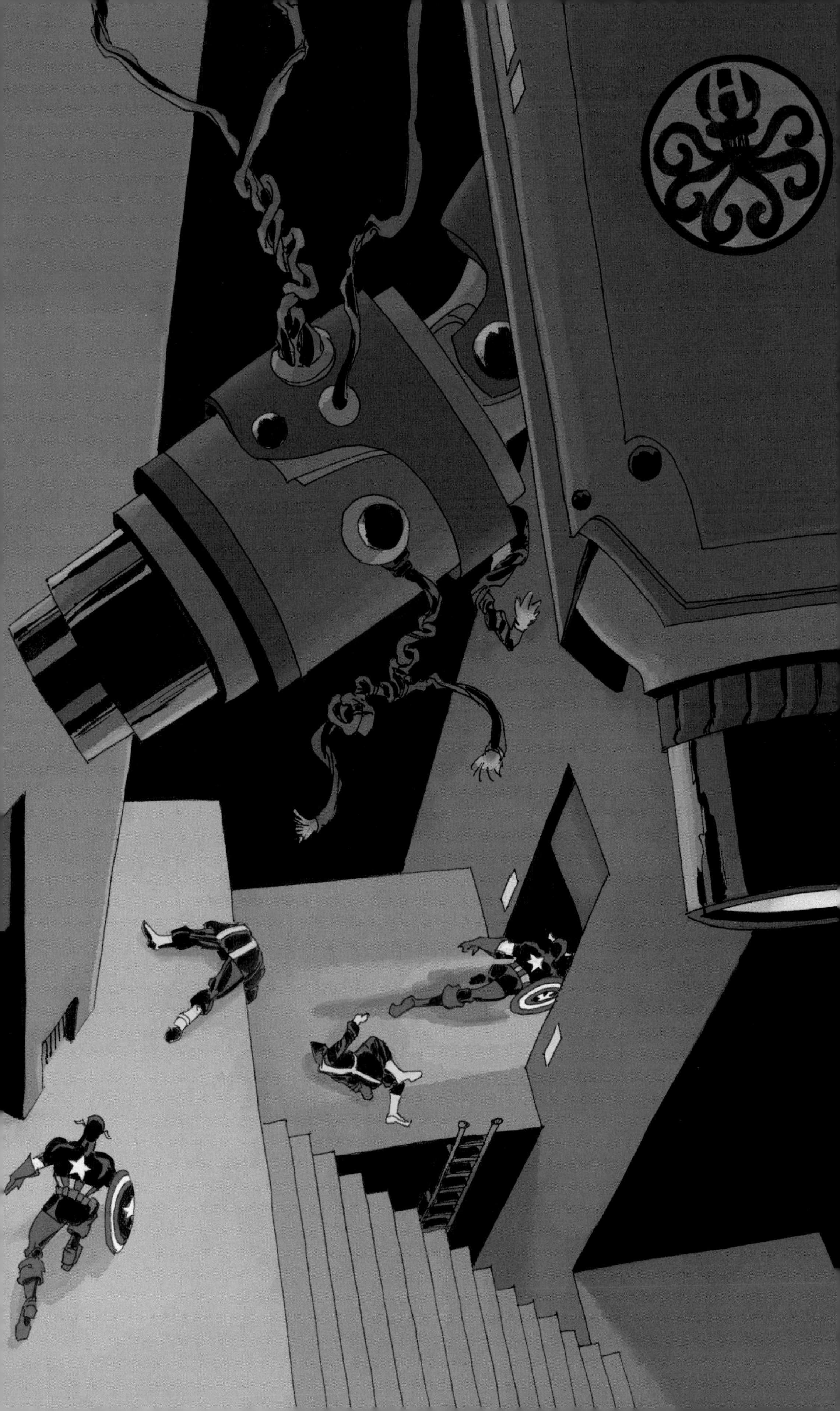

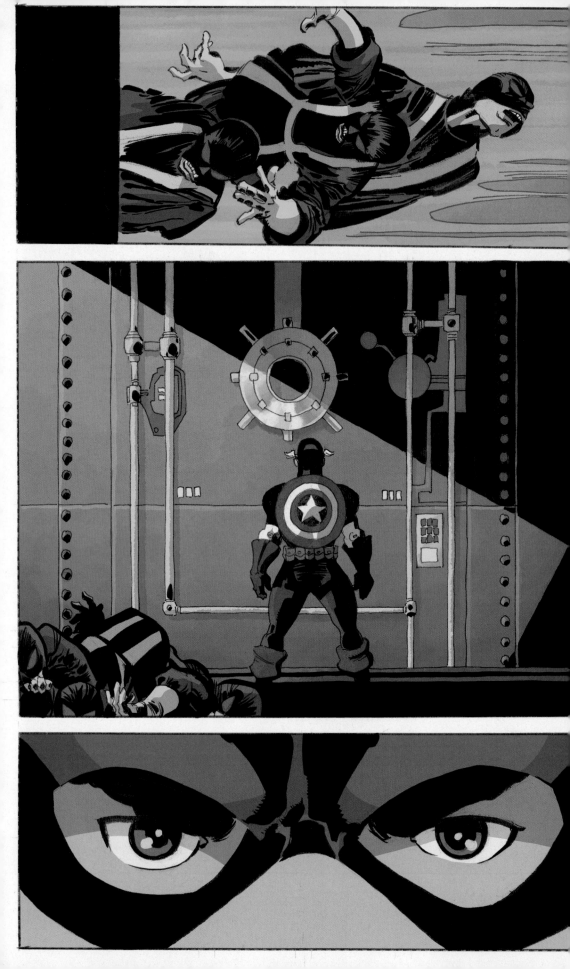

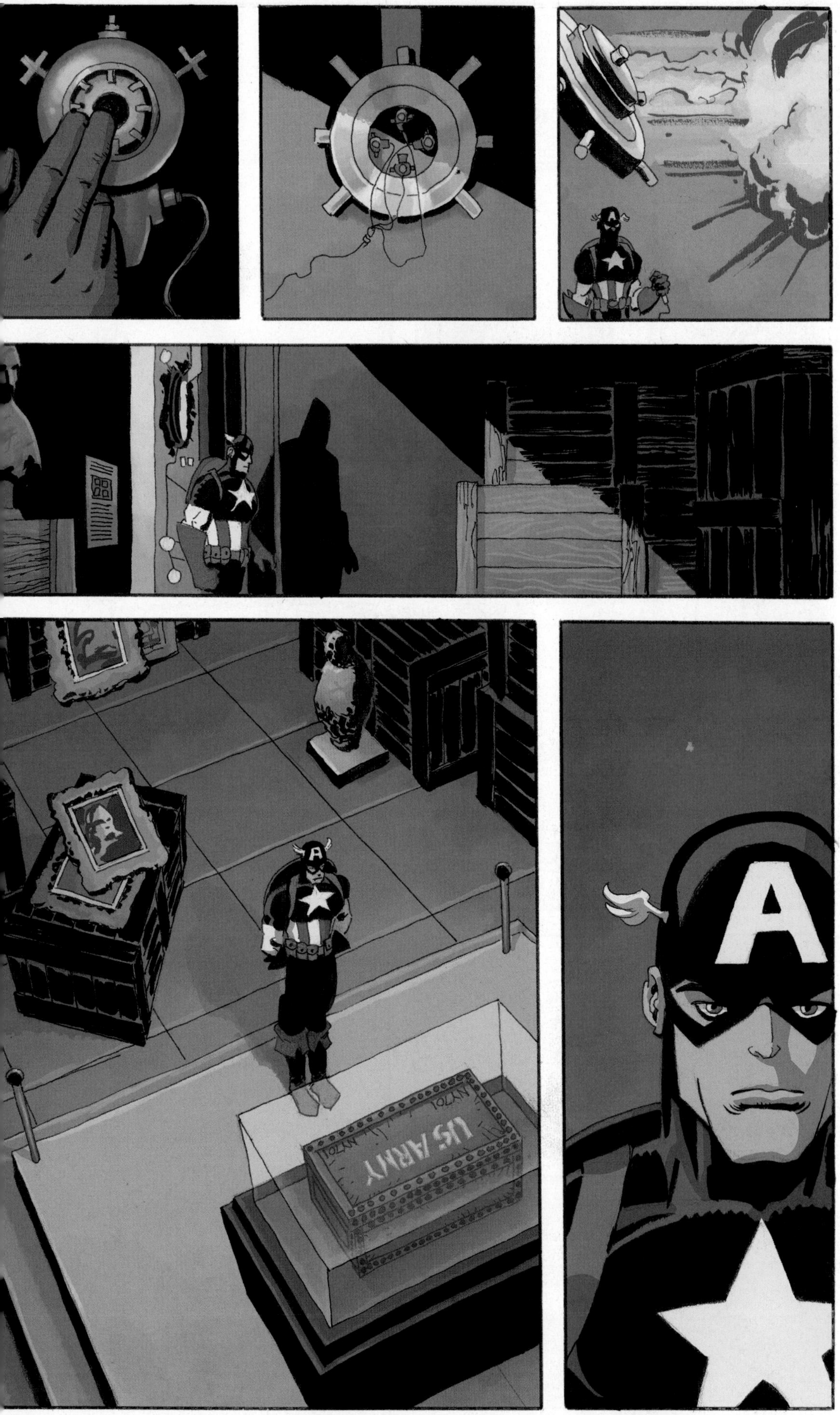
US ARMY

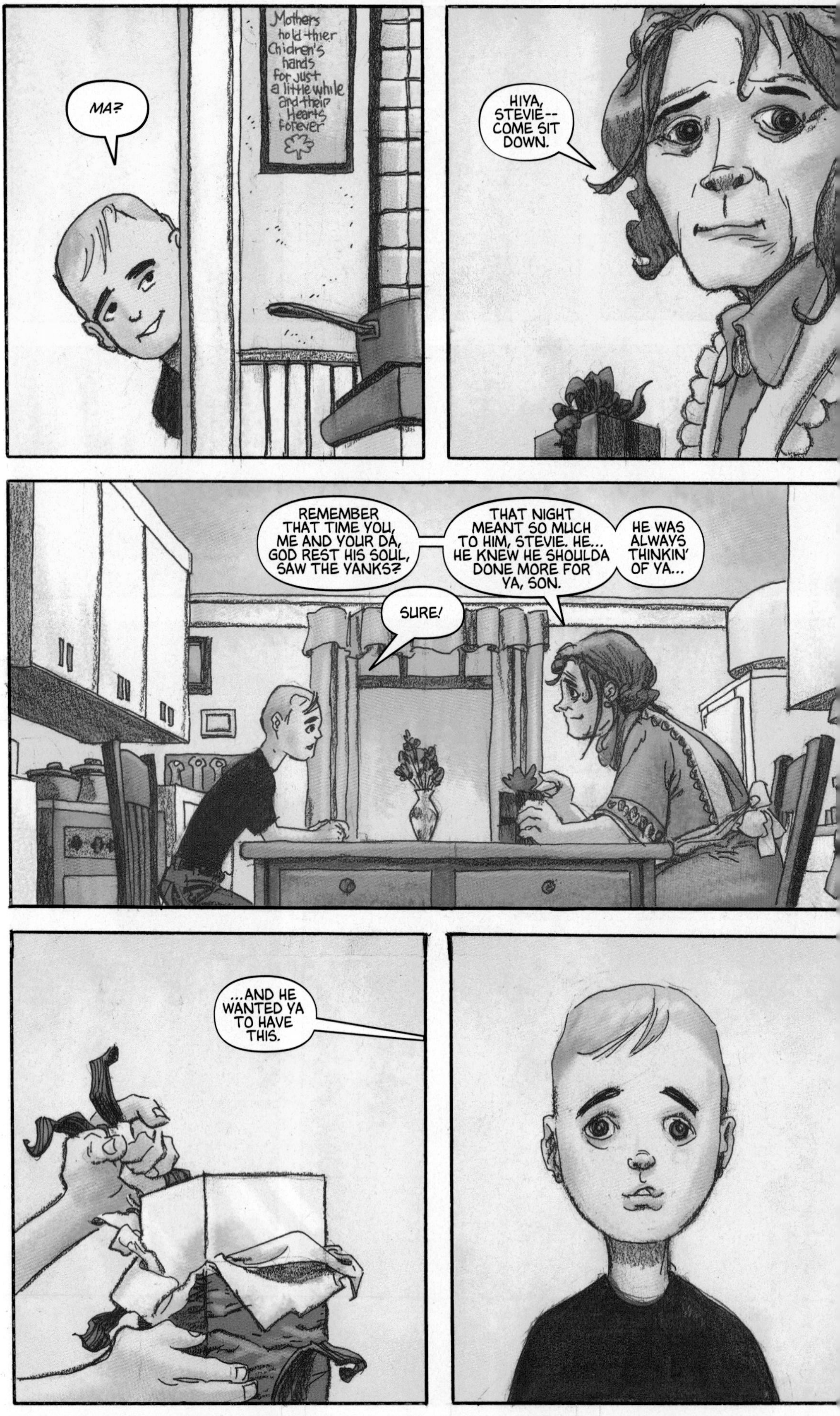
Mothers hold thier Children's hands for just a little while and their Hearts forever
MA?
HIYA, STEVIE-- COME SIT DOWN.
REMEMBER THAT TIME YOU, ME AND YOUR DA, GOD REST HIS SOUL, SAW THE YANKS?
SURE!
THAT NIGHT MEANT SO MUCH TO HIM, STEVIE. HE... HE KNEW HE SHOULDA DONE MORE FOR YA, SON.
HE WAS ALWAYS THINKIN' OF YA...
...AND HE WANTED YA TO HAVE THIS.

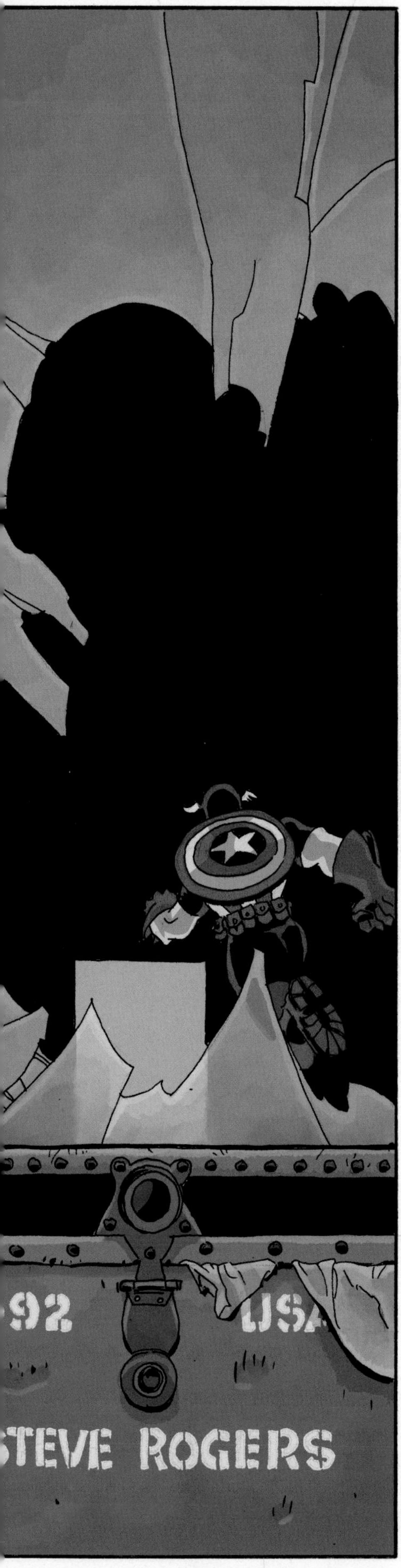
92
USA
STEVE ROGERS
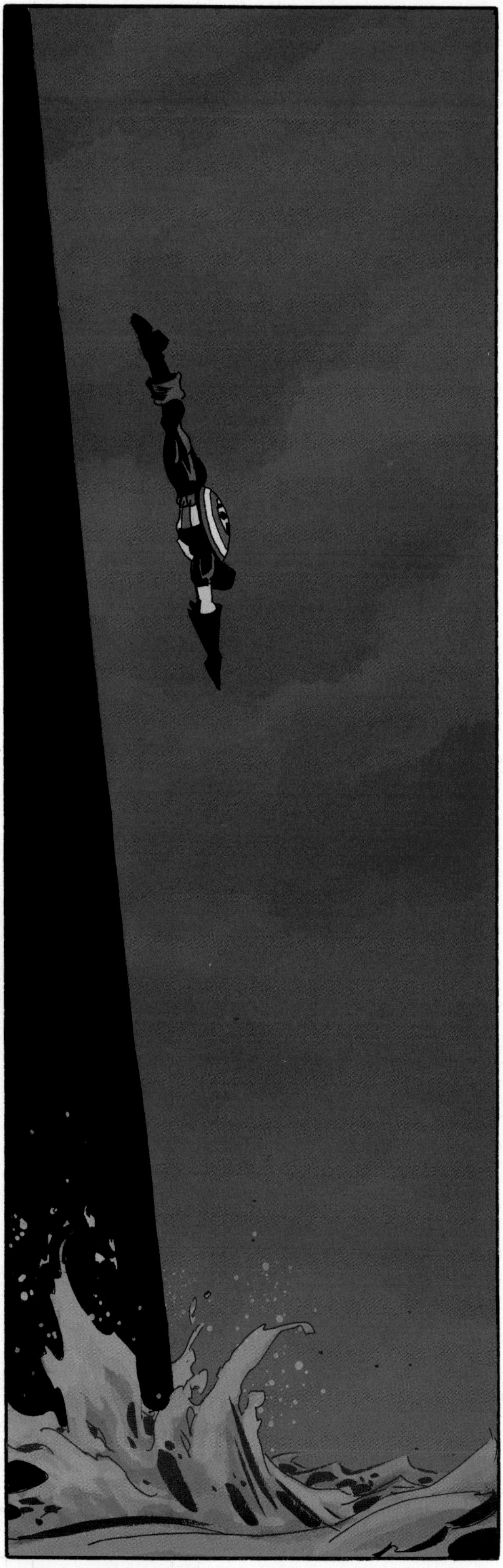

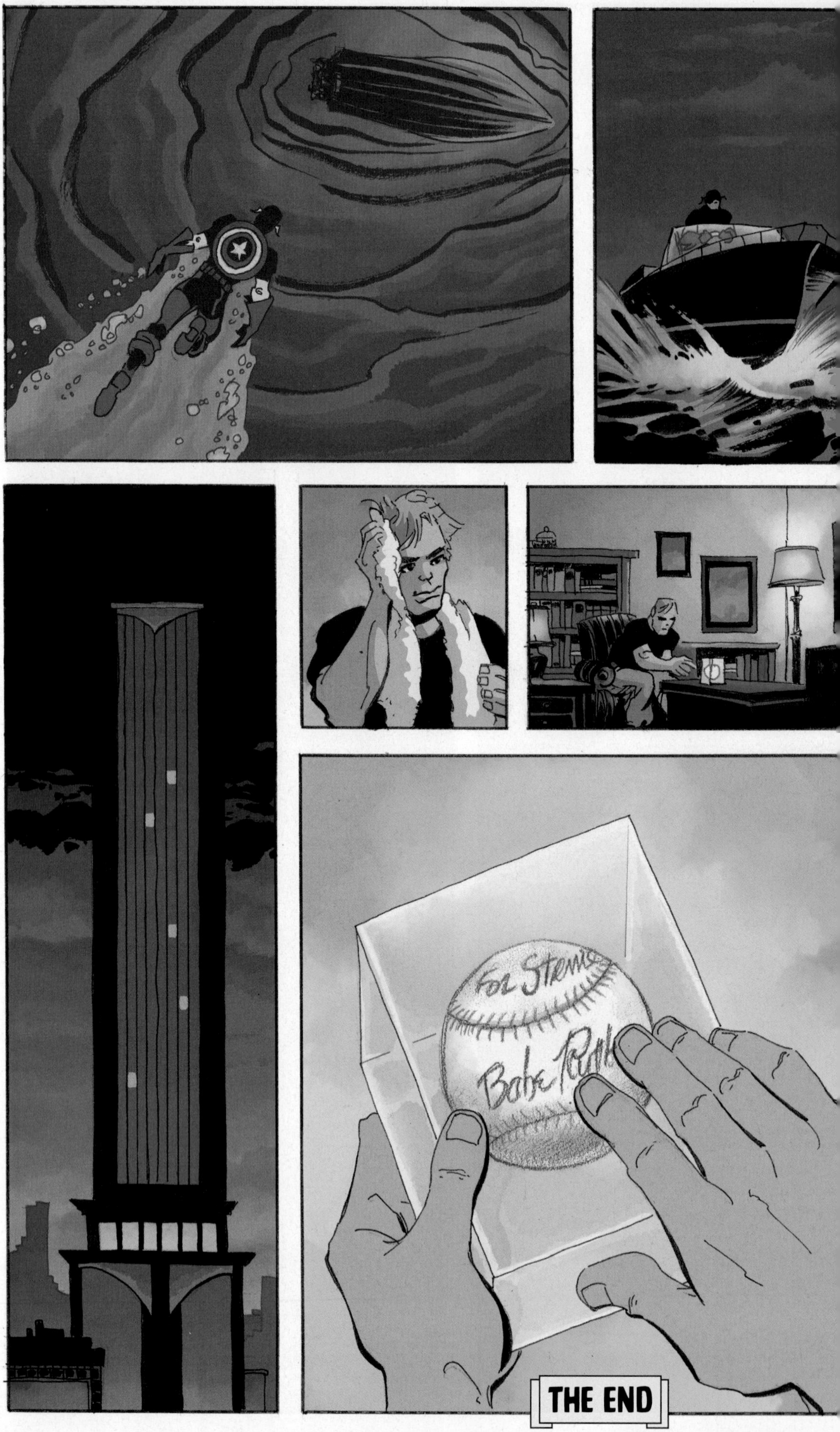
THE END

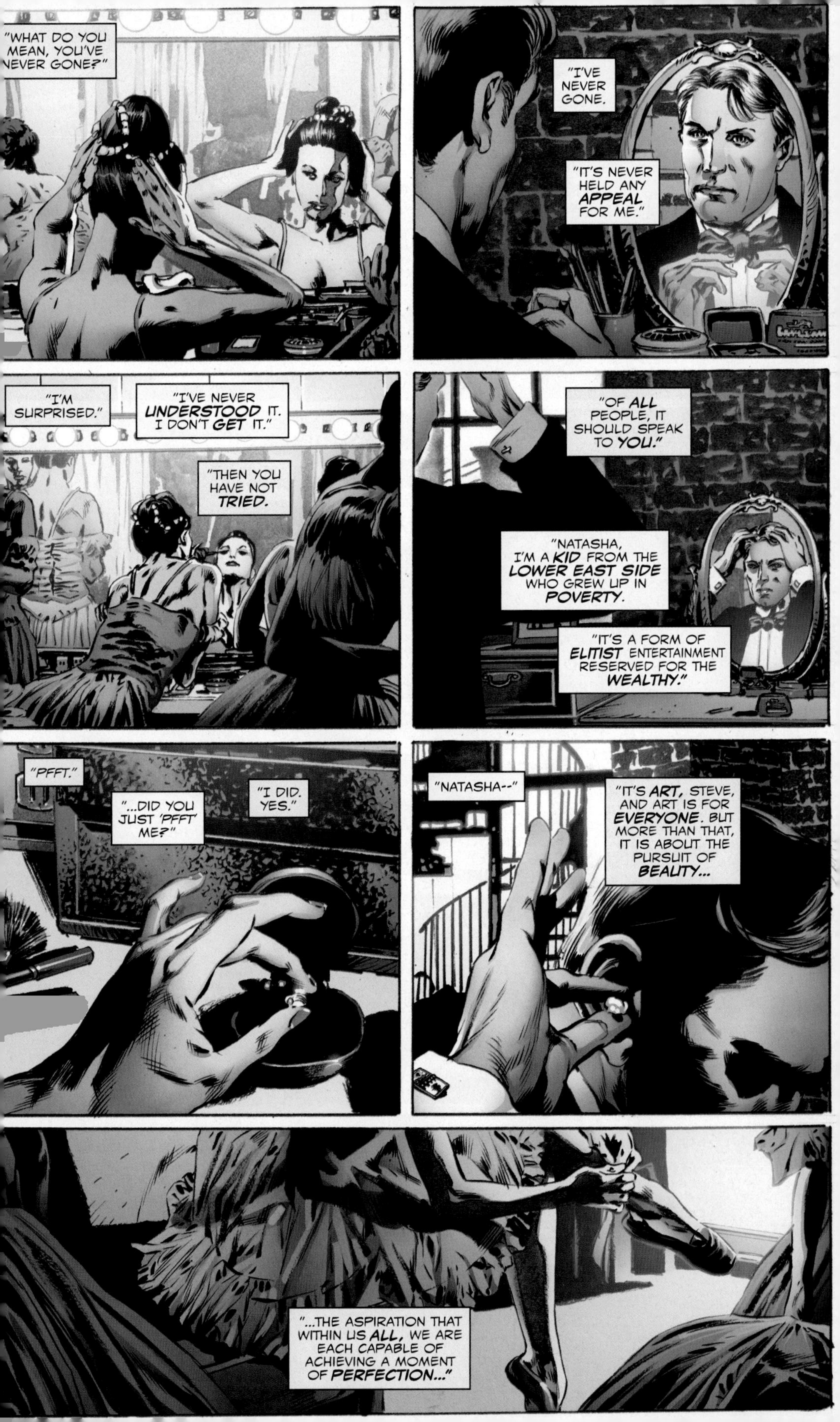
"WHAT DO YOU MEAN, YOU'VE NEVER GONE?"
"I'VE NEVER GONE.
"IT'S NEVER HELD ANY APPEAL FOR ME."
"I'M SURPRISED."
"I'VE NEVER UNDERSTOOD IT. I DON'T GET IT."
"THEN YOU HAVE NOT TRIED.
"OF ALL PEOPLE, IT SHOULD SPEAK TO YOU."
"NATASHA, I'M A KID FROM THE LOWER EAST SIDE WHO GREW UP IN POVERTY.
"IT'S A FORM OF ELITIST ENTERTAINMENT RESERVED FOR THE WEALTHY."
"PFFT."
"...DID YOU JUST 'PFFT' ME?"
"I DID. YES."
"NATASHA--"
"IT'S ART, STEVE, AND ART IS FOR EVERYONE. BUT MORE THAN THAT, IT IS ABOUT THE PURSUIT OF BEAUTY...
"...THE ASPIRATION THAT WITHIN US ALL, WE ARE EACH CAPABLE OF ACHIEVING A MOMENT OF PERFECTION..."

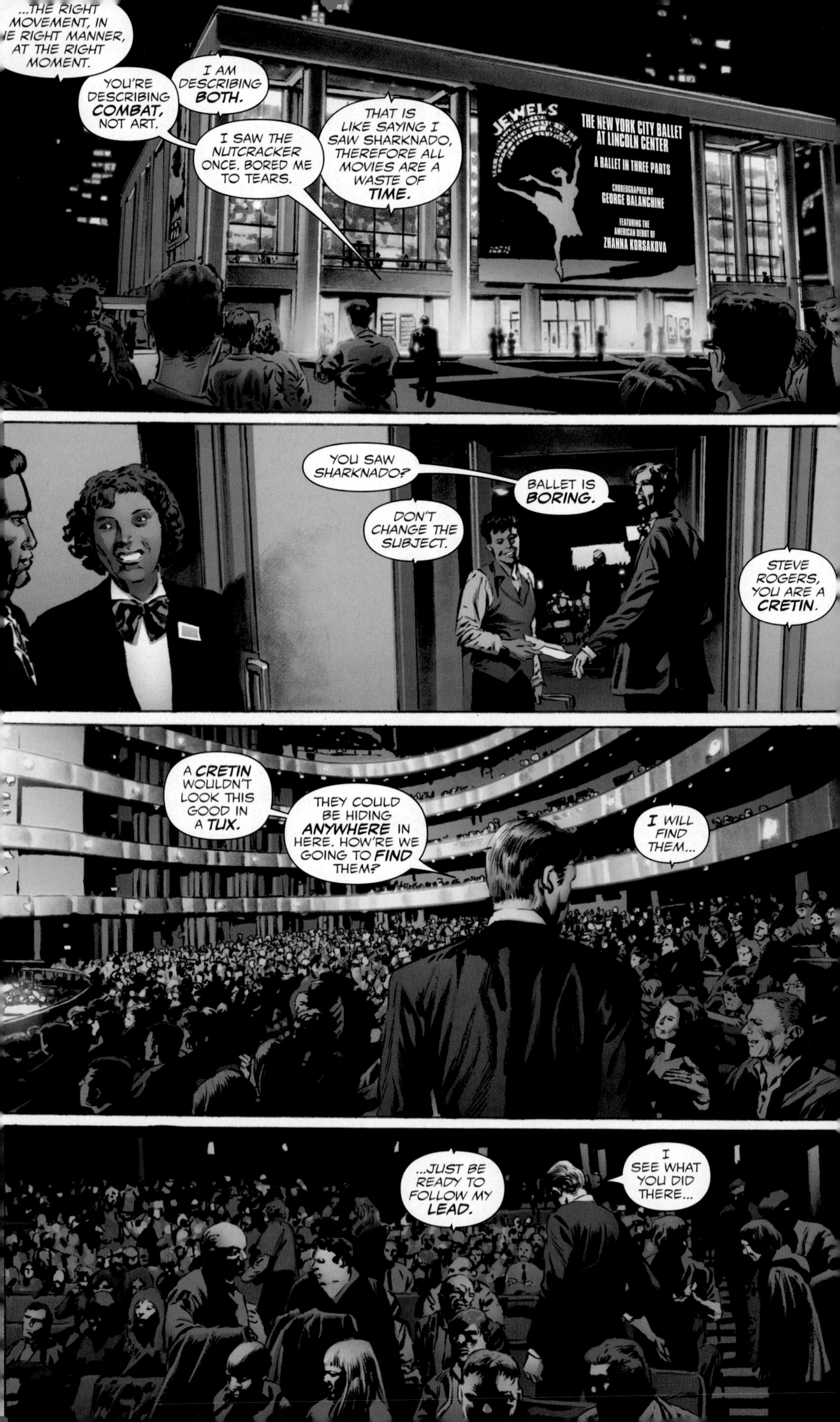
...THE RIGHT MOVEMENT, IN E RIGHT MANNER, AT THE RIGHT MOMENT.
YOU'RE DESCRIBING COMBAT, NOT ART.
I AM DESCRIBING BOTH.
I SAW THE NUTCRACKER ONCE. BORED ME TO TEARS.
THAT IS LIKE SAYING I SAW SHARKNADO, THEREFORE ALL MOVIES ARE A WASTE OF TIME.
JEWELS
THE NEW YORK CITY BALLET AT LINCOLN CENTER
A BALLET IN THREE PARTS
CHOREOGRAPHED BY GEORGE BALANCHINE
FEATURING THE AMERICAN DEBUT OF ZHANNA KORSAKOVA
YOU SAW SHARKNADO?
BALLET IS BORING.
DON'T CHANGE THE SUBJECT.
STEVE ROGERS, YOU ARE A CRETIN.
A CRETIN WOULDN'T LOOK THIS GOOD IN A TUX.
THEY COULD BE HIDING ANYWHERE IN HERE. HOW'RE WE GOING TO FIND THEM?
I WILL FIND THEM...
...JUST BE READY TO FOLLOW MY LEAD.
I SEE WHAT YOU DID THERE...

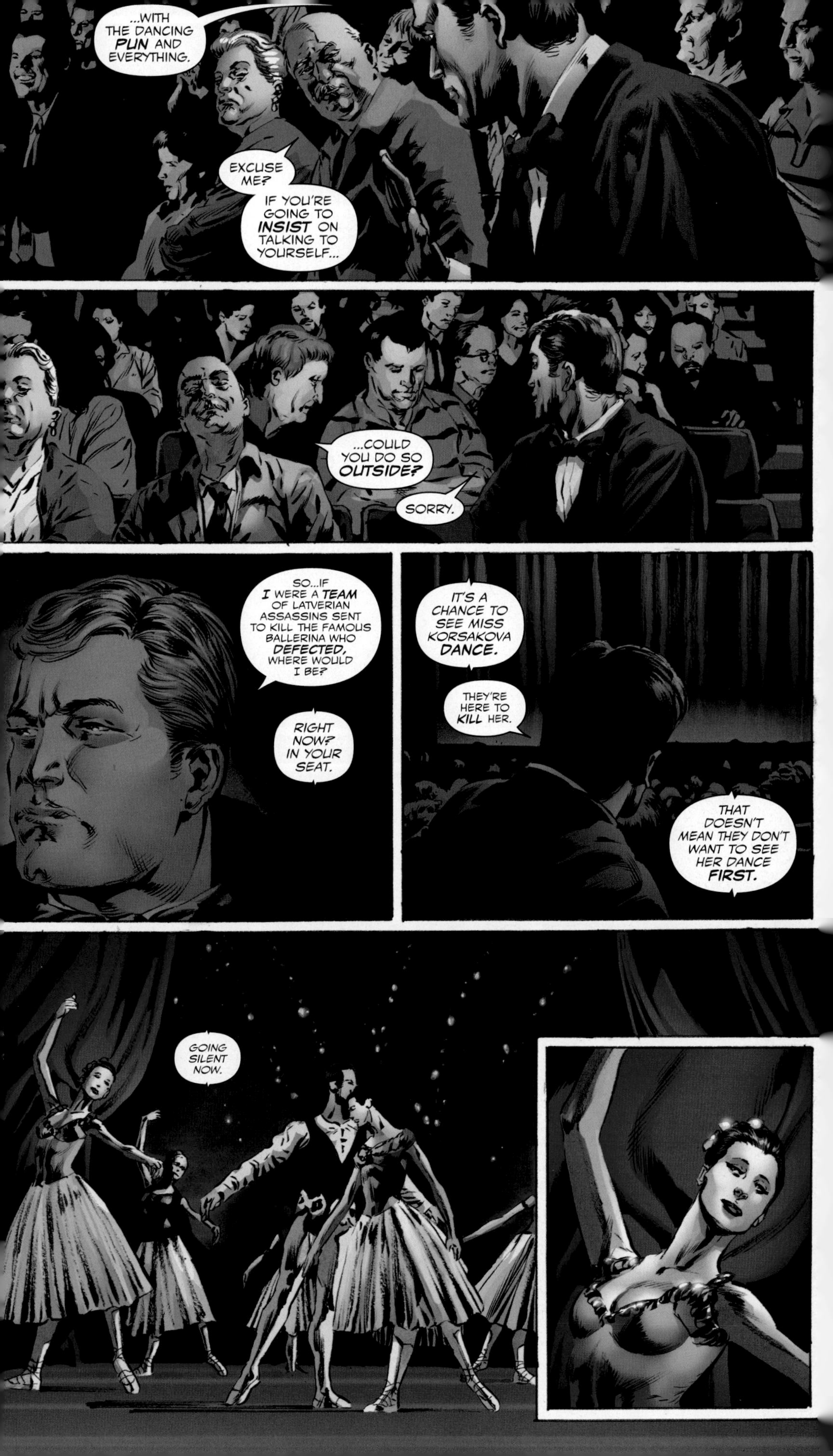

...WITH THE DANCING PUN AND EVERYTHING.
EXCUSE ME?
IF YOU'RE GOING TO INSIST ON TALKING TO YOURSELF...
...COULD YOU DO SO OUTSIDE?
SORRY.
SO...IF I WERE A TEAM OF LATVERIAN ASSASSINS SENT TO KILL THE FAMOUS BALLERINA WHO DEFECTED, WHERE WOULD I BE?
RIGHT NOW? IN YOUR SEAT.
IT'S A CHANCE TO SEE MISS KORSAKOVA DANCE.
THEY'RE HERE TO KILL HER.
THAT DOESN'T MEAN THEY DON'T WANT TO SEE HER DANCE FIRST.
GOING SILENT NOW.

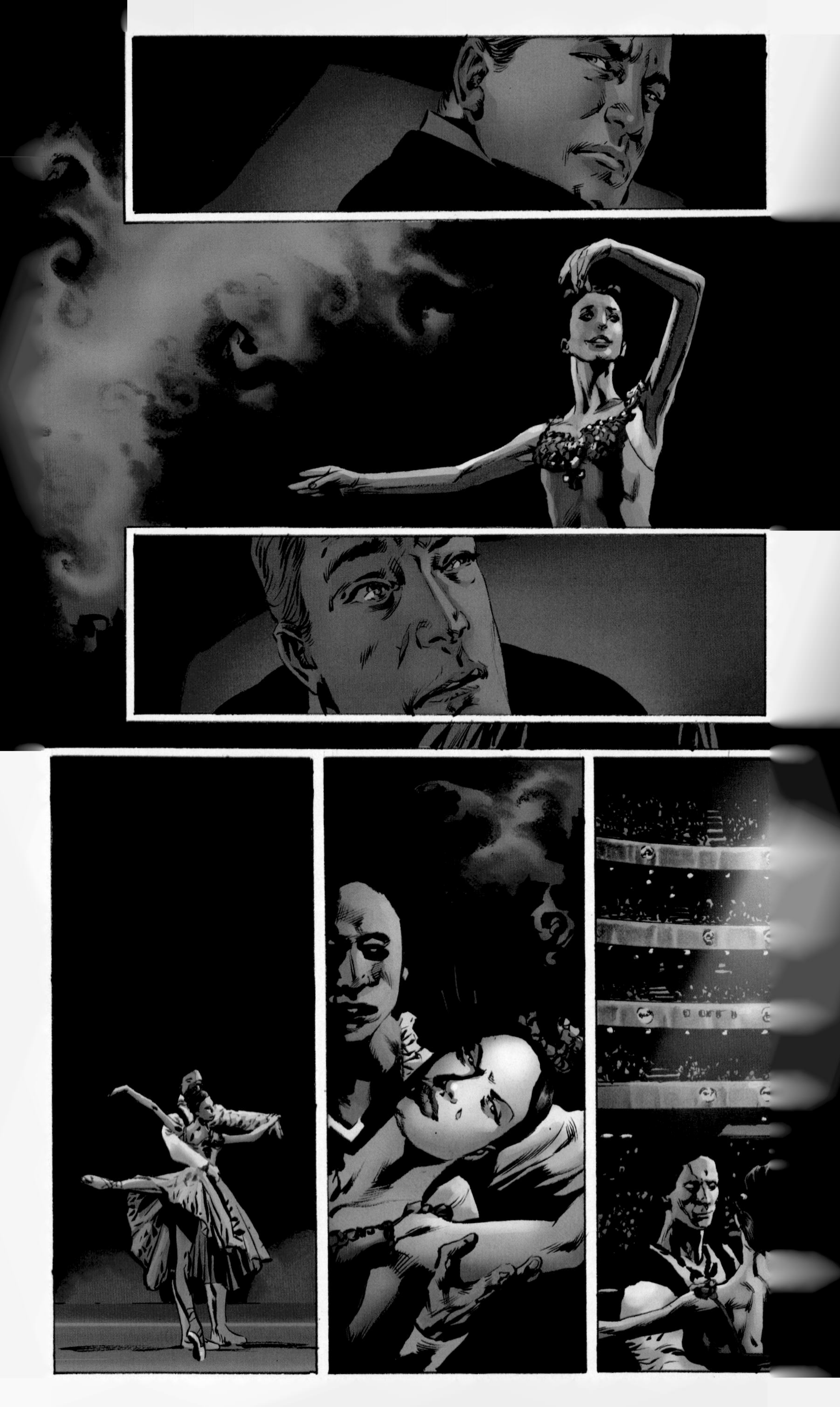

SHE'S *VERY* GOOD. IS SHE NEW? I'VE NEVER--

SHHH.

DID I JUST HEAR YOU *APPLAUD*, CAPTAIN?

NOT ME. YOUR *FEET* MUST BE *KILLING* YOU.

I'VE BEEN THROUGH *WORSE.*

ONE TEAM, *SNIPER* AND *SPOTTER*...

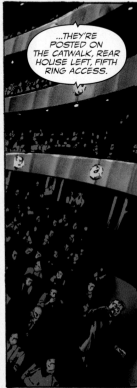
...THEY'RE POSTED ON THE CATWALK, REAR HOUSE LEFT, FIFTH RING ACCESS.

HOW MUCH TIME DO I HAVE?

LESS THAN YOU WOULD LIKE.

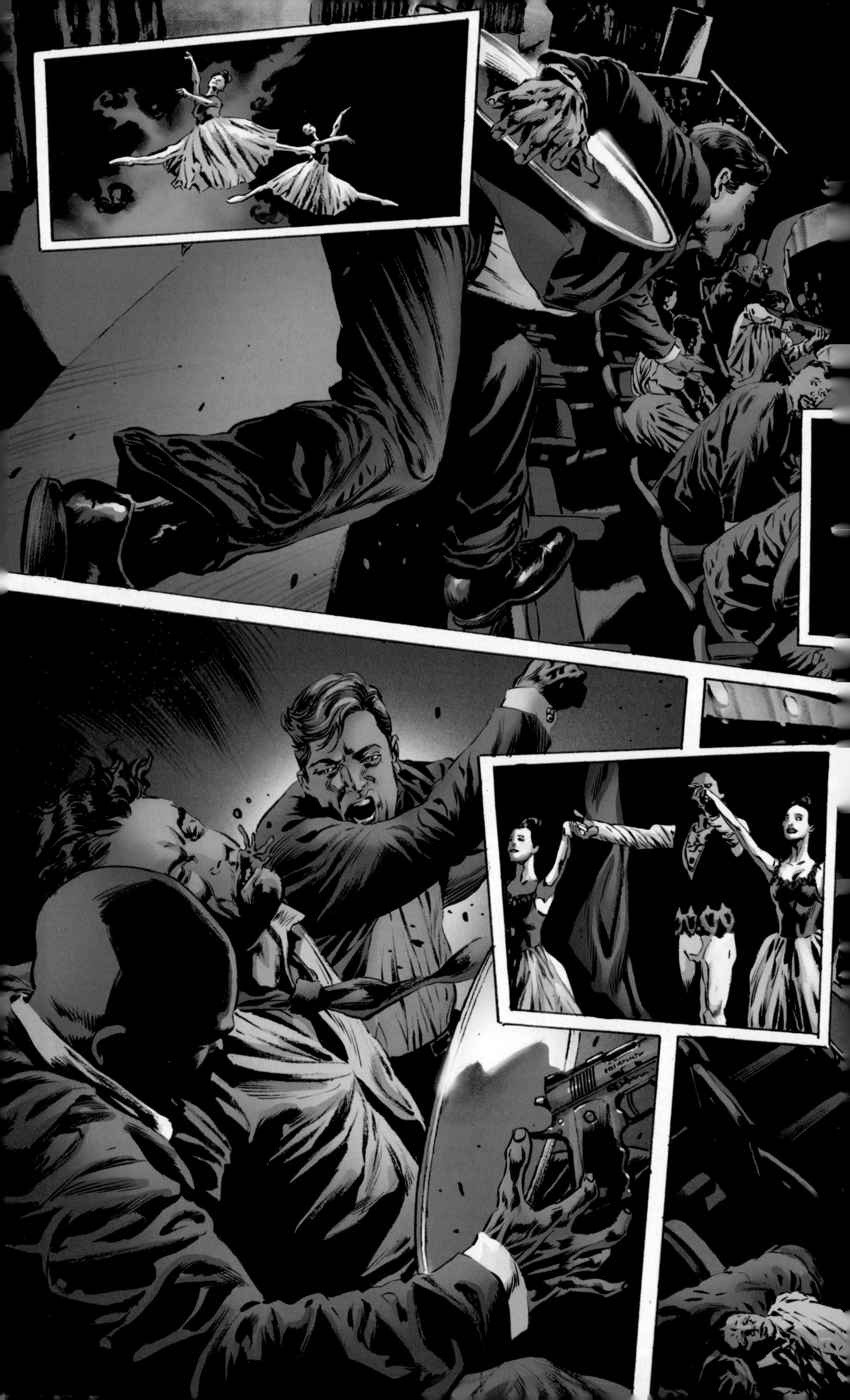

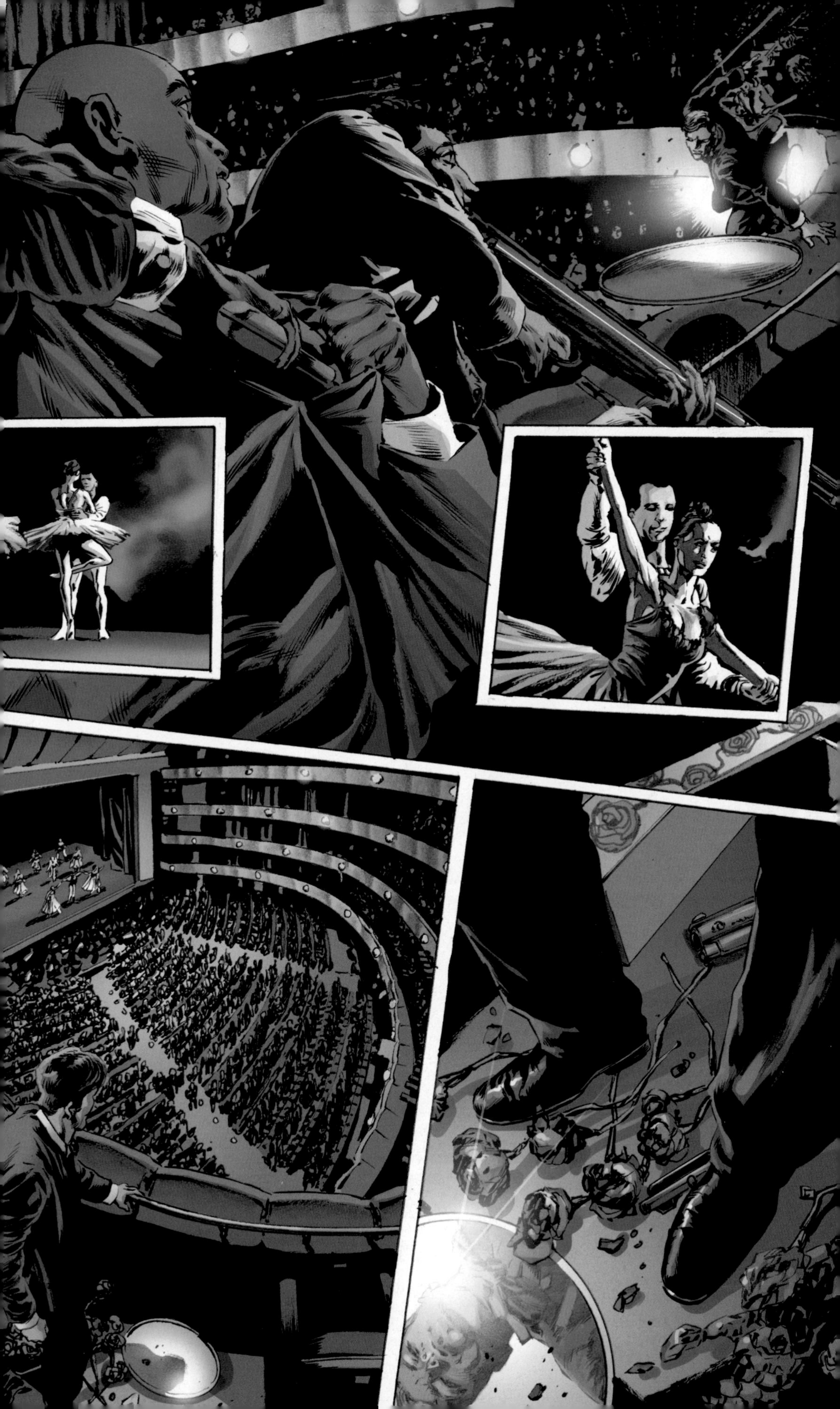

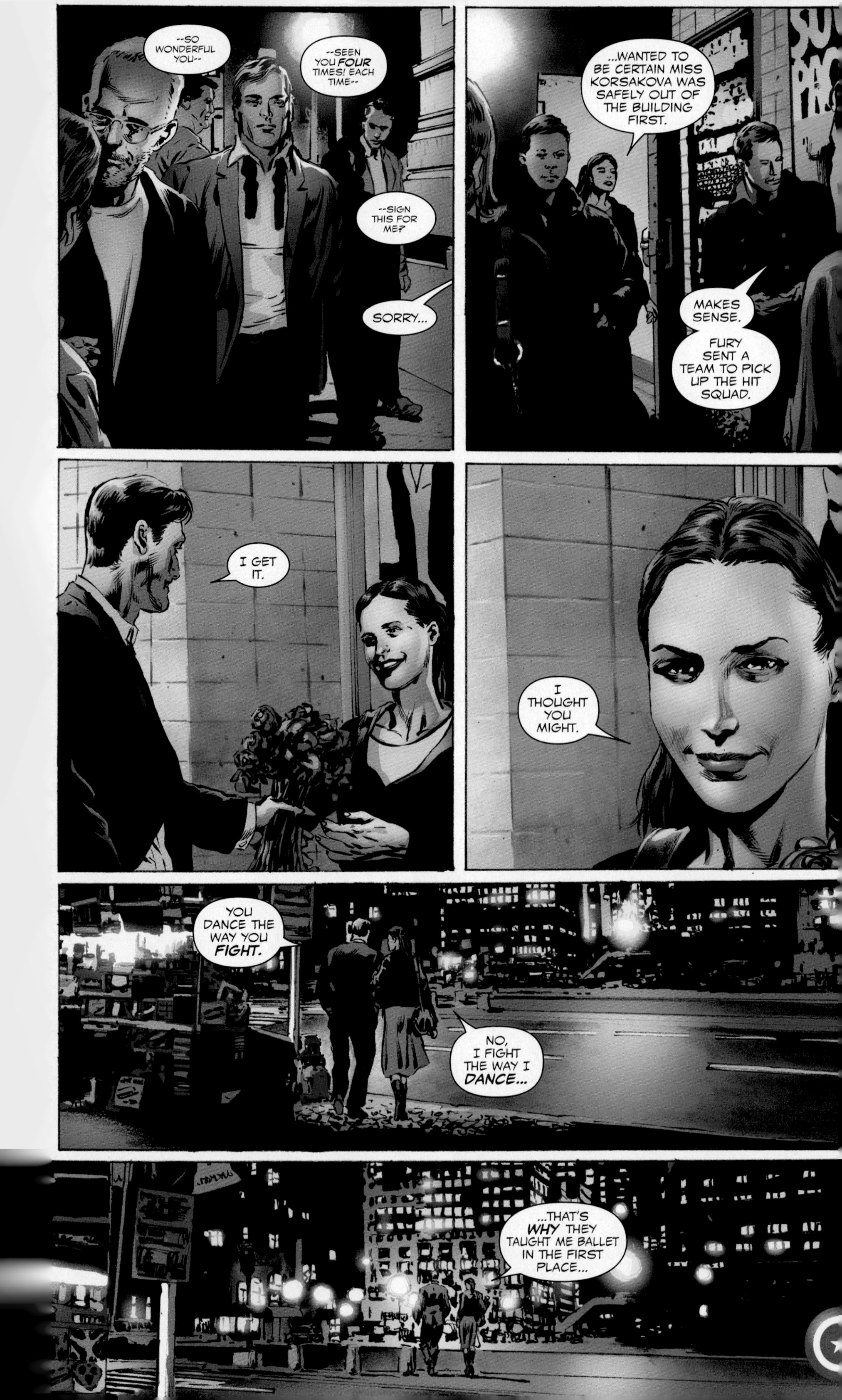
--SO WONDERFUL YOU--
--SEEN YOU FOUR TIMES! EACH TIME--
--SIGN THIS FOR ME?
SORRY...
...WANTED TO BE CERTAIN MISS KORSAKOVA WAS SAFELY OUT OF THE BUILDING FIRST.
MAKES SENSE.
FURY SENT A TEAM TO PICK UP THE HIT SQUAD.
I GET IT.
I THOUGHT YOU MIGHT.
YOU DANCE THE WAY YOU FIGHT.
NO, I FIGHT THE WAY I DANCE...
...THAT'S WHY THEY TAUGHT ME BALLET IN THE FIRST PLACE...

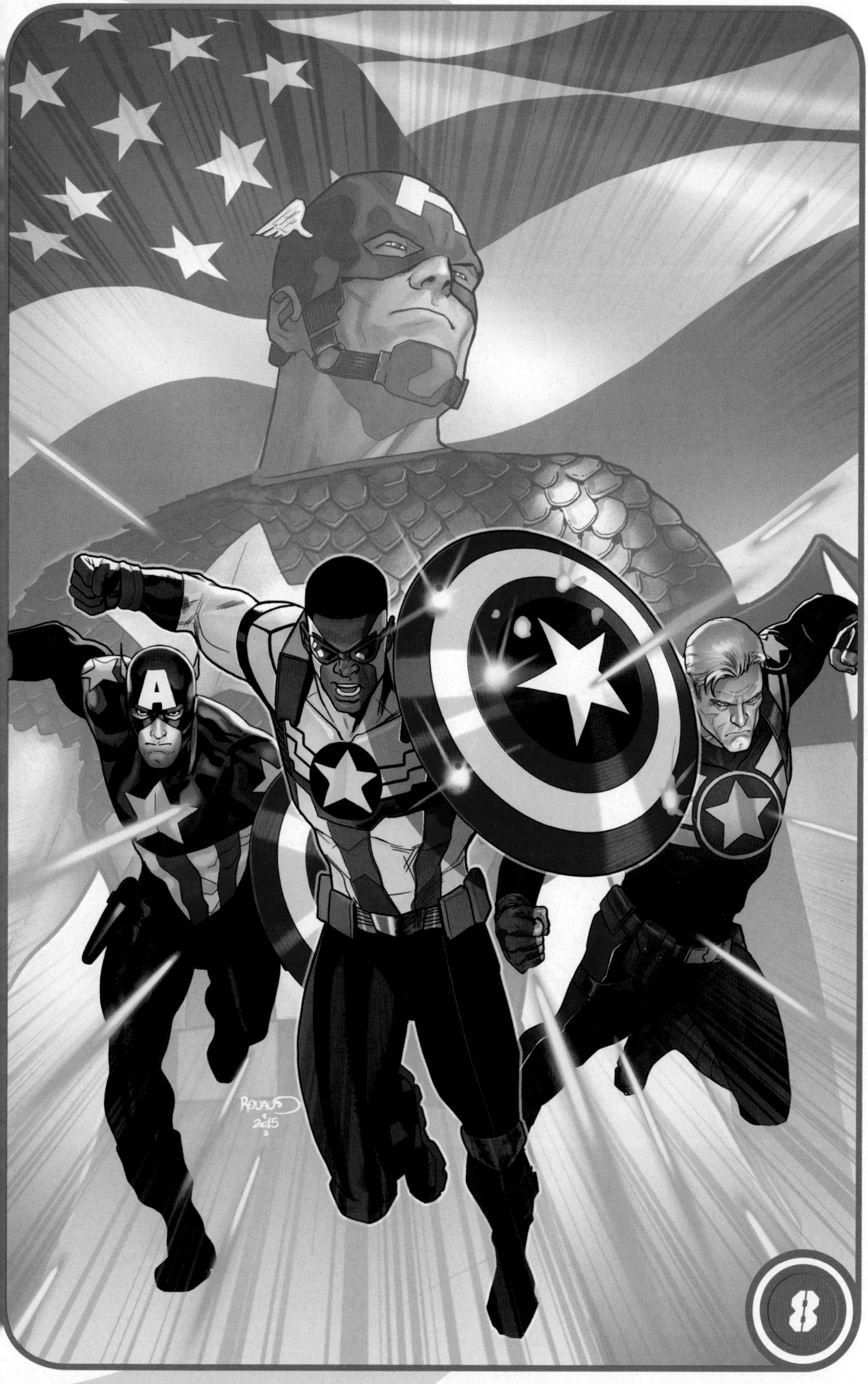
8

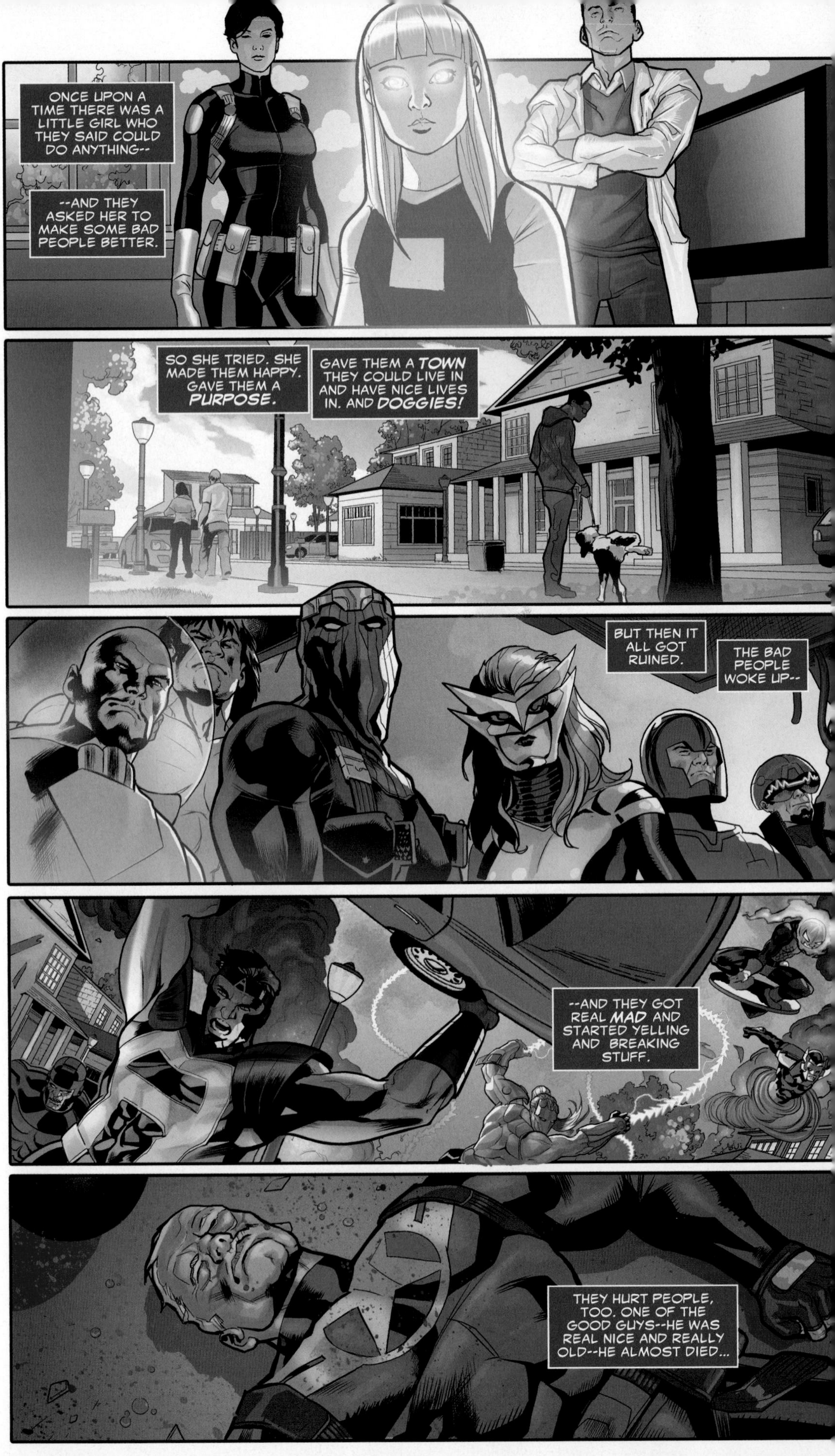
ONCE UPON A TIME THERE WAS A LITTLE GIRL WHO THEY SAID COULD DO ANYTHING--
--AND THEY ASKED HER TO MAKE SOME BAD PEOPLE BETTER.
SO SHE TRIED. SHE MADE THEM HAPPY. GAVE THEM A PURPOSE.
GAVE THEM A TOWN THEY COULD LIVE IN AND HAVE NICE LIVES IN. AND DOGGIES!
BUT THEN IT ALL GOT RUINED.
THE BAD PEOPLE WOKE UP--
--AND THEY GOT REAL MAD AND STARTED YELLING AND BREAKING STUFF.
THEY HURT PEOPLE, TOO. ONE OF THE GOOD GUYS--HE WAS REAL NICE AND REALLY OLD--HE ALMOST DIED...

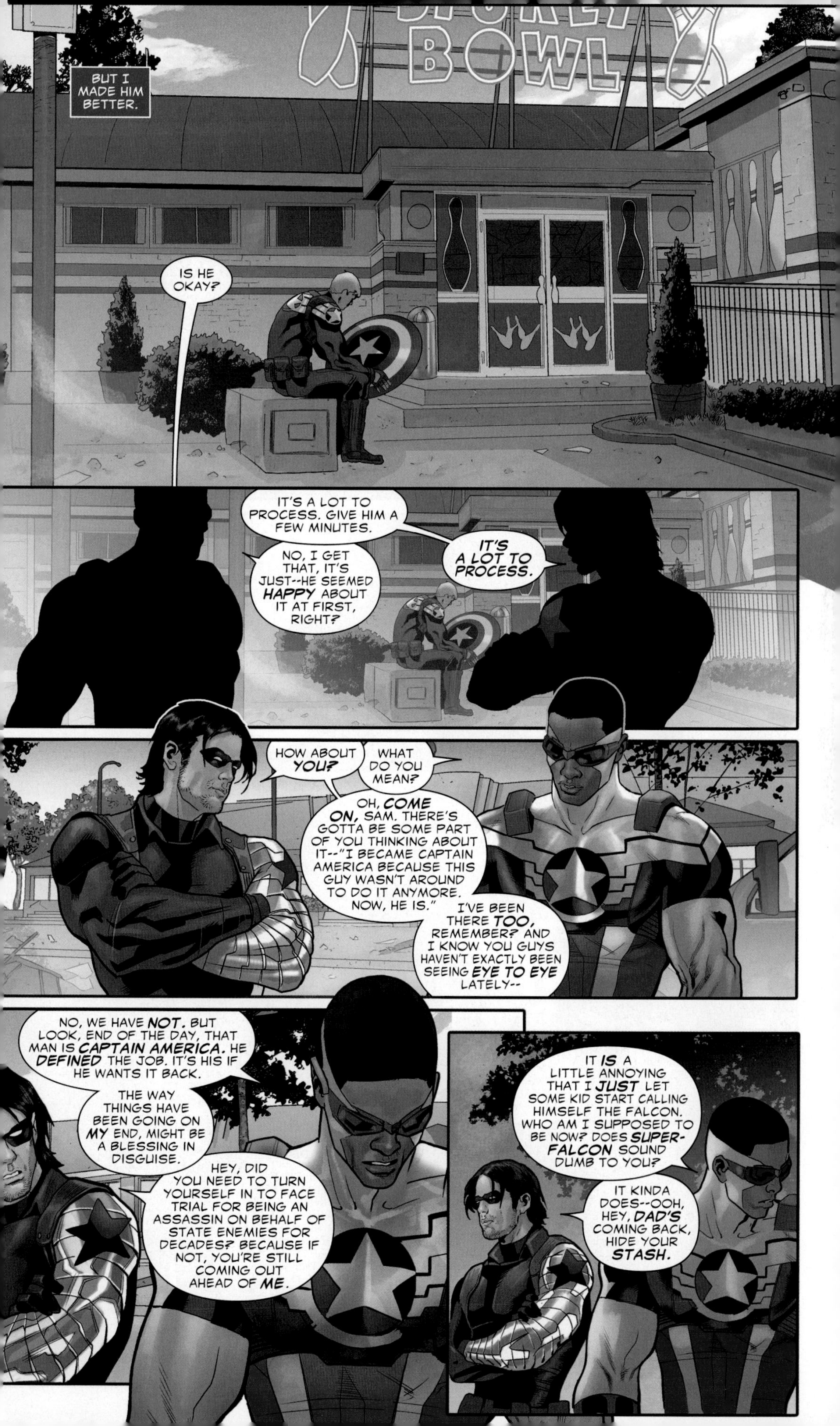
BOWL
BUT I MADE HIM BETTER.
IS HE OKAY?
IT'S A LOT TO PROCESS. GIVE HIM A FEW MINUTES.
NO, I GET THAT, IT'S JUST--HE SEEMED HAPPY ABOUT IT AT FIRST, RIGHT?
IT'S A LOT TO PROCESS.
HOW ABOUT YOU?
WHAT DO YOU MEAN?
OH, COME ON, SAM. THERE'S GOTTA BE SOME PART OF YOU THINKING ABOUT IT--"I BECAME CAPTAIN AMERICA BECAUSE THIS GUY WASN'T AROUND TO DO IT ANYMORE. NOW, HE IS."
I'VE BEEN THERE TOO, REMEMBER? AND I KNOW YOU GUYS HAVEN'T EXACTLY BEEN SEEING EYE TO EYE LATELY--
NO, WE HAVE NOT. BUT LOOK, END OF THE DAY, THAT MAN IS CAPTAIN AMERICA. HE DEFINED THE JOB. IT'S HIS IF HE WANTS IT BACK.
THE WAY THINGS HAVE BEEN GOING ON MY END, MIGHT BE A BLESSING IN DISGUISE.
HEY, DID YOU NEED TO TURN YOURSELF IN TO FACE TRIAL FOR BEING AN ASSASSIN ON BEHALF OF STATE ENEMIES FOR DECADES? BECAUSE IF NOT, YOU'RE STILL COMING OUT AHEAD OF ME.
IT IS A LITTLE ANNOYING THAT I JUST LET SOME KID START CALLING HIMSELF THE FALCON. WHO AM I SUPPOSED TO BE NOW? DOES SUPER-FALCON SOUND DUMB TO YOU?
IT KINDA DOES--OOH, HEY, DAD'S COMING BACK, HIDE YOUR STASH.

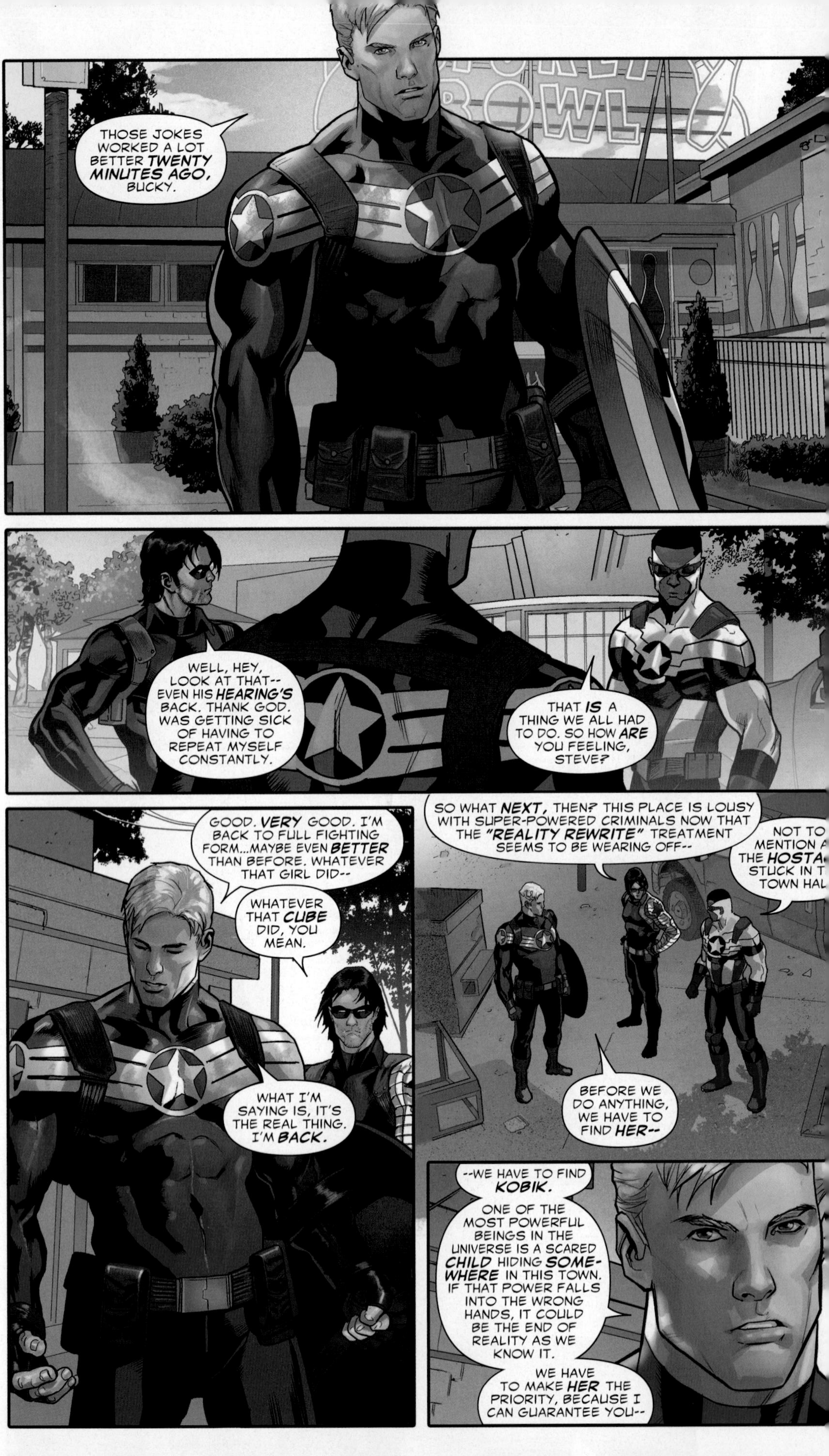
THOSE JOKES WORKED A LOT BETTER TWENTY MINUTES AGO, BUCKY.
WELL, HEY, LOOK AT THAT-- EVEN HIS HEARING'S BACK. THANK GOD. WAS GETTING SICK OF HAVING TO REPEAT MYSELF CONSTANTLY.
THAT IS A THING WE ALL HAD TO DO. SO HOW ARE YOU FEELING, STEVE?
GOOD. VERY GOOD. I'M BACK TO FULL FIGHTING FORM...MAYBE EVEN BETTER THAN BEFORE. WHATEVER THAT GIRL DID--
WHATEVER THAT CUBE DID, YOU MEAN.
WHAT I'M SAYING IS, IT'S THE REAL THING. I'M BACK.
SO WHAT NEXT, THEN? THIS PLACE IS LOUSY WITH SUPER-POWERED CRIMINALS NOW THAT THE "REALITY REWRITE" TREATMENT SEEMS TO BE WEARING OFF--
NOT TO MENTION A THE HOSTA STUCK IN T TOWN HAL
BEFORE WE DO ANYTHING, WE HAVE TO FIND HER--
--WE HAVE TO FIND KOBIK.
ONE OF THE MOST POWERFUL BEINGS IN THE UNIVERSE IS A SCARED CHILD HIDING SOME-WHERE IN THIS TOWN. IF THAT POWER FALLS INTO THE WRONG HANDS, IT COULD BE THE END OF REALITY AS WE KNOW IT.
WE HAVE TO MAKE HER THE PRIORITY, BECAUSE I CAN GUARANTEE YOU--

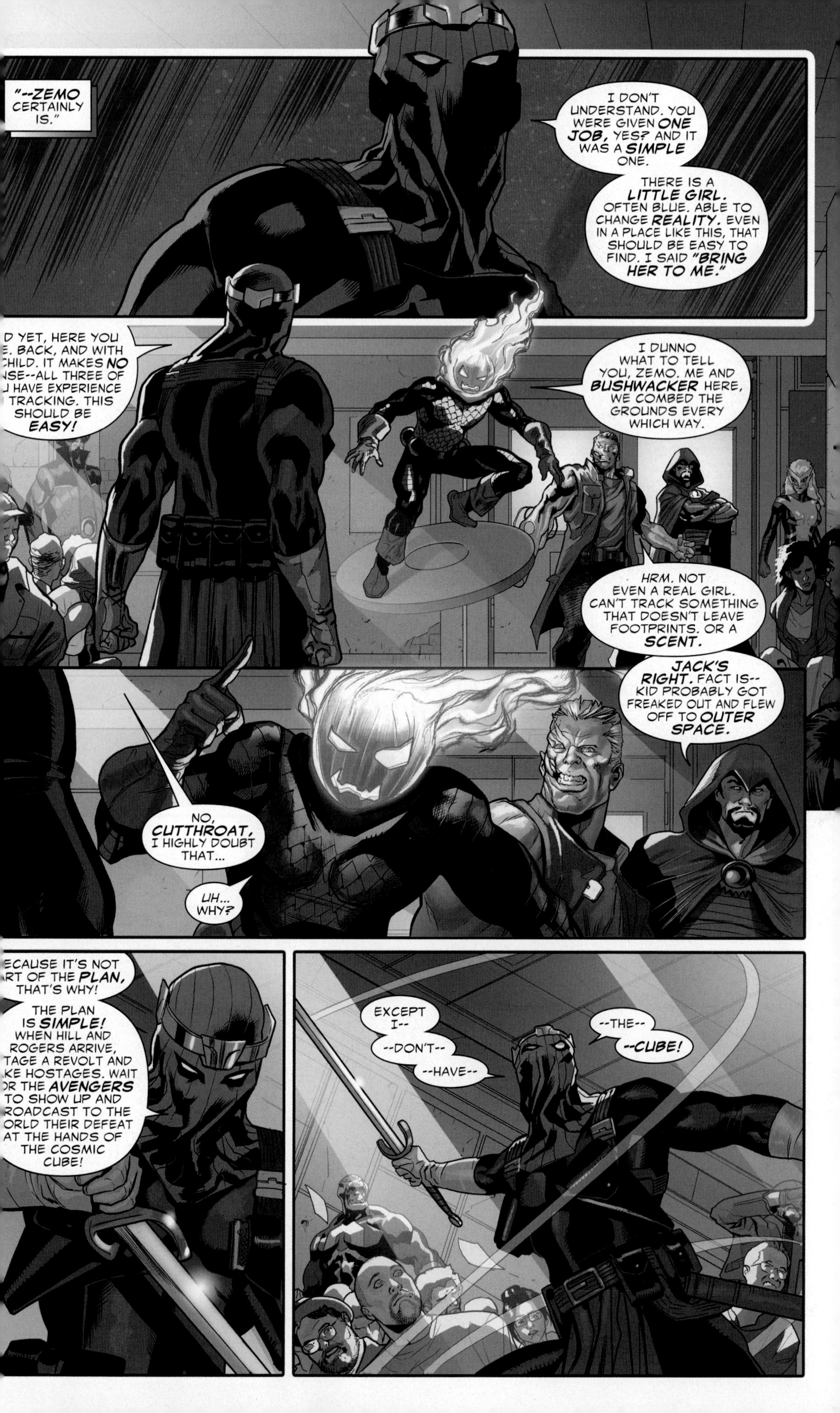
"--ZEMO CERTAINLY IS."
I DON'T UNDERSTAND. YOU WERE GIVEN ONE JOB, YES? AND IT WAS A SIMPLE ONE.
THERE IS A LITTLE GIRL. OFTEN BLUE. ABLE TO CHANGE REALITY. EVEN IN A PLACE LIKE THIS, THAT SHOULD BE EASY TO FIND. I SAID "BRING HER TO ME."
D YET, HERE YOU E. BACK, AND WITH CHILD. IT MAKES NO NSE--ALL THREE OF U HAVE EXPERIENCE TRACKING. THIS SHOULD BE EASY!
I DUNNO WHAT TO TELL YOU, ZEMO. ME AND BUSHWACKER HERE, WE COMBED THE GROUNDS EVERY WHICH WAY.
HRM. NOT EVEN A REAL GIRL. CAN'T TRACK SOMETHING THAT DOESN'T LEAVE FOOTPRINTS. OR A SCENT.
JACK'S RIGHT. FACT IS-- KID PROBABLY GOT FREAKED OUT AND FLEW OFF TO OUTER SPACE.
NO, CUTTHROAT, I HIGHLY DOUBT THAT...
UH... WHY?
ECAUSE IT'S NOT RT OF THE PLAN, THAT'S WHY!
THE PLAN IS SIMPLE! WHEN HILL AND ROGERS ARRIVE, TAGE A REVOLT AND KE HOSTAGES. WAIT OR THE AVENGERS TO SHOW UP AND ROADCAST TO THE ORLD THEIR DEFEAT AT THE HANDS OF THE COSMIC CUBE!
EXCEPT I--
--DON'T--
--HAVE--
--THE--
--CUBE!

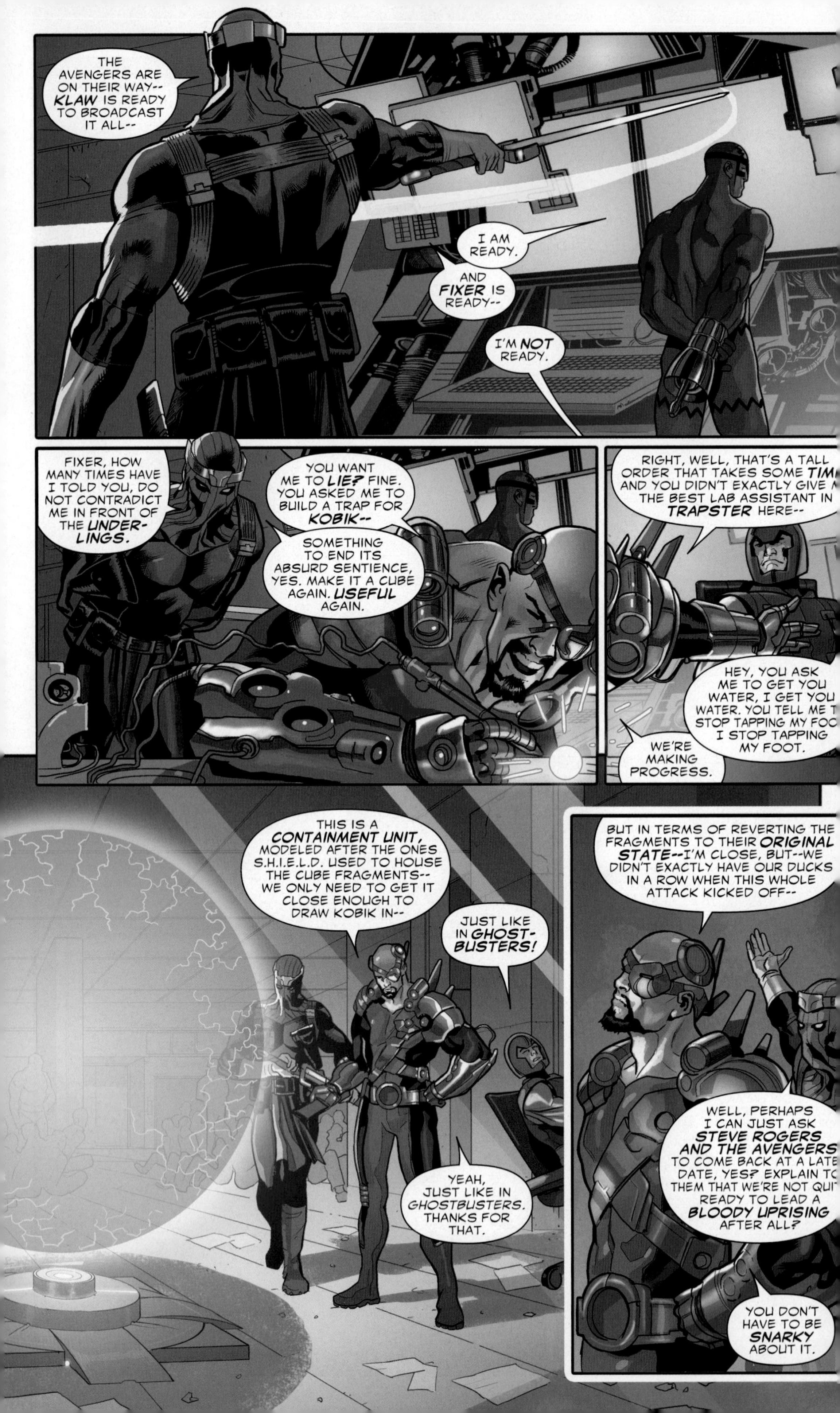

THE AVENGERS ARE ON THEIR WAY-- KLAW IS READY TO BROADCAST IT ALL--
I AM READY.
AND FIXER IS READY--
I'M NOT READY.
FIXER, HOW MANY TIMES HAVE I TOLD YOU, DO NOT CONTRADICT ME IN FRONT OF THE UNDER-LINGS.
YOU WANT ME TO LIE? FINE. YOU ASKED ME TO BUILD A TRAP FOR KOBIK--
SOMETHING TO END ITS ABSURD SENTIENCE, YES. MAKE IT A CUBE AGAIN. USEFUL AGAIN.
RIGHT, WELL, THAT'S A TALL ORDER THAT TAKES SOME TIM
AND YOU DIDN'T EXACTLY GIVE
THE BEST LAB ASSISTANT IN TRAPSTER HERE--
HEY, YOU ASK ME TO GET YOU WATER, I GET YOU WATER. YOU TELL ME T STOP TAPPING MY FOO I STOP TAPPING MY FOOT.
WE'RE MAKING PROGRESS.
THIS IS A CONTAINMENT UNIT, MODELED AFTER THE ONES S.H.I.E.L.D. USED TO HOUSE THE CUBE FRAGMENTS-- WE ONLY NEED TO GET IT CLOSE ENOUGH TO DRAW KOBIK IN--
JUST LIKE IN GHOST-BUSTERS!
YEAH, JUST LIKE IN GHOSTBUSTERS. THANKS FOR THAT.
BUT IN TERMS OF REVERTING THE FRAGMENTS TO THEIR ORIGINAL STATE--I'M CLOSE, BUT--WE DIDN'T EXACTLY HAVE OUR DUCKS IN A ROW WHEN THIS WHOLE ATTACK KICKED OFF--
WELL, PERHAPS I CAN JUST ASK STEVE ROGERS AND THE AVENGERS TO COME BACK AT A LATE DATE, YES? EXPLAIN TO THEM THAT WE'RE NOT QUI READY TO LEAD A BLOODY UPRISING AFTER ALL?
YOU DON'T HAVE TO BE SNARKY ABOUT IT.

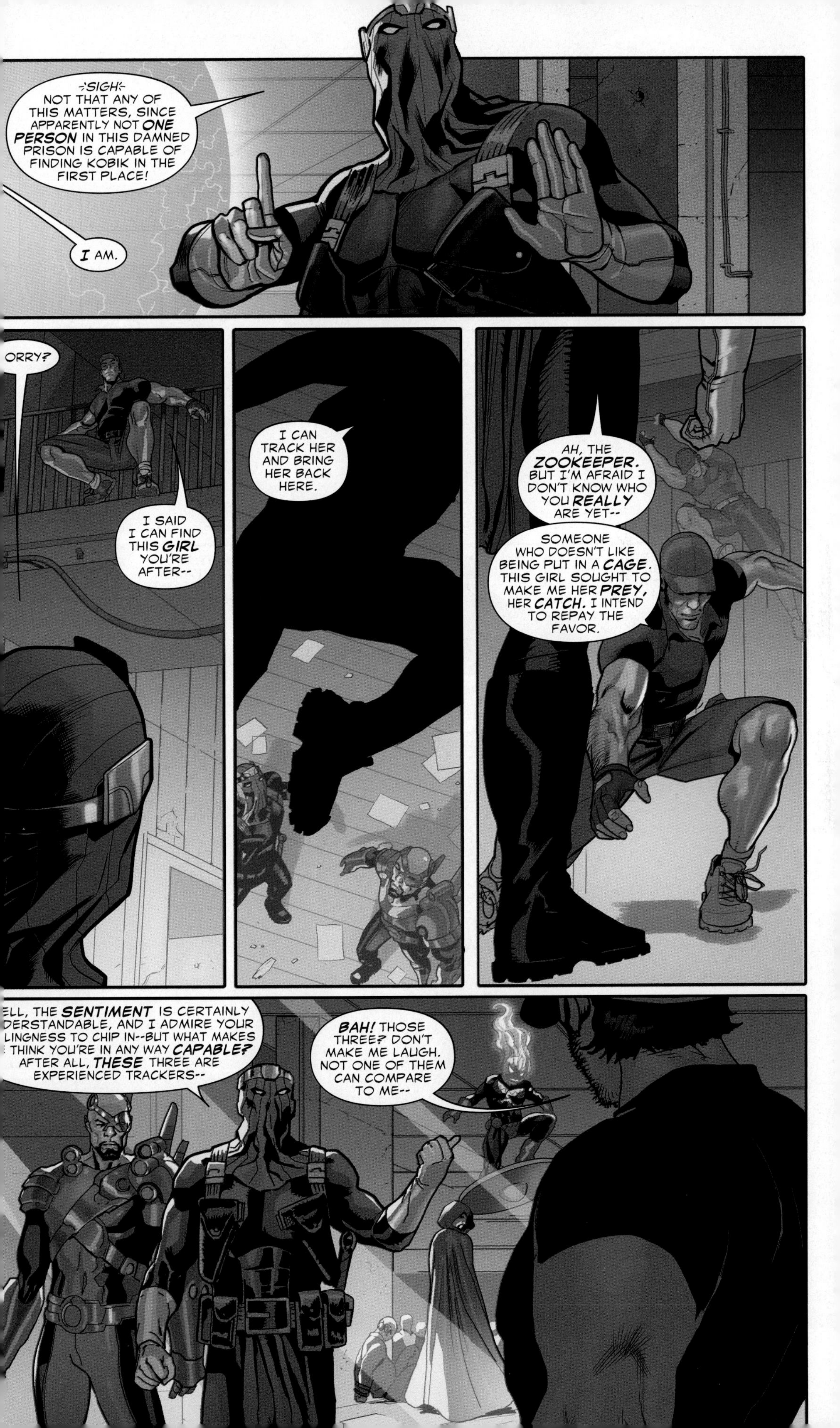

SIGH NOT THAT ANY OF THIS MATTERS, SINCE APPARENTLY NOT **ONE PERSON** IN THIS DAMNED PRISON IS CAPABLE OF FINDING KOBIK IN THE FIRST PLACE!
I AM.
ORRY?
I SAID I CAN FIND THIS **GIRL** YOU'RE AFTER--
I CAN TRACK HER AND BRING HER BACK HERE.
AH, THE **ZOOKEEPER.** BUT I'M AFRAID I DON'T KNOW WHO YOU **REALLY** ARE YET--
SOMEONE WHO DOESN'T LIKE BEING PUT IN A **CAGE**. THIS GIRL SOUGHT TO MAKE ME HER **PREY,** HER **CATCH.** I INTEND TO REPAY THE FAVOR.
ELL, THE **SENTIMENT** IS CERTAINLY DERSTANDABLE, AND I ADMIRE YOUR LINGNESS TO CHIP IN--BUT WHAT MAKES E THINK YOU'RE IN ANY WAY **CAPABLE?** AFTER ALL, **THESE** THREE ARE EXPERIENCED TRACKERS--
BAH! THOSE THREE? DON'T MAKE ME LAUGH. NOT ONE OF THEM CAN COMPARE TO ME--

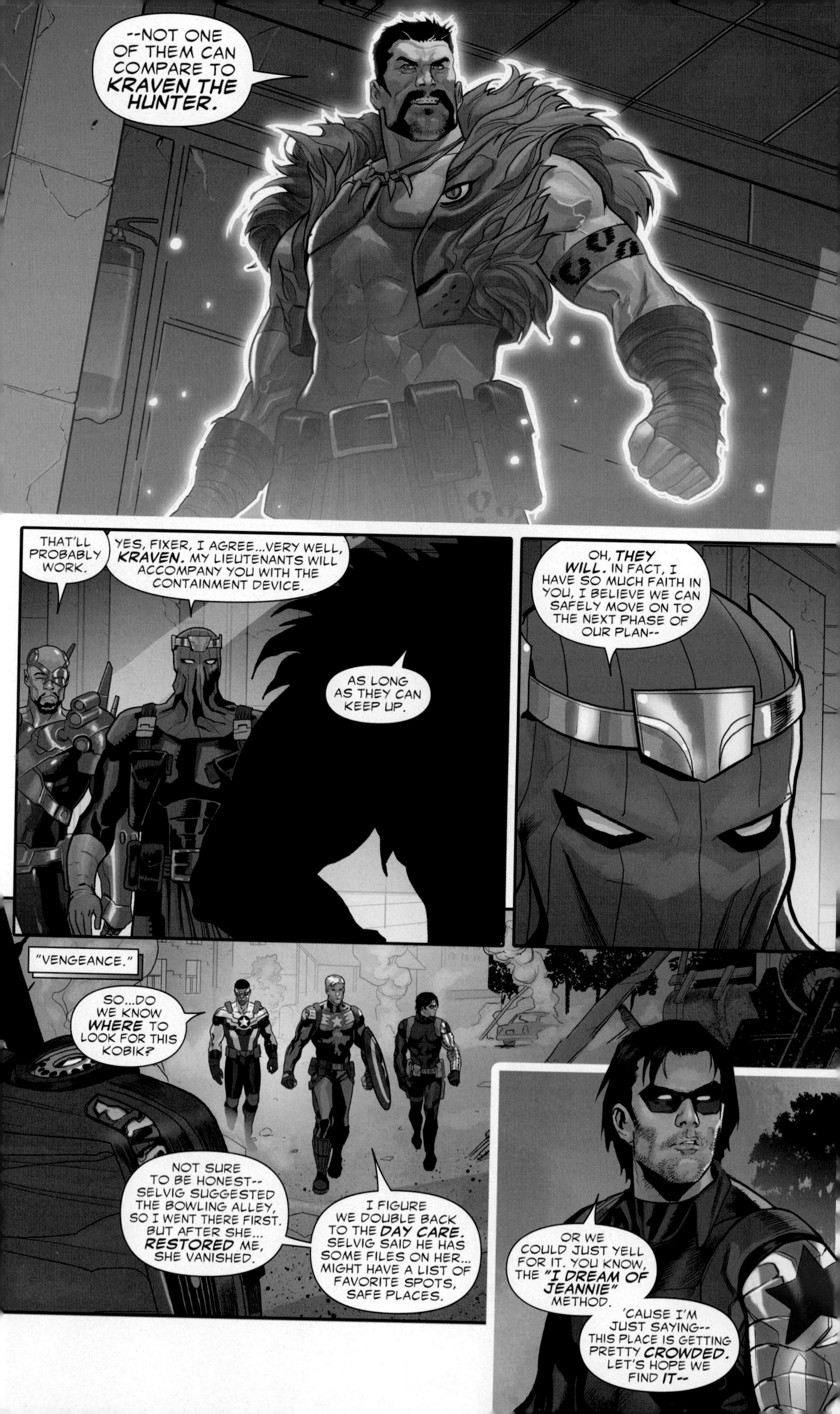
--NOT ONE OF THEM CAN COMPARE TO KRAVEN THE HUNTER.
THAT'LL PROBABLY WORK.
YES, FIXER, I AGREE...VERY WELL, KRAVEN. MY LIEUTENANTS WILL ACCOMPANY YOU WITH THE CONTAINMENT DEVICE.
AS LONG AS THEY CAN KEEP UP.
OH, THEY WILL. IN FACT, I HAVE SO MUCH FAITH IN YOU, I BELIEVE WE CAN SAFELY MOVE ON TO THE NEXT PHASE OF OUR PLAN--
"VENGEANCE."
SO...DO WE KNOW WHERE TO LOOK FOR THIS KOBIK?
NOT SURE TO BE HONEST-- SELVIG SUGGESTED THE BOWLING ALLEY, SO I WENT THERE FIRST. BUT AFTER SHE... RESTORED ME, SHE VANISHED.
I FIGURE WE DOUBLE BACK TO THE DAY CARE. SELVIG SAID HE HAS SOME FILES ON HER... MIGHT HAVE A LIST OF FAVORITE SPOTS, SAFE PLACES.
OR WE COULD JUST YELL FOR IT. YOU KNOW, THE "I DREAM OF JEANNIE" METHOD.
'CAUSE I'M JUST SAYING-- THIS PLACE IS GETTING PRETTY CROWDED. LET'S HOPE WE FIND IT--

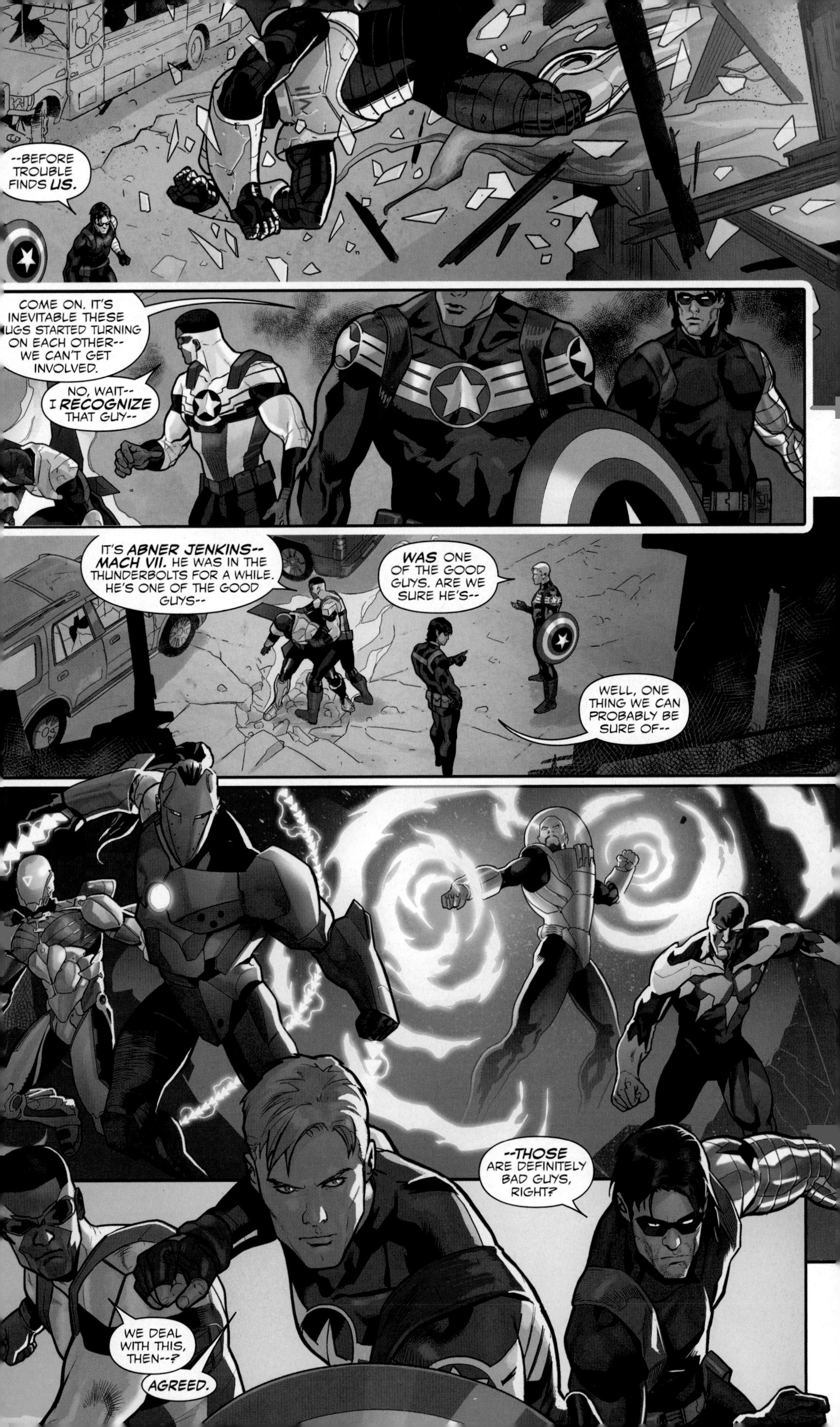

--BEFORE TROUBLE FINDS US.
COME ON. IT'S INEVITABLE THESE (M)UGS STARTED TURNING ON EACH OTHER-- WE CAN'T GET INVOLVED.
NO, WAIT-- I RECOGNIZE THAT GUY--
IT'S ABNER JENKINS-- MACH VII. HE WAS IN THE THUNDERBOLTS FOR A WHILE. HE'S ONE OF THE GOOD GUYS--
WAS ONE OF THE GOOD GUYS. ARE WE SURE HE'S--
WELL, ONE THING WE CAN PROBABLY BE SURE OF--
--THOSE ARE DEFINITELY BAD GUYS, RIGHT?
WE DEAL WITH THIS, THEN--?
AGREED.

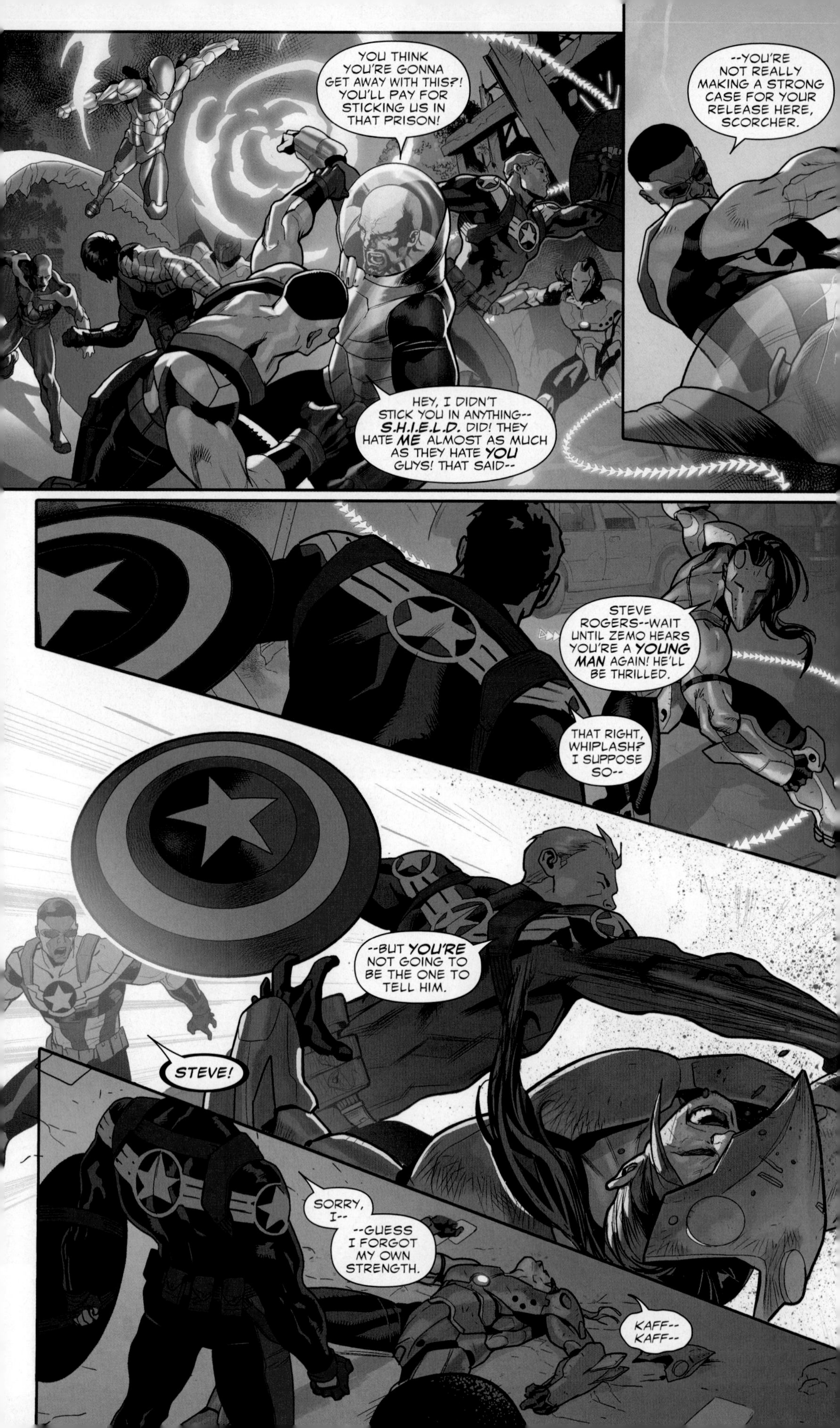
YOU THINK YOU'RE GONNA GET AWAY WITH THIS?! YOU'LL PAY FOR STICKING US IN THAT PRISON!
HEY, I DIDN'T STICK YOU IN ANYTHING-- S.H.I.E.L.D. DID! THEY HATE ME ALMOST AS MUCH AS THEY HATE YOU GUYS! THAT SAID--
--YOU'RE NOT REALLY MAKING A STRONG CASE FOR YOUR RELEASE HERE, SCORCHER.
STEVE ROGERS--WAIT UNTIL ZEMO HEARS YOU'RE A YOUNG MAN AGAIN! HE'LL BE THRILLED.
THAT RIGHT, WHIPLASH? I SUPPOSE SO--
--BUT YOU'RE NOT GOING TO BE THE ONE TO TELL HIM.
STEVE!
SORRY, I--
--GUESS I FORGOT MY OWN STRENGTH.
KAFF-- KAFF--

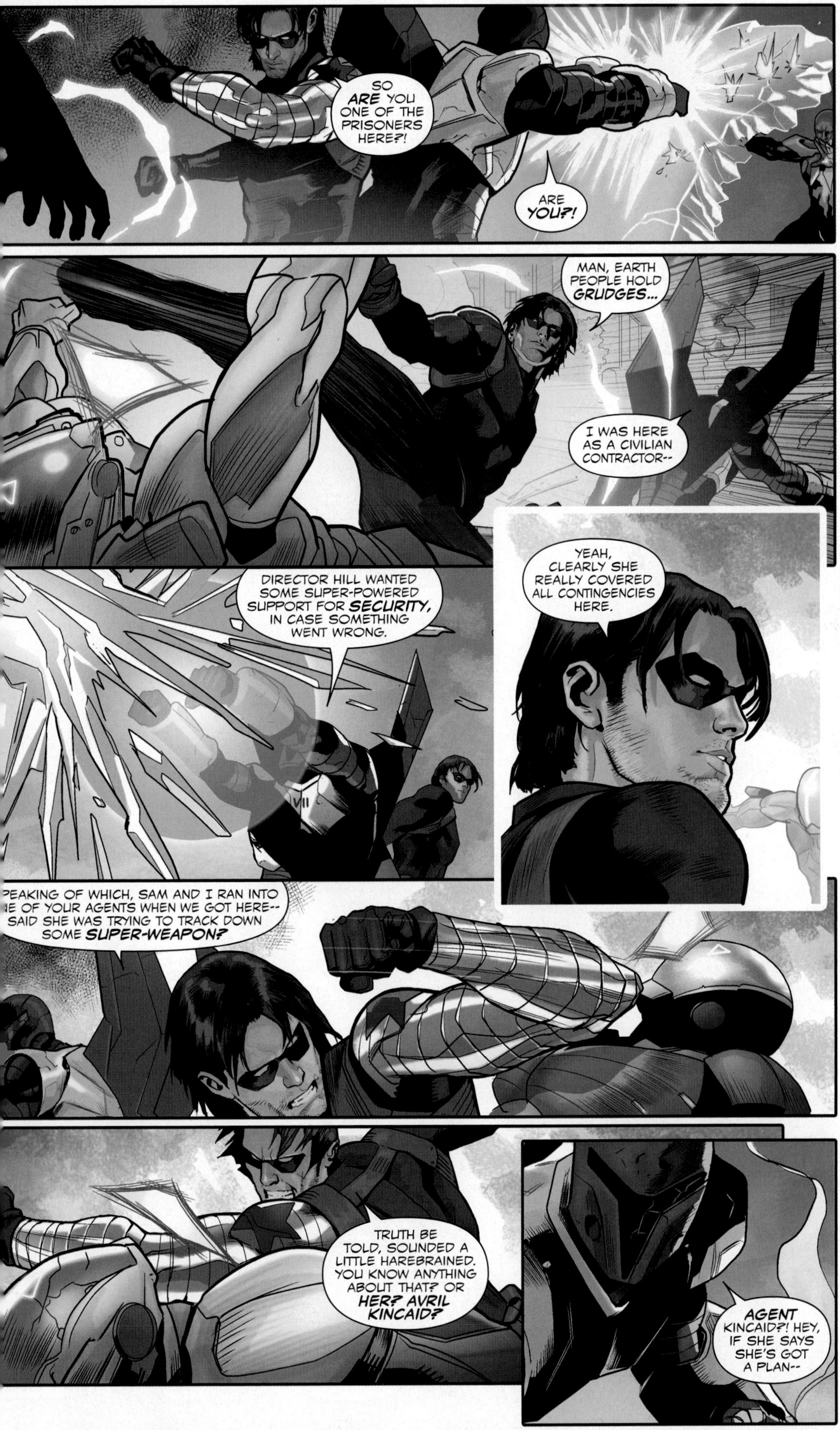
SO ARE YOU ONE OF THE PRISONERS HERE?!
ARE YOU?!
MAN, EARTH PEOPLE HOLD GRUDGES...
I WAS HERE AS A CIVILIAN CONTRACTOR--
DIRECTOR HILL WANTED SOME SUPER-POWERED SUPPORT FOR SECURITY, IN CASE SOMETHING WENT WRONG.
YEAH, CLEARLY SHE REALLY COVERED ALL CONTINGENCIES HERE.
SAID SHE WAS TRYING TO TRACK DOWN SOME SUPER-WEAPON?
TRUTH BE TOLD, SOUNDED A LITTLE HAREBRAINED. YOU KNOW ANYTHING ABOUT THAT? OR HER? AVRIL KINCAID?
AGENT KINCAID?! HEY, IF SHE SAYS SHE'S GOT A PLAN--

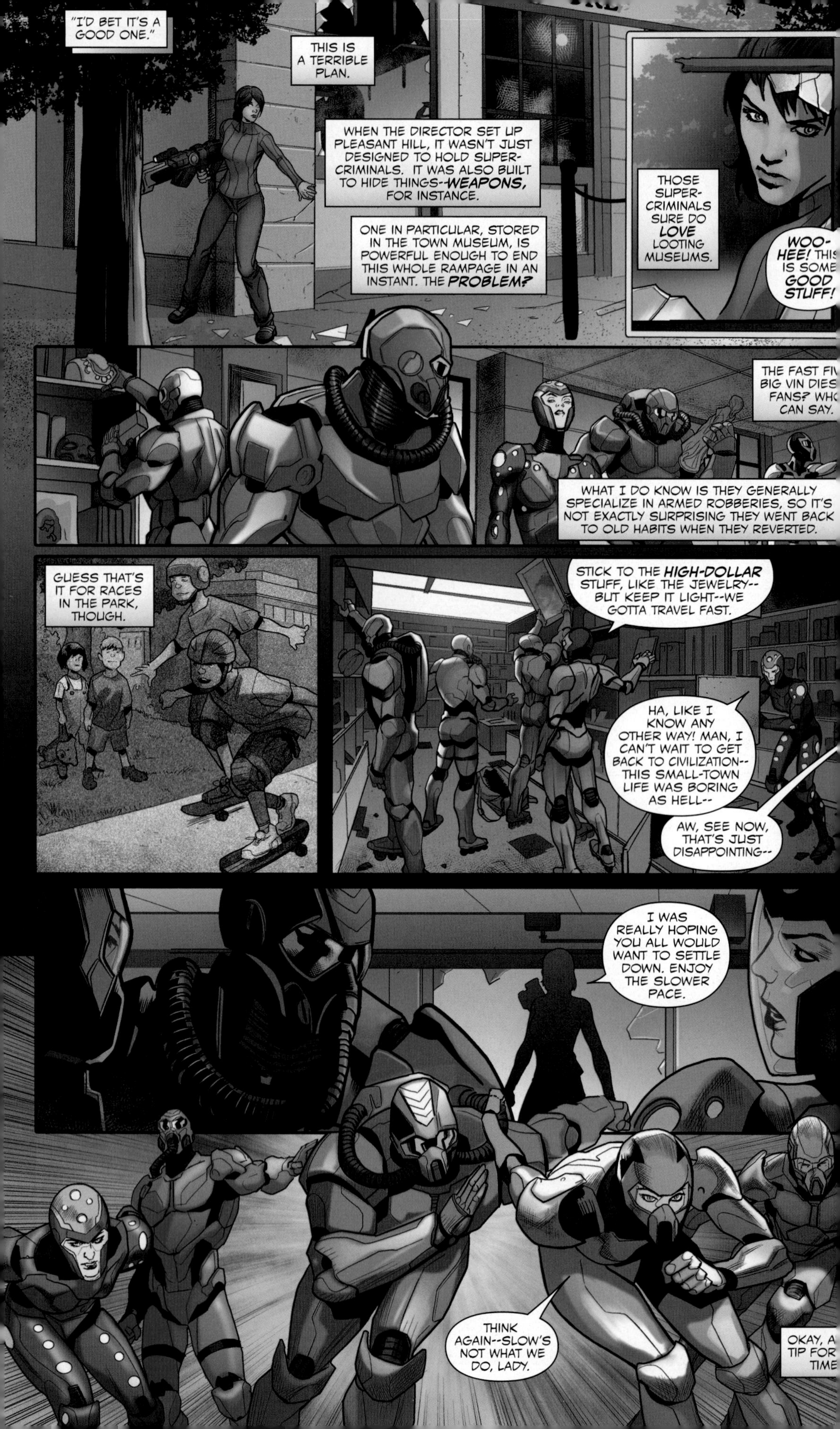
"I'D BET IT'S A GOOD ONE."
THIS IS A TERRIBLE PLAN.
WHEN THE DIRECTOR SET UP PLEASANT HILL, IT WASN'T JUST DESIGNED TO HOLD SUPER-CRIMINALS. IT WAS ALSO BUILT TO HIDE THINGS--WEAPONS, FOR INSTANCE.
ONE IN PARTICULAR, STORED IN THE TOWN MUSEUM, IS POWERFUL ENOUGH TO END THIS WHOLE RAMPAGE IN AN INSTANT. THE PROBLEM?
THOSE SUPER-CRIMINALS SURE DO LOVE LOOTING MUSEUMS.
WOO-HEE! THIS IS SOME GOOD STUFF!
THE FAST FIV BIG VIN DIES FANS? WHO CAN SAY.
WHAT I DO KNOW IS THEY GENERALLY SPECIALIZE IN ARMED ROBBERIES, SO IT'S NOT EXACTLY SURPRISING THEY WENT BACK TO OLD HABITS WHEN THEY REVERTED.
GUESS THAT'S IT FOR RACES IN THE PARK, THOUGH.
STICK TO THE HIGH-DOLLAR STUFF, LIKE THE JEWELRY-- BUT KEEP IT LIGHT--WE GOTTA TRAVEL FAST.
HA, LIKE I KNOW ANY OTHER WAY! MAN, I CAN'T WAIT TO GET BACK TO CIVILIZATION-- THIS SMALL-TOWN LIFE WAS BORING AS HELL--
AW, SEE NOW, THAT'S JUST DISAPPOINTING--
I WAS REALLY HOPING YOU ALL WOULD WANT TO SETTLE DOWN. ENJOY THE SLOWER PACE.
THINK AGAIN--SLOW'S NOT WHAT WE DO, LADY.
OKAY, A TIP FOR TIME

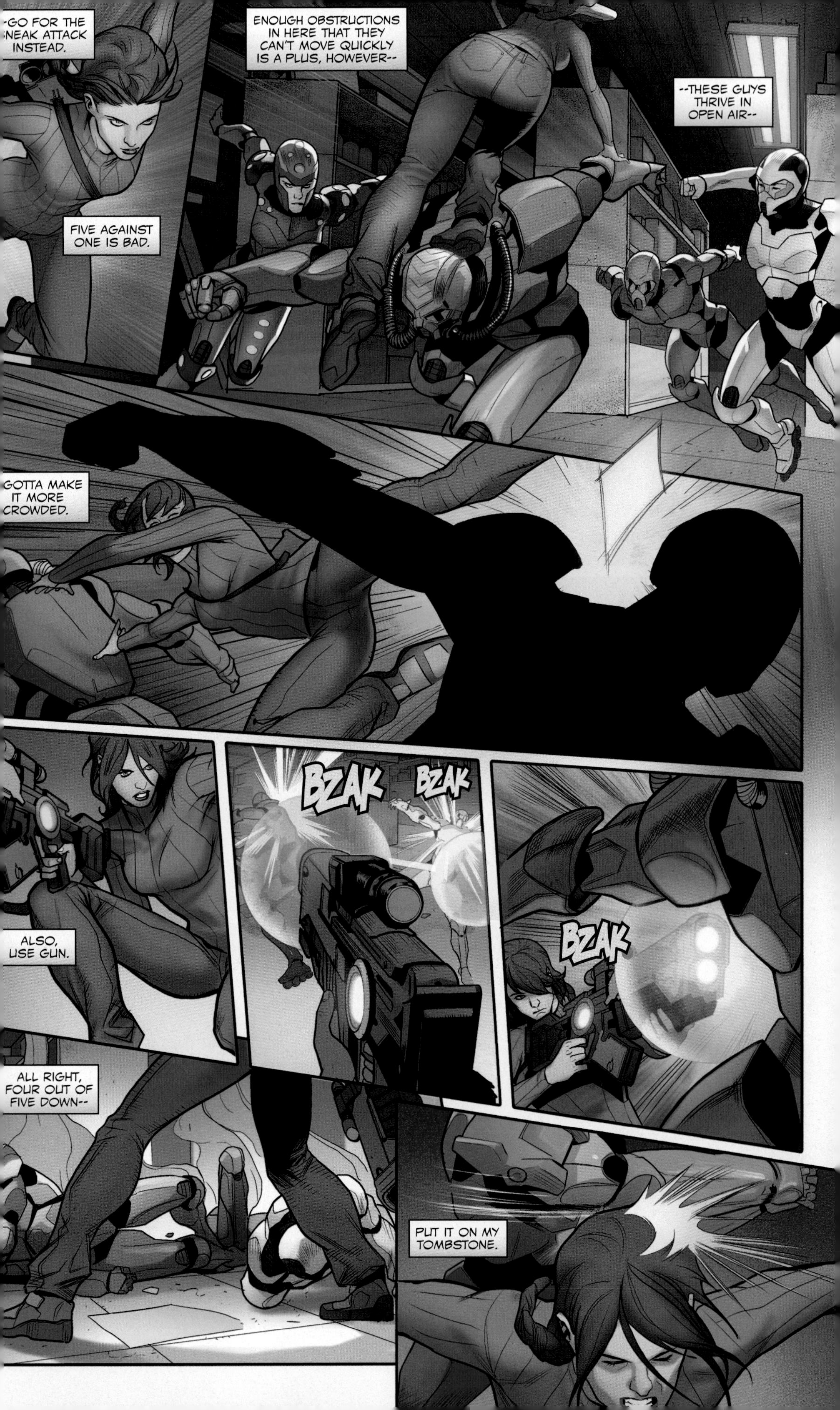
-GO FOR THE SNEAK ATTACK INSTEAD.
ENOUGH OBSTRUCTIONS IN HERE THAT THEY CAN'T MOVE QUICKLY IS A PLUS, HOWEVER--
--THESE GUYS THRIVE IN OPEN AIR--
FIVE AGAINST ONE IS BAD.
GOTTA MAKE IT MORE CROWDED.
ALSO, USE GUN.
BZAK
BZAK
BZAK
ALL RIGHT, FOUR OUT OF FIVE DOWN--
PUT IT ON MY TOMBSTONE.

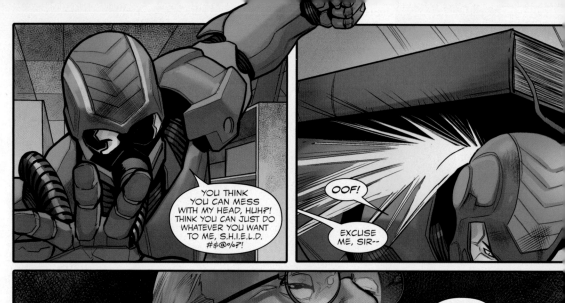

YOU THINK YOU CAN MESS WITH MY HEAD, HUH?! THINK YOU CAN JUST DO WHATEVER YOU WANT TO ME, S.H.I.E.L.D. #$@%?!

OOF!

EXCUSE ME, SIR--

--THE SIGN IN THE FRONT ASKS FOR "QUIET, PLEASE."

ARE YOU ALL RIGHT, MA'AM?

I--YEAH, I'M OKAY-- THANKS TO YOU. YOU'RE--THE CURATOR, RIGHT?

YES--AND I'VE BEEN WAITING FOR YOU. EVER SINCE THE CHAOS BROKE OUT.

YOU HAVE...?

MM. I KNOW WHO YOU ARE, AGENT KINCAID--

--AND I KNOW WHAT YOU'R LOOKING FOR...

WHICH IS REMARKAB PRESCIEN BUT HEY--

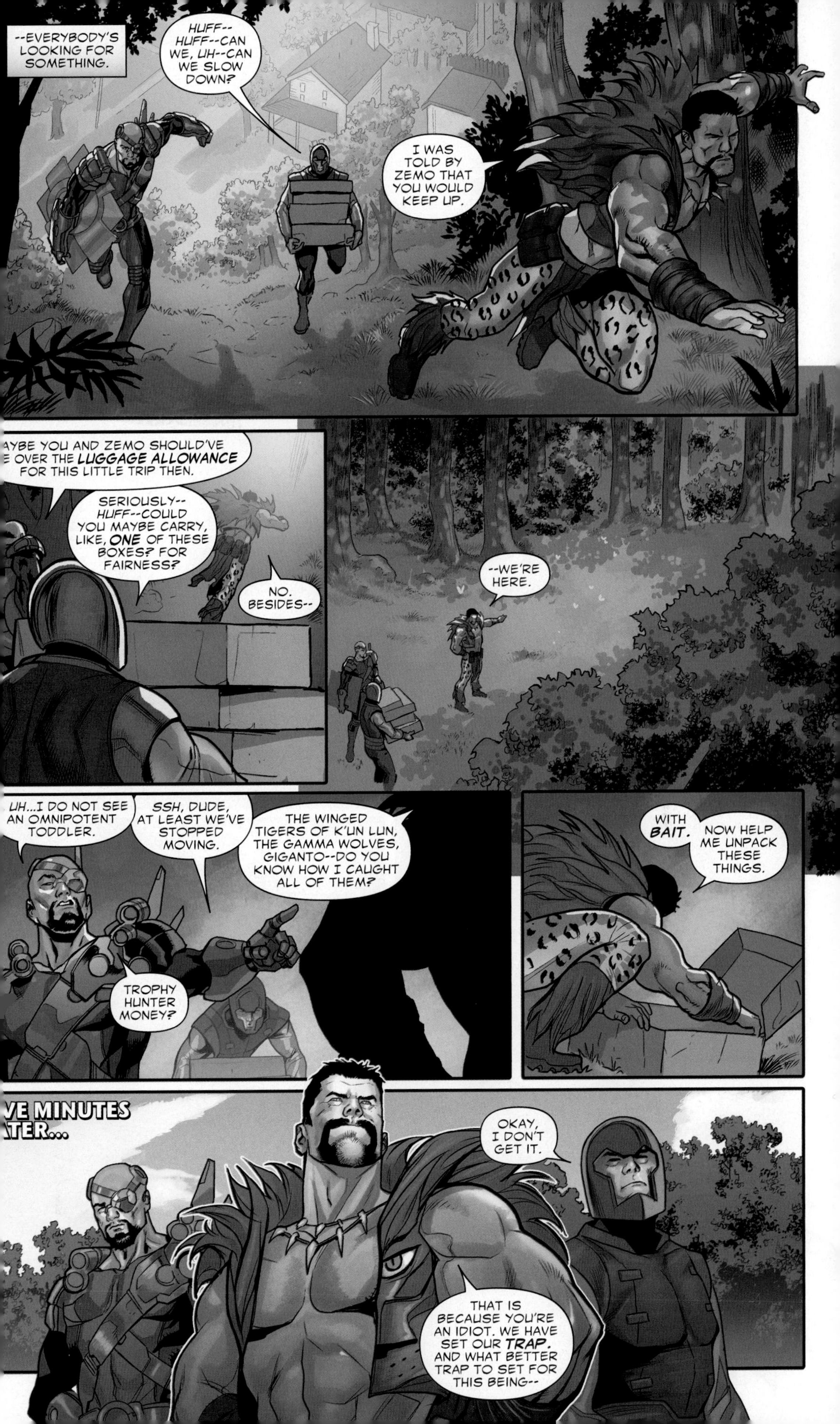
--EVERYBODY'S LOOKING FOR SOMETHING.
HUFF-- HUFF--CAN WE, UH--CAN WE SLOW DOWN?
I WAS TOLD BY ZEMO THAT YOU WOULD KEEP UP.
AYBE YOU AND ZEMO SHOULD'VE E OVER THE LUGGAGE ALLOWANCE FOR THIS LITTLE TRIP THEN.
SERIOUSLY-- HUFF--COULD YOU MAYBE CARRY, LIKE, ONE OF THESE BOXES? FOR FAIRNESS?
NO. BESIDES--
--WE'RE HERE.
UH...I DO NOT SEE AN OMNIPOTENT TODDLER.
SSH, DUDE, AT LEAST WE'VE STOPPED MOVING.
THE WINGED TIGERS OF K'UN LUN, THE GAMMA WOLVES, GIGANTO--DO YOU KNOW HOW I CAUGHT ALL OF THEM?
TROPHY HUNTER MONEY?
WITH BAIT.
NOW HELP ME UNPACK THESE THINGS.
VE MINUTES TER...
OKAY, I DON'T GET IT.
THAT IS BECAUSE YOU'RE AN IDIOT. WE HAVE SET OUR TRAP. AND WHAT BETTER TRAP TO SET FOR THIS BEING--

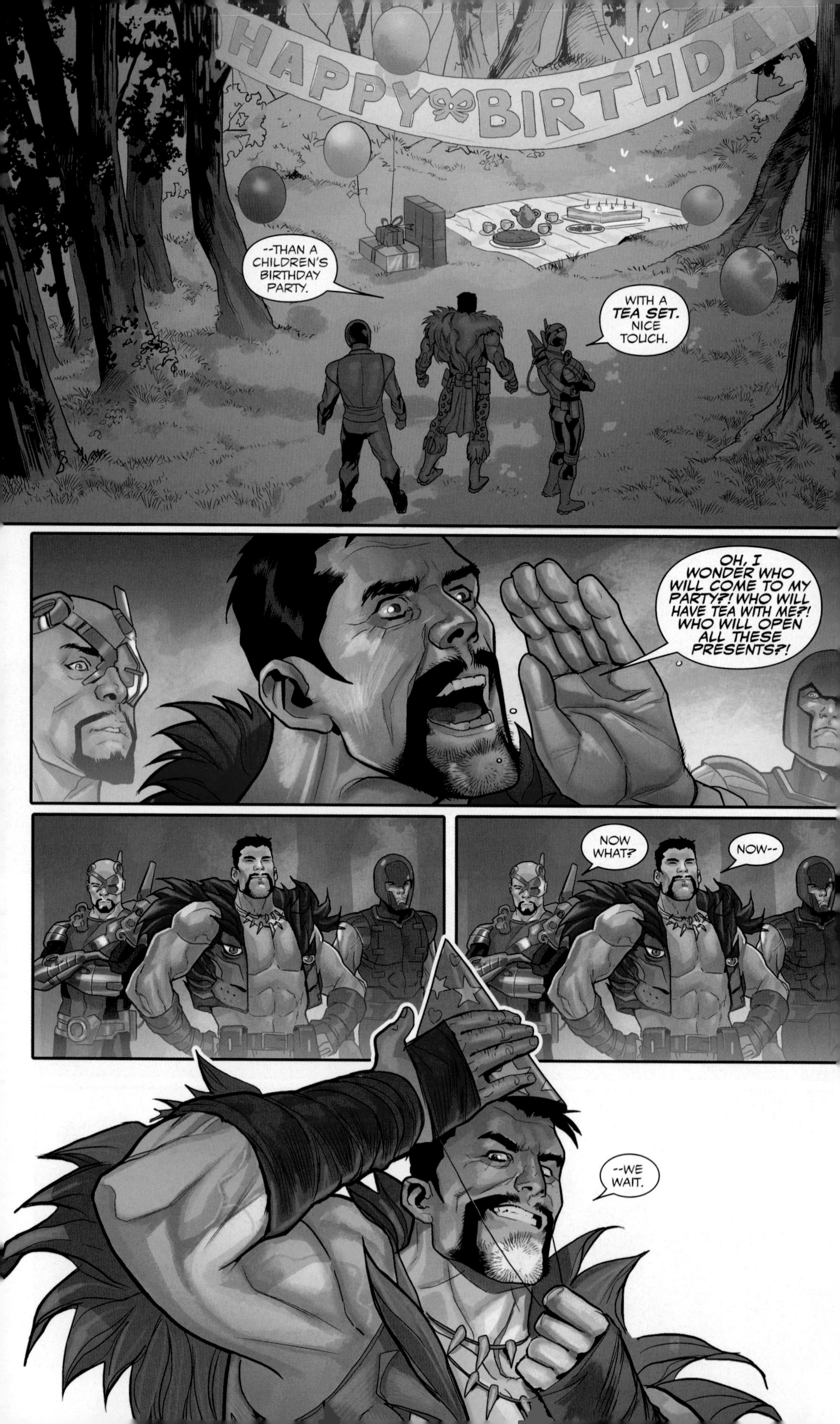
HAPPY BIRTHDA
--THAN A CHILDREN'S BIRTHDAY PARTY.
WITH A TEA SET. NICE TOUCH.
OH, I WONDER WHO WILL COME TO MY PARTY?! WHO WILL HAVE TEA WITH ME?! WHO WILL OPEN ALL THESE PRESENTS?!
NOW WHAT?
NOW--
--WE WAIT.

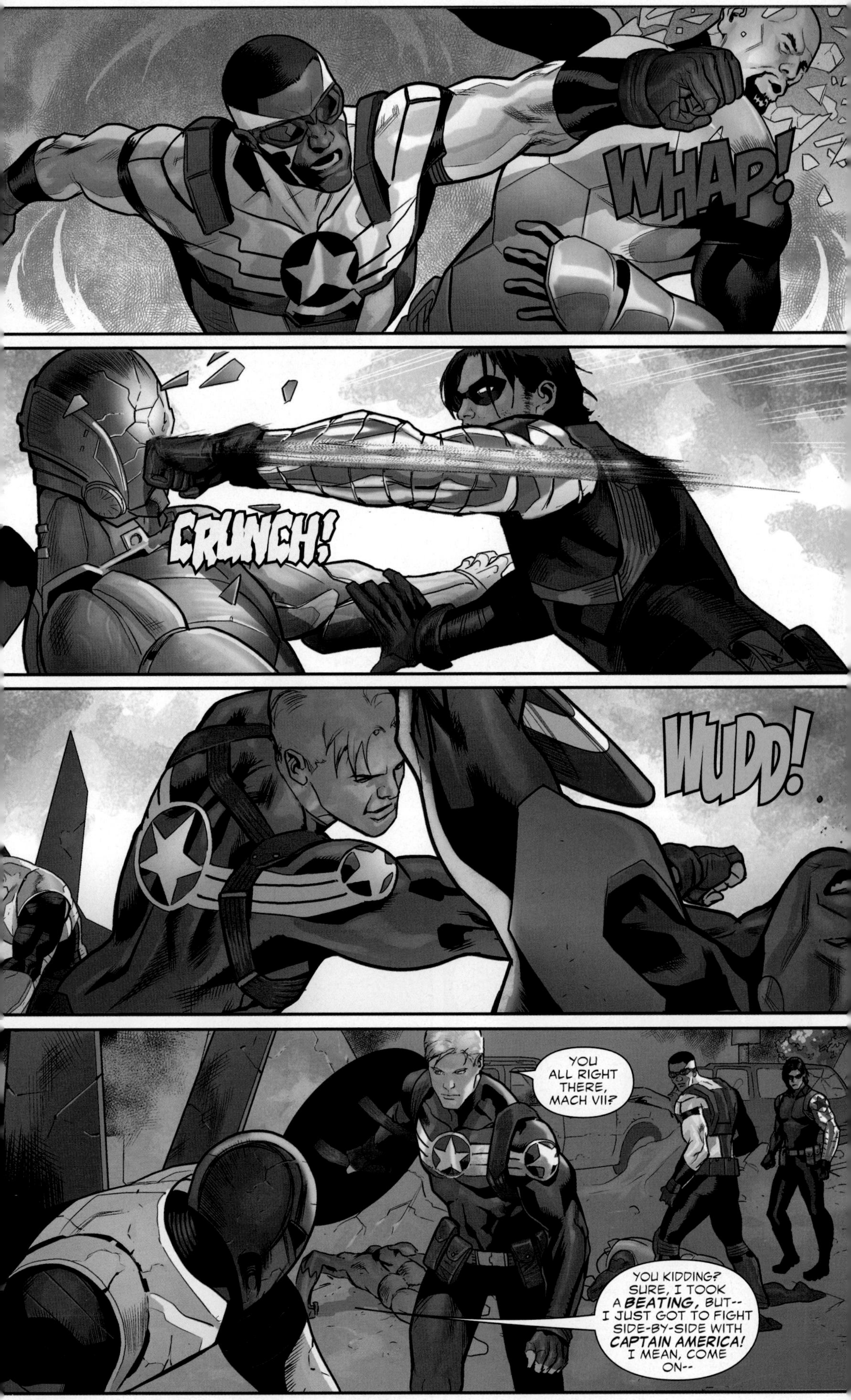
WHAP!
CRUNCH!
WUDD!
YOU ALL RIGHT THERE, MACH VII?
YOU KIDDING? SURE, I TOOK A BEATING, BUT-- I JUST GOT TO FIGHT SIDE-BY-SIDE WITH CAPTAIN AMERICA! I MEAN, COME ON--

--IT'S AN **HONOR**, SIR.

AH...

HE'S CAPTAIN AMERICA. I'M JUST **STEVE** THESE DAYS.

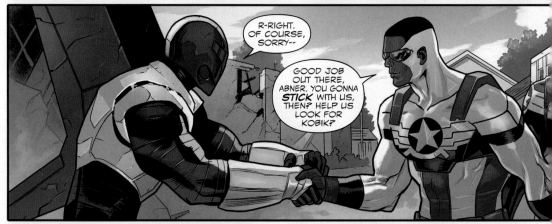

R-RIGHT. OF COURSE, SORRY--

GOOD JOB OUT THERE, ABNER. YOU GONNA **STICK** WITH US, THEN? HELP US LOOK FOR KOBIK?

I WISH I COULD. ZEMO'S GUYS HAVE DISABLED OUR COMMUNICATIONS TO S.H.I.E.L.D. OUR DISTRESS SIGNALS AREN'T GETTING THROUGH. I'M TRYING TO GET TO THE TOWER, FIGURE A WAY AROUND THE JAMMING.

GOOD LUCK, THEN. I'M SURE WE'LL BE SEEING EACH OTHER AGAIN SOON.

OH, YEAH, THAT REMINDS ME--

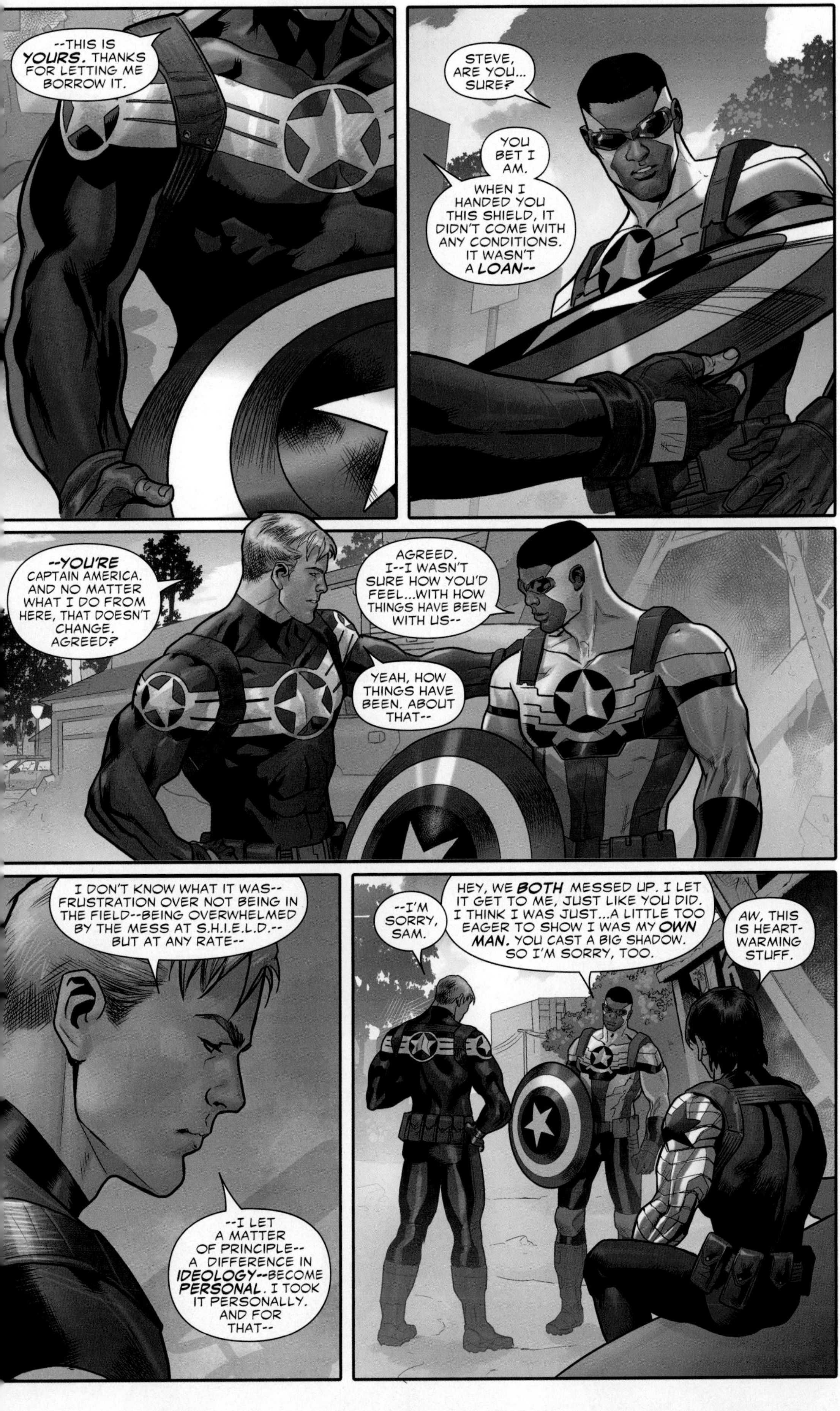
--THIS IS YOURS. THANKS FOR LETTING ME BORROW IT.
STEVE, ARE YOU... SURE?
YOU BET I AM.
WHEN I HANDED YOU THIS SHIELD, IT DIDN'T COME WITH ANY CONDITIONS. IT WASN'T A LOAN--
--YOU'RE CAPTAIN AMERICA. AND NO MATTER WHAT I DO FROM HERE, THAT DOESN'T CHANGE. AGREED?
AGREED. I--I WASN'T SURE HOW YOU'D FEEL...WITH HOW THINGS HAVE BEEN WITH US--
YEAH, HOW THINGS HAVE BEEN. ABOUT THAT--
I DON'T KNOW WHAT IT WAS--FRUSTRATION OVER NOT BEING IN THE FIELD--BEING OVERWHELMED BY THE MESS AT S.H.I.E.L.D.--BUT AT ANY RATE--
--I LET A MATTER OF PRINCIPLE--A DIFFERENCE IN IDEOLOGY--BECOME PERSONAL. I TOOK IT PERSONALLY. AND FOR THAT--
--I'M SORRY, SAM.
HEY, WE BOTH MESSED UP. I LET IT GET TO ME, JUST LIKE YOU DID. I THINK I WAS JUST...A LITTLE TOO EAGER TO SHOW I WAS MY OWN MAN. YOU CAST A BIG SHADOW. SO I'M SORRY, TOO.
AW, THIS IS HEART-WARMING STUFF.

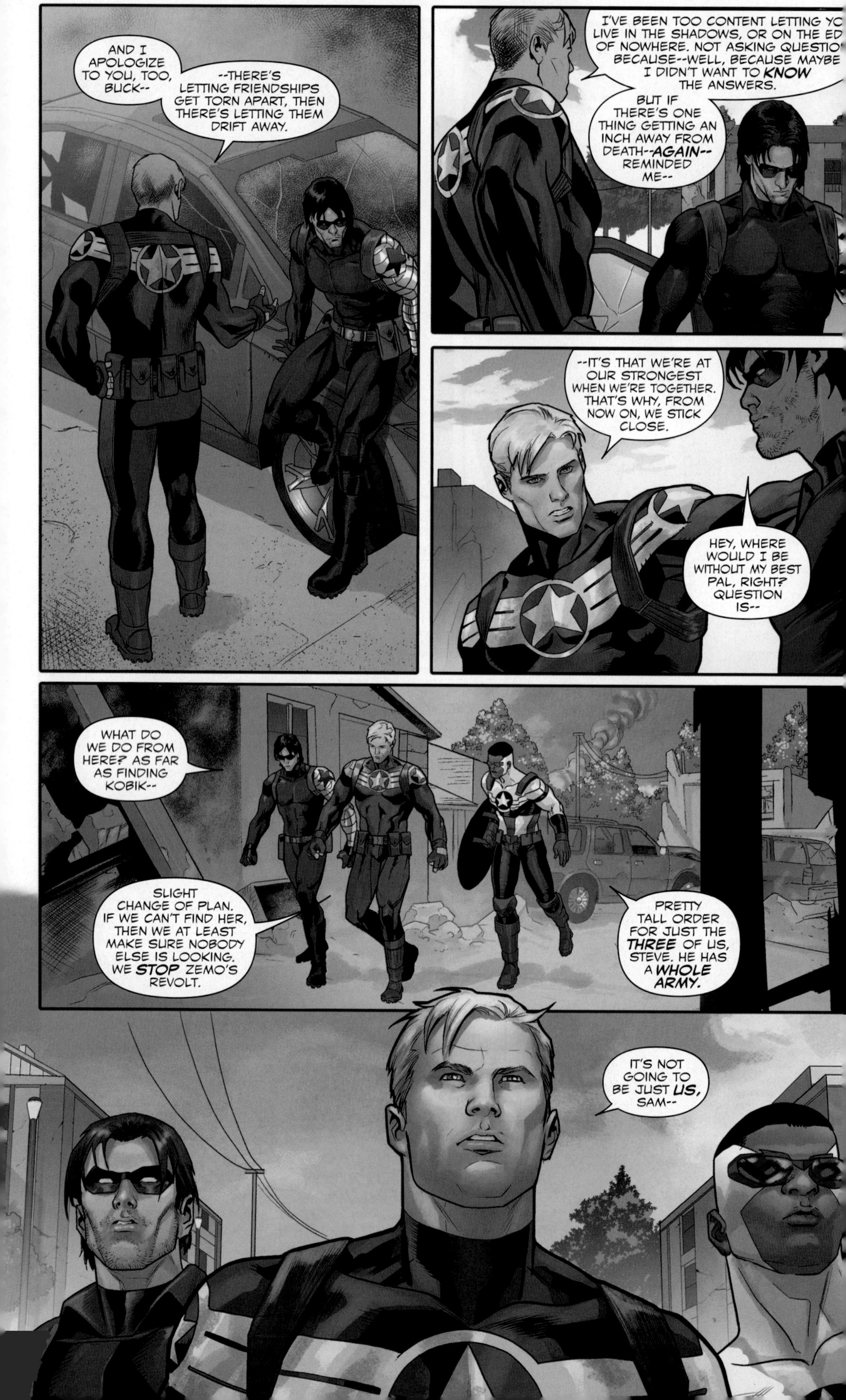
AND I APOLOGIZE TO YOU, TOO, BUCK--
--THERE'S LETTING FRIENDSHIPS GET TORN APART, THEN THERE'S LETTING THEM DRIFT AWAY.
I'VE BEEN TOO CONTENT LETTING YO LIVE IN THE SHADOWS, OR ON THE ED OF NOWHERE. NOT ASKING QUESTIO BECAUSE--WELL, BECAUSE MAYBE I DIDN'T WANT TO KNOW THE ANSWERS.
BUT IF THERE'S ONE THING GETTING AN INCH AWAY FROM DEATH--AGAIN--REMINDED ME--
--IT'S THAT WE'RE AT OUR STRONGEST WHEN WE'RE TOGETHER. THAT'S WHY, FROM NOW ON, WE STICK CLOSE.
HEY, WHERE WOULD I BE WITHOUT MY BEST PAL, RIGHT? QUESTION IS--
WHAT DO WE DO FROM HERE? AS FAR AS FINDING KOBIK--
SLIGHT CHANGE OF PLAN. IF WE CAN'T FIND HER, THEN WE AT LEAST MAKE SURE NOBODY ELSE IS LOOKING. WE STOP ZEMO'S REVOLT.
PRETTY TALL ORDER FOR JUST THE THREE OF US, STEVE. HE HAS A WHOLE ARMY.
IT'S NOT GOING TO BE JUST US, SAM--

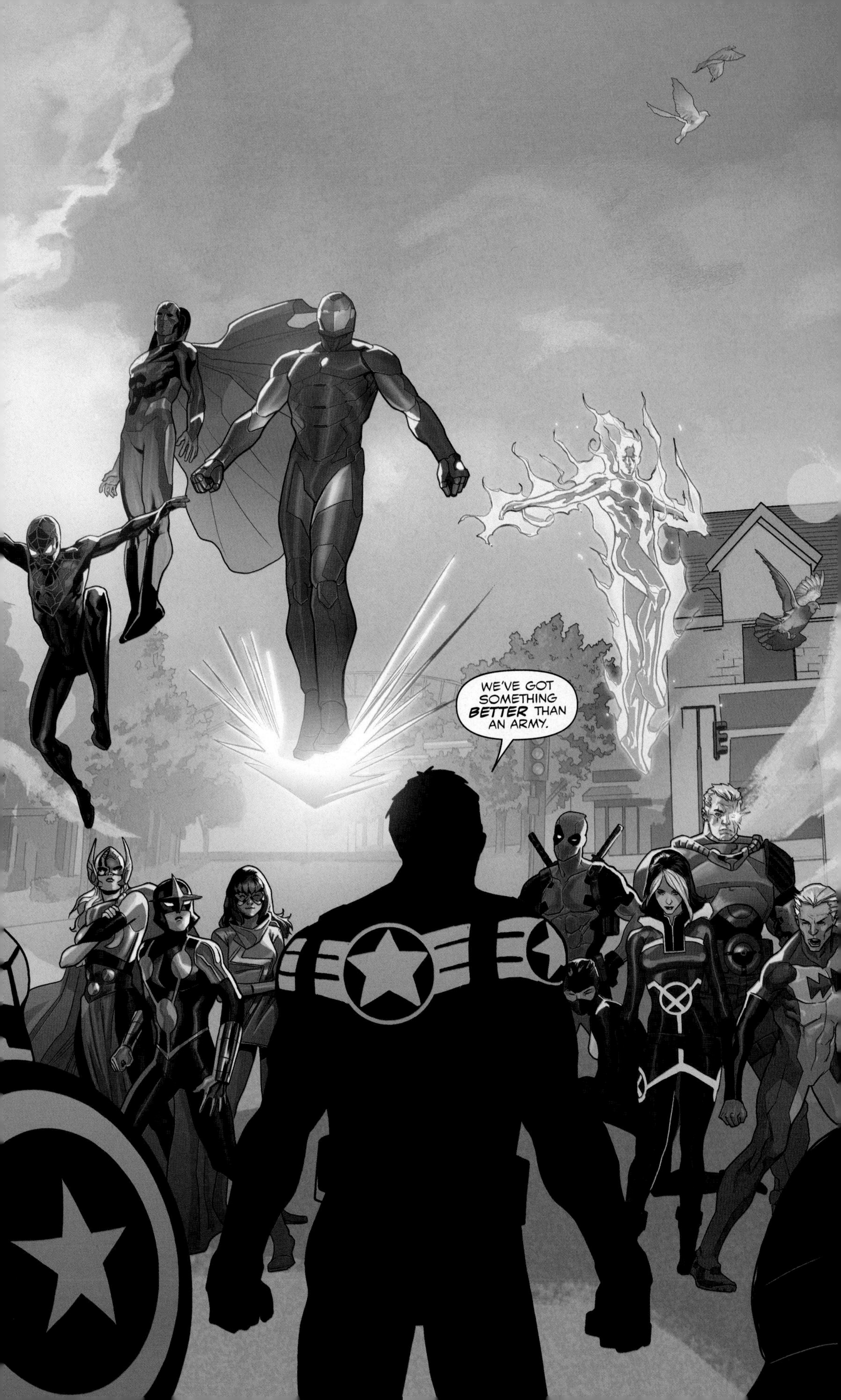
WE'VE GOT SOMETHING BETTER THAN AN ARMY.

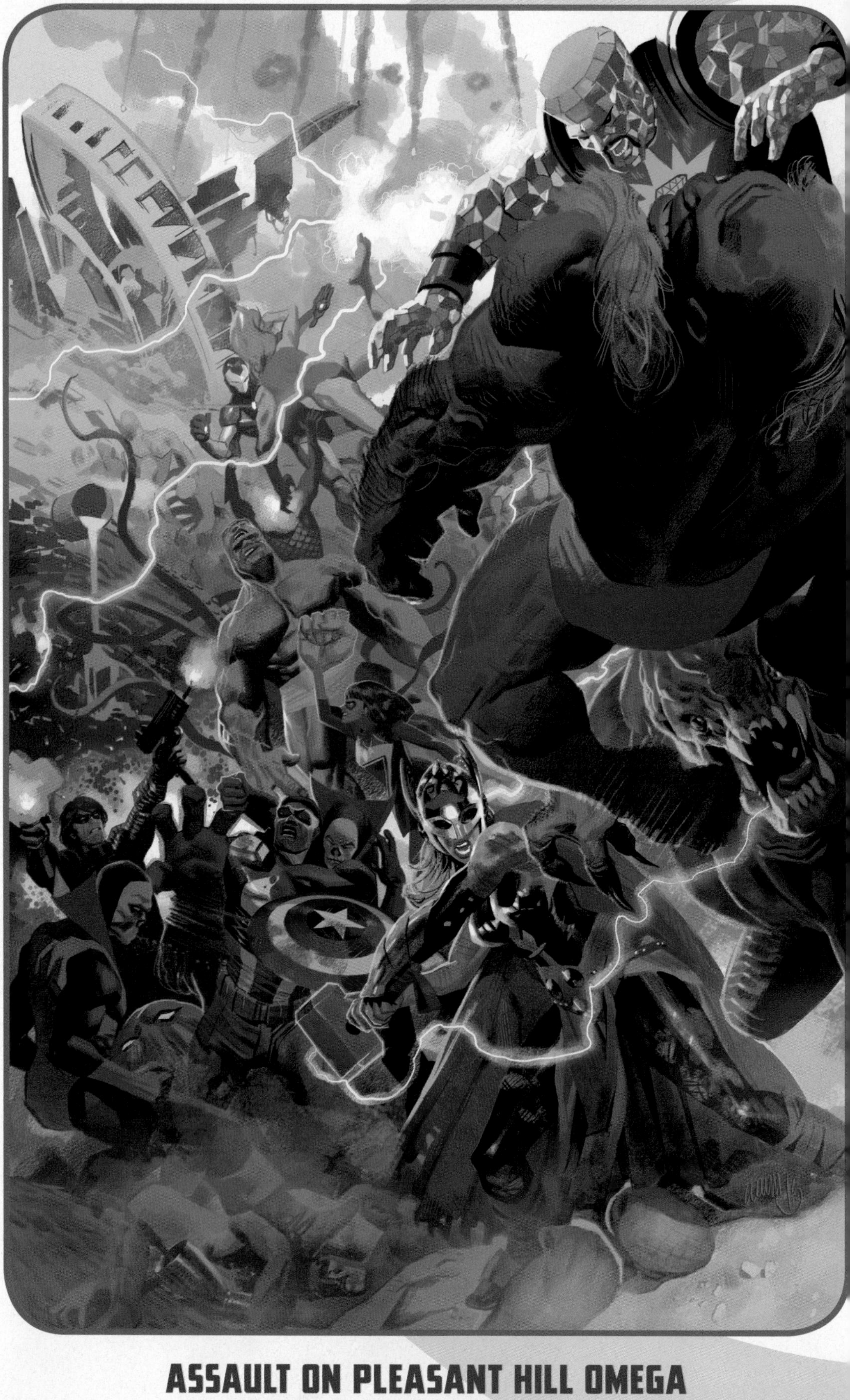

ASSAULT ON PLEASANT HILL OMEGA

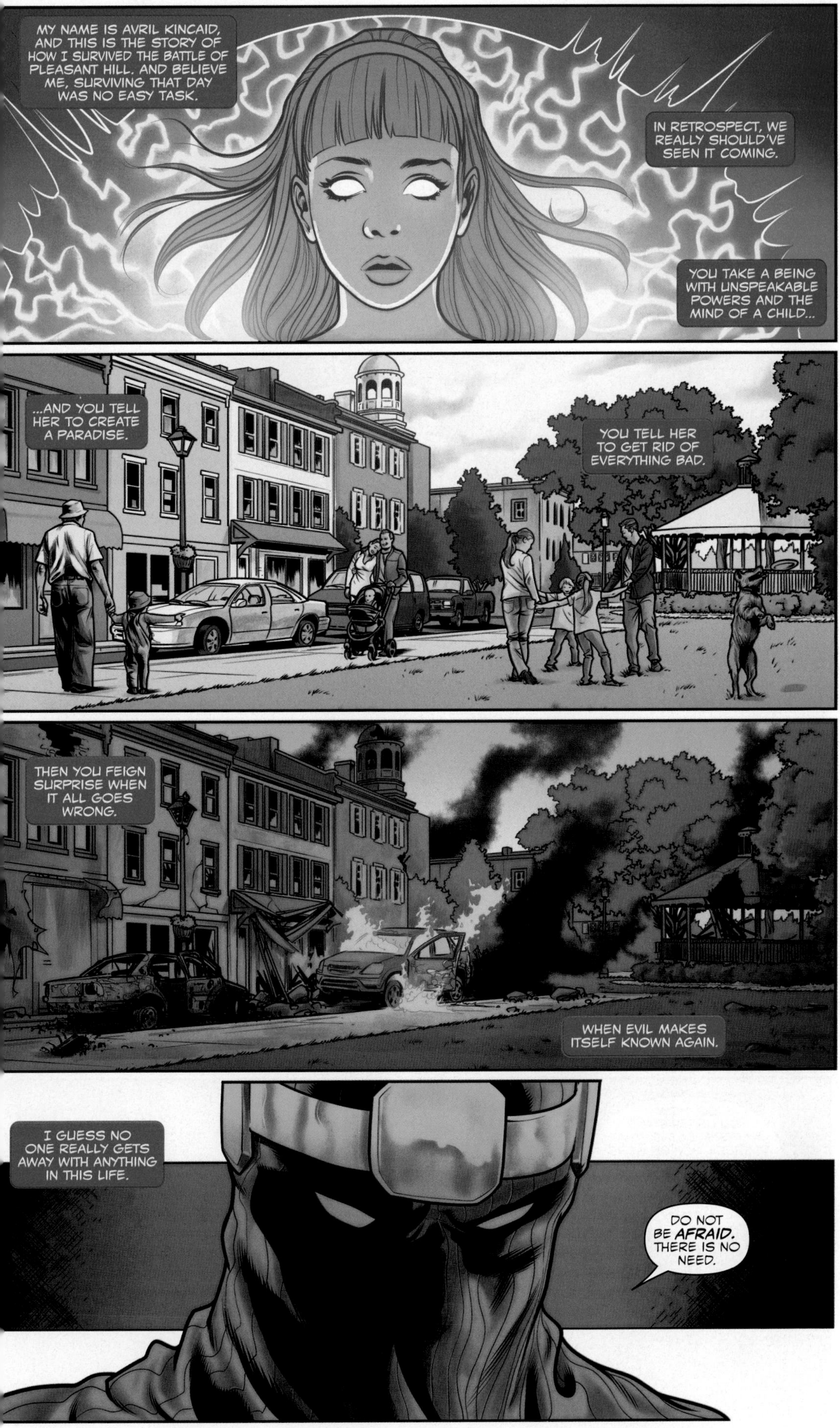
MY NAME IS AVRIL KINCAID, AND THIS IS THE STORY OF HOW I SURVIVED THE BATTLE OF PLEASANT HILL. AND BELIEVE ME, SURVIVING THAT DAY WAS NO EASY TASK.
IN RETROSPECT, WE REALLY SHOULD'VE SEEN IT COMING.
YOU TAKE A BEING WITH UNSPEAKABLE POWERS AND THE MIND OF A CHILD...
...AND YOU TELL HER TO CREATE A PARADISE.
YOU TELL HER TO GET RID OF EVERYTHING BAD.
THEN YOU FEIGN SURPRISE WHEN IT ALL GOES WRONG.
WHEN EVIL MAKES ITSELF KNOWN AGAIN.
I GUESS NO ONE REALLY GETS AWAY WITH ANYTHING IN THIS LIFE.
DO NOT BE *AFRAID.* THERE IS NO NEED.

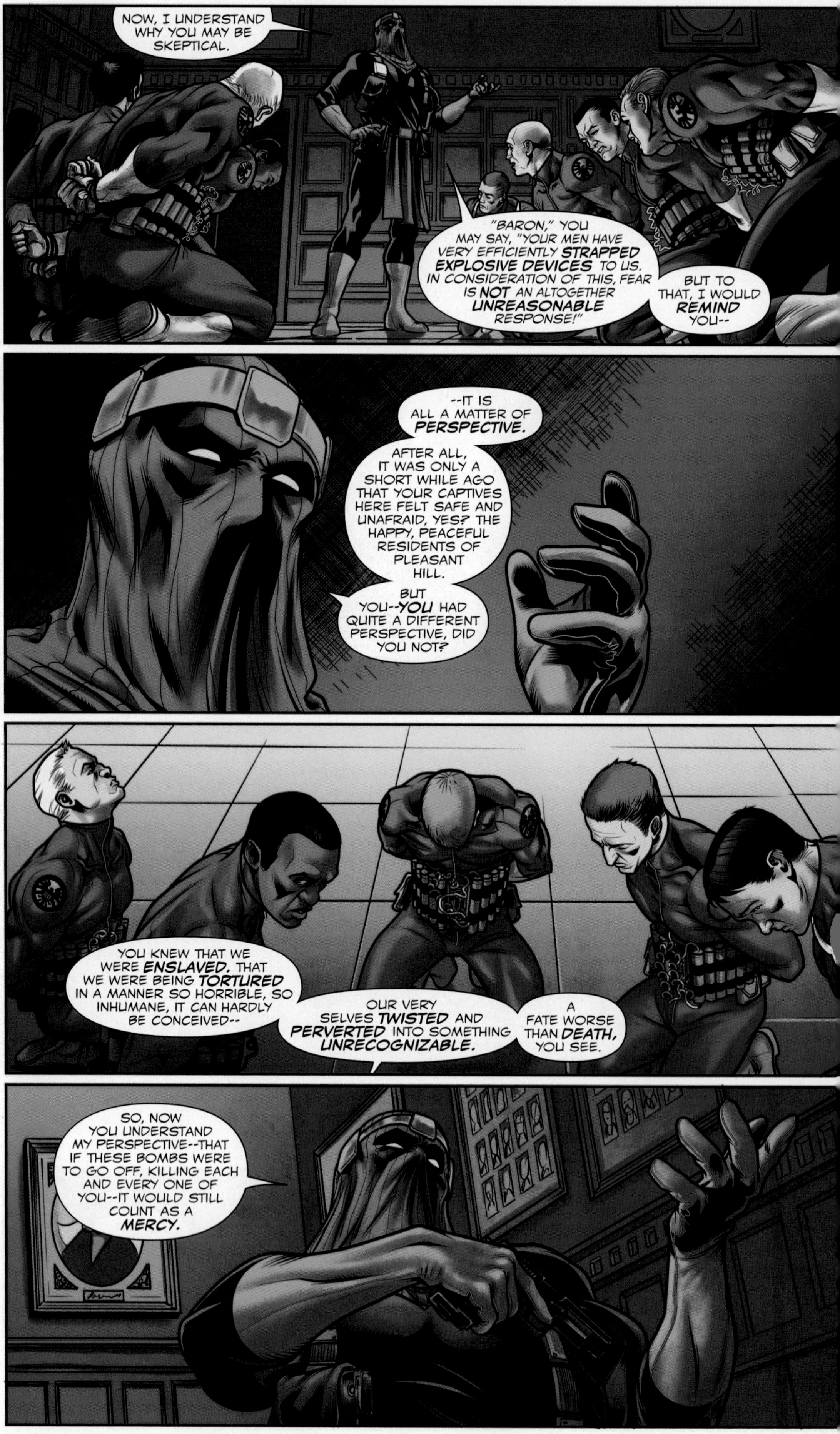
NOW, I UNDERSTAND WHY YOU MAY BE SKEPTICAL.
"BARON," YOU MAY SAY, "YOUR MEN HAVE VERY EFFICIENTLY STRAPPED EXPLOSIVE DEVICES TO US. IN CONSIDERATION OF THIS, FEAR IS NOT AN ALTOGETHER UNREASONABLE RESPONSE!"
BUT TO THAT, I WOULD REMIND YOU--
--IT IS ALL A MATTER OF PERSPECTIVE.
AFTER ALL, IT WAS ONLY A SHORT WHILE AGO THAT YOUR CAPTIVES HERE FELT SAFE AND UNAFRAID, YES? THE HAPPY, PEACEFUL RESIDENTS OF PLEASANT HILL.
BUT YOU--YOU HAD QUITE A DIFFERENT PERSPECTIVE, DID YOU NOT?
YOU KNEW THAT WE WERE ENSLAVED. THAT WE WERE BEING TORTURED IN A MANNER SO HORRIBLE, SO INHUMANE, IT CAN HARDLY BE CONCEIVED--
OUR VERY SELVES TWISTED AND PERVERTED INTO SOMETHING UNRECOGNIZABLE.
A FATE WORSE THAN DEATH, YOU SEE.
SO, NOW YOU UNDERSTAND MY PERSPECTIVE--THAT IF THESE BOMBS WERE TO GO OFF, KILLING EACH AND EVERY ONE OF YOU--IT WOULD STILL COUNT AS A MERCY.

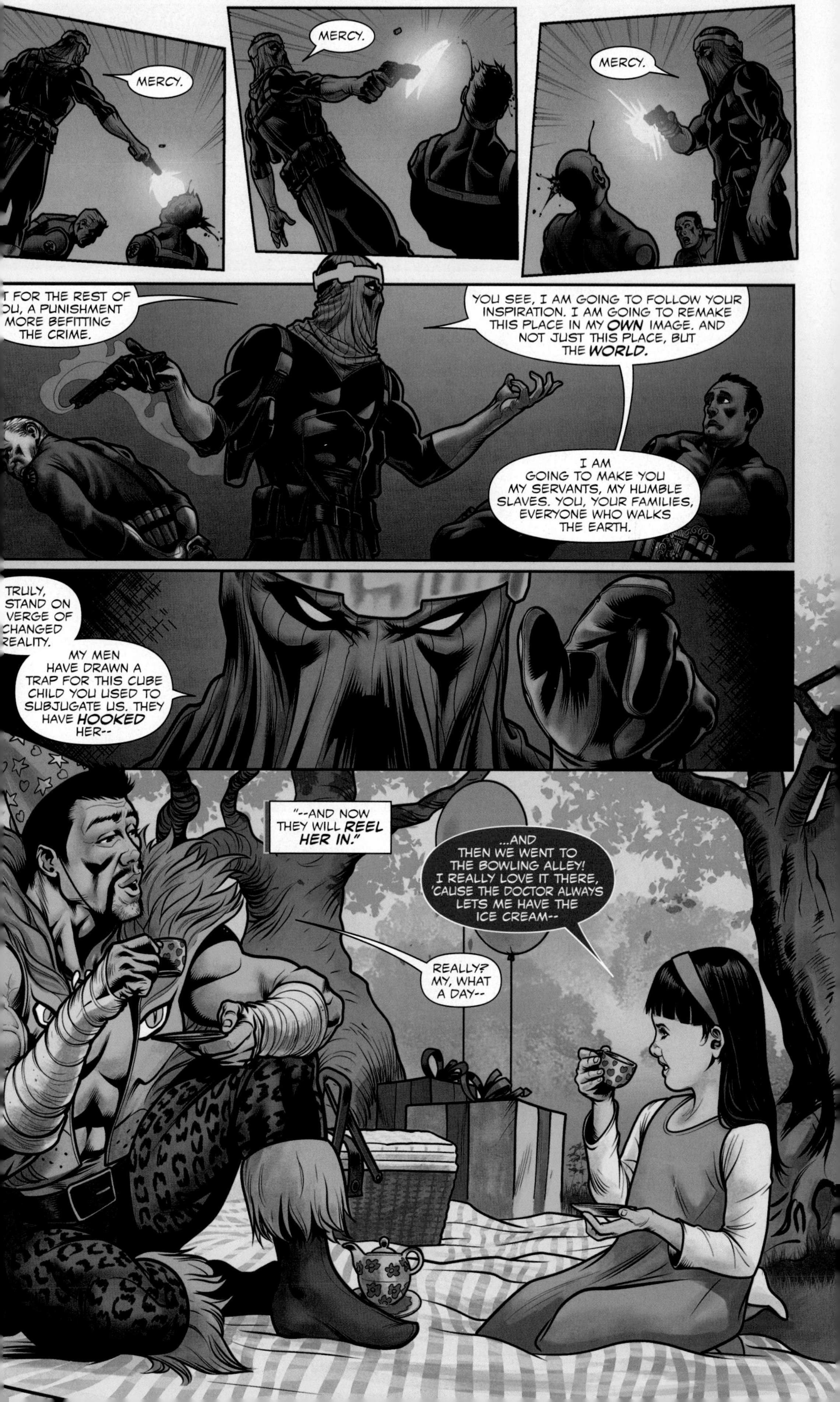
MERCY.
MERCY.
MERCY.
T FOR THE REST OF
OU, A PUNISHMENT
MORE BEFITTING
THE CRIME.
YOU SEE, I AM GOING TO FOLLOW YOUR INSPIRATION. I AM GOING TO REMAKE THIS PLACE IN MY *OWN* IMAGE. AND NOT JUST THIS PLACE, BUT THE *WORLD.*
I AM GOING TO MAKE YOU MY SERVANTS, MY HUMBLE SLAVES. YOU, YOUR FAMILIES, EVERYONE WHO WALKS THE EARTH.
TRULY, STAND ON VERGE OF CHANGED REALITY.
MY MEN HAVE DRAWN A TRAP FOR THIS CUBE CHILD YOU USED TO SUBJUGATE US. THEY HAVE *HOOKED* HER--
"--AND NOW THEY WILL *REEL HER IN.*"
...AND THEN WE WENT TO THE BOWLING ALLEY! I REALLY LOVE IT THERE, 'CAUSE THE DOCTOR ALWAYS LETS ME HAVE THE ICE CREAM--
REALLY? MY, WHAT A DAY--

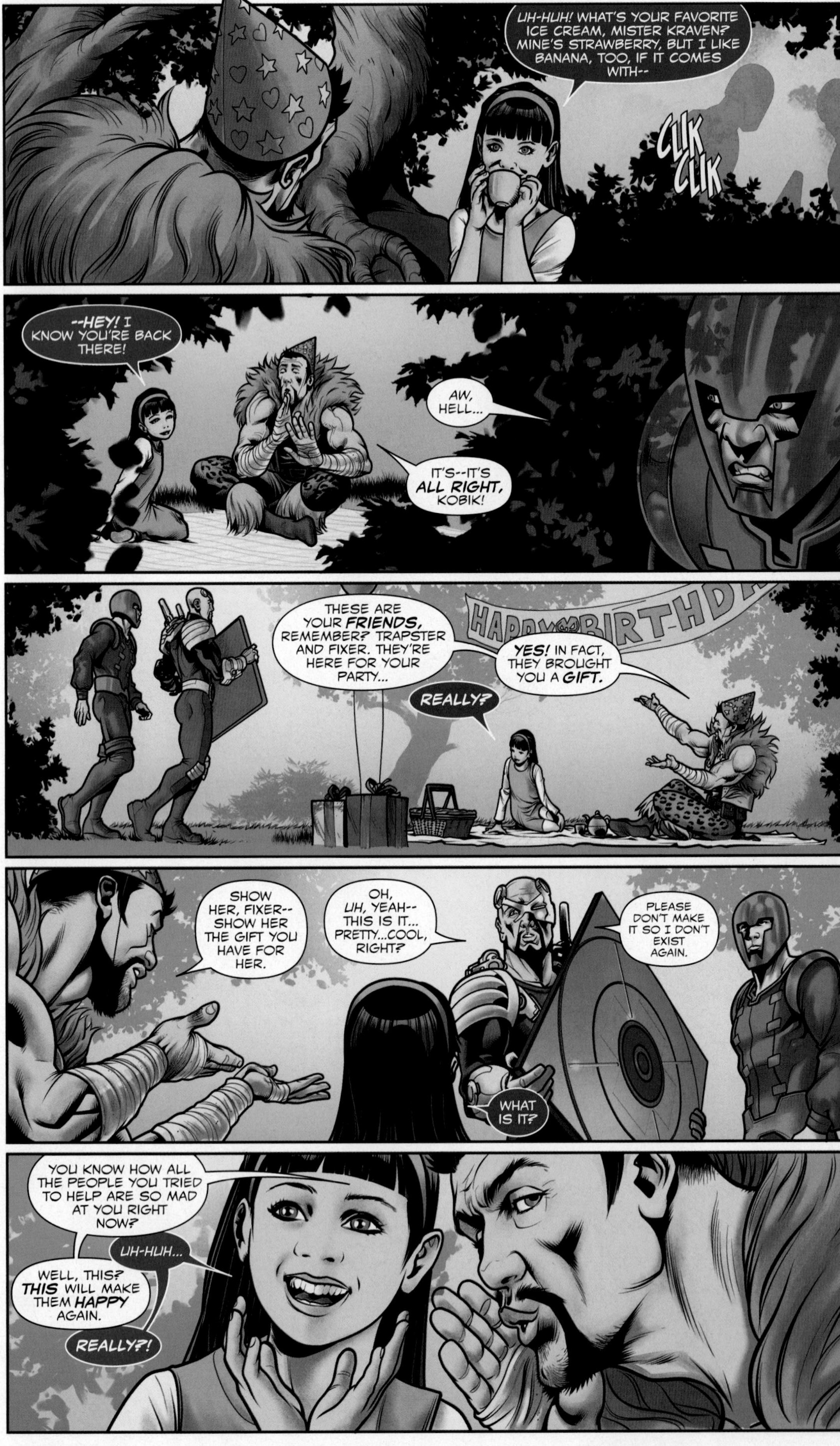
UH-HUH! WHAT'S YOUR FAVORITE ICE CREAM, MISTER KRAVEN? MINE'S STRAWBERRY, BUT I LIKE BANANA, TOO, IF IT COMES WITH--
CLIK CLIK
--HEY! I KNOW YOU'RE BACK THERE!
AW, HELL...
IT'S--IT'S ALL RIGHT, KOBIK!
THESE ARE YOUR FRIENDS, REMEMBER? TRAPSTER AND FIXER. THEY'RE HERE FOR YOUR PARTY...
YES! IN FACT, THEY BROUGHT YOU A GIFT.
REALLY?
HAPPY BIRTHD
SHOW HER, FIXER-- SHOW HER THE GIFT YOU HAVE FOR HER.
OH, UH, YEAH-- THIS IS IT... PRETTY...COOL, RIGHT?
PLEASE DON'T MAKE IT SO I DON'T EXIST AGAIN.
WHAT IS IT?
YOU KNOW HOW ALL THE PEOPLE YOU TRIED TO HELP ARE SO MAD AT YOU RIGHT NOW?
UH-HUH...
WELL, THIS? THIS WILL MAKE THEM HAPPY AGAIN.
REALLY?!

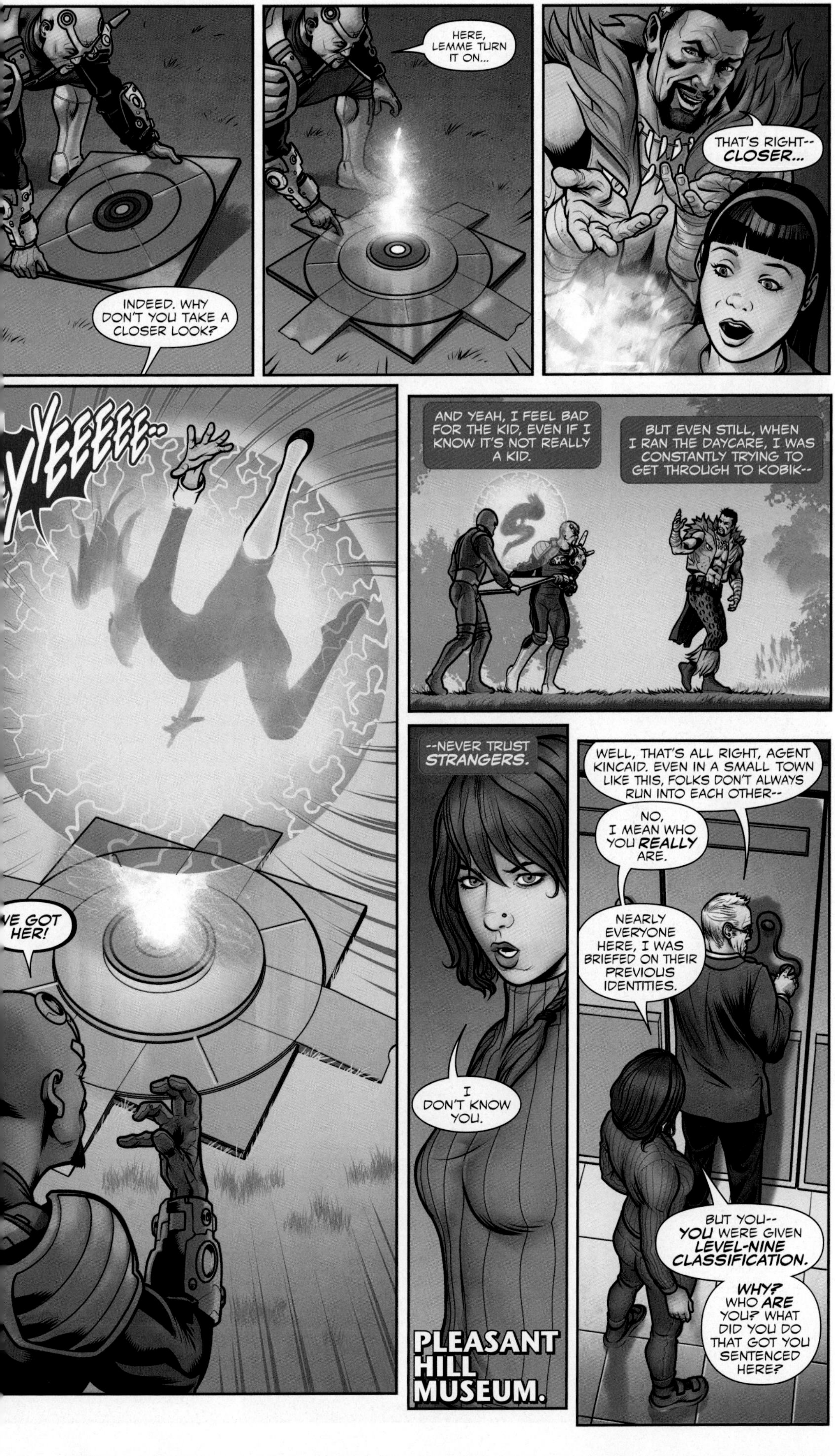

INDEED. WHY DON'T YOU TAKE A CLOSER LOOK?
HERE, LEMME TURN IT ON...
THAT'S RIGHT-- CLOSER...
YEEEEE--
WE GOT HER!
AND YEAH, I FEEL BAD FOR THE KID, EVEN IF I KNOW IT'S NOT REALLY A KID.
BUT EVEN STILL, WHEN I RAN THE DAYCARE, I WAS CONSTANTLY TRYING TO GET THROUGH TO KOBIK--
--NEVER TRUST STRANGERS.
PLEASANT HILL MUSEUM.
I DON'T KNOW YOU.
WELL, THAT'S ALL RIGHT, AGENT KINCAID. EVEN IN A SMALL TOWN LIKE THIS, FOLKS DON'T ALWAYS RUN INTO EACH OTHER--
NO, I MEAN WHO YOU REALLY ARE.
NEARLY EVERYONE HERE, I WAS BRIEFED ON THEIR PREVIOUS IDENTITIES.
BUT YOU-- YOU WERE GIVEN LEVEL-NINE CLASSIFICATION.
WHY? WHO ARE YOU? WHAT DID YOU DO THAT GOT YOU SENTENCED HERE?

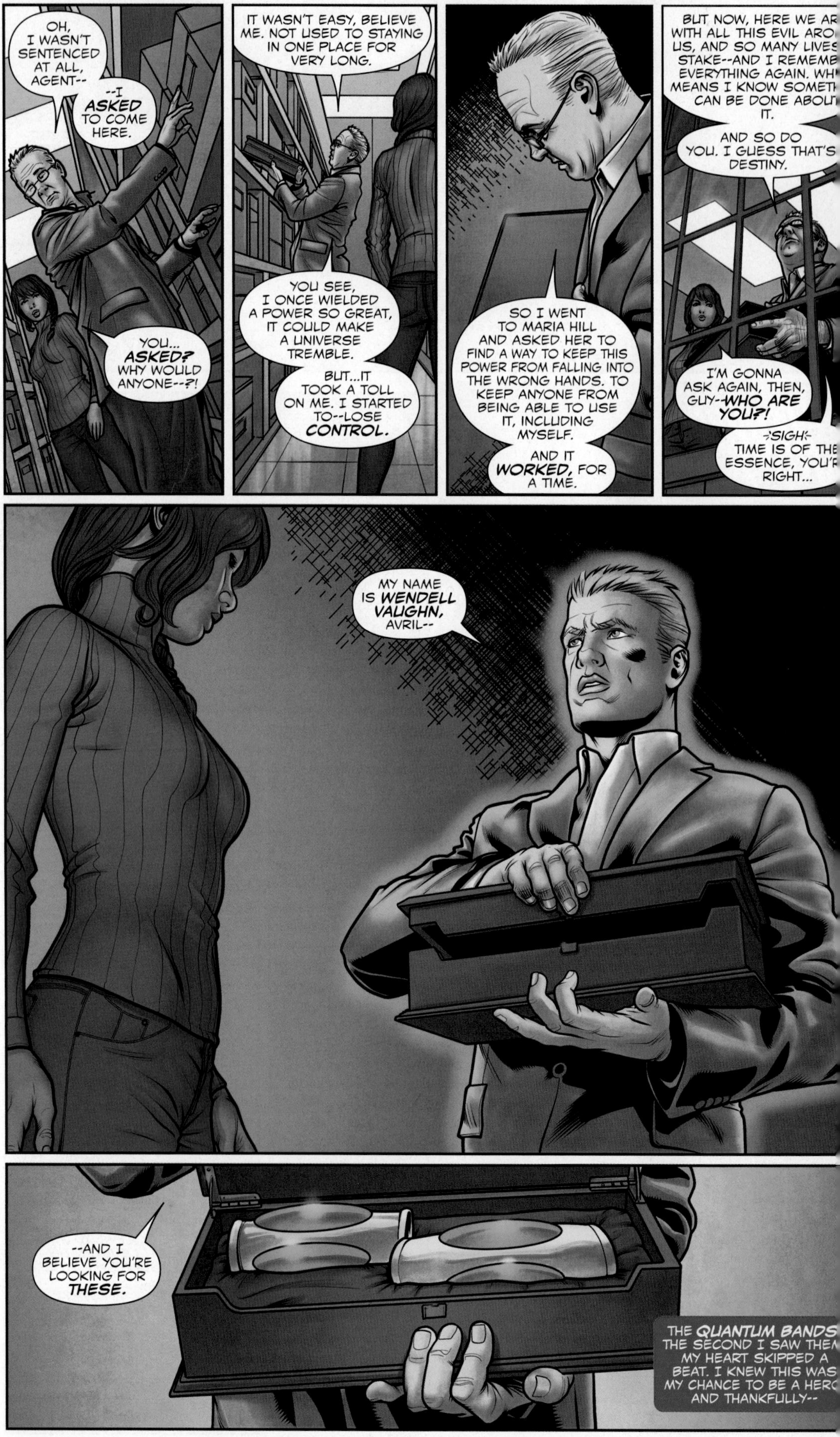

OH, I WASN'T SENTENCED AT ALL, AGENT--
--I ASKED TO COME HERE.
YOU... ASKED? WHY WOULD ANYONE--?!
IT WASN'T EASY, BELIEVE ME. NOT USED TO STAYING IN ONE PLACE FOR VERY LONG.
YOU SEE, I ONCE WIELDED A POWER SO GREAT, IT COULD MAKE A UNIVERSE TREMBLE.
BUT...IT TOOK A TOLL ON ME. I STARTED TO--LOSE CONTROL.
SO I WENT TO MARIA HILL AND ASKED HER TO FIND A WAY TO KEEP THIS POWER FROM FALLING INTO THE WRONG HANDS. TO KEEP ANYONE FROM BEING ABLE TO USE IT, INCLUDING MYSELF.
AND IT WORKED, FOR A TIME.
BUT NOW, HERE WE AR WITH ALL THIS EVIL ARO US, AND SO MANY LIVES STAKE--AND I REMEMB EVERYTHING AGAIN. WH MEANS I KNOW SOMETH CAN BE DONE ABOU IT.
AND SO DO YOU. I GUESS THAT'S DESTINY.
I'M GONNA ASK AGAIN, THEN, GUY--WHO ARE YOU?!
SIGH TIME IS OF THE ESSENCE, YOU'R RIGHT...
MY NAME IS WENDELL VAUGHN, AVRIL--
--AND I BELIEVE YOU'RE LOOKING FOR THESE.
THE QUANTUM BANDS THE SECOND I SAW THEM MY HEART SKIPPED A BEAT. I KNEW THIS WAS MY CHANCE TO BE A HER AND THANKFULLY--

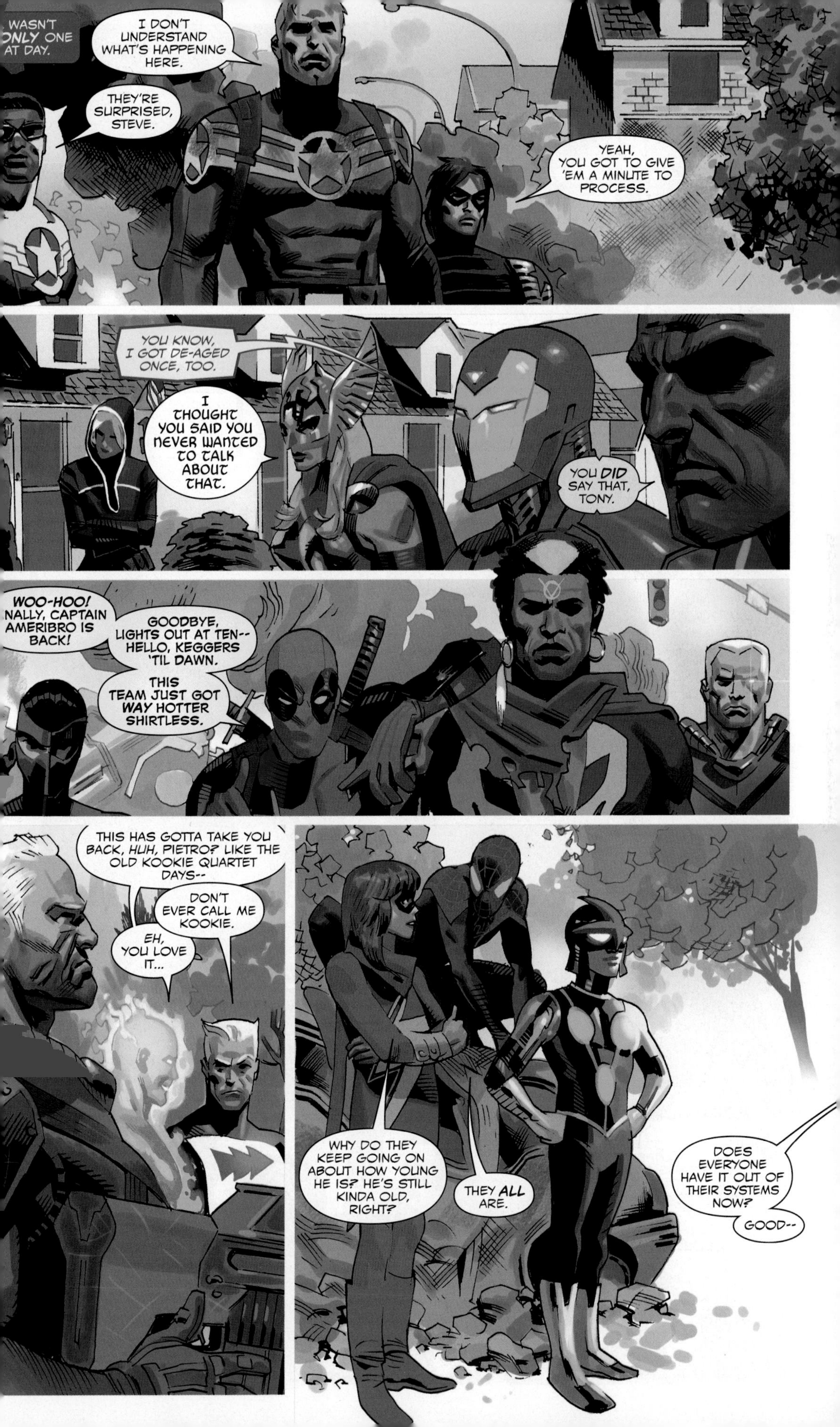
WASN'T ONLY ONE AT DAY.
I DON'T UNDERSTAND WHAT'S HAPPENING HERE.
THEY'RE SURPRISED, STEVE.
YEAH, YOU GOT TO GIVE 'EM A MINUTE TO PROCESS.
YOU KNOW, I GOT DE-AGED ONCE, TOO.
I THOUGHT YOU SAID YOU NEVER WANTED TO TALK ABOUT THAT.
YOU DID SAY THAT, TONY.
WOO-HOO! NALLY, CAPTAIN AMERIBRO IS BACK!
GOODBYE, LIGHTS OUT AT TEN-- HELLO, KEGGERS 'TIL DAWN.
THIS TEAM JUST GOT WAY HOTTER SHIRTLESS.
THIS HAS GOTTA TAKE YOU BACK, HUH, PIETRO? LIKE THE OLD KOOKIE QUARTET DAYS--
DON'T EVER CALL ME KOOKIE.
EH, YOU LOVE IT...
WHY DO THEY KEEP GOING ON ABOUT HOW YOUNG HE IS? HE'S STILL KINDA OLD, RIGHT?
THEY ALL ARE.
DOES EVERYONE HAVE IT OUT OF THEIR SYSTEMS NOW?
GOOD--

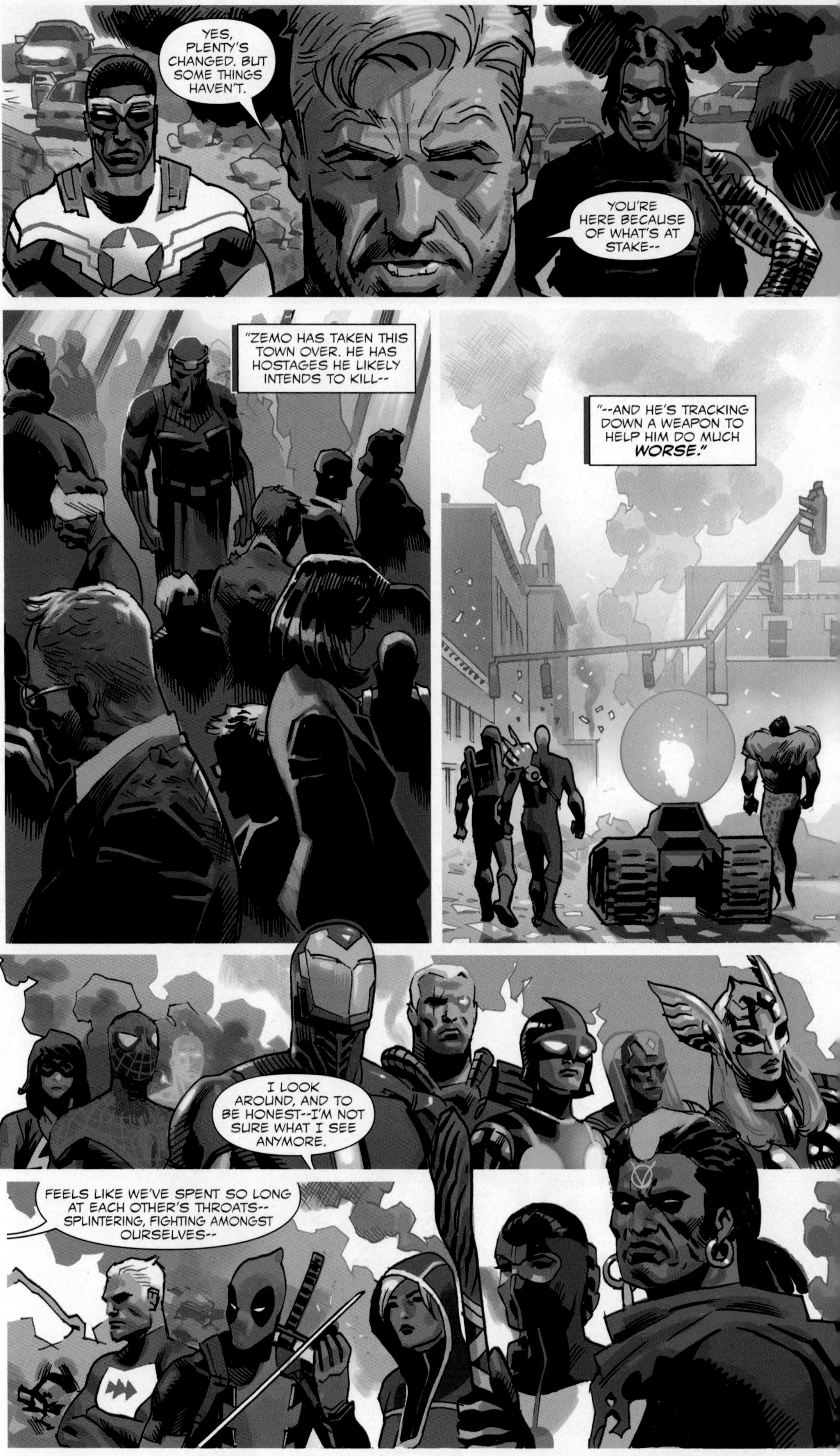
YES, PLENTY'S CHANGED. BUT SOME THINGS HAVEN'T.
YOU'RE HERE BECAUSE OF WHAT'S AT STAKE--
"ZEMO HAS TAKEN THIS TOWN OVER. HE HAS HOSTAGES HE LIKELY INTENDS TO KILL--
"--AND HE'S TRACKING DOWN A WEAPON TO HELP HIM DO MUCH WORSE."
I LOOK AROUND, AND TO BE HONEST--I'M NOT SURE WHAT I SEE ANYMORE.
FEELS LIKE WE'VE SPENT SO LONG AT EACH OTHER'S THROATS--SPLINTERING, FIGHTING AMONGST OURSELVES--

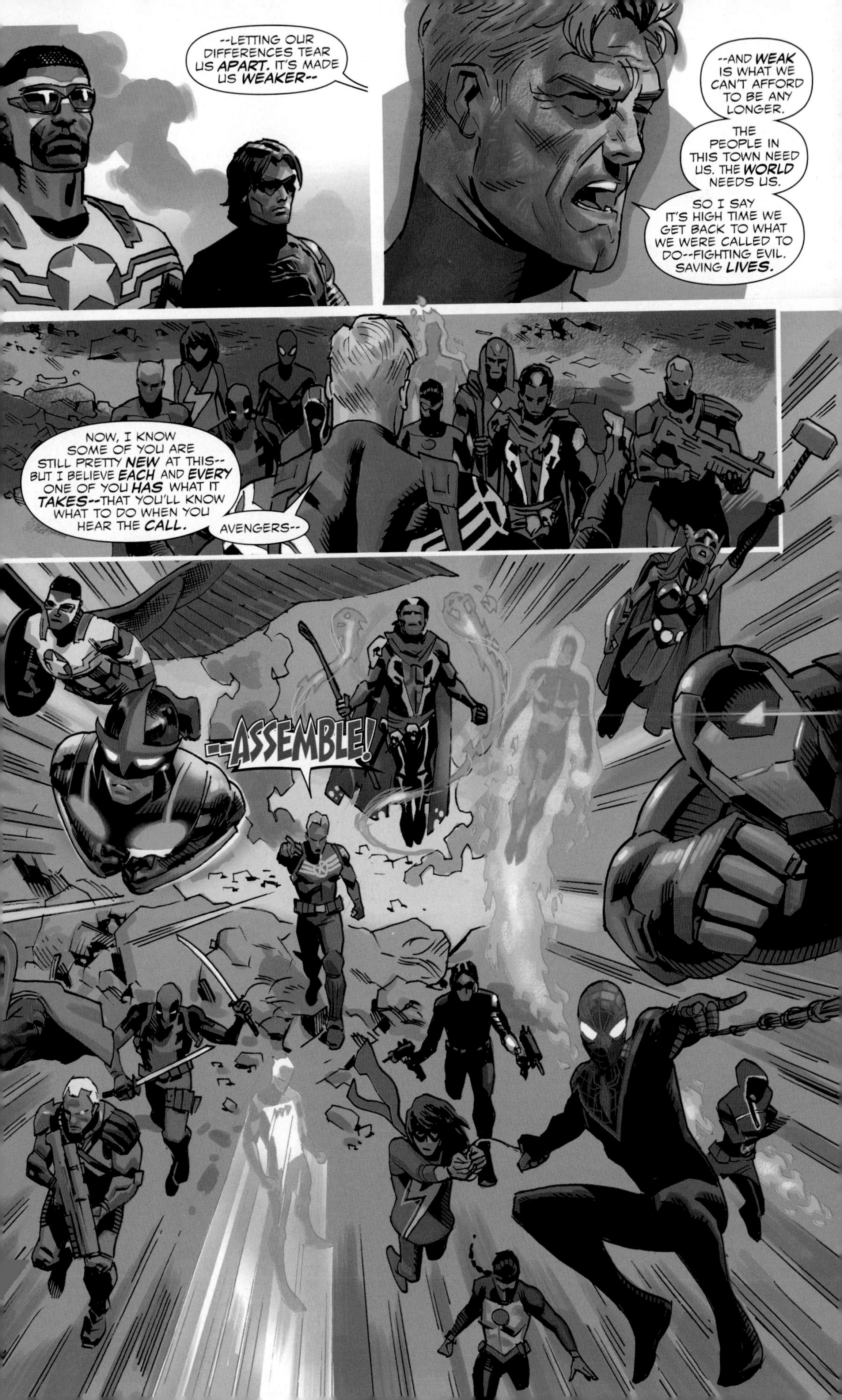

--LETTING OUR DIFFERENCES TEAR US APART. IT'S MADE US WEAKER--
--AND WEAK IS WHAT WE CAN'T AFFORD TO BE ANY LONGER.
THE PEOPLE IN THIS TOWN NEED US. THE WORLD NEEDS US.
SO I SAY IT'S HIGH TIME WE GET BACK TO WHAT WE WERE CALLED TO DO--FIGHTING EVIL. SAVING LIVES.
NOW, I KNOW SOME OF YOU ARE STILL PRETTY NEW AT THIS--BUT I BELIEVE EACH AND EVERY ONE OF YOU HAS WHAT IT TAKES--THAT YOU'LL KNOW WHAT TO DO WHEN YOU HEAR THE CALL.
AVENGERS--
--ASSEMBLE!

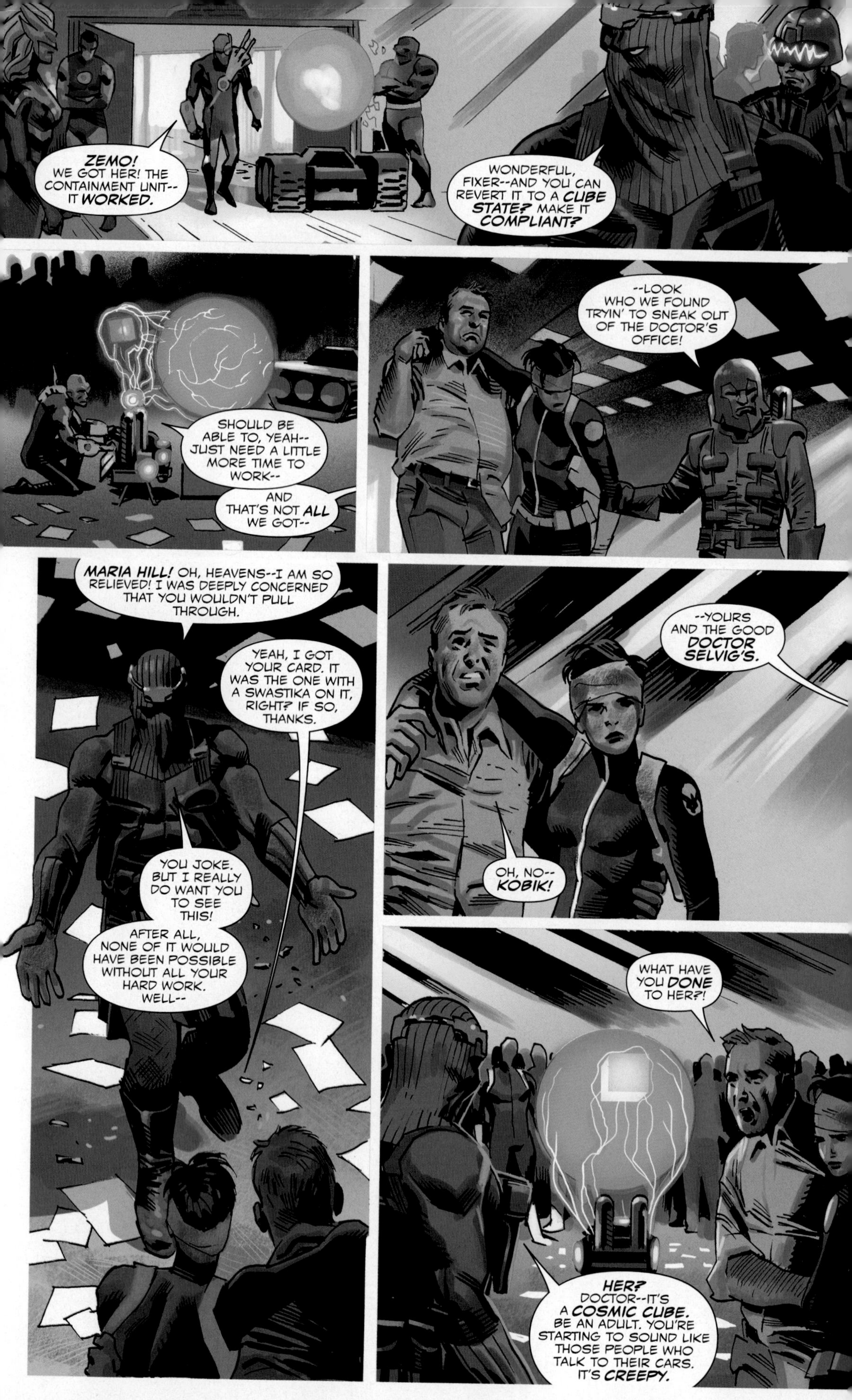
ZEMO! WE GOT HER! THE CONTAINMENT UNIT-- IT WORKED.
WONDERFUL, FIXER--AND YOU CAN REVERT IT TO A CUBE STATE? MAKE IT COMPLIANT?
SHOULD BE ABLE TO, YEAH-- JUST NEED A LITTLE MORE TIME TO WORK--
AND THAT'S NOT ALL WE GOT--
--LOOK WHO WE FOUND TRYIN' TO SNEAK OUT OF THE DOCTOR'S OFFICE!
MARIA HILL! OH, HEAVENS--I AM SO RELIEVED! I WAS DEEPLY CONCERNED THAT YOU WOULDN'T PULL THROUGH.
YEAH, I GOT YOUR CARD. IT WAS THE ONE WITH A SWASTIKA ON IT, RIGHT? IF SO, THANKS.
YOU JOKE. BUT I REALLY DO WANT YOU TO SEE THIS!
AFTER ALL, NONE OF IT WOULD HAVE BEEN POSSIBLE WITHOUT ALL YOUR HARD WORK. WELL--
--YOURS AND THE GOOD DOCTOR SELVIG'S.
OH, NO-- KOBIK!
WHAT HAVE YOU DONE TO HER?!
HER? DOCTOR--IT'S A COSMIC CUBE. BE AN ADULT. YOU'RE STARTING TO SOUND LIKE THOSE PEOPLE WHO TALK TO THEIR CARS. IT'S CREEPY.

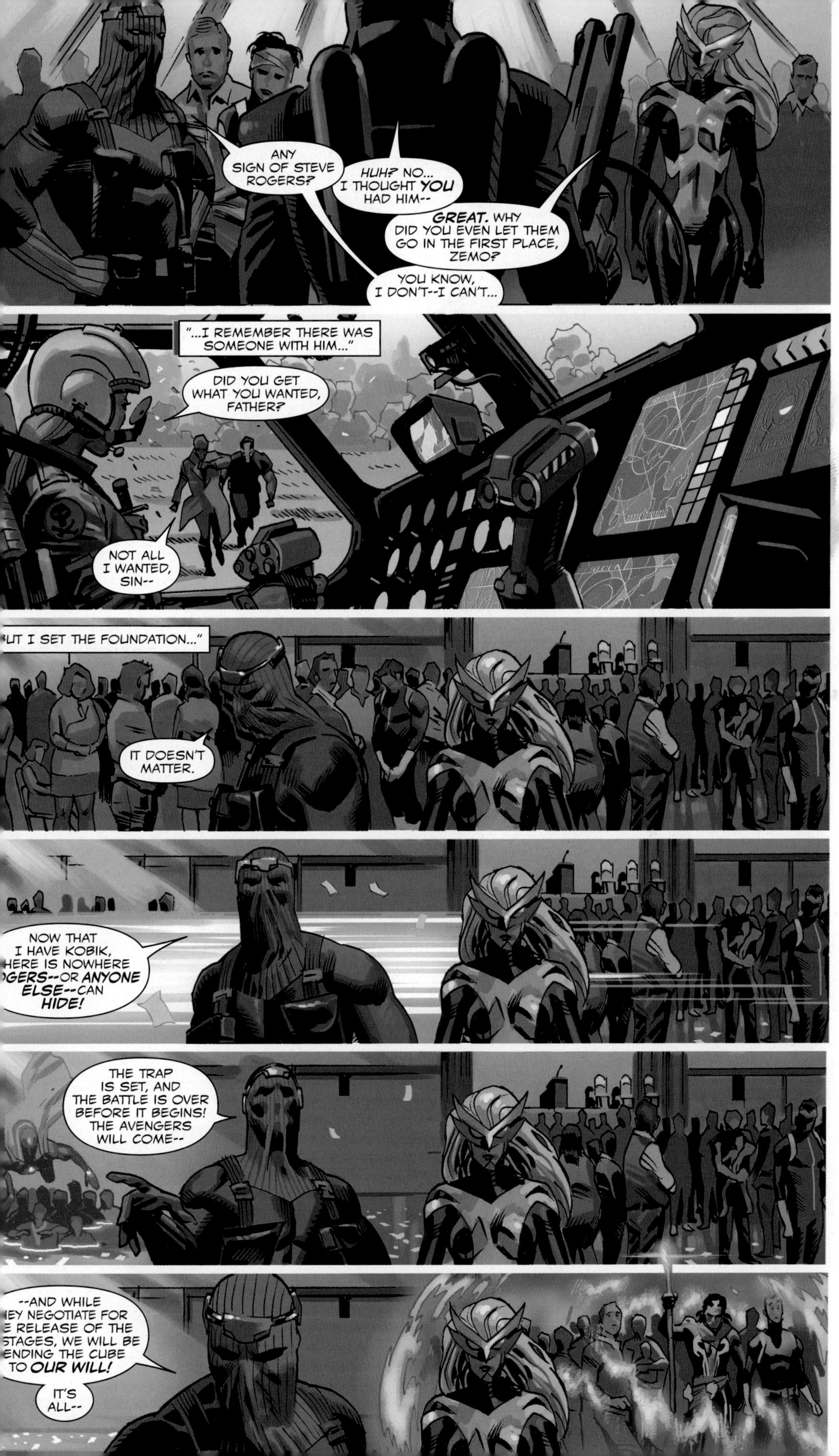
ANY SIGN OF STEVE ROGERS?
HUH? NO... I THOUGHT YOU HAD HIM--
GREAT. WHY DID YOU EVEN LET THEM GO IN THE FIRST PLACE, ZEMO?
YOU KNOW, I DON'T--I CAN'T...
"...I REMEMBER THERE WAS SOMEONE WITH HIM..."
DID YOU GET WHAT YOU WANTED, FATHER?
NOT ALL I WANTED, SIN--
UT I SET THE FOUNDATION..."
IT DOESN'T MATTER.
NOW THAT I HAVE KOBIK, HERE IS NOWHERE OGERS--OR ANYONE ELSE--CAN HIDE!
THE TRAP IS SET, AND THE BATTLE IS OVER BEFORE IT BEGINS! THE AVENGERS WILL COME--
--AND WHILE EY NEGOTIATE FOR E RELEASE OF THE STAGES, WE WILL BE ENDING THE CUBE TO OUR WILL!
IT'S ALL--

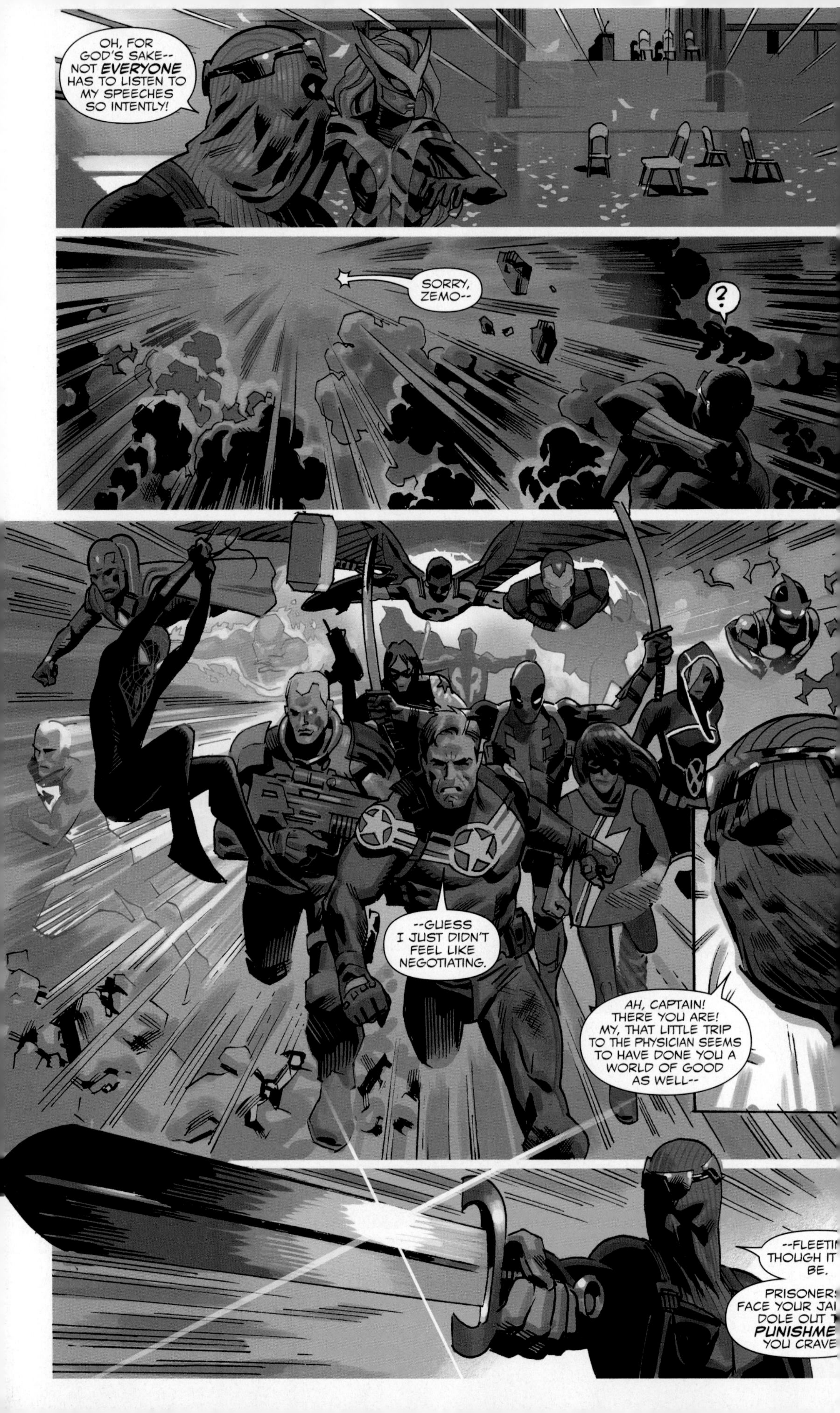
OH, FOR GOD'S SAKE-- NOT **EVERYONE** HAS TO LISTEN TO MY SPEECHES SO INTENTLY!
SORRY, ZEMO--
?
--GUESS I JUST DIDN'T FEEL LIKE NEGOTIATING.
AH, CAPTAIN! THERE YOU ARE! MY, THAT LITTLE TRIP TO THE PHYSICIAN SEEMS TO HAVE DONE YOU A WORLD OF GOOD AS WELL--
--FLEETI THOUGH IT BE.
PRISONER FACE YOUR JA DOLE OUT **PUNISHME** YOU CRAVE

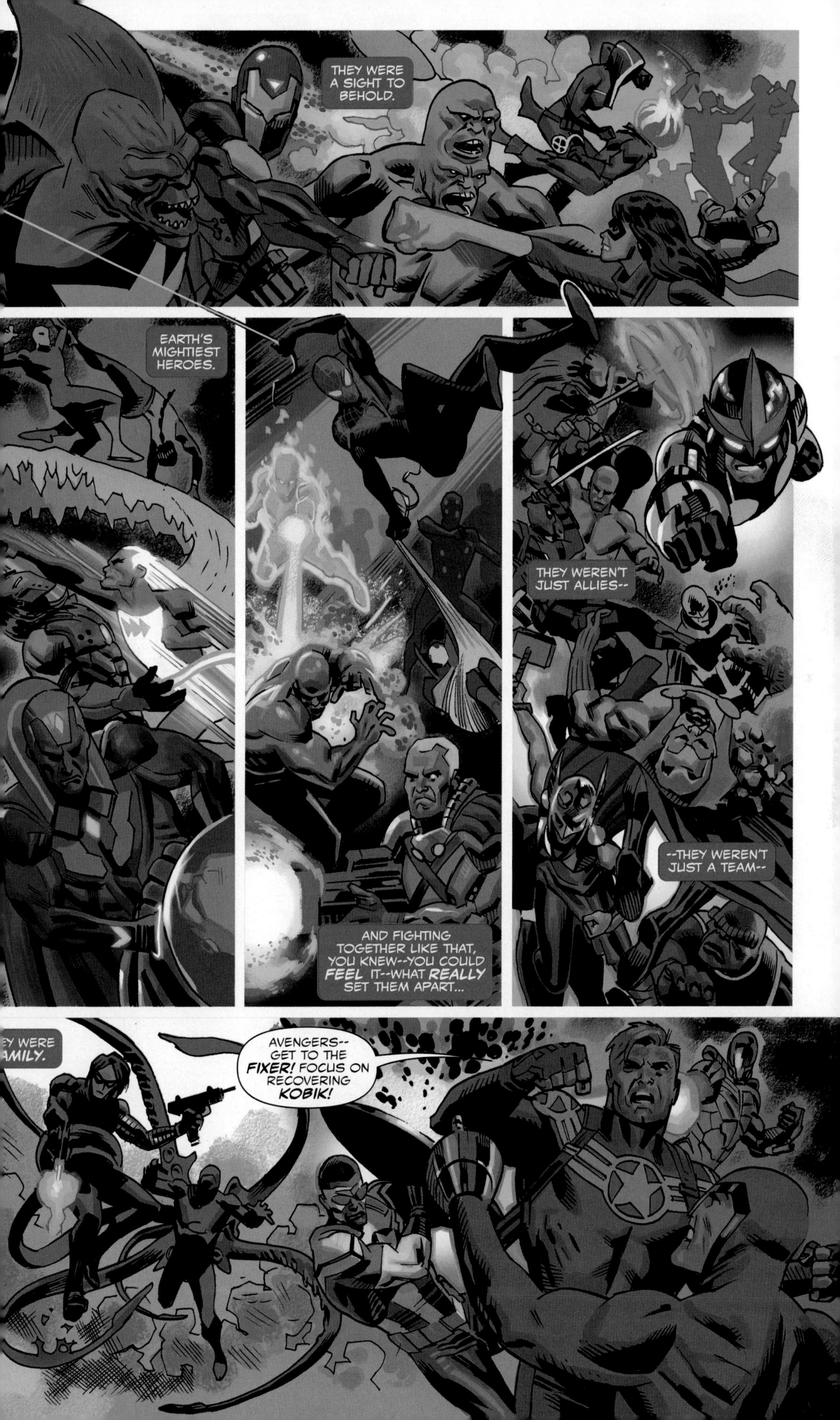
THEY WERE A SIGHT TO BEHOLD.
EARTH'S MIGHTIEST HEROES.
THEY WEREN'T JUST ALLIES--
--THEY WEREN'T JUST A TEAM--
AND FIGHTING TOGETHER LIKE THAT, YOU KNEW--YOU COULD FEEL IT--WHAT REALLY SET THEM APART...
EY WERE AMILY.
AVENGERS-- GET TO THE FIXER! FOCUS ON RECOVERING KOBIK!

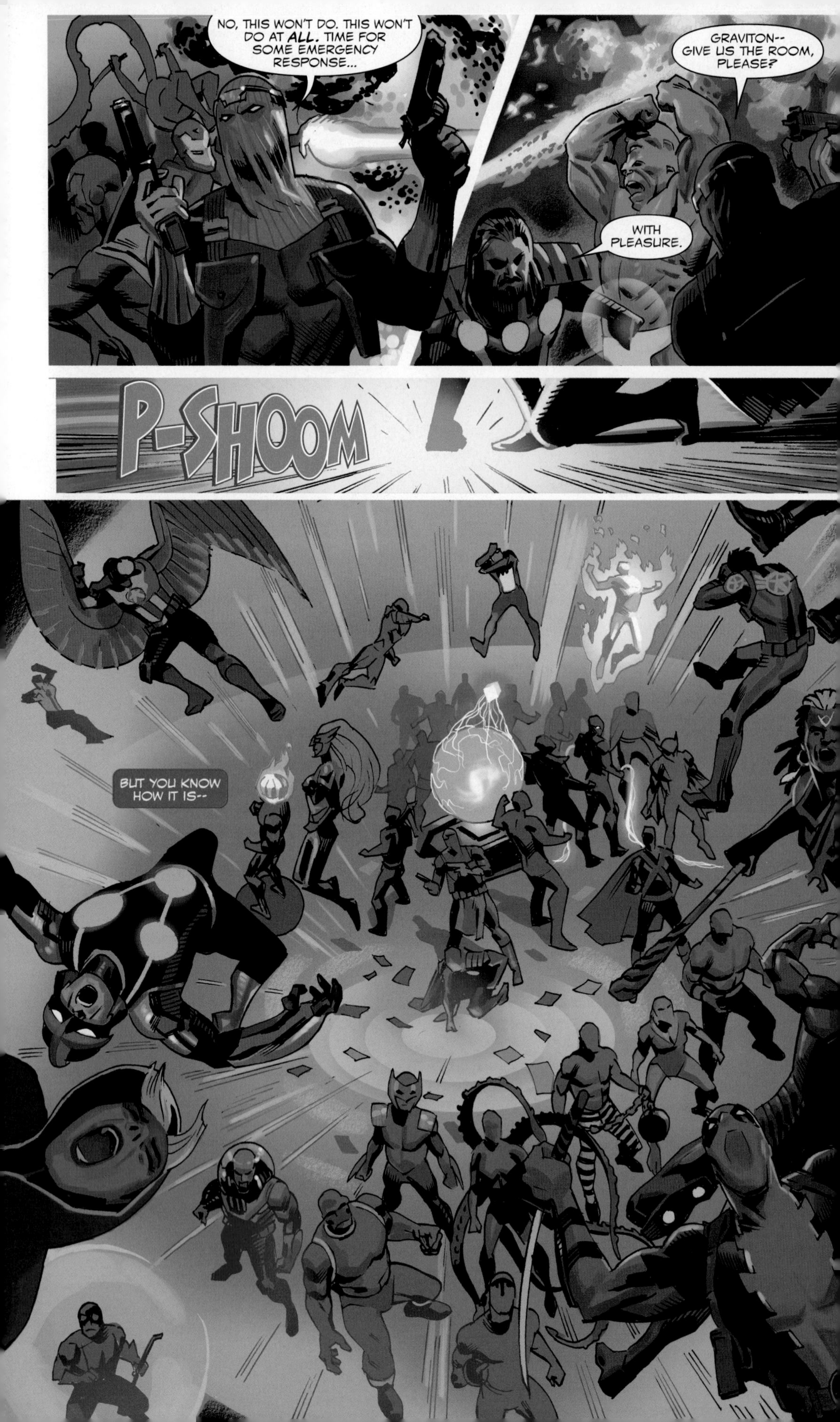
NO, THIS WON'T DO. THIS WON'T DO AT ALL. TIME FOR SOME EMERGENCY RESPONSE...
GRAVITON-- GIVE US THE ROOM, PLEASE?
WITH PLEASURE.
P-SHOOM
BUT YOU KNOW HOW IT IS--

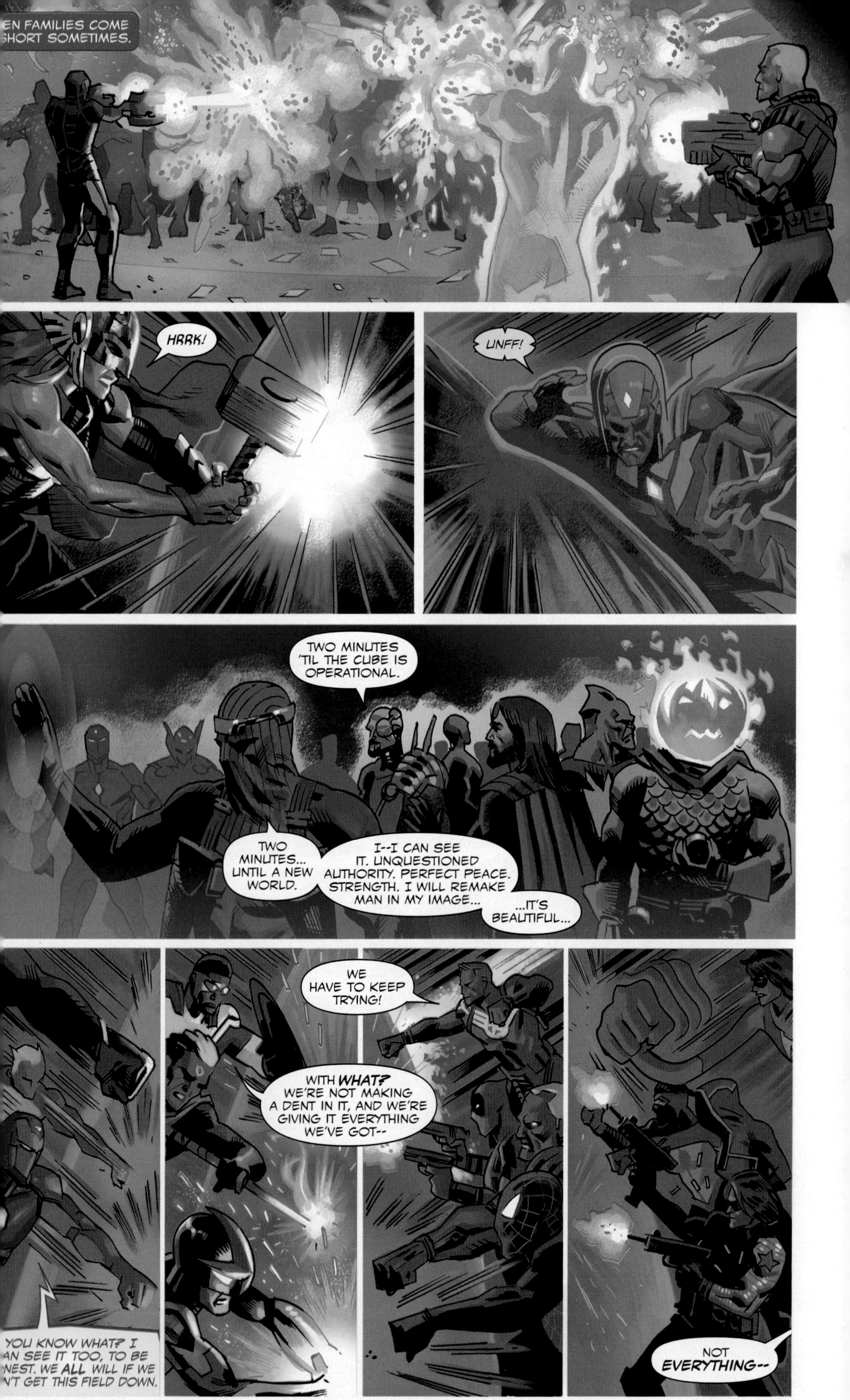
EN FAMILIES COME
SHORT SOMETIMES.
HRRK!
UNFF!
TWO MINUTES 'TIL THE CUBE IS OPERATIONAL.
TWO MINUTES... UNTIL A NEW WORLD.
I--I CAN SEE IT. UNQUESTIONED AUTHORITY. PERFECT PEACE. STRENGTH. I WILL REMAKE MAN IN MY IMAGE...
...IT'S BEAUTIFUL...
YOU KNOW WHAT? I
AN SEE IT TOO, TO BE
NEST. WE ALL WILL IF WE
N'T GET THIS FIELD DOWN.
WE HAVE TO KEEP TRYING!
WITH WHAT? WE'RE NOT MAKING A DENT IN IT, AND WE'RE GIVING IT EVERYTHING WE'VE GOT--
NOT EVERYTHING--

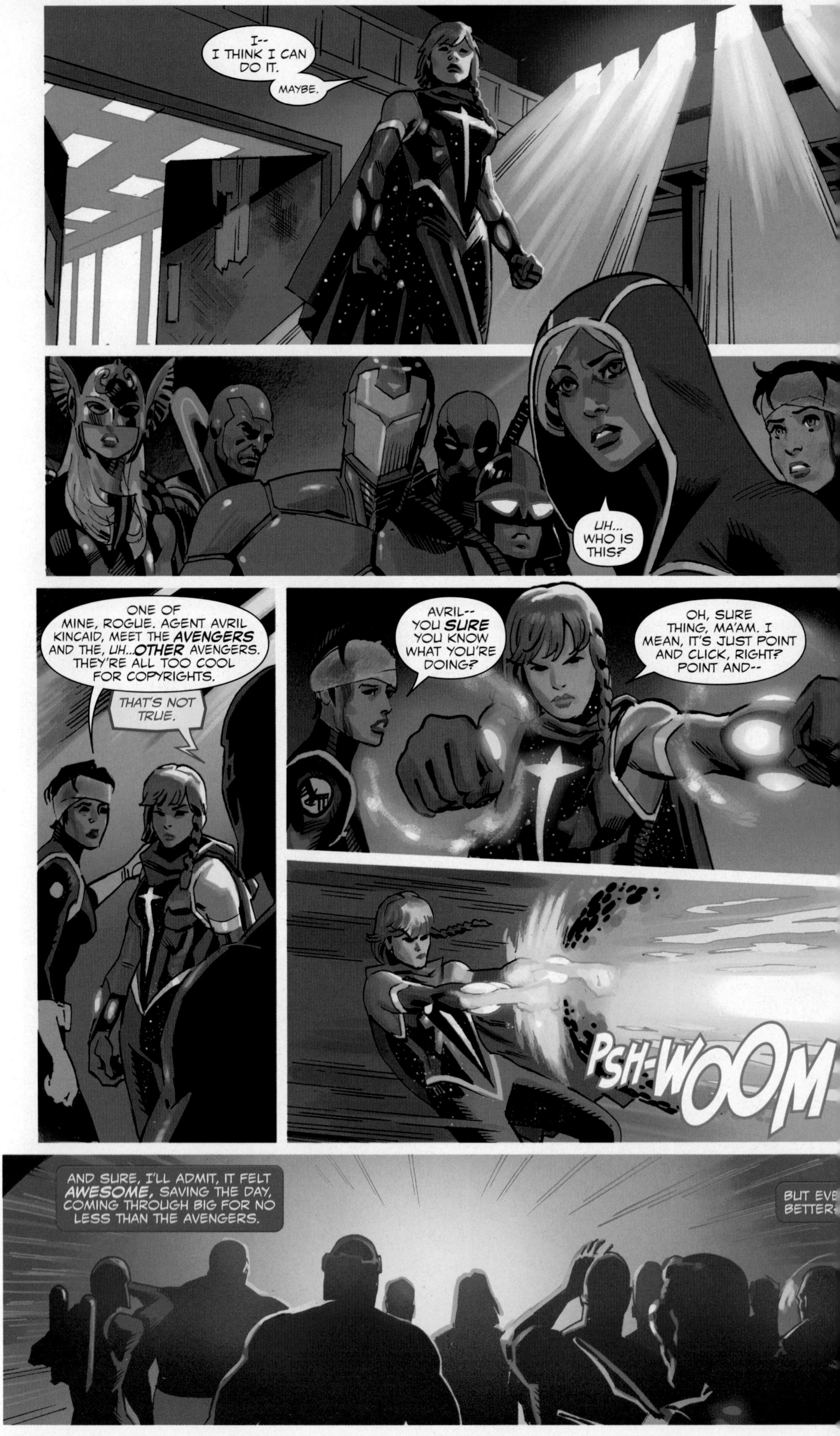
I--
I THINK I CAN DO IT.
MAYBE.
UH... WHO IS THIS?
ONE OF MINE, ROGUE. AGENT AVRIL KINCAID, MEET THE AVENGERS AND THE, UH...OTHER AVENGERS. THEY'RE ALL TOO COOL FOR COPYRIGHTS.
THAT'S NOT TRUE.
AVRIL-- YOU SURE YOU KNOW WHAT YOU'RE DOING?
OH, SURE THING, MA'AM. I MEAN, IT'S JUST POINT AND CLICK, RIGHT? POINT AND--
PSH-WOOM
AND SURE, I'LL ADMIT, IT FELT AWESOME, SAVING THE DAY, COMING THROUGH BIG FOR NO LESS THAN THE AVENGERS.

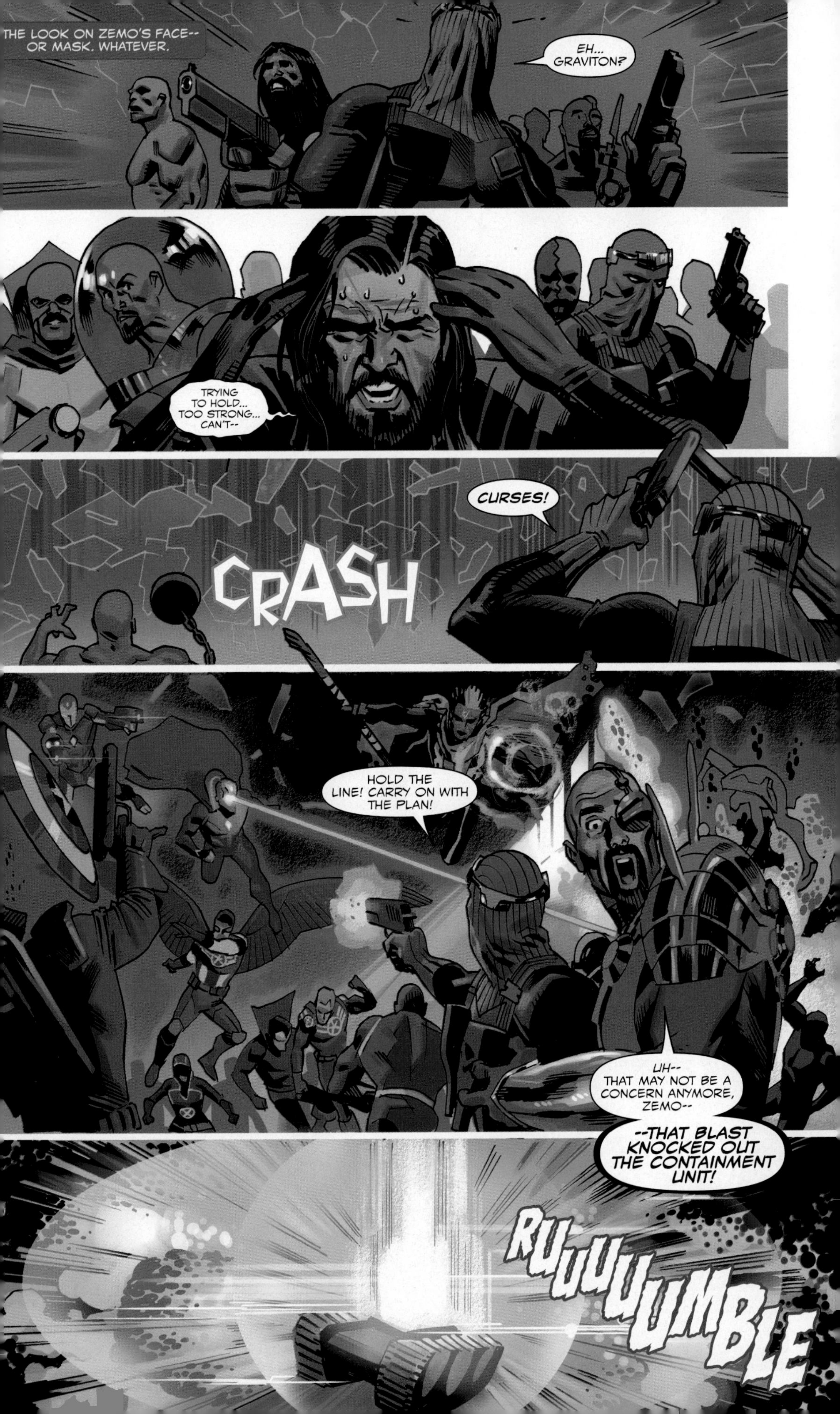
THE LOOK ON ZEMO'S FACE--
OR MASK. WHATEVER.
EH... GRAVITON?
TRYING TO HOLD... TOO STRONG... CAN'T--
CURSES!
CRASH
HOLD THE LINE! CARRY ON WITH THE PLAN!
UH-- THAT MAY NOT BE A CONCERN ANYMORE, ZEMO--
--THAT BLAST KNOCKED OUT THE CONTAINMENT UNIT!
RUUUUUMBLE

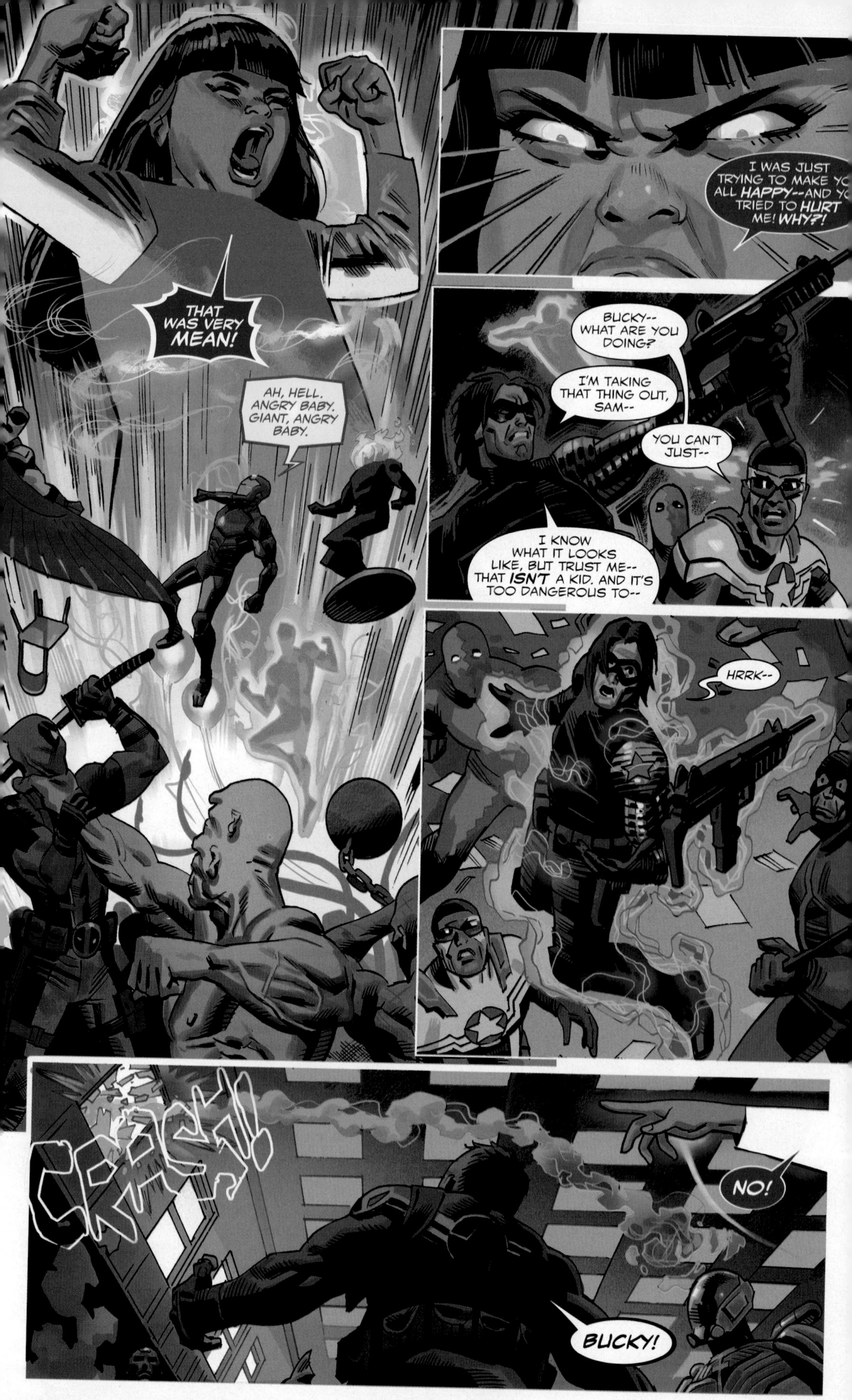

THAT WAS VERY MEAN!
AH, HELL. ANGRY BABY. GIANT, ANGRY BABY.
I WAS JUST TRYING TO MAKE YO ALL HAPPY--AND YO TRIED TO HURT ME! WHY?!
BUCKY-- WHAT ARE YOU DOING?
I'M TAKING THAT THING OUT, SAM--
YOU CAN'T JUST--
I KNOW WHAT IT LOOKS LIKE, BUT TRUST ME-- THAT ISN'T A KID. AND IT'S TOO DANGEROUS TO--
HRRK--
CRACK!!
NO!
BUCKY!

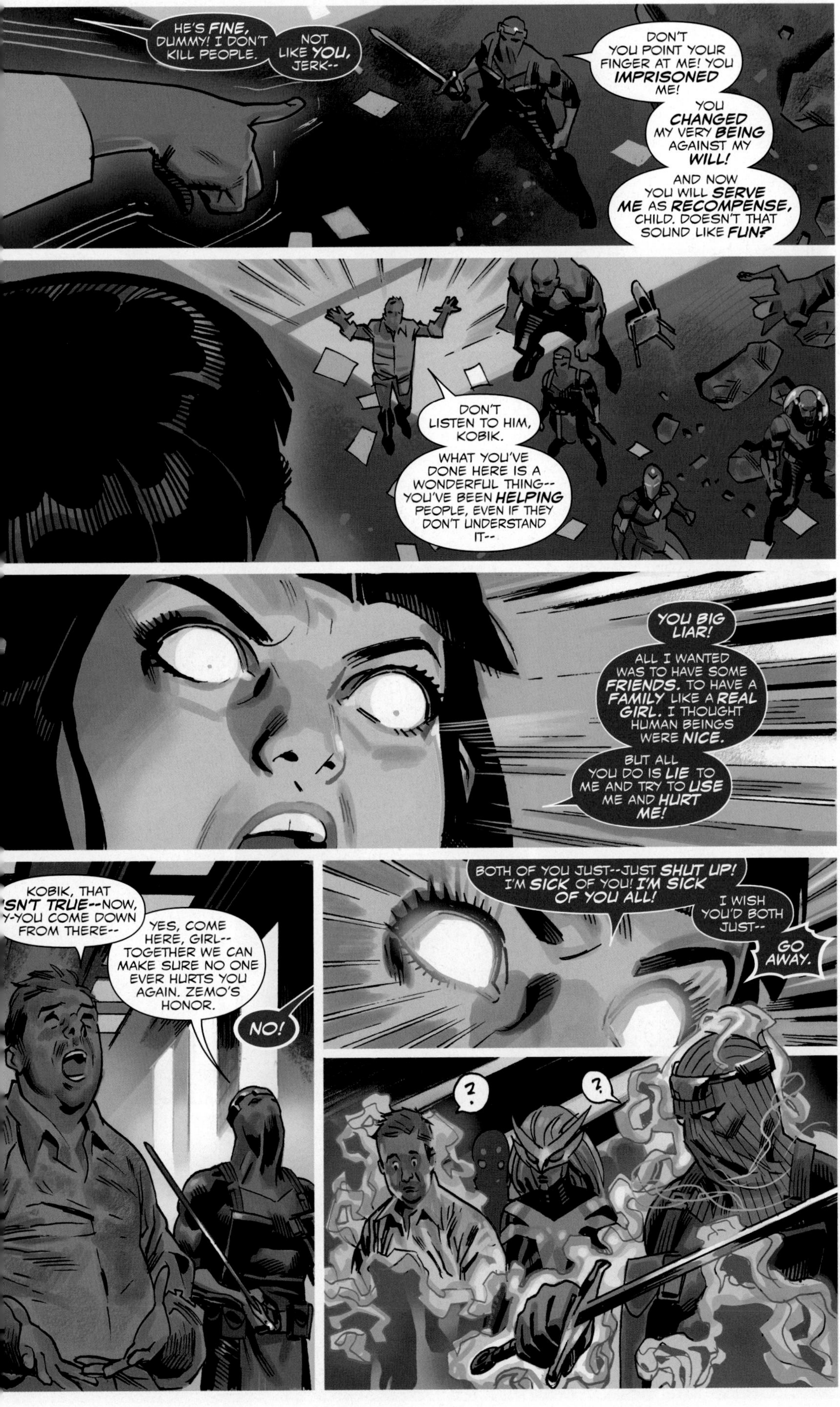
HE'S FINE, DUMMY! I DON'T KILL PEOPLE.
NOT LIKE YOU, JERK--
DON'T YOU POINT YOUR FINGER AT ME! YOU IMPRISONED ME!
YOU CHANGED MY VERY BEING AGAINST MY WILL!
AND NOW YOU WILL SERVE ME AS RECOMPENSE, CHILD. DOESN'T THAT SOUND LIKE FUN?
DON'T LISTEN TO HIM, KOBIK.
WHAT YOU'VE DONE HERE IS A WONDERFUL THING-- YOU'VE BEEN HELPING PEOPLE, EVEN IF THEY DON'T UNDERSTAND IT--
YOU BIG LIAR!
ALL I WANTED WAS TO HAVE SOME FRIENDS. TO HAVE A FAMILY LIKE A REAL GIRL. I THOUGHT HUMAN BEINGS WERE NICE.
BUT ALL YOU DO IS LIE TO ME AND TRY TO USE ME AND HURT ME!
KOBIK, THAT 'SN'T TRUE--NOW, Y-YOU COME DOWN FROM THERE--
YES, COME HERE, GIRL-- TOGETHER WE CAN MAKE SURE NO ONE EVER HURTS YOU AGAIN. ZEMO'S HONOR.
NO!
BOTH OF YOU JUST--JUST SHUT UP! I'M SICK OF YOU! I'M SICK OF YOU ALL!
I WISH YOU'D BOTH JUST--
GO AWAY.
?
?

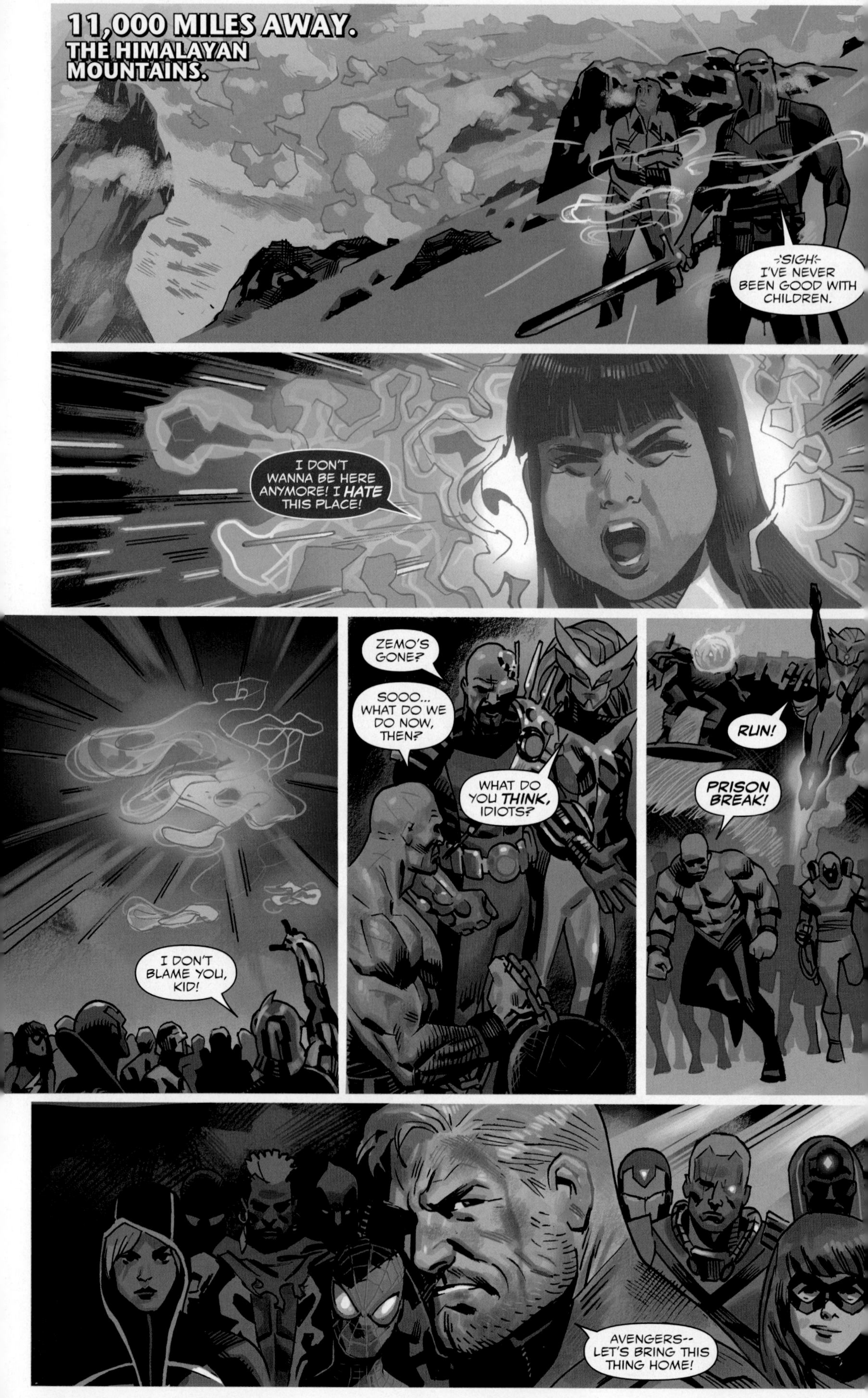
11,000 MILES AWAY. THE HIMALAYAN MOUNTAINS.
SIGH I'VE NEVER BEEN GOOD WITH CHILDREN.
I DON'T WANNA BE HERE ANYMORE! I HATE THIS PLACE!
I DON'T BLAME YOU, KID!
ZEMO'S GONE?
SOOO... WHAT DO WE DO NOW, THEN?
WHAT DO YOU THINK, IDIOTS?
RUN!
PRISON BREAK!
AVENGERS-- LET'S BRING THIS THING HOME!

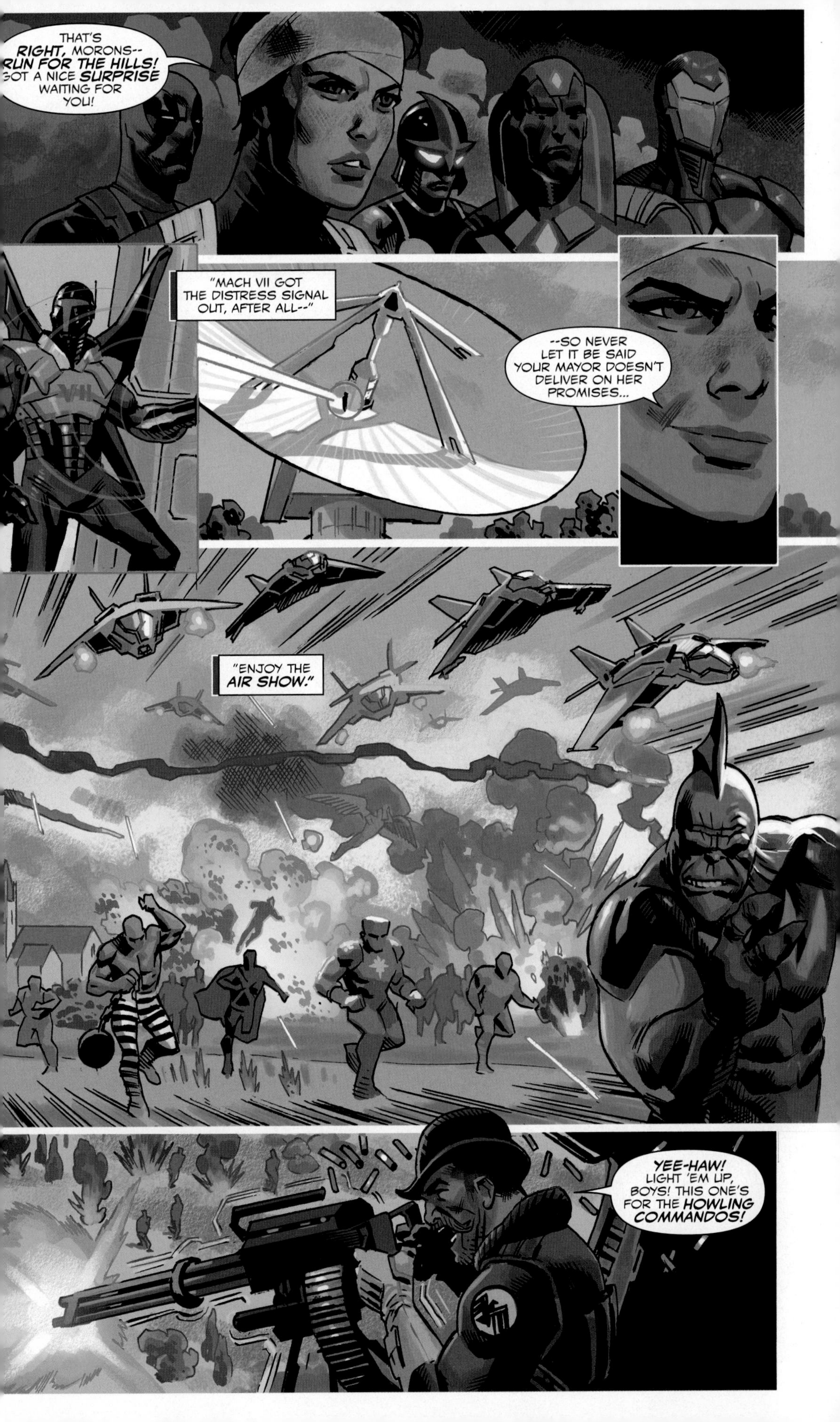
THAT'S RIGHT, MORONS-- RUN FOR THE HILLS! GOT A NICE SURPRISE WAITING FOR YOU!
"MACH VII GOT THE DISTRESS SIGNAL OUT, AFTER ALL--"
--SO NEVER LET IT BE SAID YOUR MAYOR DOESN'T DELIVER ON HER PROMISES...
"ENJOY THE AIR SHOW."
YEE-HAW! LIGHT 'EM UP, BOYS! THIS ONE'S FOR THE HOWLING COMMANDOS!

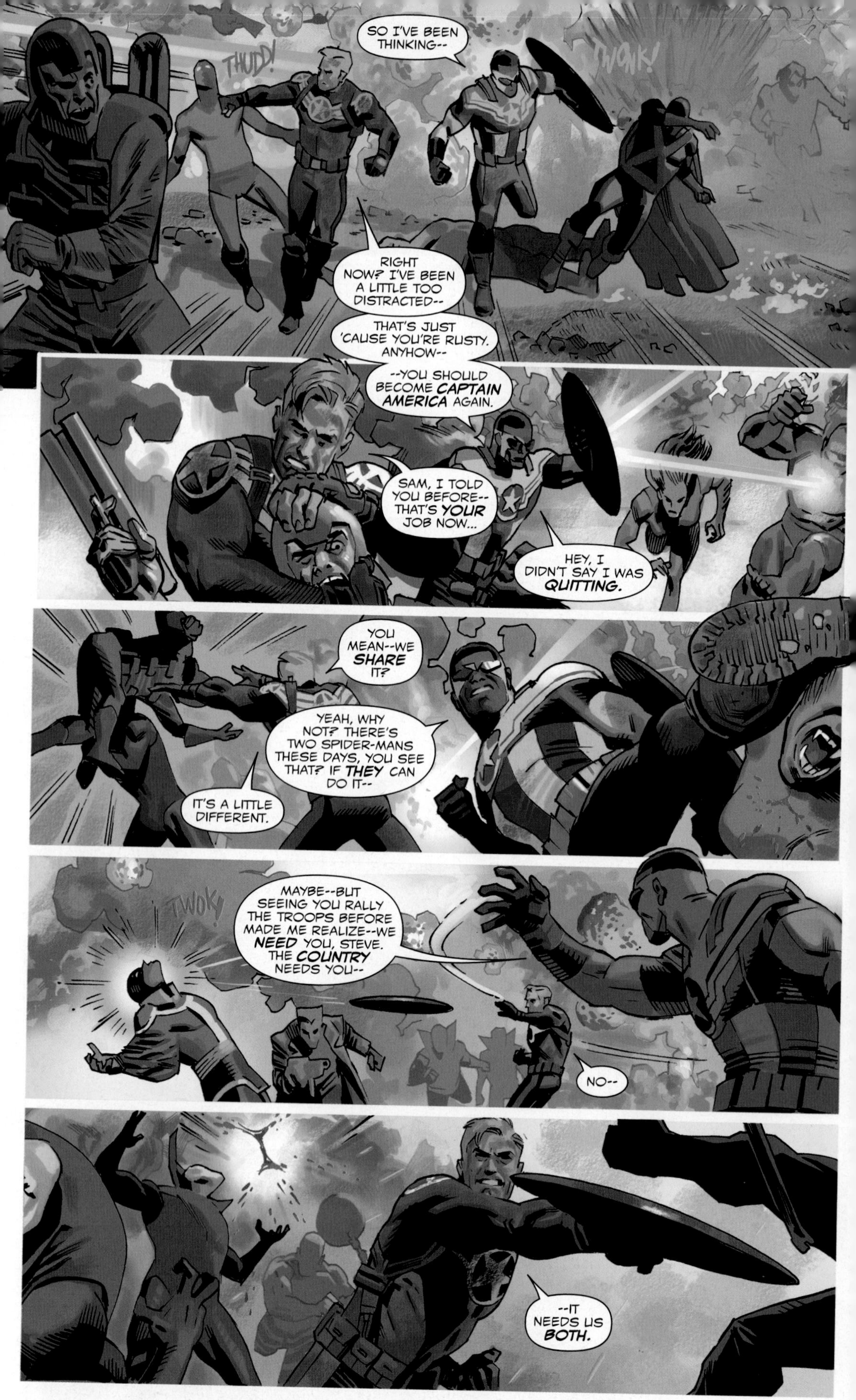
THUDD!
SO I'VE BEEN THINKING--
TWONK!
RIGHT NOW? I'VE BEEN A LITTLE TOO DISTRACTED--
THAT'S JUST 'CAUSE YOU'RE RUSTY. ANYHOW--
--YOU SHOULD BECOME CAPTAIN AMERICA AGAIN.
SAM, I TOLD YOU BEFORE-- THAT'S YOUR JOB NOW...
HEY, I DIDN'T SAY I WAS QUITTING.
YOU MEAN--WE SHARE IT?
YEAH, WHY NOT? THERE'S TWO SPIDER-MANS THESE DAYS, YOU SEE THAT? IF THEY CAN DO IT--
IT'S A LITTLE DIFFERENT.
MAYBE--BUT SEEING YOU RALLY THE TROOPS BEFORE MADE ME REALIZE--WE NEED YOU, STEVE. THE COUNTRY NEEDS YOU--
NO--
--IT NEEDS US BOTH.

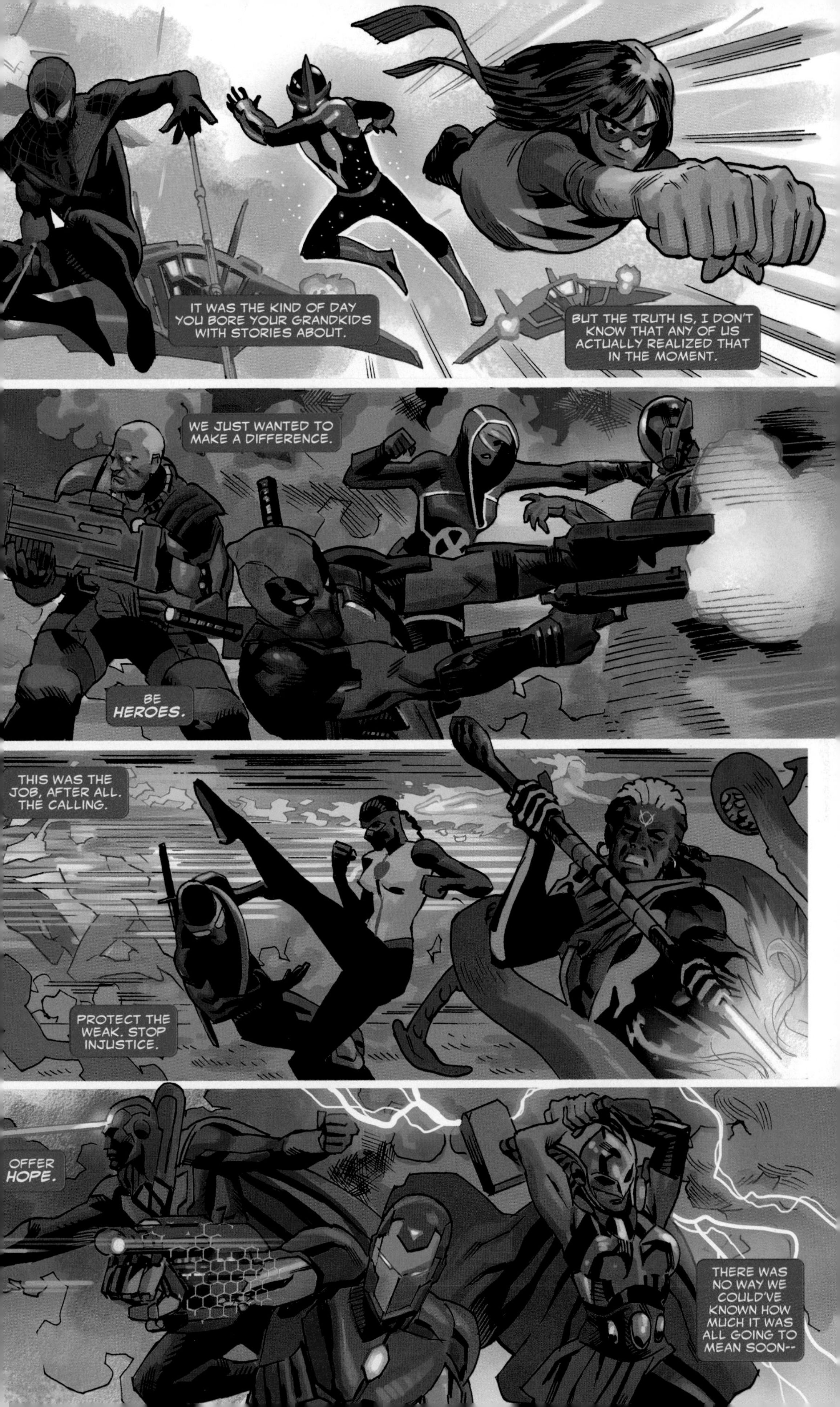
IT WAS THE KIND OF DAY YOU BORE YOUR GRANDKIDS WITH STORIES ABOUT.
BUT THE TRUTH IS, I DON'T KNOW THAT ANY OF US ACTUALLY REALIZED THAT IN THE MOMENT.
WE JUST WANTED TO MAKE A DIFFERENCE.
BE HEROES.
THIS WAS THE JOB, AFTER ALL. THE CALLING.
PROTECT THE WEAK. STOP INJUSTICE.
OFFER HOPE.
THERE WAS NO WAY WE COULD'VE KNOWN HOW MUCH IT WAS ALL GOING TO MEAN SOON--

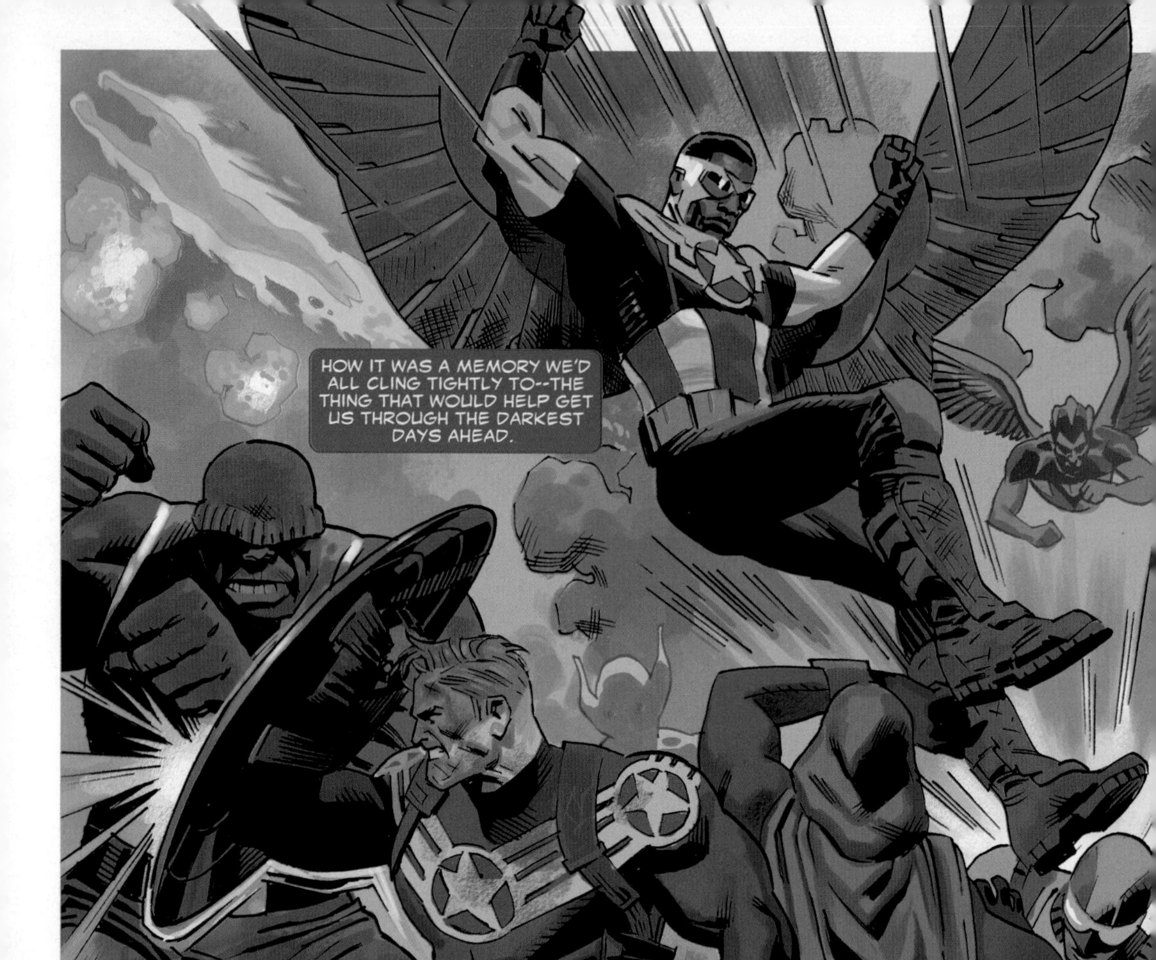
HOW IT WAS A MEMORY WE'D ALL CLING TIGHTLY TO--THE THING THAT WOULD HELP GET US THROUGH THE DARKEST DAYS AHEAD.
ONCE IT ALL STARTED TO GO WRONG--

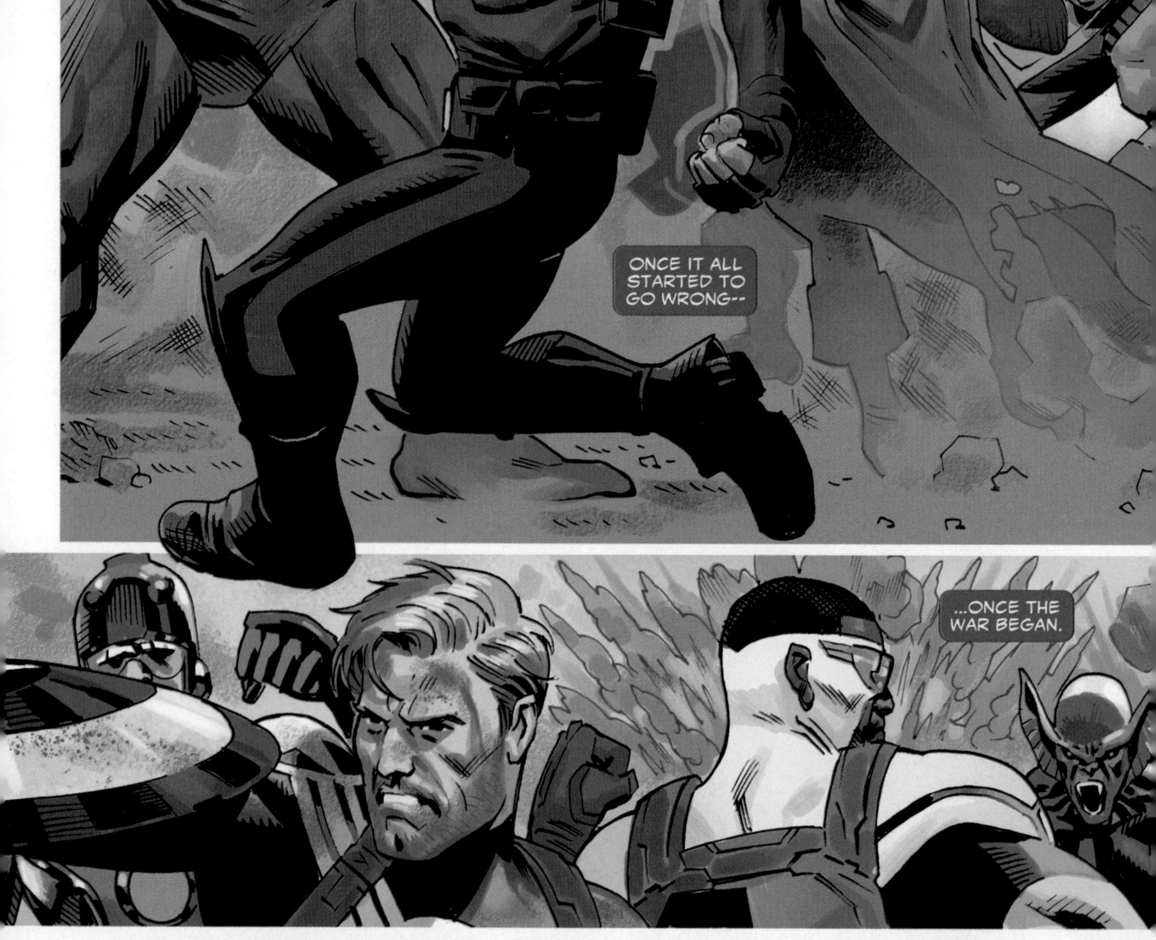
...ONCE THE WAR BEGAN.

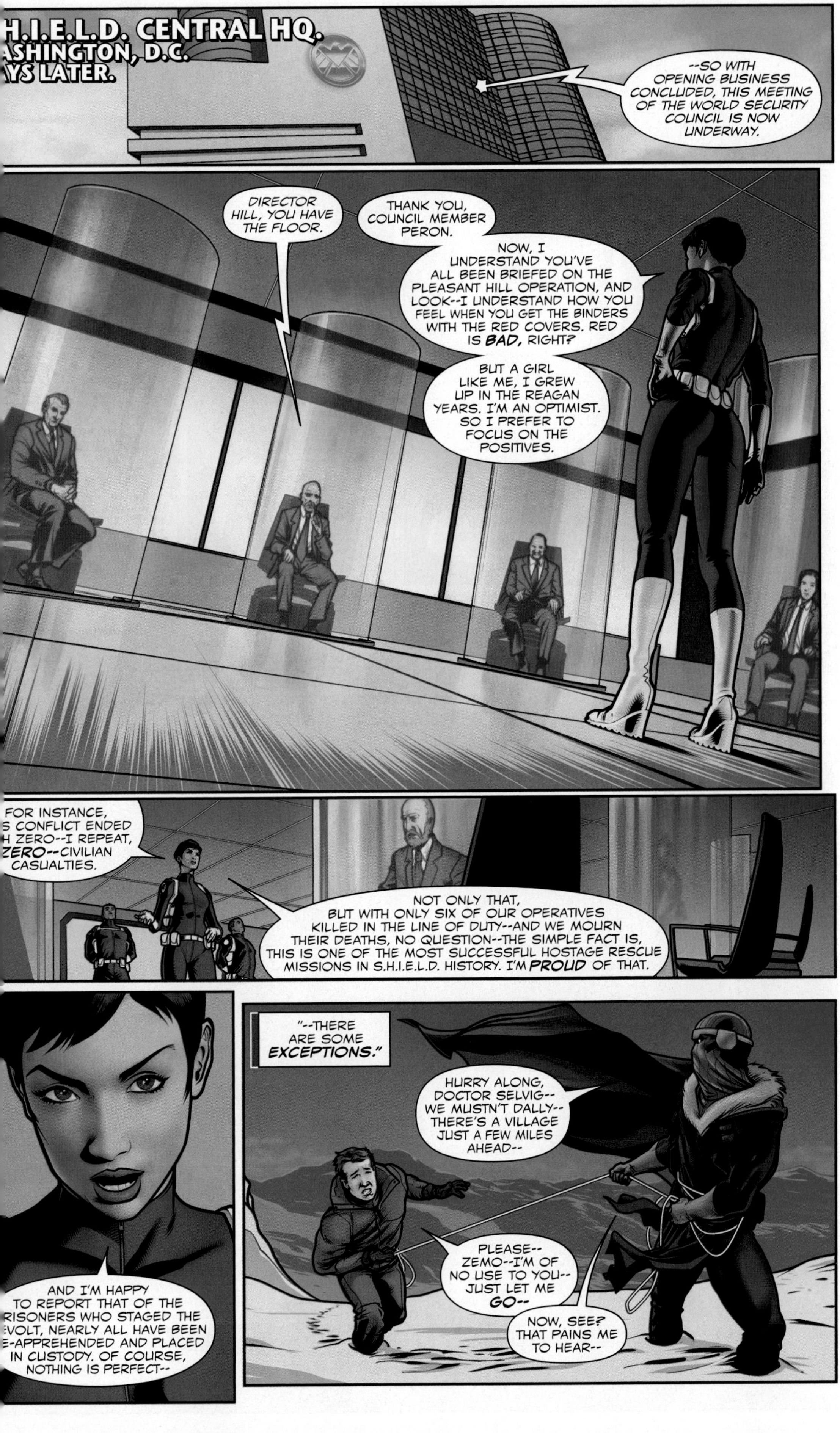
H.I.E.L.D. CENTRAL HQ.
ASHINGTON, D.C.
YS LATER.
--SO WITH OPENING BUSINESS CONCLUDED, THIS MEETING OF THE WORLD SECURITY COUNCIL IS NOW UNDERWAY.
DIRECTOR HILL, YOU HAVE THE FLOOR.
THANK YOU, COUNCIL MEMBER PERON.
NOW, I UNDERSTAND YOU'VE ALL BEEN BRIEFED ON THE PLEASANT HILL OPERATION, AND LOOK--I UNDERSTAND HOW YOU FEEL WHEN YOU GET THE BINDERS WITH THE RED COVERS. RED IS BAD, RIGHT?
BUT A GIRL LIKE ME, I GREW UP IN THE REAGAN YEARS. I'M AN OPTIMIST. SO I PREFER TO FOCUS ON THE POSITIVES.
FOR INSTANCE, S CONFLICT ENDED H ZERO--I REPEAT, ZERO--CIVILIAN CASUALTIES.
NOT ONLY THAT, BUT WITH ONLY SIX OF OUR OPERATIVES KILLED IN THE LINE OF DUTY--AND WE MOURN THEIR DEATHS, NO QUESTION--THE SIMPLE FACT IS, THIS IS ONE OF THE MOST SUCCESSFUL HOSTAGE RESCUE MISSIONS IN S.H.I.E.L.D. HISTORY. I'M PROUD OF THAT.
AND I'M HAPPY TO REPORT THAT OF THE RISONERS WHO STAGED THE EVOLT, NEARLY ALL HAVE BEEN E-APPREHENDED AND PLACED IN CUSTODY. OF COURSE, NOTHING IS PERFECT--
"--THERE ARE SOME EXCEPTIONS."
HURRY ALONG, DOCTOR SELVIG--WE MUSTN'T DALLY--THERE'S A VILLAGE JUST A FEW MILES AHEAD--
PLEASE--ZEMO--I'M OF NO USE TO YOU--JUST LET ME GO--
NOW, SEE? THAT PAINS ME TO HEAR--

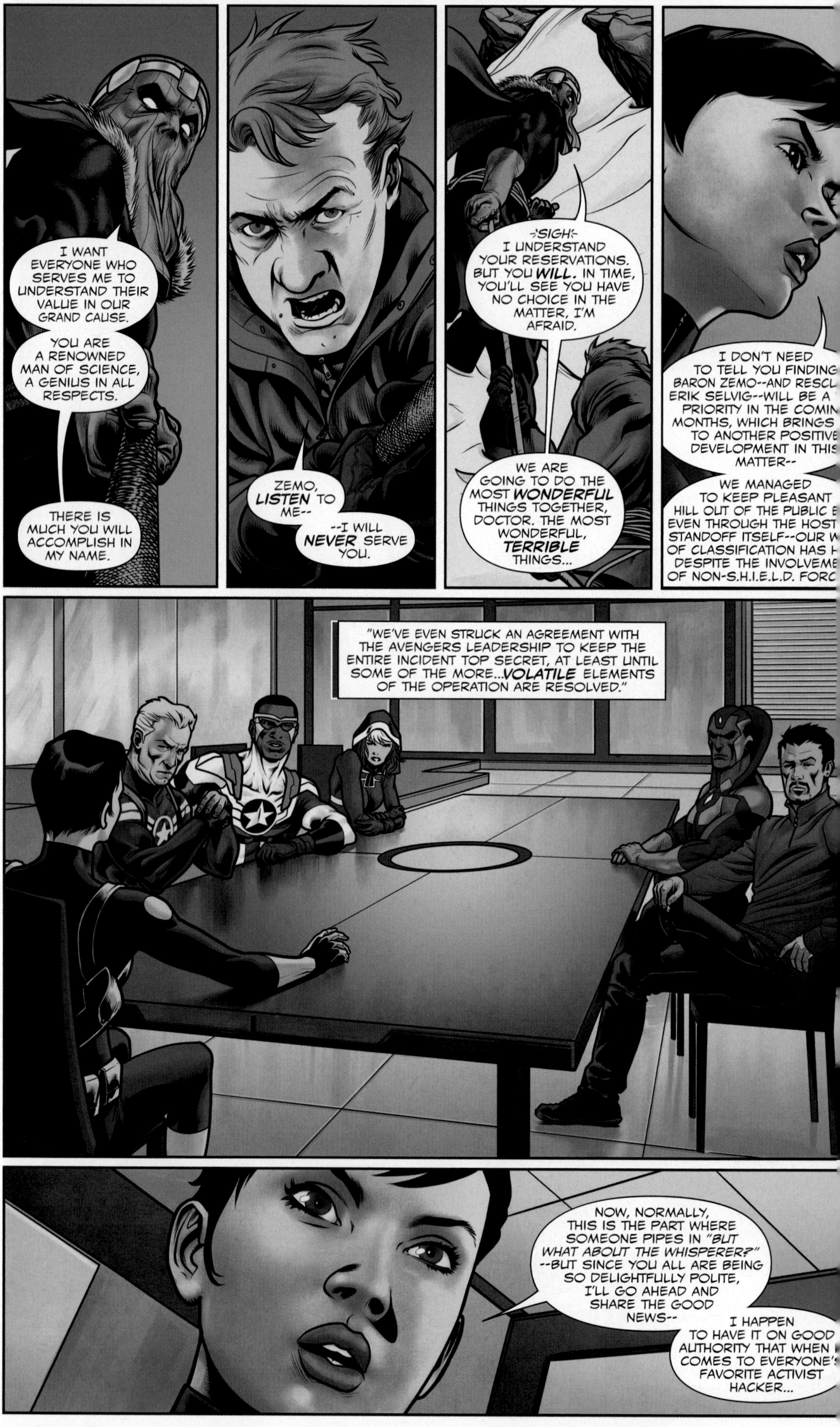
I WANT EVERYONE WHO SERVES ME TO UNDERSTAND THEIR VALUE IN OUR GRAND CAUSE.
YOU ARE A RENOWNED MAN OF SCIENCE, A GENIUS IN ALL RESPECTS.
THERE IS MUCH YOU WILL ACCOMPLISH IN MY NAME.
ZEMO, LISTEN TO ME--
--I WILL NEVER SERVE YOU.
-SIGH- I UNDERSTAND YOUR RESERVATIONS. BUT YOU WILL. IN TIME, YOU'LL SEE YOU HAVE NO CHOICE IN THE MATTER, I'M AFRAID.
WE ARE GOING TO DO THE MOST WONDERFUL THINGS TOGETHER, DOCTOR. THE MOST WONDERFUL, TERRIBLE THINGS...
I DON'T NEED TO TELL YOU FINDING BARON ZEMO--AND RESCU ERIK SELVIG--WILL BE A PRIORITY IN THE COMIN MONTHS, WHICH BRINGS TO ANOTHER POSITIVE DEVELOPMENT IN THIS MATTER--
WE MANAGED TO KEEP PLEASANT HILL OUT OF THE PUBLIC E EVEN THROUGH THE HOST STANDOFF ITSELF--OUR W OF CLASSIFICATION HAS H DESPITE THE INVOLVEME OF NON-S.H.I.E.L.D. FORC
"WE'VE EVEN STRUCK AN AGREEMENT WITH THE AVENGERS LEADERSHIP TO KEEP THE ENTIRE INCIDENT TOP SECRET, AT LEAST UNTIL SOME OF THE MORE...VOLATILE ELEMENTS OF THE OPERATION ARE RESOLVED."
NOW, NORMALLY, THIS IS THE PART WHERE SOMEONE PIPES IN "BUT WHAT ABOUT THE WHISPERER?" --BUT SINCE YOU ALL ARE BEING SO DELIGHTFULLY POLITE, I'LL GO AHEAD AND SHARE THE GOOD NEWS--
I HAPPEN TO HAVE IT ON GOOD AUTHORITY THAT WHEN COMES TO EVERYONE' FAVORITE ACTIVIST HACKER...

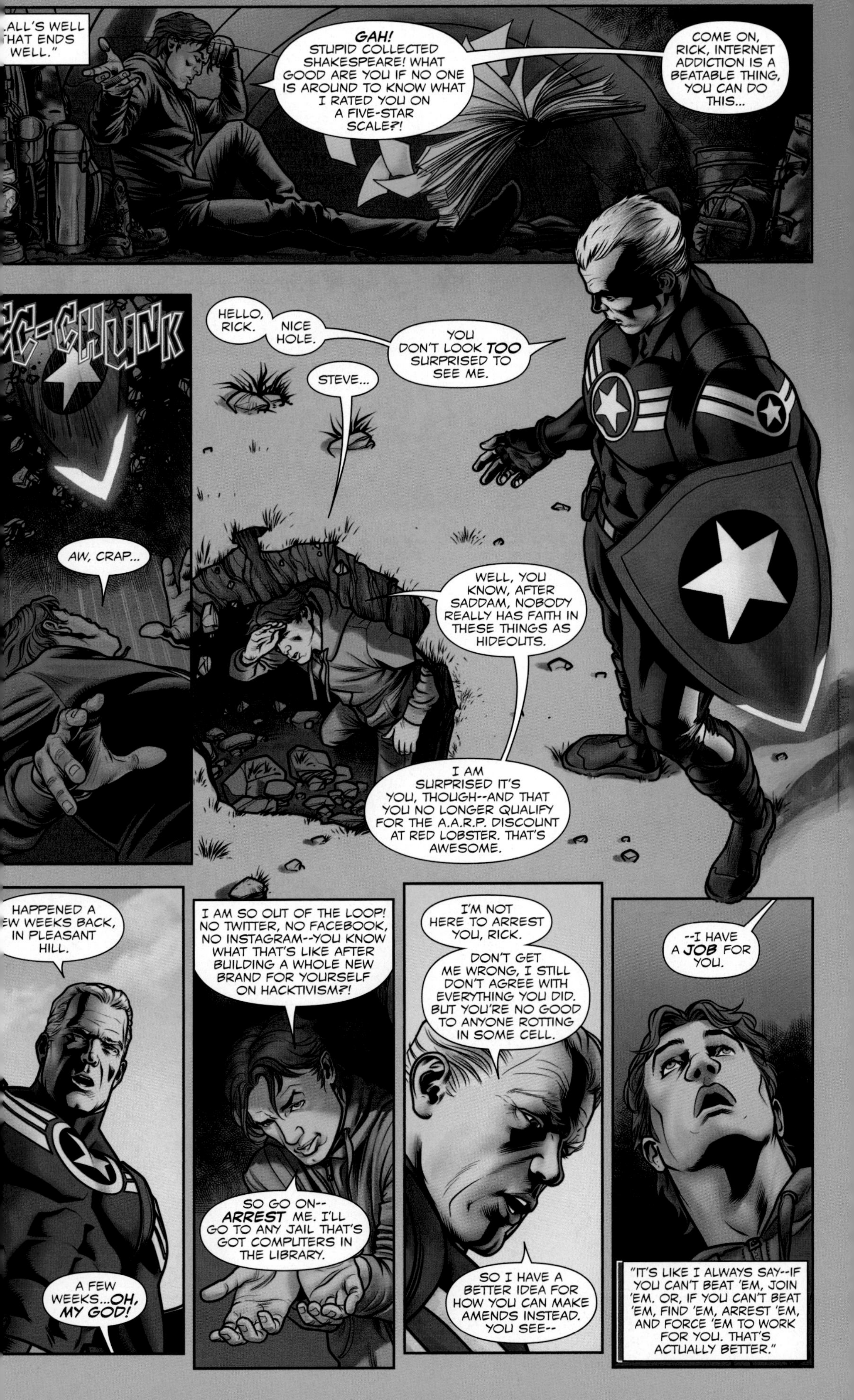
...ALL'S WELL THAT ENDS WELL."
GAH! STUPID COLLECTED SHAKESPEARE! WHAT GOOD ARE YOU IF NO ONE IS AROUND TO KNOW WHAT I RATED YOU ON A FIVE-STAR SCALE?!
COME ON, RICK, INTERNET ADDICTION IS A BEATABLE THING, YOU CAN DO THIS...
C-CHUNK
AW, CRAP...
HELLO, RICK.
NICE HOLE.
YOU DON'T LOOK TOO SURPRISED TO SEE ME.
STEVE...
WELL, YOU KNOW, AFTER SADDAM, NOBODY REALLY HAS FAITH IN THESE THINGS AS HIDEOUTS.
I AM SURPRISED IT'S YOU, THOUGH--AND THAT YOU NO LONGER QUALIFY FOR THE A.A.R.P. DISCOUNT AT RED LOBSTER. THAT'S AWESOME.
HAPPENED A FEW WEEKS BACK, IN PLEASANT HILL.
A FEW WEEKS...OH, MY GOD!
I AM SO OUT OF THE LOOP! NO TWITTER, NO FACEBOOK, NO INSTAGRAM--YOU KNOW WHAT THAT'S LIKE AFTER BUILDING A WHOLE NEW BRAND FOR YOURSELF ON HACKTIVISM?!
SO GO ON--ARREST ME. I'LL GO TO ANY JAIL THAT'S GOT COMPUTERS IN THE LIBRARY.
I'M NOT HERE TO ARREST YOU, RICK.
DON'T GET ME WRONG, I STILL DON'T AGREE WITH EVERYTHING YOU DID. BUT YOU'RE NO GOOD TO ANYONE ROTTING IN SOME CELL.
SO I HAVE A BETTER IDEA FOR HOW YOU CAN MAKE AMENDS INSTEAD. YOU SEE--
--I HAVE A JOB FOR YOU.
"IT'S LIKE I ALWAYS SAY--IF YOU CAN'T BEAT 'EM, JOIN 'EM. OR, IF YOU CAN'T BEAT 'EM, FIND 'EM, ARREST 'EM, AND FORCE 'EM TO WORK FOR YOU. THAT'S ACTUALLY BETTER."

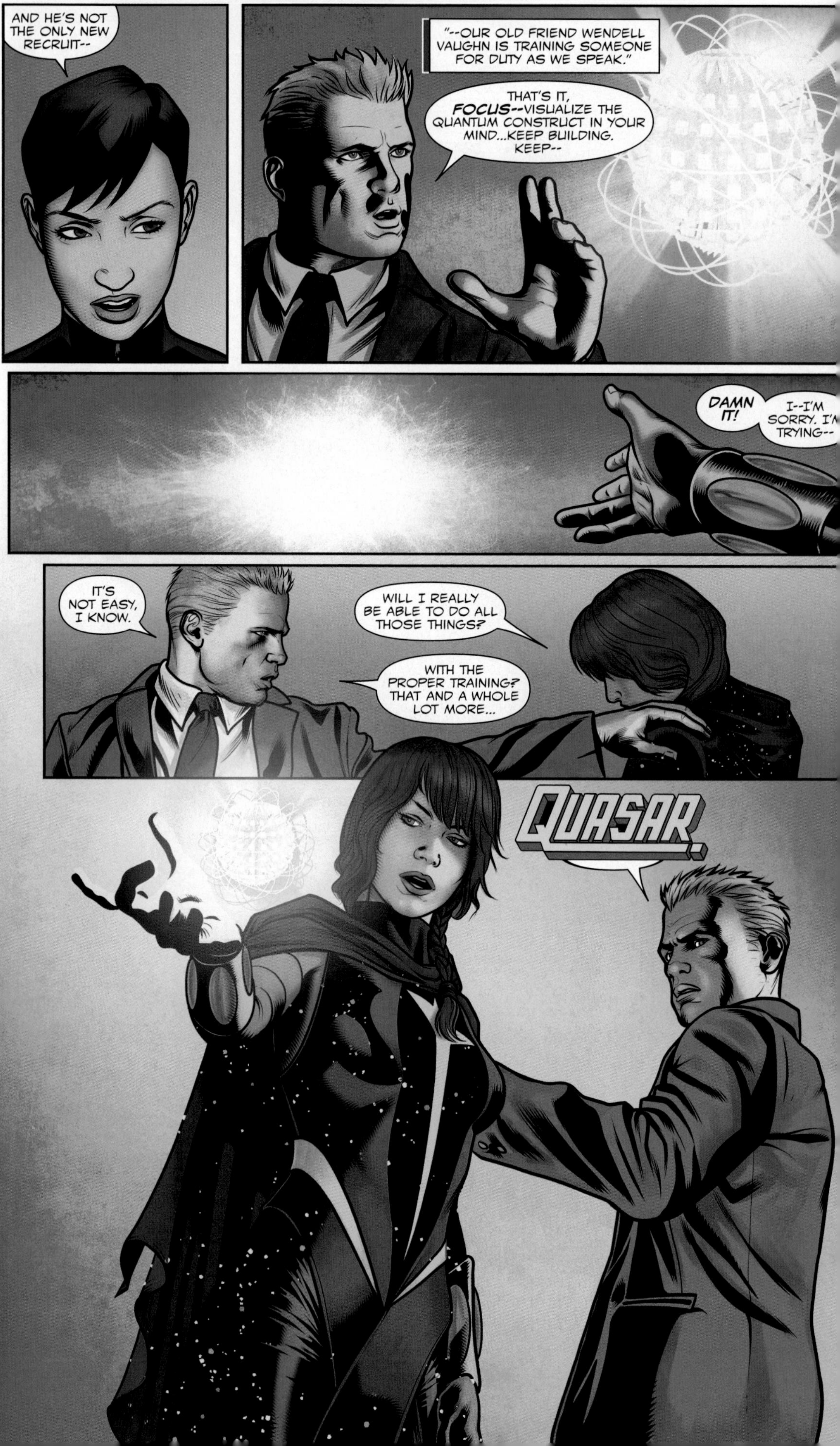
AND HE'S NOT THE ONLY NEW RECRUIT--
"--OUR OLD FRIEND WENDELL VAUGHN IS TRAINING SOMEONE FOR DUTY AS WE SPEAK."
THAT'S IT, FOCUS--VISUALIZE THE QUANTUM CONSTRUCT IN YOUR MIND...KEEP BUILDING. KEEP--
DAMN IT!
I--I'M SORRY. I'M TRYING--
IT'S NOT EASY, I KNOW.
WILL I REALLY BE ABLE TO DO ALL THOSE THINGS?
WITH THE PROPER TRAINING? THAT AND A WHOLE LOT MORE...
QUASAR.

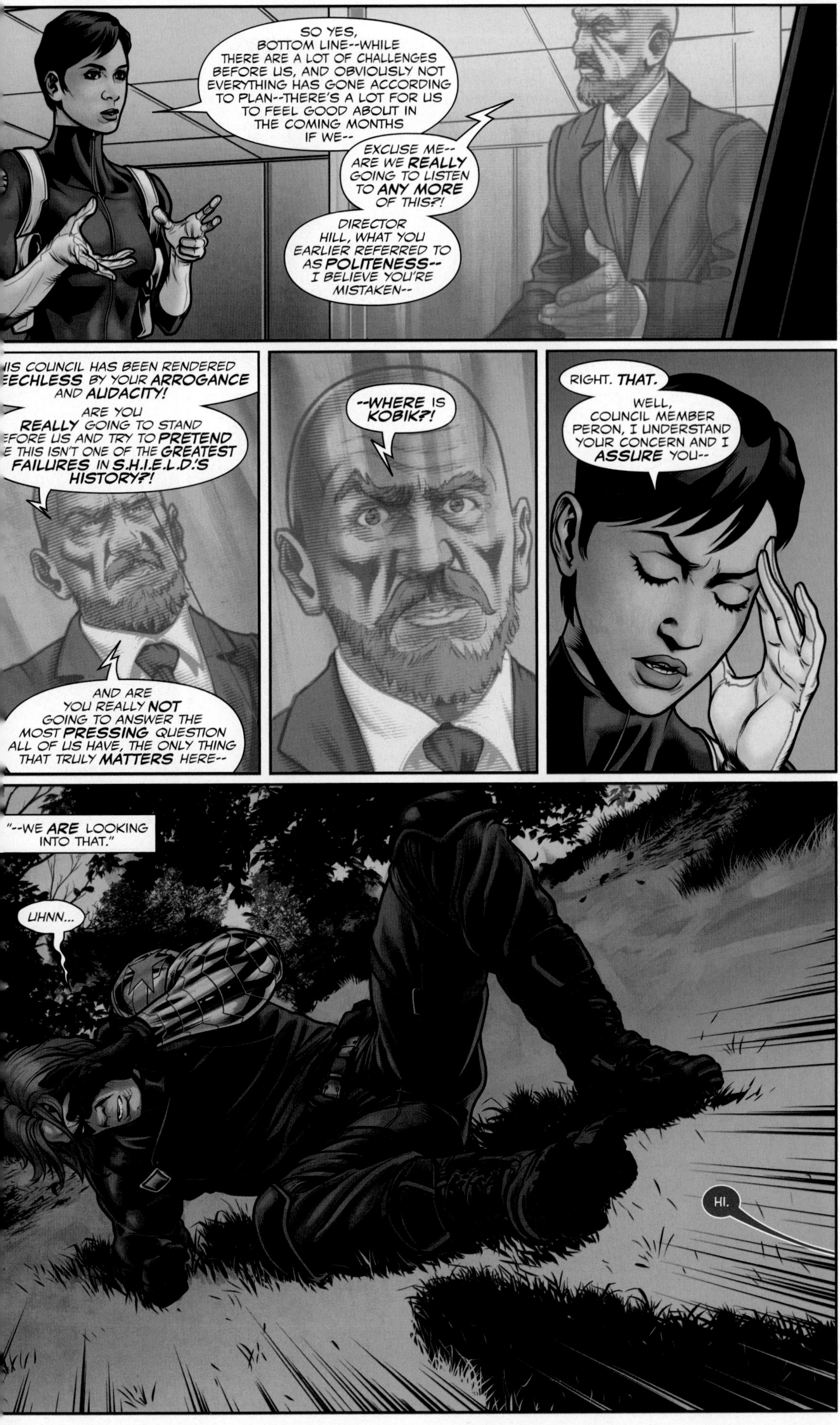
SO YES, BOTTOM LINE--WHILE THERE ARE A LOT OF CHALLENGES BEFORE US, AND OBVIOUSLY NOT EVERYTHING HAS GONE ACCORDING TO PLAN--THERE'S A LOT FOR US TO FEEL GOOD ABOUT IN THE COMING MONTHS IF WE--
EXCUSE ME--ARE WE REALLY GOING TO LISTEN TO ANY MORE OF THIS?!
DIRECTOR HILL, WHAT YOU EARLIER REFERRED TO AS POLITENESS--I BELIEVE YOU'RE MISTAKEN--
IS COUNCIL HAS BEEN RENDERED EECHLESS BY YOUR ARROGANCE AND AUDACITY!
ARE YOU REALLY GOING TO STAND EFORE US AND TRY TO PRETEND E THIS ISN'T ONE OF THE GREATEST FAILURES IN S.H.I.E.L.D.'S HISTORY?!
AND ARE YOU REALLY NOT GOING TO ANSWER THE MOST PRESSING QUESTION ALL OF US HAVE, THE ONLY THING THAT TRULY MATTERS HERE--
--WHERE IS KOBIK?!
RIGHT. THAT.
WELL, COUNCIL MEMBER PERON, I UNDERSTAND YOUR CONCERN AND I ASSURE YOU--
"--WE ARE LOOKING INTO THAT."
UHNN...
HI.

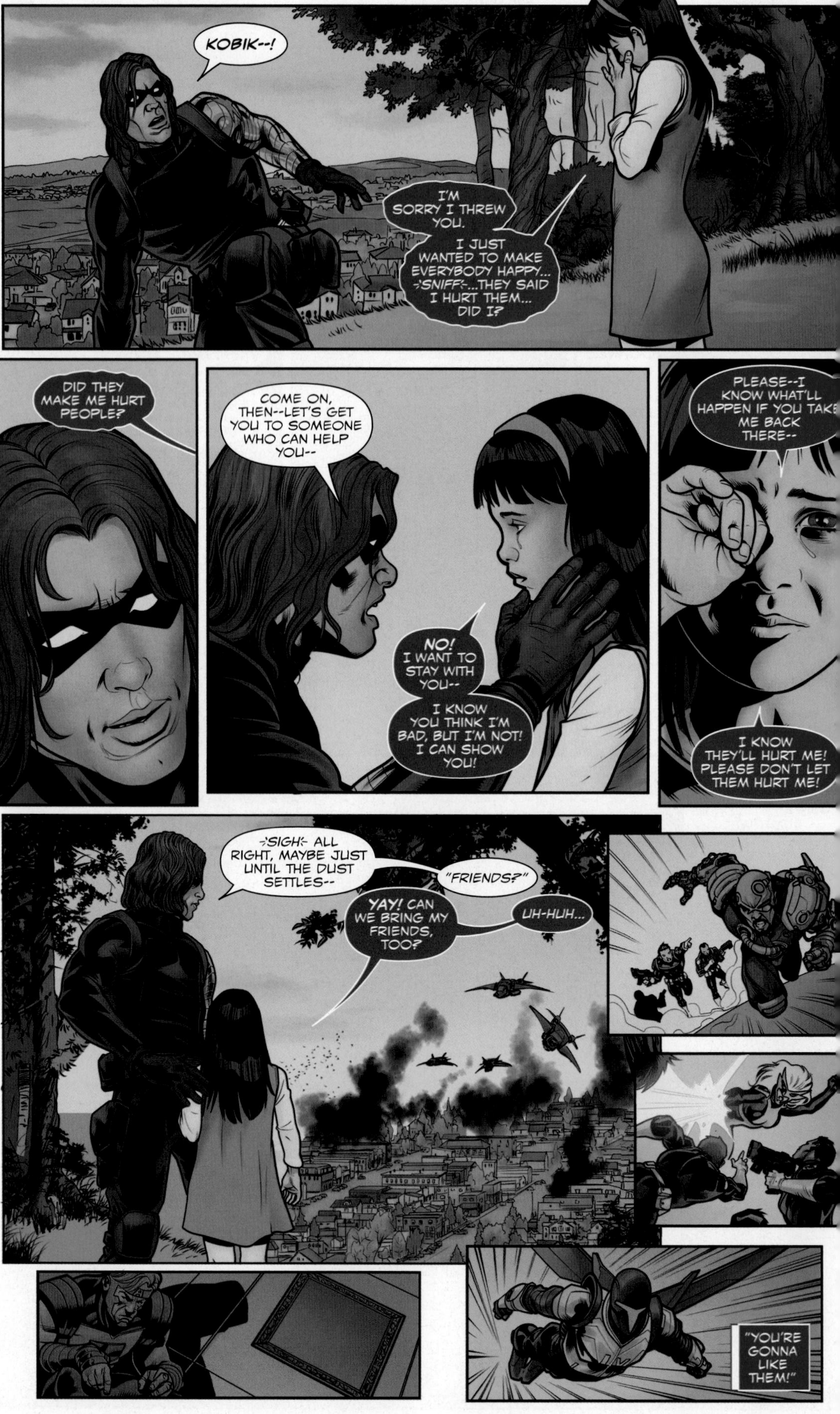
KOBIK--!
I'M SORRY I THREW YOU.
I JUST WANTED TO MAKE EVERYBODY HAPPY... -SNIFF- ...THEY SAID I HURT THEM... DID I?
DID THEY MAKE ME HURT PEOPLE?
COME ON, THEN--LET'S GET YOU TO SOMEONE WHO CAN HELP YOU--
NO! I WANT TO STAY WITH YOU--
I KNOW YOU THINK I'M BAD, BUT I'M NOT! I CAN SHOW YOU!
PLEASE--I KNOW WHAT'LL HAPPEN IF YOU TAKE ME BACK THERE--
I KNOW THEY'LL HURT ME! PLEASE DON'T LET THEM HURT ME!
-SIGH- ALL RIGHT, MAYBE JUST UNTIL THE DUST SETTLES--
YAY! CAN WE BRING MY FRIENDS, TOO?
"FRIENDS?"
UH-HUH...
"YOU'RE GONNA LIKE THEM!"

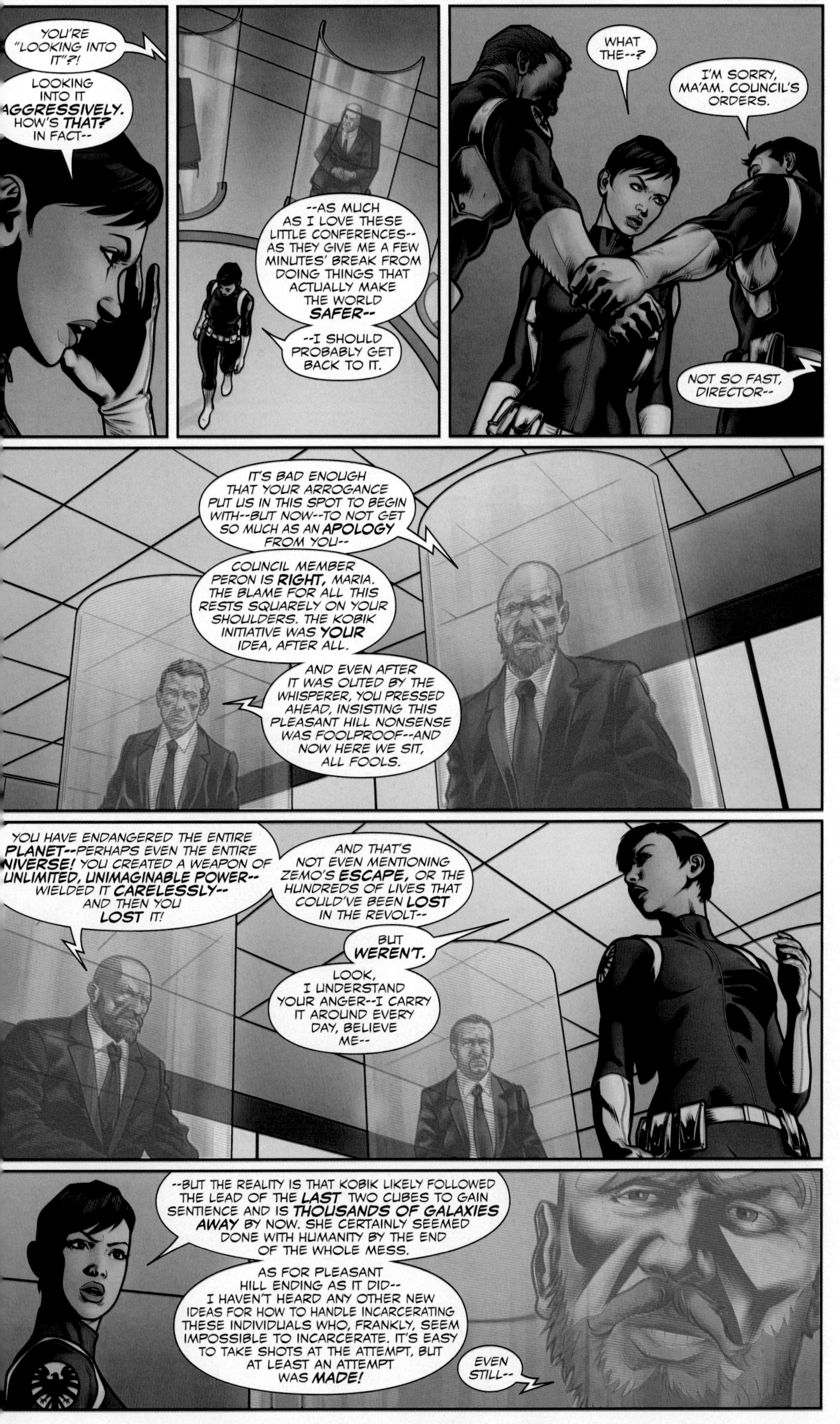
YOU'RE "LOOKING INTO IT"?!
LOOKING INTO IT AGGRESSIVELY. HOW'S THAT? IN FACT--
--AS MUCH AS I LOVE THESE LITTLE CONFERENCES-- AS THEY GIVE ME A FEW MINUTES' BREAK FROM DOING THINGS THAT ACTUALLY MAKE THE WORLD SAFER--
--I SHOULD PROBABLY GET BACK TO IT.
WHAT THE--?
I'M SORRY, MA'AM. COUNCIL'S ORDERS.
NOT SO FAST, DIRECTOR--
IT'S BAD ENOUGH THAT YOUR ARROGANCE PUT US IN THIS SPOT TO BEGIN WITH--BUT NOW--TO NOT GET SO MUCH AS AN APOLOGY FROM YOU--
COUNCIL MEMBER PERON IS RIGHT, MARIA. THE BLAME FOR ALL THIS RESTS SQUARELY ON YOUR SHOULDERS. THE KOBIK INITIATIVE WAS YOUR IDEA, AFTER ALL.
AND EVEN AFTER IT WAS OUTED BY THE WHISPERER, YOU PRESSED AHEAD, INSISTING THIS PLEASANT HILL NONSENSE WAS FOOLPROOF--AND NOW HERE WE SIT, ALL FOOLS.
YOU HAVE ENDANGERED THE ENTIRE PLANET--PERHAPS EVEN THE ENTIRE UNIVERSE! YOU CREATED A WEAPON OF UNLIMITED, UNIMAGINABLE POWER-- WIELDED IT CARELESSLY-- AND THEN YOU LOST IT!
AND THAT'S NOT EVEN MENTIONING ZEMO'S ESCAPE, OR THE HUNDREDS OF LIVES THAT COULD'VE BEEN LOST IN THE REVOLT--
BUT WEREN'T.
LOOK, I UNDERSTAND YOUR ANGER--I CARRY IT AROUND EVERY DAY, BELIEVE ME--
--BUT THE REALITY IS THAT KOBIK LIKELY FOLLOWED THE LEAD OF THE LAST TWO CUBES TO GAIN SENTIENCE AND IS THOUSANDS OF GALAXIES AWAY BY NOW. SHE CERTAINLY SEEMED DONE WITH HUMANITY BY THE END OF THE WHOLE MESS.
AS FOR PLEASANT HILL ENDING AS IT DID-- I HAVEN'T HEARD ANY OTHER NEW IDEAS FOR HOW TO HANDLE INCARCERATING THESE INDIVIDUALS WHO, FRANKLY, SEEM IMPOSSIBLE TO INCARCERATE. IT'S EASY TO TAKE SHOTS AT THE ATTEMPT, BUT AT LEAST AN ATTEMPT WAS MADE!
EVEN STILL--

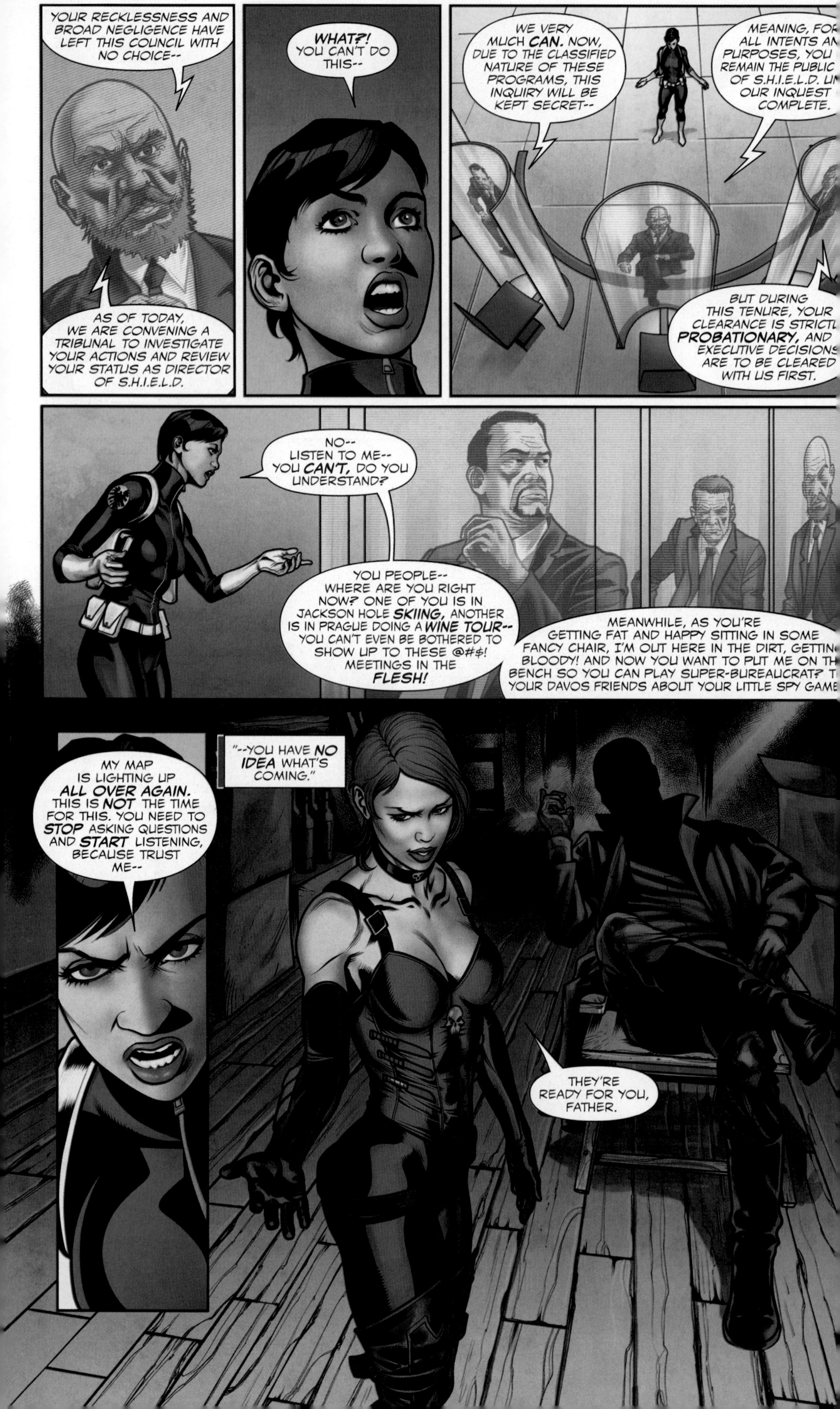
YOUR RECKLESSNESS AND BROAD NEGLIGENCE HAVE LEFT THIS COUNCIL WITH NO CHOICE--
AS OF TODAY, WE ARE CONVENING A TRIBUNAL TO INVESTIGATE YOUR ACTIONS AND REVIEW YOUR STATUS AS DIRECTOR OF S.H.I.E.L.D.
WHAT?! YOU CAN'T DO THIS--
WE VERY MUCH CAN. NOW, DUE TO THE CLASSIFIED NATURE OF THESE PROGRAMS, THIS INQUIRY WILL BE KEPT SECRET--
MEANING, FOR ALL INTENTS AN PURPOSES, YOU REMAIN THE PUBLIC OF S.H.I.E.L.D. UN OUR INQUEST COMPLETE.
BUT DURING THIS TENURE, YOUR CLEARANCE IS STRICTL PROBATIONARY, AND EXECUTIVE DECISIONS ARE TO BE CLEARED WITH US FIRST.
NO-- LISTEN TO ME-- YOU CAN'T, DO YOU UNDERSTAND?
YOU PEOPLE-- WHERE ARE YOU RIGHT NOW? ONE OF YOU IS IN JACKSON HOLE SKIING, ANOTHER IS IN PRAGUE DOING A WINE TOUR-- YOU CAN'T EVEN BE BOTHERED TO SHOW UP TO THESE @#$! MEETINGS IN THE FLESH!
MEANWHILE, AS YOU'RE GETTING FAT AND HAPPY SITTING IN SOME FANCY CHAIR, I'M OUT HERE IN THE DIRT, GETTIN BLOODY! AND NOW YOU WANT TO PUT ME ON TH BENCH SO YOU CAN PLAY SUPER-BUREAUCRAT? T YOUR DAVOS FRIENDS ABOUT YOUR LITTLE SPY GAME
MY MAP IS LIGHTING UP ALL OVER AGAIN. THIS IS NOT THE TIME FOR THIS. YOU NEED TO STOP ASKING QUESTIONS AND START LISTENING, BECAUSE TRUST ME--
"--YOU HAVE NO IDEA WHAT'S COMING."
THEY'RE READY FOR YOU, FATHER.

WONDERFUL, SIN. HOW MANY ANSWERED OUR CALL?

CLOSE TO FIFTY. MOSTLY RECRUITED FROM FASCIST AND NEO-NAZI ORGANIZATIONS IN THE AREA. THEY'RE ALL VERY EAGER TO HEAR WHAT YOU HAVE TO SAY.

DAMN WELL OUGHTA BE--

THEY'RE NOT MUCH TO LOOK AT. NO DECENT TRAINING, ONLY A COUPLE KILLERS IN THE WHOLE BUNCH--IF YOU'RE LOOKIN' FOR AN ARMY, I CAN FIND YOU BETTER--

NO, CROSSBONES. WE ARE NOT LOOKING FOR AN ARMY. WE ARE LOOKING FOR BELIEVERS...

IT'S QUITE THE BEAUTIFUL IDEA, ISN'T IT?

EN STRUCKER BROUGHT BACK FROM THE EAST, IT NDED LIKE MADNESS TO ME. N'T RECOGNIZE ITS BEAUTY, R ITS MAGNIFICENCE. ITS RESILIENCE IN THE FACE OF TIME.

SURE DIDN'T SEEM RESILIENT ENOUGH TO SAVE ZEMO...

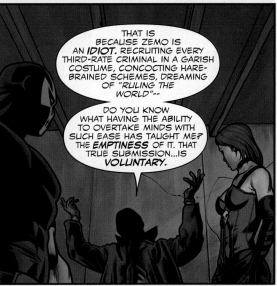

THAT IS BECAUSE ZEMO IS AN IDIOT. RECRUITING EVERY THIRD-RATE CRIMINAL IN A GARISH COSTUME, CONCOCTING HARE-BRAINED SCHEMES, DREAMING OF "RULING THE WORLD"--

DO YOU KNOW WHAT HAVING THE ABILITY TO OVERTAKE MINDS WITH SUCH EASE HAS TAUGHT ME? THE EMPTINESS OF IT. THAT TRUE SUBMISSION...IS VOLUNTARY.

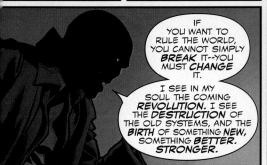

IF YOU WANT TO RULE THE WORLD, YOU CANNOT SIMPLY BREAK IT--YOU MUST CHANGE IT.

I SEE IN MY SOUL THE COMING REVOLUTION. I SEE THE DESTRUCTION OF THE OLD SYSTEMS, AND THE BIRTH OF SOMETHING NEW, SOMETHING BETTER, STRONGER.

"CUT OFF ONE HEAD, AND TWO MORE SHALL TAKE ITS PLACE."

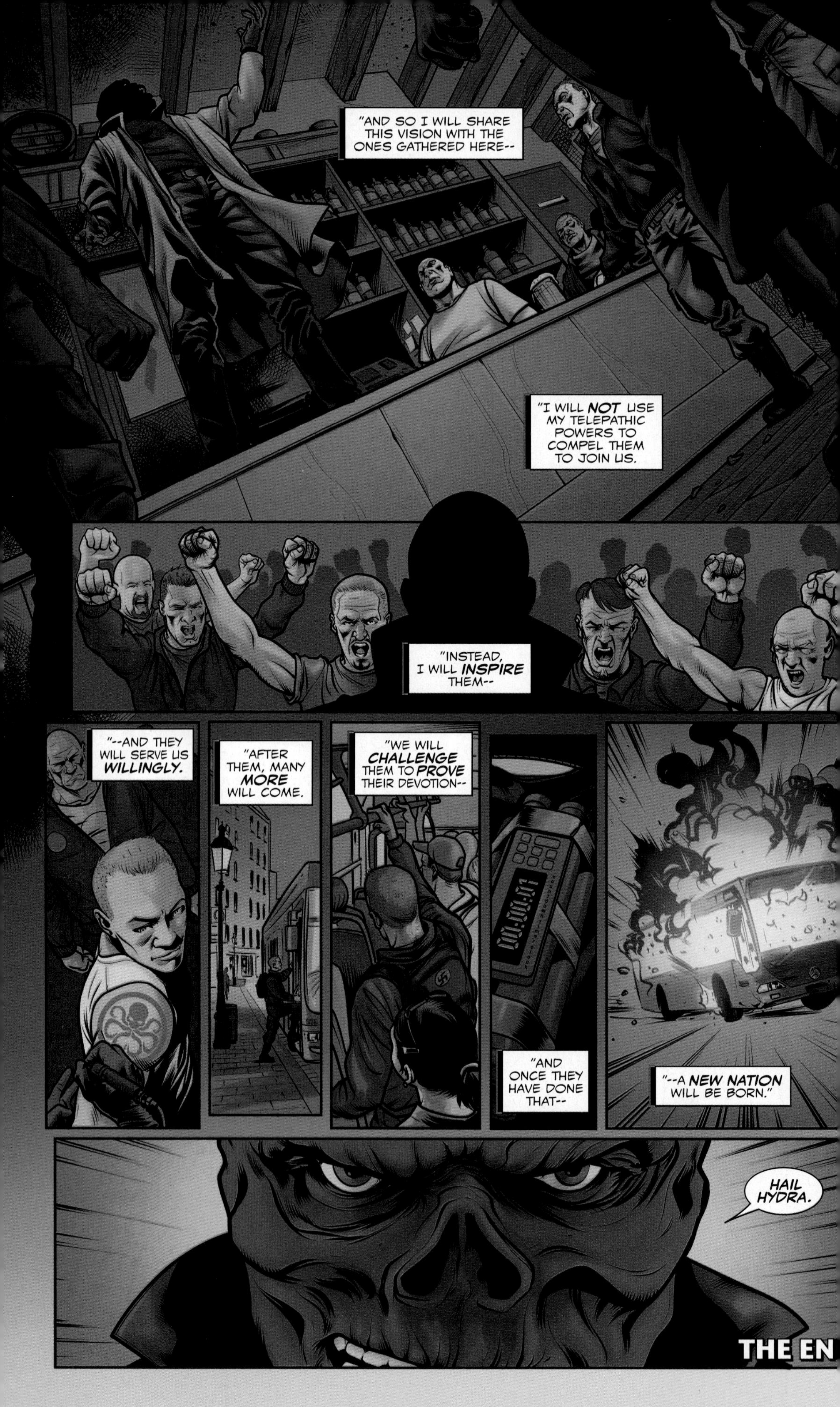

"AND SO I WILL SHARE THIS VISION WITH THE ONES GATHERED HERE--
"I WILL NOT USE MY TELEPATHIC POWERS TO COMPEL THEM TO JOIN US.
"INSTEAD, I WILL INSPIRE THEM--
"--AND THEY WILL SERVE US WILLINGLY.
"AFTER THEM, MANY MORE WILL COME.
"WE WILL CHALLENGE THEM TO PROVE THEIR DEVOTION--
"AND ONCE THEY HAVE DONE THAT--
"--A NEW NATION WILL BE BORN."
HAIL HYDRA.
THE EN

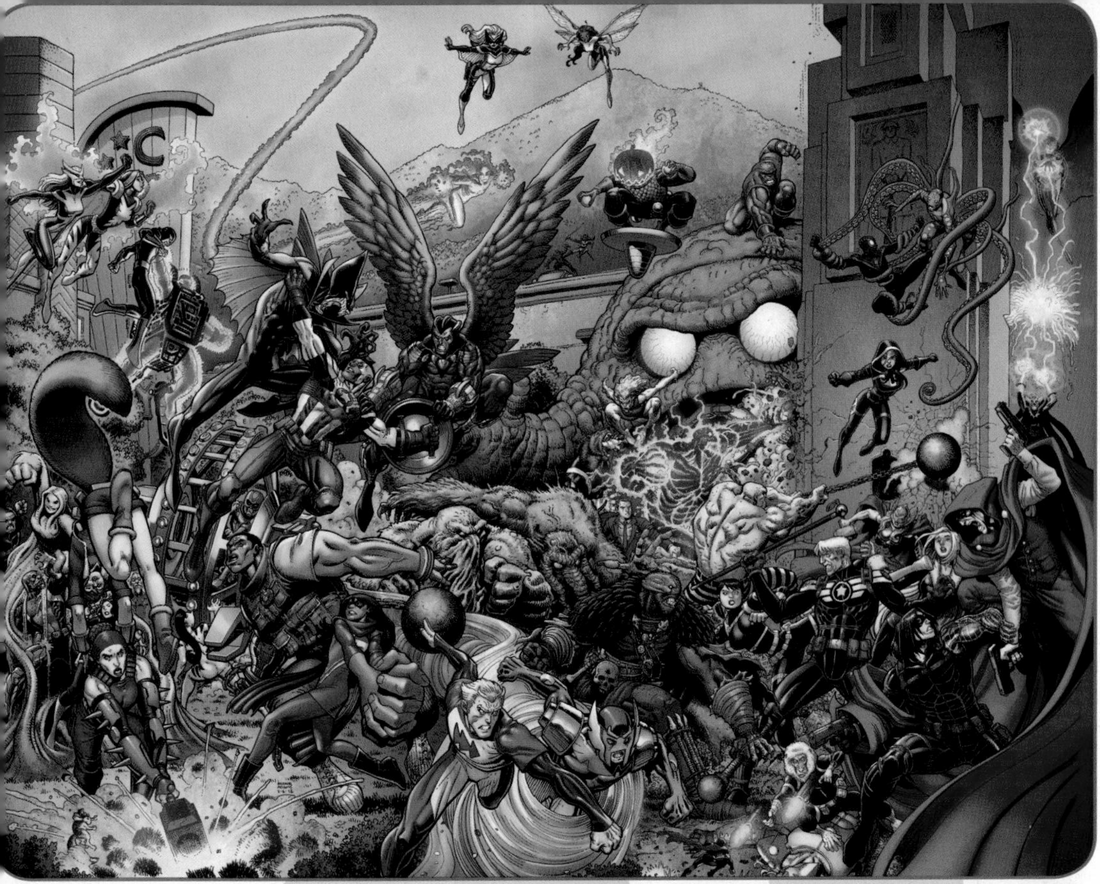

Assault on Pleasant Hill Alpha & Omega connecting variants by
ART ADAMS & CHRIS SOTOMAYOR

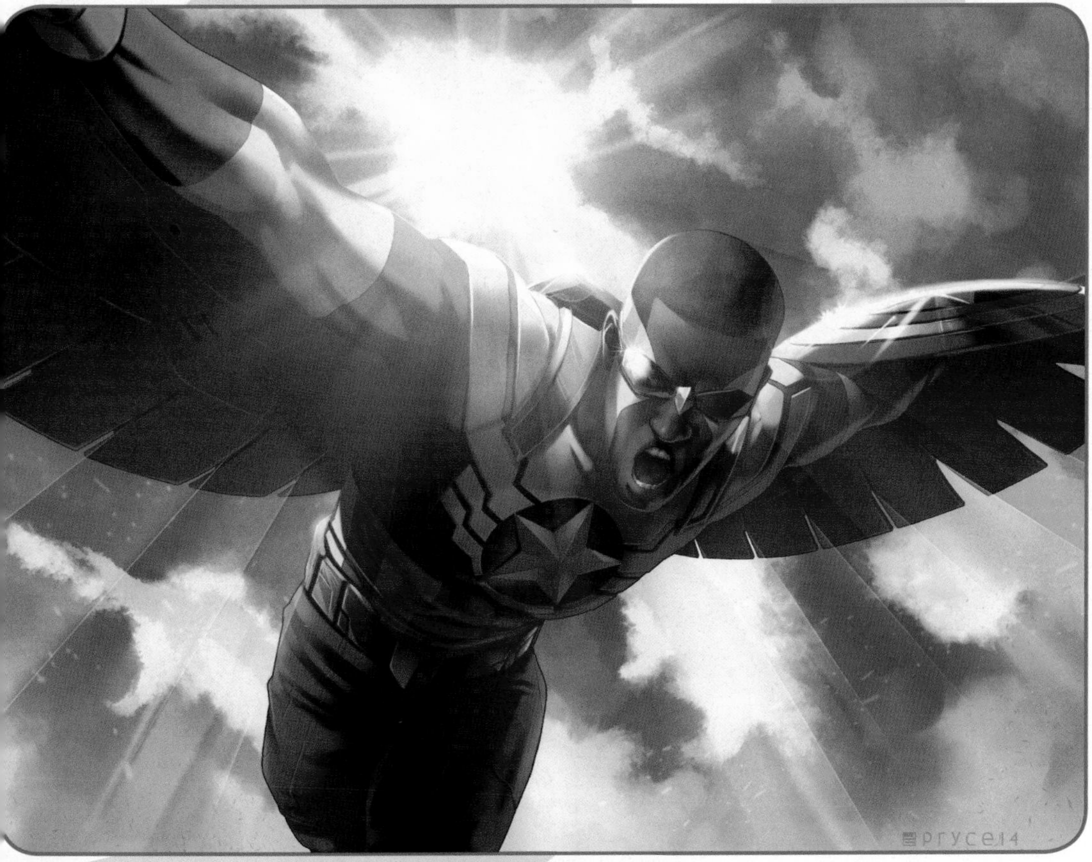

#8 Civil War II variant by
JAMAL CAMPBELL

Assault on Pleasant Hill Alpha
variant by
ART ADAMS & DAVE MCCAIG

Assault on Pleasant Hill Alpha
Gwenpool Party variant by
JAY FOSGITT

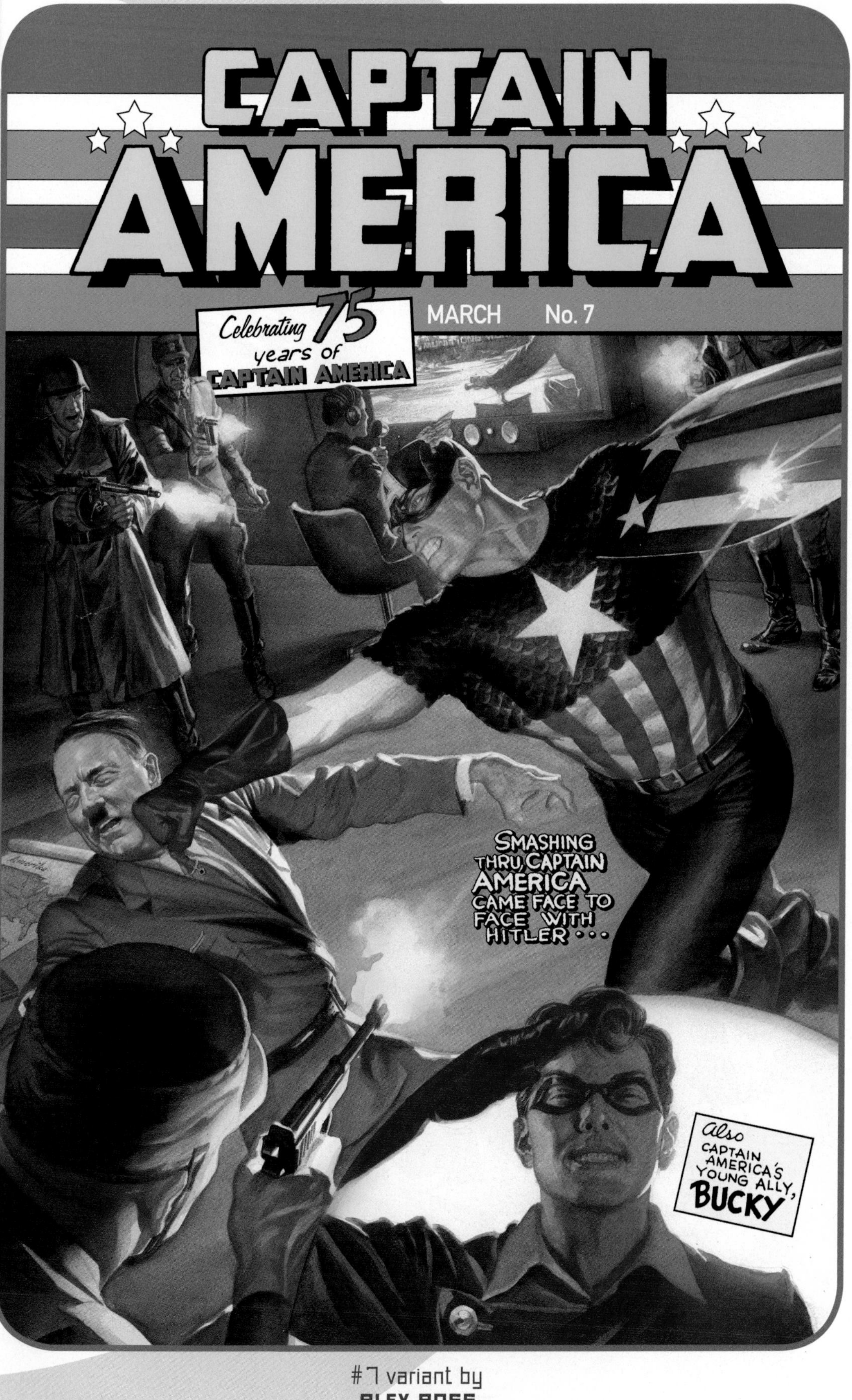
CAPTAIN AMERICA
Celebrating 75 years of CAPTAIN AMERICA
MARCH No. 7
SMASHING THRU, CAPTAIN AMERICA CAME FACE TO FACE WITH HITLER...
Also CAPTAIN AMERICA'S YOUNG ALLY, BUCKY

#7 variant by
ALEX ROSS

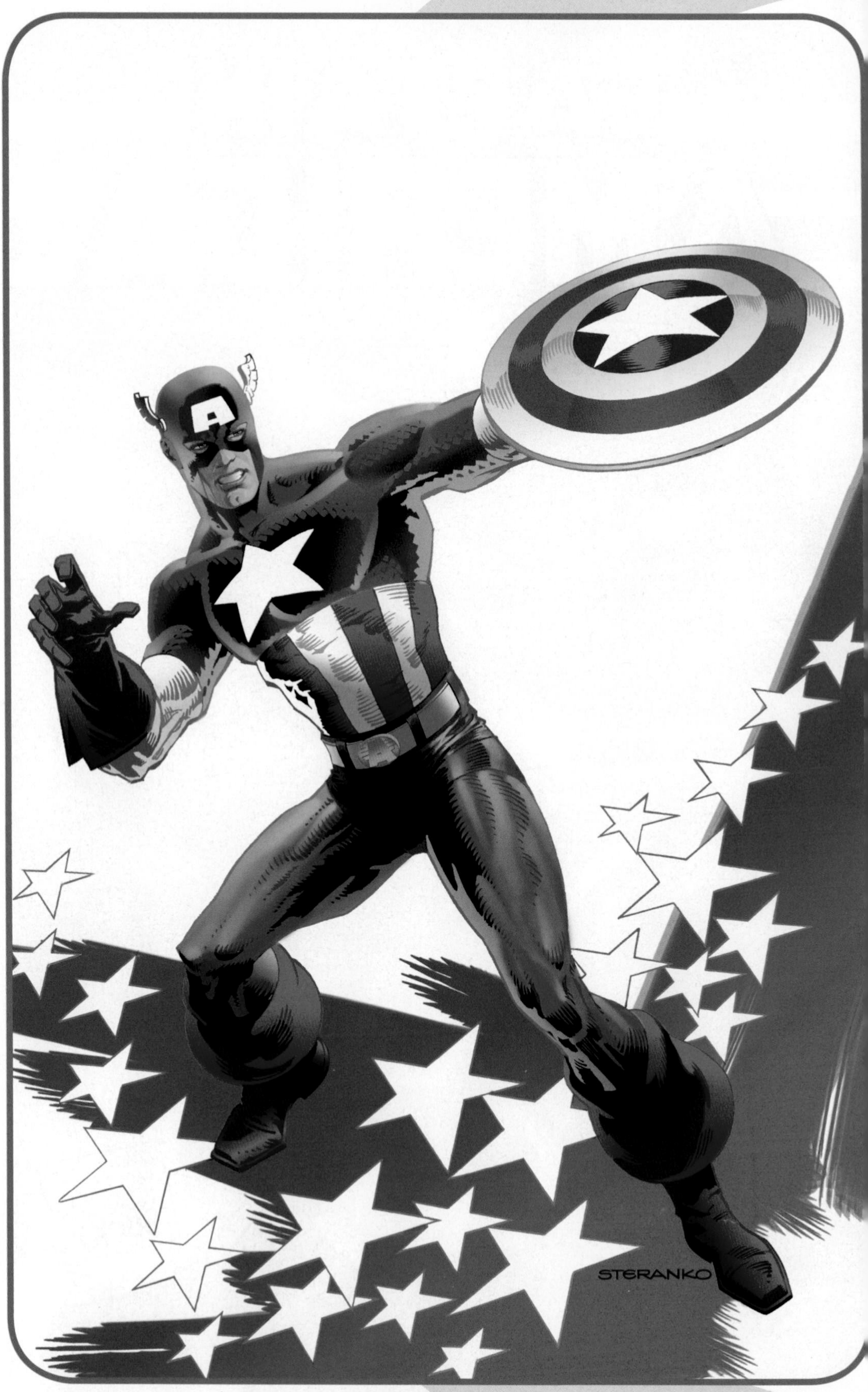
STERANKO

#7 variant by
JIM STERANKO

#7 Women of Power variant by
NEN CHANG

#7 variant by
**MAHMUD ASRAR &
DAVE McCAIG**

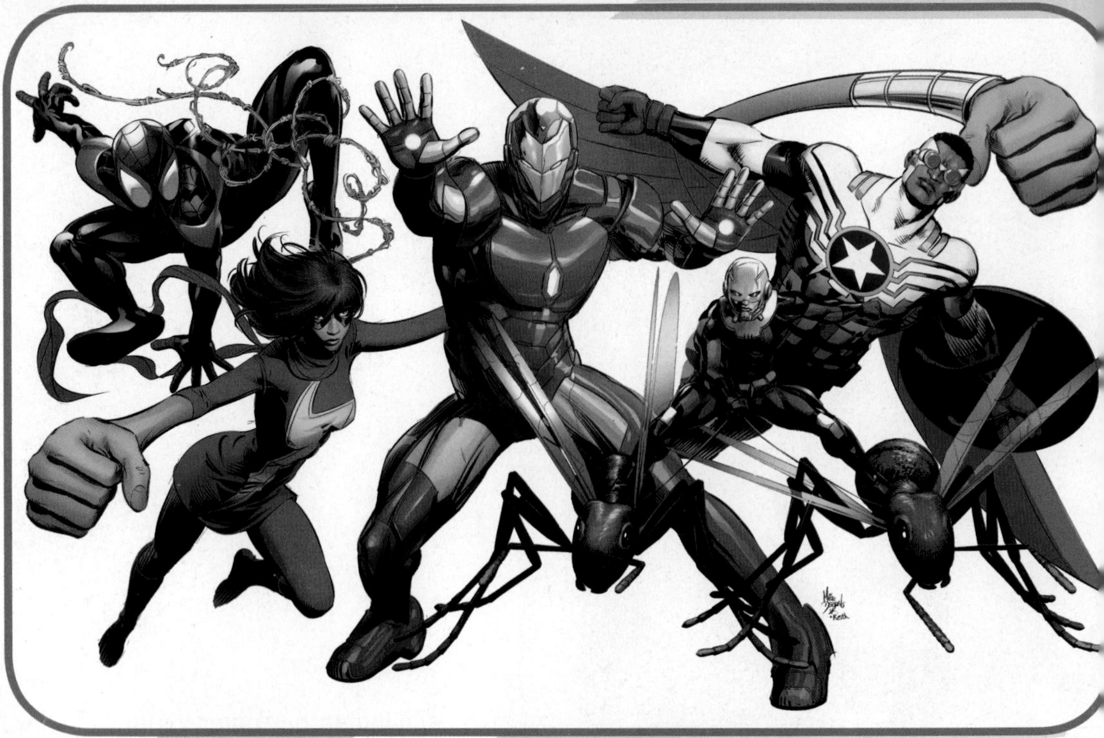

Assault on Pleasant Hill Omega wraparound variant by
MIKE DEODATO & FRANK MARTIN

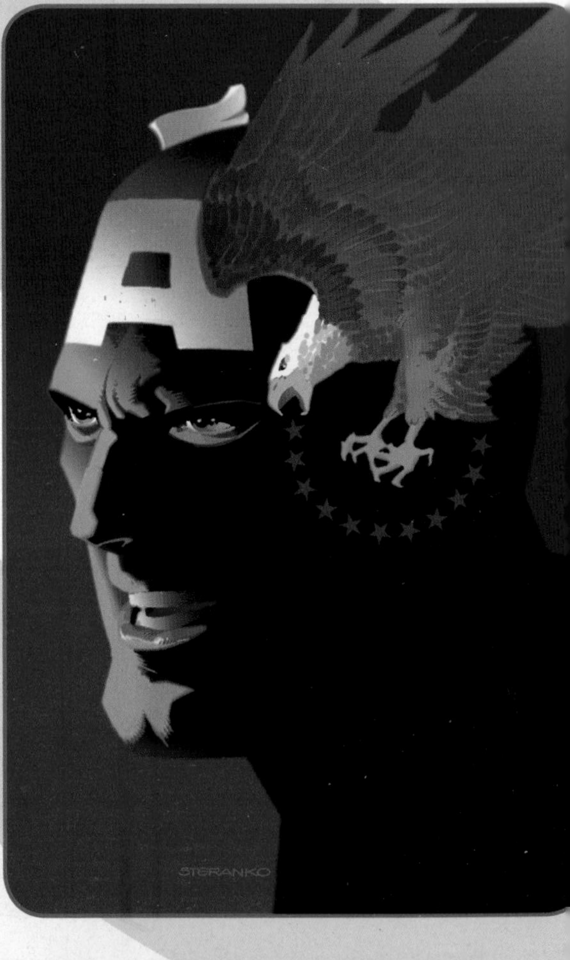
STERANKO

Assault on Pleasant Hill Omega
variant by
JIM STERANKO